Critical Essays on Henry David Thoreau's Walden

Critical Essays on Henry David Thoreau's Walden

Joel Myerson

G. K. Hall & Co. • **Boston, Massachusetts**

Library of Congress Cataloging-in-Publication Data

Critical essays on Henry David Thoreau's Walden.
  (Critical essays on American literature)
  Includes bibliographies and index.
  1. Thoreau, Henry David, 1817–1862. Walden.
I. Myerson, Joel. II. Series.
PS3048.C75   1988   818'.303   88-1818
ISBN 0-8161-8885-8 (alk. paper)

This publication is printed on permanent/durable acid-free paper
MANUFACTURED IN THE UNITED STATES OF AMERICA

CRITICAL ESSAYS ON AMERICAN LITERATURE

This series seeks to anthologize the most important criticism on a wide variety of topics and writers in American Literature. Our readers will find in various volumes not only a generous selection of reprinted articles and reviews but original essays, bibliographies, manuscript sections, and other materials brought to public attention for the first time. This volume is a collection of reviews and essays on Henry David Thoreau's *Walden*. It contains the most complete record of critical reaction to this American masterpiece ever published, including all the contemporary reviews and a broad selection of more modern scholarship. Among noted early reviewers are Horace Greeley and George Eliot, along with many anonymous reviewers in the leading periodicals of the day. There are reprinted articles by Sherman Paul, Lauriat Lane, Jr., Joseph J. Moldenhauer, Michael T. Gilmore, and Robert A. Gross, among others. In addition to an introduction that traces the history of critical reaction to *Walden*, there are also three original essays commissioned specifically for publication in this volume, new studies by Philip Gura, Linck Johnson, and Robert Richardson. We are confident that this book, edited by Joel Myerson, a distinguished scholar of American literature, will make a permanent and significant contribution to literary study.

JAMES NAGEL, GENERAL EDITOR

Northeastern University

To Greta

CONTENTS

INTRODUCTION

When, on 4 July 1845, Henry David Thoreau moved to some land at Walden Pond owned by his Concord neighbor Ralph Waldo Emerson in order to "transact some private business,"[1] he was unaware that he had set in motion one of the masterpieces of American literature. His twenty-six months at Walden, as artistically created and re-created over the next seven years, resulted in *Walden; or, Life in the Woods*, published in 1854.[2] John Greenleaf Whittier called the book, "very wicked and heathenish";[3] Emerson found it "cheerful, sparkling, readable, with all kinds of merits, & rising sometimes to very great heights" and praised its author as "the undoubted King of all American Lions";[4] contemporary reviewers nearly all commented favorably. Yet one may argue that of all the major American authors, Thoreau has been the subject of the most vapid and uninformative critical and biographical studies. There are many reasons for this, including the lack of easily found documentation with which to trace Thoreau's life, the enthusiast-inspirational tone of many critics that belies Thoreau's artistic abilities, and a general failure to take Thoreau seriously as a careful and artistic writer.

Critical Essays on Henry David Thoreau's "Walden" is the first volume to reprint all the known contemporary reviews of the book.[5] I have also tried to include in my selection a series of twentieth-century articles that accurately reflects what I believe are worthwhile types of approaches to *Walden*.[6] Because nearly every book-length study of Thoreau is in print and readily available in libraries, I have prepared this volume to complement these studies rather than reprint sections therefrom.[7]

Walden had a long gestation.[8] In March 1846, Thoreau noted in his journal that "some of my townsmen had expected of me some account of my life at the pond."[9] He returned to his journal for materials and on 10 and 17 February 1847 lectured before the Concord Lyceum on "The History of myself."[10] He continued adding to this account up until the time he left Walden Pond in September 1847. He then dropped the *Walden* manuscript to work on lectures and *A Week on the Concord and Merrimack Rivers*, which he finished in February 1849.[11] Planning to publish *Walden* on the heels of *A Week*, Thoreau created a second and

1

then a third version of *Walden* in 1848–49. By early 1849, he was trying to find a publisher for his "History of myself."[12] And when James Munroe of Boston published *A Week* on 30 May 1849, it contained an advertising page announcing that *Walden* would "be published soon."

But *A Week* was a commercial failure—out of 1,000 copies printed, only 219 copies were sold.[13] The prospects for publishing *Walden* immediately were now nonexistent, and Thoreau only tinkered with the manuscript over the next few years. But by January 1852 he was at work on a fourth version,[14] which he dropped in late 1852 or early 1853 to begin a fifth version. Late in 1853 he began a sixth version, which he completed at the beginning of 1854. In the late winter and spring of 1854, he created a seventh version of *Walden* by adding to the existing manuscript, and then prepared a clean (and revised) copy for the printer, the eighth and final version. He began receiving proofs on 28 March, while still sending in copy. Thoreau continued reading proofs and supplying copy through May, heavily revising the proofs with over one thousand corrections.[15] Ticknor and Fields of Boston published *Walden* on 9 August 1854 for a price of one dollar, with Thoreau receiving a fifteen-cent royalty on each copy sold.[16]

In 1849, the *New-York Daily Tribune* had described a lecture on "Life in the Woods" by "Henry D. Thoreau of Concord, Mass.," a "young student, who has imbibed (or rather refused to stifle) the idea that a man's soul is better worth living for than his body."[17] Within a week, "Timothy Thorough" responded that his wife "will have it that the young man is either a whimsy or else a good-for-nothing, selfish, crab-like sort of chap, who tries to shirk the duties whose hearty and honest discharge is the only thing that in her view entitles a man to be regarded as a good example."[18] This occasioned an official defense of Thoreau by the *Tribune* (probably by its editor, Horace Greeley) and of the "large class of young men who aspire to Mental Culture through Study, Reading, Reflection, &c.," which also noted that no one had "proposed or suggested that it becomes everybody to go off into the woods, each build himself a hut and live hermit-like, on the vegetable products of his very moderate labor."[19] This public debate over a lecture that would eventually be incorporated into the text of *Walden* foreshadowed what would become major points of discussion five years later when *Walden* was published: body versus spirit; philosophy versus practicality; individualism versus social responsibility; physical isolation versus social involvement; and the implied hypocrisy of the author.

In general, the response of reviewers to *Walden* was very positive. Although most of the reviews were short, general, or both, they did contain such effusions as "one of the most remarkable books for originality of thought and beauty of style yet written in our day"; "one of the most remarkable publications of the day"; "a prose poem . . . [with] classical elegance, and New England homeliness, with a sprinkle of Oriental magnificence in it"; "the most readable and original volume we have seen in a long time"; "[s]ometimes strikingly original, sometimes merely eccentric and odd, it is always racy and stimulating"; and "one of the most original, eccentric and suggestive books which the season has brought out."[20]

The body versus spirit argument of *Walden* was perhaps best recognized by the Oneida community's *Circular*, which called the book "a picturesque and unique continuation of the old battle between the flesh and the spirit."[21] In "Higher Laws," Thoreau himself overtly stated this dichotomy as being of interest to him: "I found in myself, and still find, an instinct toward a higher, or, as it is named, spiritual life, as do most men, and another toward a primitive rank and savage one, and I reverence them both" (210). But the *Boston Atlas* found that Thoreau's pursuit of higher laws had led to his loss of humanity: while praising the "strong, vigorous, nervous truth" of the spiritual passages of *Walden*, the *Atlas* complained that "there is not a page, a paragraph giving one sign of liberality, charitableness, kind feeling, generosity, in a word—HEART." In *Walden*, body had lost to spirit and there was a "total absence of human affection."[22]

Another dichotomy in *Walden*—that of philosophy versus practicality—was recognized by reviewers. Although Thoreau gave plenty of evidence in *Walden* that good ideas must be built upon solid bases ("If you have built castles in the air, your work need not be lost; that is where they should be. Now put the foundations under them" [324]), not all reviewers noticed this. Some, like the Boston *Daily Evening Traveller*, simply pointed out the combination of "many shrewd and sensible suggestions" and "a fair share of nonesense [*sic*]" in the book.[23] To the *Providence Daily Journal*, since the practical "incidents [of Thoreau's life] were not remarkably stirring, he has filled up the pages with his philosophy, which is shrewd and eccentric."[24] Similarly, the *North American Review* found the "suggestive capacity" of *Walden* to be superior to the practical "economical details and calculations," which were "more curious than useful."[25] The *National Anti-Slavery Standard* also liked the philosophical parts of *Walden*, but for a different reason:

> The striking peculiarity of Mr. Thoreau's attitude is . . . that the loftiest dreams of the imagination are the solidest realities, and so the only foundation for us to build upon, while the affairs in which men are everywhere busying themselves so intensely are comparatively the merest froth and foam.[26]

In its odd comparison of *Walden* and P. T. Barnum's *Autobiography*, the *Knickerbocker Magazine* noted that the only similarity between the two authors was the rejection of practicality (neither would labor "very hard with their hands for a living") for a type of philosophy (both were "determined to support themselves principally by their wits").[27] In the English *Westminster Review*, George Eliot called attention to "that practical as well as theoretical independence of formulae, which is peculiar to some of the finer American minds."[28] A few reviewers saw in *Walden's* philosophical passages vestiges of transcendentalism. Elizabeth Stoddard, writing in the *Daily Alta California*, called *Walden* "the latest effervescence of the peculiar school, at the head of which stands Ralph Waldo Emerson,"[29] and the *Yankee Blade* thought the "Conclusion," in which Thoreau "tries to Emersonize," the "poorest" chapter of the book.[30] But John Sullivan Dwight, himself earlier aligned with the transcendentalists, defended Thoreau as "one of those men who has put such a determined trust in the simple dictates of common sense, as to earn the vulgar title of 'transcendentalist' from his sophisticated neighbors."[31]

Most reviewers touched on the theme of individual versus social responsibility in *Walden*. But while they did discuss it, few recognized the truly antisocial basis of Thoreau's individualistic philosophy, which warned that "[p]ublic opinion is a weak tyrant compared with our own private opinion" (7) and that "[n]ot until we are lost, in other words, not till we have lost the world, do we begin to find ourselves, and realize where we are and the infinite extent of our relations" (171). That this theme is a major one in *Walden* can be seen by the generations who have made one of the book's most famous lines to be "If a man does not keep pace with his companions, perhaps it is because he hears a different drummer" (326). Typical of the reactions to this theme is the comment of the English *Albion* that readers can "admire [Thoreau], without wishing to imitate him."[32] On the other hand, the *Boston Atlas* recognized that, unlike his "brother moralizers" who "think and speak of mankind as being themselves" units of it, Thoreau "fondly deems himself emancipated from this thraldom, and looks down upon them as an inferior tribe."[33] In a similar fashion, the *National Anti-Slavery Standard* presented the strongest recognition of Thoreau's belief that individuals need to emancipate themselves before attempting to emancipate society:

> In a deeper sense than we commonly think, charity begins at home. The man who, with any fidelity, obeys his own genius, serves men infinitely more by so doing, becoming an encouragement, a strengthener, a fountain of inspiration to them, than if he were to turn aside from his path and exhaust his energies in striving to meet their superficial needs.[34]

Following upon the previous theme is the one of physical isolation versus social involvement. Thoreau had made it clear which he preferred: "I had this advantage, at least, in my mode of life, over those who were obliged to look abroad for amusement, to society and the theatre, that my life itself was become my amusement and never ceased to be novel" (112). He made this point over and over in *Walden*, sometimes by using paradox ("We are for the most part more lonely when we go abroad among men than when we stay in our chambers" [135]) and sometimes by using humor

("I would rather sit on a pumpkin and have it all to myself, than to be crowded on a velvet cushion" [37]). Again, most reviewers missed the antisocial implications of this theme, choosing instead to harp upon what the *Boston Atlas* called "the one great, fatal error, which completely vitiates the experiment," that Thoreau was "no true hermit . . . He only played savage on the borders of civilization."[35] In other words, while Thoreau denounced society in print, in life he snuck back into town for meals and companionship.

Finally, many reviewers complained of Thoreau's hypocrisy. Indeed, this is probably the most complained about aspect of *Walden*, both by Thoreau's contemporaries and by twentieth-century readers. As the *National Era* described *Walden*, it contained "many acute observations on the follies of mankind, but enough of such follies to show that its author has his full share of the infirmities of human nature, without being conscious of it."[36] A corollary to this was the argument made by Charles Frederick Briggs in *Putnam's Monthly Magazine*: "although he paints his shanty-life in rose-colored tints, we do not believe he liked it, else why not stick to it?"[37] Obviously, these reviewers missed the many comments in the book in which Thoreau said he was making a case for all people, not just himself ("If I seem to boast more than is becoming, my excuse is that I brag for humanity rather than for myself" [49]); wants his readers to rethink their own lives and not merely imitate him ("I would not have any one adopt *my* mode of living on any account" [71]); and explains that "I left the woods for as good a reason as I went there. Perhaps it seemed to me that I had several more lives to live, and could not spare any more time for that one" [323]). Indeed, Thoreau clearly stated that his purpose in *Walden* was not to encourage clones of himself, but to free people to think; he proposed—in a line which appeared on the title page of the first edition—"to brag as lustily as chanticleer in the morning, standing on his roost, if only to wake my neighbors up" (84).

Sales for *Walden* were much better than those for *A Week*. Of the 2,000 copies printed, 1,744 were sold within a year, and the book was out of print by 1859.[38] *Walden* was first reprinted in 1862,[39] the year of Thoreau's death; it has been in print ever since. Between 1862 and 1890, nearly 8,000 copies were printed from the 1854 plates. In 1886, Walter Scott published the first English edition of *Walden*, although an American printing for English sale had been completed two years earlier. As Thoreau's popularity gradually increased, Houghton, Mifflin (successors to Ticknor and Fields) published the first collected edition of his works, the "Riverside Edition," in 1894. Today, *Walden* is arguably the most widely translated and available book by an American author.

With few exceptions, publications about *Walden* between the Civil War and World War II could only be described as "criticism" by the most generous reader; there were, in effect, many spirited defenses of Thoreau as an inspirational writer or a few attacks on him as a fraud.[40] Only slowly was there general recognition of Thoreau as a careful and original literary artist, one who could be compared in all seriousness with such contemporaries as Emerson and Herman Melville.[41] The twentieth-century essays reprinted in this volume begin with works which carry forward the early consideration of Thoreau as a serious artist which really began with F. O. Matthiessen's 1941 *American Renaissance*: John C. Broderick discusses Thoreau's style, Lauriat Lane, Jr., *Walden*'s structure, and Joseph J. Moldenhauer the use of a particular literary device, paradox.[42] Llewelyn Powys offers caveats about Thoreau, which are indirectly refuted by the intellectual approach to *Walden* of Sherman Paul.[43] Articles by Joseph Allen Boone deal with the search for truth in *Walden*, Richard H. Dillman with rhetoric, Robert Hodges with satire, Richard J. Schneider with optics, and James S. Tillman with Thoreau's use of the georgic.[44] All are indebted to Walter Harding's essay on the various ways in which *Walden* can be interpreted.[45] The possibilities of more recent criticism can be seen in Michael T. Gilmore's discussion of contemporary socioeconomic values as reflected in *Walden*, Robert A. Gross's placing *Walden* in the context of contemporary agricultural reform books, and Walter Benn Michaels's "new critical" approach to the indeterminedness of *Walden*'s text.[46] Original essays, commissioned especially for this volume, provide wide-ranging discussions of Thoreau's social ethics by Robert D. Richardson, Jr., the various literary genres that can be found in *Walden* by Linck C. Johnson, and Thoreau's use of language by Philip F. Gura.[47]

Bibliographical aids for the study of Thoreau are generally good, if widely scattered. Francis H. Allen's *A Bibliography of Henry David Thoreau* is a good place to start for nineteenth-century criticism. Raymond R. Borst has recently published an annotated bibliography of nineteenth-century criticism.[48] For twentieth-century work, Allen's book goes through 1908; it is supplemented by William White for the 1908–37 period, J. S. Wade for 1909–36, Philip E. Burnham and Carvel Collins for 1930–45, and Christopher A. Hildenbrand for 1940–67.[49] Beginning in 1941, the quarterly *Thoreau Society Bulletin* has published a bibliography in each issue; the ones through 1969 have been cumulated (sadly, without an index) by Walter Harding and Jean Cameron Advena.[50] Jeanetta Boswell and Sara Crouch pillaged the previous works to compile *Henry David Thoreau and the Critics*, covering the period between 1900 and 1978 in a poorly indexed, error filled book.[51] Much better are Walter Harding, *A Thoreau Handbook*, revised with Michael Meyer as *A New Thoreau Handbook*, and Meyer's chapter on Thoreau in *The Transcendentalists: A Review of Research and Criticism*; all these works evaluate the scholarship on Thoreau in a solid, evenhanded fashion.[52] An excellent annotated list of material devoted especially to *Walden* has been prepared by Annette M. Woodlief.[53] *American Literary Scholarship: An Annual* gives an ongoing evaluation of publications since 1963.[54] Specialized bibliographies of use are by William L. Howarth on Thoreau's literary manuscripts, an often erroneous work; and by Walter Harding on Thoreau's career as a lecturer and the books in his library.[55]

The standard list of works by Thoreau is *Henry David Thoreau: A Descriptive Bibliography*, by Raymond R. Borst.[56] The twenty-volume 1906 edition of *The Writings of Henry David Thoreau*, fourteen volumes of which are Thoreau's journal, is slowly being replaced by *The Writings of Henry D. Thoreau* from the Princeton University Press.[57] *The Correspondence of Henry David Thoreau*, edited by Walter Harding and Carl Bode, will be reedited for the latter edition; until that is published, users should be aware that the present edition's annotations are skimpy and the index incomplete.[58] Bode has edited Thoreau's poetry, which Elizabeth Hall Wetherell is editing anew for the Princeton edition.[59]

The Princeton edition of *Walden*, edited by J. Lyndon Shanley in 1971, is the standard text, but disappointing in its lack of complete editorial disclosure;[60] it has been reprinted in paperback with turn-of-the-century photographs by Herbert W. Gleason.[61] Other landmark editions of *Walden* are the Bibliophile Society edition, in which F. B. Sanborn cheerfully added an additional 12,000 words from Thoreau's various manuscript drafts; a variorum *Walden*, edited by Walter Harding with annotations and summaries of critical comments on various passages; and an annotated *Walden*, with a facsimile of the 1854 text, edited by Philip Van Doren Stern.[62] A concordance to *Walden* has been done by Marlene A. Ogden and Clifton Keller.[63]

Two early biographies of Thoreau are still useful: Ellery Channing, *Thoreau: The Poet-Naturalist*, is rich in anecdotes, and F. B. Sanborn, *The Life of Henry David Thoreau*, has much detailed information, but must be used with care, since Sanborn is often inaccurate.[64] Henry Seidel Canby's *Thoreau* adds new information, but is marred by an overly Freudian viewpoint.[65] Walter Harding, *The Days of Henry Thoreau*, is the standard biography, but is now outdated in many of its particulars.[66] An interesting Eriksonian approach to Thoreau may be found in *Young Man Thoreau* and *Thoreau's Seasons*, both by Richard Lebeaux.[67] A brilliant and incisive view of Thoreau's mind is presented in Robert D. Richardson, Jr., *Henry Thoreau: A Life of the Mind*, which is the one book to read on Thoreau as both introduction and overview.[68] Thomas Blanding is currently working on a series of studies that will shed much new light on Thoreau's life and his relations with contemporaries. Also of use are the well-written pictorial biography of Thoreau by Milton Meltzer and Harding, *A Thoreau Profile*, and Roland Robbins's account of his excavation of the remains of Thoreau's cabin at Walden Pond in the 1940s.[69]

Virtually every book on Thoreau has a section dealing with *Walden*; a survey of the contents may be gleaned from Woodlief's checklist of *Walden* criticism, Harding and Meyer's *A New Thoreau Handbook*, Meyer's chapter on Thoreau in *The Transcendentalists*, and *American Literary Scholarship*. Of particular use are Sherman Paul, *The Shores of*

America: Thoreau's Inward Exploration, for Thoreau's ideas; Lawrence Buell, *Literary Transcendentalism: Style and Vision in the American Renaissance*, for Thoreau's transcendental environment; Richard Bridgman, *Dark Thoreau*, for Thoreau's supposed morbidness; Frederick Garber, *Thoreau's Redemptive Imagination*, and James McIntosh, *Thoreau as Romantic Naturalist: His Shifting Stance Toward Nature*, for Thoreau and Romanticism; J. Golden Taylor, *Neighbor Thoreau's Critical Humor*, for Thoreau's humor; Joan Burbick, *Thoreau's Alternative History: Changing Perspectives on Nature, Culture, and Language* for Thoreau's use of history; and Philip F. Gura, *The Wisdom of Words: Language, Theology, and Literature in the New England Renaissance*, for Thoreau's knowledge and use of contemporary theories of language.[70]

Some books deal exclusively with *Walden*. J. Lyndon Shanley, *The Making of Walden with the Text of the First Draft*, is a brilliant suggestive work, but no one has yet taken up Shanley's own call for a complete study of the *Walden* manuscripts and proofs, now at the Henry E. Huntington Library.[71] Charles R. Anderson, *The Magic Circle of Walden*, reads the book as an extended prose poem, and Stanley Cavell, *The Senses of Walden*, is a philosophical study of *Walden* as a book "about its own writing and reading."[72] All three books are required reading for anyone seriously interested in *Walden*.

There are well over one hundred articles and sections of books dealing solely with *Walden*; they are evaluated in Woodlief's checklist of *Walden* criticism, Harding and Meyer's *A New Thoreau Handbook*, Meyer's chapter on Thoreau in *The Transcendentalists*, and *American Literary Scholarship*.

Now that Thoreau has finally been accepted as a major literary artist, as well as a major American author, better scholarship about him is being published. Of particular interest are those works discussing Thoreau's use of language, his comments on the role of the artist, his indebtedness to the English Romantics, his views of history, his connection to the luminist movement in painting, his general intellectual background, and the changing socioeconomic environment in which he worked. We may now join with Thoreau in saying that there is "more day to dawn" (333).

I am grateful to Thomas Blanding, Philip F. Gura, Walter Harding, Michael Meyer, Leonard Neufeldt, Robert D. Richardson, Jr., and Albert J. von Frank for suggestions about the contents for this book. James Nagel continues to be a gem of a series editor, and I thank him for the Critical Essays on American Literature series. Raymond R. Borst has generously allowed me an advance look at his bibliography of nineteenth-century writings on Thoreau. I am grateful to Armida Gilbert for assistance in preparing the manuscript of this book. The University of South Carolina has supported my work, and I am especially grateful to Carol McGinnis

Kay, Dean of the College of Humanities and Social Sciences. And, of course, my gratitude to Greta for love and patience.

JOEL MYERSON

University of South Carolina

Notes

1. *Walden*, ed. J. Lyndon Shanley (Princeton: Princeton University Press, 1971), 19. Further references to *Walden* are to this edition and will be cited parenthetically in the text.

2. Thoreau himself asked that the subtitle be dropped from later editions; see his letter to Ticknor and Fields, 4 March 1862, in *The Correspondence of Henry David Thoreau*, ed. Walter Harding and Carl Bode (New York: New York University Press, 1958), 639.

3. Letter to James T. Fields, 14 August 1854, in *The Letters of John Greenleaf Whittier*, ed. John B. Pickard, 3 vols. (Cambridge: Harvard University Press, 1975), 2:267.

4. Letter to George Partridge Bradford, 28 August 1854, in *The Letters of Ralph Waldo Emerson*, ed. Ralph L. Rusk, 6 vols. (New York: Columbia University Press, 1939), 4:460.

5. In addition to items listed in numerous bibliographies of Thoreau, I assembled contemporary reviews from the advance sheets of Raymond R. Borst's bibliography of nineteenth-century writings on Thoreau, Walter Harding's prodigious researches, and, for particular reviews, Walter Fertig, "John Sullivan Dwight's Pre-publication Notice of *Walden*," *New England Quarterly* 30 (March 1957):84–90; George Monteiro, "*Walden* in the *Albion*," *Thoreau Society Bulletin*, no. 149 (Fall 1979):1–2; Gary Scharnhorst, "James T. Fields and Early Notices of *Walden*," *New England Quarterly* 55 (March 1982):114–17, and "Five Uncollected Contemporary Reviews of *Walden*," *Thoreau Society Bulletin*, no. 160 (Summer 1982):1–3; Kent P. Ljungquist, "Further Responses to Thoreau's Worcester Lectures and a Review of *Walden*," *Thoreau Society Bulletin*, no. 177 (Fall 1986):2–5; and Bradley P. Dean, "Another Uncollected Contemporary Review of *Walden*," *Thoreau Society Bulletin*, no. 179 (Spring 1987):4.

6. Unfortunately, limitations of space forced me to leave out four fine works: Robert A. Gross, "Culture and Cultivation: Agriculture and Society in Thoreau's Concord," *Journal of American History* 69 (June 1982):42–61; Richard N. Masteller and Jean Carwile Masteller, "Rural Architecture in Andrew Jackson Downing and Henry David Thoreau: Pattern Book Parody in *Walden*," *New England Quarterly* 57 (December 1984):483–510; Thomas Woodson, "The Two Beginnings of *Walden*: A Distinction of Styles," *ELH* 35 (September 1968):440–73; and Philip R. Yannella, "Socio-Economic Disarray and Literary Response: Concord and *Walden*," *Mosaic* 14 (Winter 1981):1–24.

7. I have also chosen, for reasons of space, not to reprint the sections on Thoreau from general book-length works such as F. O. Matthiessen, *American Renaissance: Art and Expression in the Age of Emerson and Whitman* (New York: Oxford University Press, 1941). Most such sections are too long and really need to be read in the context of the book as a whole.

8. Information on the writing of *Walden* is from J. Lyndon Shanley, *The Making of Walden with the Text of the First Draft* (Chicago: University of Chicago Press, 1957), and Shanley's "Historical Introduction" to the Princeton Edition of *Walden*, 360–67. Also of interest is the chapter on *Walden* in Stephen J. Adams and Donald Ross, Jr., *Revising Mythologies: The Composition of Thoreau's Major Works* (Charlottesville: University Press of Virginia, forthcoming).

9. *Journal*, in *The Writings of Henry David Thoreau*, ed. Bradford Torrey and Francis H. Allen, 20 vols. (Boston: Houghton Mifflin, 1906), 1:485.

10. Walter Harding, "A Check List of Thoreau's Lectures," *Bulletin of the New York Public Library* 52 (February 1948):80. Harding also notes that Thoreau gave lectures from materials which would later be incorporated into *Walden* on 22 November 1848 at Salem, 3 January 1849 at Concord, 28 February 1849 at Salem, March 1849 at Portland, Maine, 20 and 27 April 1849 at Worcester, 22 January 1851 at Medford, and April 1852 at Boston (80–82).

11. Information about *A Week* is from Linck C. Johnson's *Thoreau's Complex Weave: The Writing of "A Week on the Concord and Merrimack Rivers" with the Text of the First Draft* (Charlottesville: University Press of Virginia, 1986) and "Historical Introduction" to *A Week*, ed. Carl F. Hovde et al. (Princeton: Princeton University Press, 1980), xvi–xxxvi.

12. Ticknor and Fields to Thoreau, 8 February 1849, *Correspondence*, 236.

13. 28 October 1853, *Journal*, 5:459. In this entry, Thoreau notes that when the 706 remaining copies of *A Week* (1,000 printed less those sold and 75 distributed to friends and for review) were sent to him, he now had "a library of nearly nine hundred volumes, over seven hundred of which I wrote myself." The book eventually cost Thoreau $290, paid to the publisher to reimburse them for their costs.

14. Portions of this version were published as "The Iron Horse" (from "Sounds") and "A Poet Buying a Farm" (from "Where I Lived, and What I Lived for") in *Sartain's Union Magazine* 11 (July, August 1852):66–68, 127.

15. Shanley, "Textual Introduction," *Walden*, 382.

16. Raymond R. Borst, *Henry David Thoreau: A Descriptive Bibliography* (Pittsburgh: University of Pittsburgh Press, 1982), 17.

17. ["Life in the Woods"], *New-York Daily Tribune*, 2 April 1849, 3.

18. "Timothy Thorough," "How to Live—Mr. Thoreau's Example," *New-York Daily Tribune*, 7 April 1849, 5.

19. "Reply," *New-York Daily Tribune*, 7 April 1849, 5.

20. [Notice of *Walden*], *Boston Transcript*, 21 July 1854, 1; [Notice of *Walden*], *Boston Atlas*, 10 August 1854, 2; [Review of *Walden*], *Worcester Palladium*, 16 August 1954, 3; [Review of *Walden*], *Portland Transcript*, 19 August 1854, 151; [Review of *Walden*], *Graham's Magazine* 45 (September 1854):298; [Review of *Walden*], *Watchman and Reflector*, 5 October 1854, 158.

21. [Review of *Walden*], *Circular*, 28 March 1864.

22. "D'A," [Review of *Walden*], *Boston Atlas*, 21 October 1854, 1.

23. [Review of *Walden*], Boston *Daily Evening Traveller*, 9 August 1854, 1.

24. [Review of *Walden*], *Providence Daily Journal*, 11 August 1854, 1.

25. [Andrew Preston Peabody?], [Review of *Walden*], *North American Review* 79 (October 1854):536.

26. [Lydia Maria Child?], [Review of *A Week on the Concord and Merrimack Rivers* and *Walden*], *National Anti-Slavery Standard*, 16 December 1854, 3.

27. "Town and Rural Humbugs," *Knickerbocker Magazine* 45 (March 1855):239.

28. [George Eliot], [Review of *Walden*], *Westminster Review* 65 (January 1856):302.

29. [Elizabeth Barstow Stoddard], [Review of *Walden*], *Daily Alta California* 5 (8 October 1854):279.

30. [Review of *Walden*], *Yankee Blade*, 28 October 1854, 3.

31. [John Sullivan Dwight], "Editorial Correspondence," *Dwight's Journal of Music* 5 (12 August 1854):150.

32. [Review of *Walden*], *Albion*, n.s. 13 (9 September 1854):429.

33. "D'A," [Review of *Walden*], 1.

34. [Lydia Maria Child?], [Review of *A Week*], 3.

35. "D'A," [Review of *Walden*], 1.

36. [Gamaliel Bailey?], [Review of *Walden*], *National Era* 8 (28 September 1854):155.

37. [Charles Frederick Briggs], "A Yankee Diogenes," *Putnam's Monthly Magazine* 4 (October 1854):443.

38. Walter Harding, *The Days of Henry Thoreau* (New York: Alfred A. Knopf, 1965), 340; Harding, "The First Year's Sales of Thoreau's *Walden*," *Thoreau Society Bulletin*, no. 117 (Fall 1971):1–3.

39. Information on reprintings of *Walden* comes from Shanley, "Historical Introduction" to *Walden*, 368–71, and Borst, *Thoreau*, 18–21.

40. These attacks continue to the present day: see, for example, Leon Edel, "*Walden*: The Myth and the Mystery," *American Scholar* 44 (Spring 1975):272–81, an attack continued in his *The Stuff of Sleep and Dreams* (New York: Harpers, 1982), 47–65.

41. When in 1980 Walter Harding revised his *A Thoreau Handbook* (1959), a new chapter was added on "Thoreau's Art."

42. John C. Broderick, "The Movement of Thoreau's Prose," *American Literature* 33 (May 1961):133–42; Lauriat Lane, Jr., "On the Organic Structure of *Walden*," *College English* 21 (January 1960):195–202; Joseph J. Moldenhauer, "The Extra-vagant Maneuver: Paradox in *Walden*," *Graduate Journal* 6 (Winter 1964):132–46.

43. Llewelyn Powys, "Thoreau: A Disparagement," *Bookman* (New York) 69 (April 1929):163–65; Sherman Paul, "Resolution at Walden," *Accent* 13 (Spring 1953):101–13.

44. Joseph Allen Boone, "Delving and Diving for Truth: Breaking Through to Bottom in Thoreau's *Walden*," *ESQ: A Journal of the American Renaissance* 27 (3d Quarter 1981):135–46; Richard H. Dillman, "The Psychological Rhetoric of *Walden*," *ESQ: A Journal of the American Renaissance* 25 (2d Quarter 1979):79–91; Robert R. Hodges, "The Functional Satire of Thoreau's Hermit and Poet," *Satire Newsletter* 8 (Spring 1971):105–8; Richard J. Schneider, "Reflections in Walden Pond: Thoreau's Optics," *ESQ: A Journal of the American Renaissance* 21 (2d Quarter 1975):65–75; and James S. Tillman, "The Transcendental Georgic in *Walden*," *ESQ: A Journal of the American Renaissance* 21 (3d Quarter 1975):137–41.

45. Walter Harding, "Five Ways of Looking at *Walden*," *Massachusetts Review* 4 (Autumn 1962):149–62.

46. Michael T. Gilmore, "*Walden* and the 'Curse of Trade,'" in his *American Romanticism and the Marketplace* (Chicago: University of Chicago Press, 1985), 35–51; Robert A. Gross, "The Great Bean Field Hoax: Thoreau and the Agricultural Reformers," *Virginia Quarterly Review* 61 (Summer 1985):483–97; Walter Benn Michaels, "*Walden's* False Bottoms," *Glyph* 1 (1977):132–49.

47. See Robert D. Richardson, Jr., "The Social Ethics of *Walden*," Linck C. Johnson, "Revolution and Renewal: The Genres of *Walden*," and Philip F. Gura, "Henry Thoreau and the Wisdom of Words," all printed below.

48. Francis H. Allen, *A Bibliography of Henry David Thoreau* (Boston: Houghton Mifflin, 1908); Raymond R. Borst, *Henry David Thoreau: A Reference Guide, 1835–1899* (Boston: G. K. Hall, 1987).

49. William White, "A Henry David Thoreau Bibliography, 1908–37," *Bulletin of Bibliography* 16 (January–April, May–August, September–December 1938, January–April, May–August, September–December 1939): 90–92, 111–13, 131–32, 163, 181–82, 199–202, rpt. as *A Henry David Thoreau Bibliography, 1908–37* (Boston: Faxon, 1939); J. S. Wade, "A Contribution to a Bibliography from 1909 to 1939 of Henry David Thoreau," *Journal of the New York Entomological Society* 47 (June 1939):163–203; Philip E. Burnham and Carvel Collins, "Contributions Toward a Bibliography of Thoreau, 1938–1945," *Bulletin of Bibliog-*

raphy 19 (September–December 1946, January–April 1947):16–19, 37–39; and Christopher A. Hildenbrand, *A Bibliography of Scholarship About Henry David Thoreau: 1940–1967* (Fort Hays, Kans.: Fort Hays State College, 1967).

50. Walter Harding and Jean Cameron Advena, *A Bibliography of the Thoreau Society Bulletin Bibliographies, 1941–1969* (Troy, N.Y.: Whitston, 1971).

51. Jeanetta Boswell and Sara Crouch, *Henry David Thoreau and the Critics* (Metuchen, N.J.: Scarecrow, 1981).

52. Walter Harding, *A Thoreau Handbook* (New York: New York University Press, 1959); Harding and Michael Meyer, *A New Thoreau Handbook* (New York: New York University Press, 1980); Michael Meyer, "Henry David Thoreau," in *The Transcendentalists: A Review of Research and Criticism*, ed. Joel Myerson (New York: Modern Language Association, 1984), 260–85.

53. Annette M. Woodlief, "*Walden*: A Checklist of Literary Criticism Through 1973," *Resources for American Literary Study* 5 (Spring 1975):15–58.

54. *American Literary Scholarship: An Annual* (Durham: Duke University Press, 1965–   ).

55. William L. Howarth, *The Literary Manuscripts of Henry David Thoreau* (Columbus: Ohio State University Press, 1974); Walter Harding, "A Check List of Thoreau's Lectures," *Bulletin of the New York Public Library* 52 (February 1948):78–87, and *Thoreau's Library* (Charlottesville: University Press of Virginia, 1957), revised as "A New Checklist of the Books in Henry David Thoreau's Library," *Studies in the American Renaissance 1983*, ed. Joel Myerson (Charlottesville: University Press of Virginia, 1983), 151–86.

56. Raymond R. Borst, *Henry David Thoreau: A Descriptive Bibliography* (Pittsburgh: University of Pittsburgh Press, 1982).

57. *The Writings of Henry David Thoreau*, ed Bradford Torrey and Francis H. Allen, 20 vols. (Boston: Houghton Mifflin, 1906); *The Writings of Henry D. Thoreau*, ed. Walter Harding et al, 8 vols. to date (Princeton: Princeton University Press, 1971–   ).

58. *The Correspondence of Henry David Thoreau*, ed. Walter Harding and Carl Bode (New York: New York University Press, 1958).

59. *Collected Poems of Henry Thoreau*, ed. Carl Bode (Chicago: Packard, 1943; enl. ed., Baltimore: Johns Hopkins University Press, 1964).

60. For a criticism of this edition, see Joseph R. McElrath, Jr., "The First Two Volumes of The Writings of Henry D. Thoreau: A Review Article," *Proof* 4 (1975):215–35.

61. *The Illustrated Walden*, ed. J. Lyndon Shanley (Princeton: Princeton University Press, 1973).

62. *Walden*, ed. F. B. Sanborn, 2 vols. (Boston: Bibliophile Society, 1909); *The Variorum Walden*, ed. Walter Harding (New York: Twayne, 1962); and *The Annotated Walden*, ed. Philip Van Doren Stern (New York: Clarkson N. Potter, 1970).

63. Marlene A. Ogden and Clifton Keller, *Walden: A Concordance* (New York: Garland, 1985).

64. William Ellery Channing II, *Thoreau: The Poet-Naturalist* (Boston: Roberts Brothers, 1873; enl. ed., ed. F. B. Sanborn, Boston: Charles E. Goodspeed, 1902); F. B. Sanborn, *The Life of Henry David Thoreau* (Boston: Houghton Mifflin, 1917).

65. Henry Seidel Canby, *Thoreau* (Boston: Houghton Mifflin, 1939).

66. Walter Harding, *The Days of Henry Thoreau* (New York: Alfred A. Knopf, 1965).

67. Richard Lebeaux, *Young Man Thoreau* (Amherst: University of Massachusetts Press, 1977), and *Thoreau's Seasons* (Amherst: University of Massachusetts Press, 1984).

68. Robert D. Richardson, Jr., *Henry Thoreau: A Life of the Mind* (Berkeley: University of California Press, 1986).

69. Milton Meltzer and Walter Harding, *A Thoreau Profile* (New York: Thomas Y.

Crowell, 1962; rpt. Concord: Thoreau Foundation, 1970); Roland Robbins, *Discovery at Walden* (Stoneham, Mass.: The Author, 1947; rpt., Concord: Thoreau Foundation, 1970).

70. Sherman Paul, *The Shores of America: Thoreau's Inward Exploration* (Urbana: University of Illinois Press, 1958); Lawrence Buell, *Literary Transcendentalism: Style and Vision in the American Renaissance* (Ithaca: Cornell University Press, 1973); Richard Bridgman, *Dark Thoreau* (Lincoln: University of Nebraska Press, 1981); Frederick Garber, *Thoreau's Redemptive Imagination* (New York: New York University Press, 1977); James McIntosh, *Thoreau as Romantic Naturalist: His Shifting Stance Toward Nature* (Ithaca: Cornell University Press, 1974); J. Golden Taylor, *Neighbor Thoreau's Critical Humor* (Logan: Utah State University Press, 1958); Joan Burbick, *Thoreau's Alternative History: Changing Perspectives on Nature, Culture, and Language* (Philadelphia: University of Pennsylvania Press, 1987); Philip F. Gura, *The Wisdom of Words: Language, Theology, and Literature in the New England Renaissance* (Middletown, Conn.: Wesleyan University Press, 1981).

71. Ronald Clapper has produced a dissertation with a variorum text of *Walden*, in which manuscript readings from the various versions are keyed (inexplicably) to the 1906 text: "The Development of *Walden*: A Genetic Text," Ph.D. diss., University of California at Los Angeles, 1967.

72. Charles R. Anderson, *The Magic Circle of Walden* (New York: Holt, Rinehart, and Winston, 1968); Stanley Cavell, *The Senses of Walden* (New York: Viking, 1972; exp. ed., San Francisco: North Point Press, 1971).

["Life in the Woods"]

Anonymous*

Henry D. Thoreau of Concord, Mass. has recently been lecturing on "Life in the Woods," in Portland and elsewhere. There is not a young man in the land — and very few old ones — who would not profit by an attentive hearing of that lecture. Mr. Thoreau is a young student, who has imbibed (or rather refused to stifle), the idea that a man's soul is better worth living for than his body. Accordingly, he has built him a house ten by fifteen feet in a piece of unfrequented woods by the side of a pleasant little lakelet, where he devotes his days to study and reflection, cultivating a small plat of ground, living frugally on vegetables, and working for the neighboring farmers whenever he is in need of money or additional exercise. It thus costs him some six to eight week's rugged labor per year to earn his food and clothes, and perhaps an hour or two per day extra to prepare his food and fuel, keep his house in order, &c. — He has lived in this way four years, and his total expenses for last year were $41.25, and his surplus earnings at the close were $13.21, which he considers a better result than almost any of the farmers of Concord could show, though they have worked all the time. By this course Mr. Thoreau lives free from pecuniary obligation or dependence on others, except that he borrows some books, which is an equal pleasure to lender and borrower. The man on whose land he is a squatter is no wise injured nor inconvenienced thereby. If all our young men would but hear this lecture, we think some among them would feel less strongly impelled either to come to New York or go to California.

*Reprinted from the *New-York Daily Tribune*, 2 April 1849, 3.

"How to Live—
Mr. Thoreau's Example" and
"Reply"   "Timothy Thorough" and [Horace Greeley?]*

To the Editor of the Tribune:

I notice in your paper this morning a strong commendation of one Mr. Thoreau for going out into the woods and living in a hut all by himself at the rate of about $45 per annum, in order to illustrate the value of the soul. Having always found in The Tribune a friend of sociability and neighborly helping-each-other-along, I felt a little surprise at seeing such a performance held up as an example for the young men of this country, and supposed I must have mistaken the sense of your article. Accordingly I called in my wife, Mrs. Thorough, and we studied it over together, and came to the conclusion that you really believed the Concord hermit had done a fine thing. Now I am puzzled, and write in a friendly way to ask for a little light on this peculiar philosophy. Mrs. T. is more clear in her mind than I am. She will have it that the young man is either a whimsy or else a good-for-nothing, selfish, crab-like sort of chap, who tries to shirk the duties whose hearty and honest discharge is the only thing that in her view entitles a man to be regarded as a good example. She declares that nobody has a right to live for himself alone, away from the interests, the affections, and the sufferings of his kind. Such a way of going on, she says, is not living, but a cold and snailish kind of existence, which, as she maintains, is both infernal and internally stupid.

Yours, truly   Timothy Thorough.
Le Roy Place, April 2, 1849

Reply.

Mr. Thorough is indeed in a fog—in fact, we suspect there is a mistake in his name, and that he must have been changed at nurse for another boy whose true name was Shallow. Nobody has proposed or suggested that it becomes everybody to go off into the woods, each build himself a hut and live hermit-like, on the vegetable products of his very moderate labor. But there is a large class of young men who aspire to Mental Culture through Study, Reading, Reflection, &c. These are too apt to sacrifice their proper independence in the pursuit of their object—to run in debt, throw themselves on the tender mercies of some patron, relative, Education Society, or something of the sort, or to descend into the lower deep of roping out a thin volume of very thin poems, to be inflicted on a much-enduring public, or to importune some one for a sub-Editorship or the like. Now it does seem to us that Mr. Thoreau has set all his brother aspirants to self-culture, a very wholesome example, and

*Reprinted from the *New-York Daily Tribune*, 7 April 1849, 5.

shown them how, by chastening their physical appetites, they may preserve their proper independence without starving their souls. When they shall have conned that lesson, we trust, with Mr. Thorough otherwise Shallow's permission, he will give them another.   [*Ed. Trib.*

[Notice of *Walden*]   Anonymous*

Life in the Woods. Ticknor and Fields have allowed us to read the proof sheets of one of the most remarkable books for originality of thought and beauty of style yet written in our day. "Walden; or Life in the Woods, by Henry D. Thoreau," will attract as much attention and be as widely read as if it were a new book by Hawthorne or Emerson. Indeed we predict for it the same interest as a new *Scarlet Letter*, or a new *Hyperion* would elicit in the reading world. Thoreau was for many years the neighbor of Emerson and Hawthorne, and other fine spirits who have made the little town of Concord famous. He says in this eloquent record of his sojourn in the woods that he lived alone two years, a mile from any neighbor, in a house which he built himself, on the shore of Walden Pond, in Concord, Massachusetts, where he earned his living by the labor of his own hands. How he lived a few extracts from his own story will best delineate.[1]

Note

1. Omitted is a quotation from "Economy," not in the 1982 reprinting.

Thoreau's *Life in the Woods*   Anonymous*

Messrs. Ticknor & Fields, of Boston, will shortly publish a work by Henry D. Thoreau, which will take its place as one of the most unique and original accessions that have been made to American literature. Mr. Thoreau is the Orson of New England transcendentalism, and his two years' experience of hermit life in the forest that skirts the shores of Walden Pond—a beautiful sheet of water in Concord, Mass.—is the subject of

*Reprinted from *Boston Transcript*, 21 July 1854, 1. Text from Gary Scharnhorst, "James T. Fields and Early Notices of *Walden*," *New England Quarterly* 55 (March 1982):115.

*Reprinted from the *New York Evening Post*, 24 July 1854, 1. Text from Gary Scharnhorst, "James T. Fields and Early Notices of *Walden*," *New England Quarterly* 55 (March 1982):116.

Walden's [*sic*] forthcoming volume, which, in almost every particular, is a decided advance on *Merrimack*, the preceding work of this author. The minuteness and accuracy of his descriptions of the various forms of outward nature which came under his notice during his isolation from the world are hardly paralleled by any previous American production, while its quaint style and the poetic-philosophic tone of the writer's reveries suggest a comparison with the best passages of Sir Thomas Browne or Emerson.

The subjoined extracts from *Walden*, which are furnished for the *Evening Post* in advance of publication, are good specimens of its contents.[1] . . .

Note

1. Omitted are quotations from "The Pond in Winter," "Former Inhabitants and Winter Visitors," and "Conclusion," not in the 1982 reprinting.

[Review of *Walden*]   Anonymous*

This is a sort of autobiography of a hermit, who lived two years alone in the woods of Concord, Mass., a mile from any neighbor. Mr. Thoreau's object in thus turning hermit, appears to have been — so far as he had any particular end in view — to ascertain by experiment, what are the absolute necessities of man, to illustrate in his own person the truth of Watts's line: "Man wants but little here below." And his return to civilized life again, confirmed that companion line of Watts — "Nor wants that little long;" though it must be confessed Mr. Thoreau held out on little or nothing, longer than most men could have done. It is a curious and amusing book, written in the Emersonian style, but containing many shrewd and sensible suggestions, with a fair share of nonesense.

[Notice of *Walden*]   Anonymous*

This is one of the most remarkable publications of the day, and one that will not fail to be read with mingled interest and pleasure, by all who find a charm in life-like sketches of solitary and rural life. Its author is well known as one of our most eccentric and original writers and thinkers, and Walden abounds in exquisite sketches and many fine thoughts.

*Reprinted from the *Boston Daily Evening Traveller*, 9 August 1854, 1.

*Reprinted from the *Boston Atlas*, 10 August 1854, 2. I am grateful to Bradley P. Dean for discovering and transcribing this notice.

[Review of *Walden*]   Anonymous*

The author of this book, having his own ideas about life, built him a shanty on the banks of Walden Pond, in Concord, Mass., and lived there upon the labor of his hands for more than two years. This book is the story of his life; and as the incidents were not remarkably stirring, he has filled up the pages with his philosophy, which is shrewd and eccentric; and, altogether, the book is worth reading, which is saying a good deal in these times.

[Review of *Walden*]   [John Sullivan Dwight]*

. . . For indoor reading, in the interims of physical fatigue and the lull of social excitement, say, for a few minutes after the evening company have dispersed and left us to our thoughts which will not sleep without some soothing efficacy of thoughts printed and impersonal, we have another book: — kindly placed in our hands upon the eve of starting on our journey, and with a delicate instinct of what was fitting, by our friend Fields, the poet partner in the firm of Ticknor and Co., the publishers, — a copy in advance of publication. In such hours one retires from Nature only to live her over in dreams and by whatever rush-light of his own reflections; and for such hours no truer friend and text book have we ever found than this wonderful new book called *Walden, or Life in the Woods*, by Henry D. Thoreau, the young Concord hermit, as he has sometimes been called. Thoreau is one of those men who has put such a determined trust in the simple dictates of common sense, as to earn the vulgar title of "transcendentalist" from his sophisticated neighbors. He is one of the few who really thinks and acts and tries life for himself, honestly weighing and reporting thereof, and in his own way (which he cares not should be others' ways) enjoying. Of course, they find him strange, fantastical, a humorist, a theorist, a dreamer. It may be or may not. One thing is certain, that his humor has led him into a life experiment, and that into a literary report or book, that is full of information, full of wisdom, full of wholesome, bracing moral atmosphere, full of beauty, poetry and entertainment for all who have the power to relish a good book. He built himself a house in the woods by Walden pond, in Concord, where he lived alone for more than two years, thinking it false economy to eat so that life must be spent in procuring what to eat, but cultivating sober, simple,

*Reprinted from the *Providence Daily Journal*, 11 August 1854, 1.

*Reprinted from "Editorial Correspondence," *Dwight's Journal of Music* 5 (12 August 1854):149–50. Material not dealing with *Walden* has been omitted.

philosophic habits, and daily studying the lesson which nature and the soul of nature are perpetually teaching to the individual soul, would that but listen. Every chapter of the book is redolent of pine and hemlock. With a keen eye and love for nature, many are the rare and curious facts which he reports for us. He has become the confidant of all plants and animals, and writes the poem of their lives for us. Read that chapter upon sounds, that of the owl, the bull-frog, &c.; or that in which he commemorates the battle of the red and black ants, "red-republicans and black imperialists," which "took place in the Presidency of Polk, five years before the passage of Webster's Fugitive Slave Bill." Truer touches of humor and quaint, genuine, first-hand observation you will seldom find. And then his vegetable planting — read how he was "determined to know beans!" And his shrewd criticisms, from his woodland seclusion, upon his village neighbors and upon civilized life generally, in which men are slaves to their own thrift, are worthy of a philosophic, though by no means a "melancholy, Jacques." It is the most thoroughly original book that has been produced these many days. Its literary style is admirably clear and terse and elegant; the pictures wonderfully graphic; for the writer is a poet and a scholar as well as a tough wrestler with the first economical problems of nature, and a winner of good cheer and of free glorious leisure out of what men call the "hard realities" of life. Walden pond, a half mile in diameter, in Concord town, becomes henceforth as classical as any lake of Windermere. And we doubt not, men are beginning to look to transcendentalists for the soberest reports of good hard common-sense, as well as for the models of the clearest writing. . . .

[Review of *Walden*]   Anonymous*

We do not suppose any of our readers need be informed who Thoreau is; but if any are ignorant of his name or existence, this book will be their best introduction. Looked upon as one of the Concord oddities, as a wayward genius, many have smiled and turned away their heads as they would at a clown who for a moment might make them stare and laugh, but leave them no wiser in the end. A few interested themselves in the Walden philosopher, amused with his quaintness, struck with the sense of some of his philosophy, and pleased with his originality. Almost the only opportunity he has given the public to become acquainted with him, has been through the medium of lectures. These will be eclipsed in popularity by the book which has many decided advantages over the lectures. A man can write about himself with better effect than he can talk about himself.

*Reprinted from the *Worcester Palladium*, 16 August 1854, 3. I am grateful to Bradley P. Dean for transcribing this review.

The pen is a more modest communicator than the tongue, and is not so easily charged with egotism.

Walden is a prose poem. It has classical elegance, and New England homeliness, with a sprinkle of Oriental magnificence in it. It is a book to be read and re-read, and read again, until another is written like it; so great is the popular tendency towards artificialities. It can not be complained against the book that it is not practical in its theories. Does not its author tell us of every board that built his house? Also the cost of the laths, the windows, the chimney, and the food he eats? He shows us that life is too hard work now-a-days; that it grows harder and more perplexing the farther it advances from primitive simplicity. With portions of the volume the public are familiar, but the whole of it is well worth being acquainted with. Our readers will find extracts from it on our first page. Elegantly published in a neat and convenient form, it is for sale at Livermore's.

[Review of *Walden*]   Anonymous*

Mr. Thoreau spent two years of his life alone in the woods, a mile from any neighbor, in a house which he built himself, on the shores of Walden Pond in Concord, Mass. In a lecture which he delivered before our Lyceum, he gave some of the experiences of this episode in his life — and this book is that lecture revised and extended. It is the same quaint production of a crooked genius — only, a good deal more so. Beneath all its seemingly paradoxical philosophy, however, there is a stream of true thought, in which some of the illusions of civilization are clearly shown. We only wish some of our good dames who make themselves such complete slaves to their furniture and their "best rooms," would read Mr. Thoreau's chapter on household economy. We think they might gather a few ideas there that would be of great advantage to them. This book contains many pleasant thoughts, quaintly expressed, some sound philosophy, and numerous passages of poetic power. It is thoroughly redolent of the woods, and brings all their pleasant sights and sounds graphically before the reader's senses. Walden Pond and its surroundings will be known of all men, from this time forth. The book is the most readable and original volume we have seen in a long time. For sale by J. S. Bailey.

*Reprinted from the *Portland Transcript*, 19 August 1854, 151.

[Review of *Walden*]   Anonymous*

Whatever may be thought or said of this curious volume, nobody can deny its claims to individuality of opinion, sentiment, and expression. Sometimes strikingly original, sometimes merely eccentric and odd, it is always racy and stimulating. The author, an educated gentleman, disgusted with the compliances and compromises which society enjoins on those to whom it gives "a living," goes off alone into Concord woods, builds his own house, cooks his own victuals, makes and mends his own clothes, works, reads, thinks as he pleases, and writes this book to chronicle his success in the experiment. Mr. Thoreau, it is well known, belongs to the class of transcendentalists who lay the greatest stress on the "I," and knows no limitation on the exercise of the rights of that important pronoun. The customs, manners, occupations, religion, of society, he "goes out" from, and brings them before his own inward tribunal for judgment. He differs from all mankind with wonderful composure; and, without any of the fuss of the come-outers, goes beyond them in asserting the autocracy of the individual. Making himself the measure of truth, he is apt to think that "difference from me is the measure of absurdity"; and occasionally he obtains a startling paradox, by the simple inversion of a stagnant truism. He likes to say that four and four make nine, in order to assert his independence of the contemptible trammels of the world's arithmetic. He has a philosophical fleer and gibe for most axioms, and snaps his fingers in the face of the most accredited proprieties and "do-me-goodisms" of conventional life. But if he has the wildness of the woods about him, he has their sweetness also. Through all the audacities of his eccentric protests, a careful eye can easily discern the movement of a powerful and accomplished mind. He has evidently read the best books, and talked with the best people. His love for nature, and his eye for nature, are altogether beyond the ordinary love and insight of nature's priests; and his descriptions have a kind of De Foe-like accuracy and reality in their eloquence, peculiar to himself among all American writers. We feel, in reading him, that such a man has earned the right to speak of nature, for he has taken her in all moods, and given the same "frolic welcome" to her "thunder and her sunshine."

But we doubt if anybody can speak so well of Mr. Thoreau as Mr. Thoreau himself. He has devoted so much of his life to the perusal of his own consciousness, that we feel it would be a kind of impertinence to substitute our impressions for his knowledge. We will first extract his account of his expenses for eight months in his woodland home: —[1]. . . .

As the article of food, put down at $8,74, is unaccompanied by the items thereof, we subjoin them in order that our readers may see on how little a philosopher can live: —[2]. . . .

*Reprinted from *Graham's Magazine* 45 (September 1854):298–300.

One of the great trials of authors and sages has its source in the necessity of being clothed. Mr. Thoreau has discussed this matter with unusual sagacity, and what thinker, after reading the following, can mourn over the fact of being out at the elbows: — [3]. . . .

In a description of his visitors, occurs the following testimonial to a Concord philosopher, who occasionally penetrated to his residence. Although the name is not given, we suppose Mr. Thoreau refers to A. Bronson Alcott: — [4]

Here is a defense of individualism, in its large sense of following one's genius, the sense in which Mr. Thoreau uses it:[5]. . . .

The volume is so thickly studded with striking descriptions that it is difficult to select an average specimen of Mr. Thoreau's power and felicity. We take the following as one of the best: — [6]. . . .

We fear that our extracts have not done justice to the attractiveness of this curious and original volume. We might easily fill a page with short, sharp, quotable sentences, embodying some flash of wit or humor, some scrap of quaint or elevated wisdom, or some odd or beautiful image. Every chapter in the book is stamped with sincerity. It is genuine and genial throughout. Even its freaks of thought are full of suggestions. When the author turns his eye seriously on an object, no matter how remote from the sphere of ordinary observation, he commonly sees into it and through it. He has a good deal of Mr. Emerson's piercing quality of mind, which he exercises on the more elusive and fitting phenomena of consciousness, with a metaphysician's subtilty, and a poet's expressiveness. And as regards the somewhat presumptuous manner in which he dogmatizes, the reader will soon learn to pardon it for the real wealth of individual thinking by which it is accompanied, always remembering that Mr. Thoreau, in the words of his own motto, does not intend to write an "ode to dejection, but to brag as lustily as chanticleer in the morning, standing on his roost, if only to wake his neighbors up."

Notes

1. Omitted is the section from "Economy," p. 60.10–16.
2. Omitted is the section from "Economy," p. 59.7–21.
3. Omitted is the section from "Economy," pp. 21.16–22.21 and 23.21–24.11.
4. Omitted is the section quoted from "Former Inhabitants; and Winter Visitors," pp. 268.17–270.12.
5. Omitted is the section quoted from "Higher Laws," pp. 216.13–217.2
6. Omitted is the section quoted from "Baker Farm," pp. 201.1–203.2.

[Review of *Walden*]   Anonymous*

I have just fallen upon a proof-sheet of a new work, now in the press of Ticknor & Co., which is so cooling and refreshing in the glaring blaze of this high summer day, that I cannot resist the temptation to copy it. It is from Thoreau's "Walden; or Life in the Woods." The author is a resident of Concord, Massachusetts, and a neighbor, and, as can readily be imagined, a friend of Mr. Emerson. Some time since, he built himself a hut in the woods, and retired to it for two years that he might hold undisturbed communion with nature. And he seems to have passed through her objective covering into her very subjective life. The extract might be appropriately entitled "Morning." Thus he discourses: — [1]

Notes

1. Omitted is the section quoted from "Where I Lived, and What I Lived For," pp. 88.24–90.31.

[Review of *Walden*]   Anonymous*

A large class of readers will be pleased by the fresh rural scenes and descriptions of Mr. Thoreau, and his volume is a delightful companion for a loll under the rustling leaves of some oak, far in the country. He paints rural scenes and habits, works and pleasures with a gusto most refreshing. The book is published in the uniform style of Messrs. Ticknor and Fields, and is very handsome. We commend it to our readers.

[Review of *Walden*]   Anonymous*

One of those rare books that stand apart from the herd of new publications under which the press absolutely groans; moderate in compass but eminently suggestive, being a compound of thought, feeling, and observation. Its author, it seems, during 1845, 6, and 7, played the philosophic hermit in a wood that overlooks Walden Pond, in the neighbourhood of Concord, Massachusetts. Here he tested at how cheap a rate physical existence may healthfully be maintained, and how, apart

*Reprinted from *National Magazine* 5 (September 1854):284–85.
*Reprinted from the *Southern Literary Messenger* 20 (September 1854):575.
*Reprinted from *Albion*, n.s. 13 (9 September 1854):429.

from the factitious excitement of society and the communion of mind with mind, he could cultivate a tranquil and contemplative spirit, yet resolute withal. This experiment was undeniably successful; and he has here set forth the record of his sylvan life and the musings of his happy solitude. He probably errs in believing, that life is an isolated shanty, and the strict vegetarian system, could be made profitable or pleasant to the men and women of this age. But we shall not discuss the question with this voluntary and most practical hermit. We can admire, without wishing to imitate him; and we can thank him cordially for hints on many topics that interest humanity at large, as well as for page upon page of research and ancedote, showing how lovingly he studied the instincts and the habits of the dumb associates by whom he was surrounded. The choicest and most popular works on natural history contain no descriptions more charming than those that abound in this volume. A little humour and a little satire are the pepper and salt to this part of the entertainment that Mr. Thoreau serves up. Into it we advise the reader—of unvitiated taste and unpalled appetite—to dip deeply. We at least do not come across a Walden, every day.

Possibly our strong commendation may be borne out by the two lengthened and characteristic extracts that we quote. The first may well be called the "The Battle of the Ants."[1]

We might have found something writ in gentler strain; but there is a point and a quaintness in the above warlike episode, that catches our fancy. Our second borrowing from this clever book—a sketch of character and a striking one—may be found on another page.[2]

Notes

1. Omitted is the section quoted from "Brute Neighbors," pp. 228.25–232.11.

2. In the same issue, the *Albion* quoted from "Visitors," pp. 114.13–150.22, under the title of "The Canadian Wood-Cutter" (p. 424).

[Review of *Walden*]   Anonymous*

This is a very strange book, the history of a philosopher living in the woods, a sort of Robinson Crusoe life. It shows the simplicity with which life can be conducted, stripped of some of its conventionalities, and the whole narrative is imbued with a deep philosophic spirit. Altogether besides being beautifully written, it has an air of originality which is quite taking. We commend it to our readers.

*Reprinted from the *Daily Alta California* 5 (23 September 1854):264.

[Review of *Walden*]   [Gamaliel Bailey?]*

In its narrative, this book is unique, in its philosophy quite Emersonian. It is marked by genius of a certain order, but just as strongly, by pride of intellect. It contains many acute observations on the follies of mankind, but enough of such follies to show that its author has his full share of the infirmities of human nature, without being conscious of it. By precept and example he clearly shows how very little is absolutely necessary to the subsistence of a man, what a Robinson Crusoe life he may lead in Massachusetts, how little labor he need perform, if he will but reduce his wants to the philosophical standard, and how much time he may then have for meditation and study. To go out and squat, all alone, by a pretty pond in the woods, dig, lay the foundation of a little cabin, and put it up, with borrowed tools, furnish it, raise corn, beans, and potatoes, and do one's own cooking, hermit like, so that the total cost of the whole building, furnishing, purchasing necessaries, and living for eight months, shall not exceed forty or fifty dollars, may do for an experiment, by a highly civilized man, with Yankee versatility, who has had the full benefit of the best civilization of the age. All men are not "up to" everything. But, if they were, if they all had the universal genius of the "Yankee nation," how long would they remain civilized, by squatting upon solitary duck-ponds, eschewing matrimony, casting off all ties of family, each one setting his wits to work to see how little he could do with, and how much of that little he could himself accomplish? At the end of eight months, Mr. Thoreau might remain a ruminating philosopher, but he would have few but ruminating animals to write books for.

But, with all its extravagances, its sophisms, and its intellectual pride, the book is acute and suggestive, and contains passages of great beauty.

A Yankee Diogenes   [Charles Frederick Briggs]*

The New England character is essentially anti-Diogenic; the Yankee is too shrewd not to comprehend the advantages of living in what we call the world; there are no bargains to be made in the desert, nobody to be taken advantage of in the woods, while the dwellers in tubs and shanties have slender opportunities of bettering their condition by barter. When the New Englander leaves his home, it is not for the pleasure of living by himself; if he is migratory in his habits, it is not from his fondness for solitude, nor from any impatience he feels at living in a crowd. Where

*Reprinted from *National Era* 8 (28 September 1854):155.
*Reprinted from *Putnam's Monthly Magazine* 4 (October 1854):443–48.

there are most men, there is, generally, most money, and there is where the strongest attractions exist for the genuine New Englander. A Yankee Diogenes is a *lusus*, and we feel a peculiar interest in reading the account which an oddity of that kind gives of himself. The name of Thoreau has not a New England sound; but we believe that the author of *Walden* is a genuine New Englander, and of New England antecedents and education. Although he plainly gives the reasons for publishing his book, at the outset, he does not clearly state the causes that led him to live the life of a hermit on the shore of Walden Pond. But we infer from his volume that his aim was the very remarkable one of trying to be something, while he lived upon nothing; in opposition to the general rule of striving to live upon something, while doing nothing. Mr. Thoreau probably tried the experiment long enough to test its success, and then fell back again into his normal condition. But he does not tell us that such was the case. He was happy enough to get back among the good people of Concord, we have no doubt; for although he paints his shanty-life in rose-colored tints, we do not believe he liked it, else why not stick to it? We have a mistrust of the sincerity of the St. Simon Sylites', and suspect that they come down from their pillars in the night-time, when nobody is looking at them. Diogenes placed his tub where Alexander would be sure of seeing it, and Mr. Thoreau ingenuously confesses that he occasionally went out to dine, and when the society of woodchucks and chipping-squirrels were insufficient for his amusement, he liked to go into Concord and listen to the village gossips in the stores and taverns. Mr. Thoreau informs us that he lived alone in the woods, by the shore of Walden Pond, in a shanty built by his own hands, a mile from any neighbor, two years and half. What he did there besides writing the book before us, cultivating beans, sounding Walden Pond, reading Homer, baking johnny-cakes, studying Brahminical theology, listening to chipping-squirrels, receiving visits, and having high imaginations, we do not know. He gives us the results of his bean cultivation with great particularity, and the cost of his shanty; but the actual results of his two years and a half of hermit life he does not give. But there have been a good many lives spent and a good deal of noise made about them, too, from the sum total of whose results not half so much good could be extracted as may be found in this little volume. Many a man will find pleasure in reading it, and many a one, we hope, will be profited by its counsels. A tour in Europe would have cost a good deal more, and not have produced half as much. As a matter of curiosity, to show how cheaply a gentleman of refined tastes, lofty aspirations and cultivated intellect may live, even in these days of high prices, we copy Mr. Thoreau's account of his first year's operations; he did better, he informs us, the second year. The entire cost of his house, which answered all his purposes, and was as comfortable and showy as he desired, was $28 12½. But one cannot live on a house unless he rents it to somebody else, even though he be a philosopher and a believer in Vishnu. Mr. Thoreau felt the need of a little ready money, one of the most convenient things in the world to have by one, even before his house was finished.

"Wishing to earn ten or twelve dollars by some agreeable and honest method," he observes, "I planted about two acres and a half of light and sandy soil, chiefly with beans, but also a small part with potatoes and corn, peas and turnips." As he was a squatter, he paid nothing for rent, and as he was making no calculation for future crops, he expended nothing for manure, so that the results of his farming will not be highly instructive to young agriculturists, nor be likely to be held up as excitements to farming pursuits by agricultural periodicals. . . .¹

We will not extract the other items which Mr. Thoreau favors us with in the accounts of his *ménage*; according to his figures it cost him twenty-seven cents a week to live, clothes included; and for this sum he lived healthily and happily, received a good many distinguished visitors, who, to humor his style, used to leave their names on a leaf or a chip, when they did not happen to find him at home. But, it strikes us that all the knowledge which the "Hermit of Walden" gained by his singular experiment in living might have been done just as well, and as satisfactorily, without any experiment at all. We know what it costs to feed prisoners, paupers and soldiers; we know what the cheapest and most nutritious food costs, and how little it requires to keep up the bodily health of a full-grown man. A very simple calculation will enable any one to satisfy himself in regard to such points, and those who wish to live upon twenty-seven cents a week, may indulge in that pleasure. The great Abernethy's prescription for the attainment of perfect bodily health was, "live on sixpence a day and earn it." But that would be Sybaritic indulgence compared with Mr. Thoreau's experience, whose daily expenditure hardly amounted to a quarter of that sum. And he lived happily, too, though it don't exactly speak volumes in favor of his system to announce that he only continued his economical mode of life two years. If it was "the thing," why did he not continue it? But, if he did not always live like a hermit, squatting on other people's property, and depending upon chance perch and pickerel for his dinner, he lived long enough by his own labor, and carried his system of economy to such a degree of perfection,² . . . .

There is nothing of the mean or sordid in the economy of Mr. Thoreau, though to some his simplicity and abstemiousness may appear trivial and affected; he does not live cheaply for the sake of saving, nor idly to avoid labor; but, that he may live independently and enjoy his great thoughts; that he may read the Hindoo scriptures and commune with the visible forms of nature. We must do him the credit to admit that there is no mock sentiment, nor simulation of piety or philanthropy in his volume. He is not much of a cynic, and though we have called him a Yankee Diogenes, the only personage to whom he bears a decided resemblance is that good humored creation of Dickens, Mark Tapley, whose delight was in being jolly under difficulties. The following passage might have been written by

Mr. Tapley if that person had ever turned author, for the sake of testing the provocatives to jollity, which may be found in the literary profession:[3]. . . .

There is a true vagabondish disposition manifested now and then by Mr. Thoreau, which, we imagine, was more powerful in leading him to his eremite way of life, than his love of eastern poetry, and his fondness for observing the ways of snakes and shiners. If there had been a camp of gipsies in the neighborhood of Concord, he would have become a king among them, like Lavengro. It breaks out here with unmistakable distinctness:[4]. . . .

There is much excellent good sense delivered in a very comprehensive and by no means unpleasant style in Mr. Thoreau's book, and let people think as they may of the wisdom or propriety of living after his fashion, denying oneself all the luxuries which the earth can afford, for the sake of leading a life of lawless vagabondage, and freedom from starched collars, there are but few readers who will fail to find profit and refreshment in his pages. Perhaps some practical people will think that a philosopher like Mr. Thoreau might have done the world a better service by purchasing a piece of land, and showing how much it might be made to produce, instead of squatting on another man's premises, and proving how little will suffice to keep body and soul together. But we must allow philosophers, and all other men, to fulfill their missions in their own way. If Mr. Thoreau had been a practical farmer, we should not have been favored with his volume; his corn and cabbage would have done but little towards profiting us, and we might never have been the better for his labors. As it is, we see how much more valuable to mankind is our philosophical vagabond than a hundred sturdy agriculturists; any plodder may raise beans, but it is only one in a million who can write a readable volume. With the following extract from his volume, and heartily recommending him to the class of readers who exact thoughts as well as words from an author, we must take leave, for the present, of the philosopher of Walden Pond.[5]. . . .

Notes

1. Omitted is the section quoted from "Economy," p. 55.3–24.
2. Omitted is the section quoted from "Economy," pp. 69.7–71.3.
3. Omitted is the section quoted from "Solitude," pp. 131.22–134.2.
4. Omitted is the section quoted from "Higher Laws," pp. 210.1–211.24.
5. Omitted is the section quoted from "Economy," pp. 35.30–37.16.

[Review of *Walden*]   [Andrew Preston Peabody?]*

The economical details and calculations in this book are more curious than useful; for the author's life in the woods was on too narrow a scale to find imitators. But in describing his hermitage and his forest life, he says so many pithy and brilliant things, and offers so many piquant, and, we may add, so many just, comments on society as it is, that his book is well worth reading, both for its actual contents and its suggestive capacity.

[Review of *Walden*]   Anonymous*

"A Life in the Woods," within twenty miles of Boston may strike the reader as hardly affording enough of material in the shape of incident and adventure, for a fair sized volume like the present. But he must read and learn his mistake, for this beyond dispute is one of the most original, eccentric and suggestive books which the season has brought out. The writer, in relating his own experience, which he does with *naivete*, shows much power of reflection, and a philosophic knowledge of men and things.

[Review of *Walden*]   [Elizabeth Barstow Stoddard]*

. . . If my limits would allow, the Book I would most like to expatiate upon, would be Thoreau's *Walden, or Life in the Woods*, published by Ticknor and Fields, Boston. It is the result of a two or three years' sojourn in the woods, and it is a most minute history of Thoreau's external life, and internal speculation. It is the latest effervescence of the peculiar school, at the head of which stands Ralph Waldo Emerson. Of *Walden*, Emerson says, that Thoreau has cornered nature in it. Several years ago Thoreau sought the freedom of the woods, and built him a little house with his two hands, on the margin of Walden Pond, near Concord, Massachusetts. There he contemplated, on "cornered" nature, and hoed beans, determined, as he said, to know them. Notwithstanding an apparent contempt for utility, he seems a sharp accountant, and not a little interest is attached to his bills of expense, they are so ludicrously

*Reprinted from *North American Review* 79 (October 1854):536.
*Reprinted from *Watchman and Reflector*, 5 October 1854, 158.
*Reprinted from "Letter from a Lady Correspondent," *Daily Alta California* 5 (8 October 1854):279. Material not dealing with *Walden* has been omitted.

small. Coarse bread, occasional molasses and rice, now and then a fish taken from Walden Pond, and philosophically matured vegetables, (he sold his beans) were his fare. His ideas of beauty are positive, but limited. The world of art is beyond his wisdom. Individualism is the altar at which he worships. Philanthropy is an opposite term, and he does not scruple to affirm that Philanthropy and he are two. The book is full of talent, curious and interesting. I recommend it as a study to all fops, male and female. . . .

[Review of *Walden*]   Anonymous*

To the Editor of the Transcript: The volume with the above title, recently issued by Messrs. Ticknor & Fields, is a very remarkable book; one which appeals to the loftiest instincts of men, and which, we are sure, is already making a deep impression upon some souls. Few books have sprung from a genius so clear of extraneous influences, whether from Church, State, Society or Literature. Here is one person, at least, who is not swallowed up by the whirlpool of civilization, who though feeling no respect for any special form of religion, so that he would be scouted at by many as an infidel, yet has such a sense of the greatness of our nature, such an appreciation of intellectual and spiritual satisfactions, that it is no sacrifice, but rather a pleasure for him to resign many of the so-called advantages of society, as being obstacles in the way of his true life.

There can be no question that even in the best *class* of society, however it may be with here and there an individual, intellectual culture does not hold the first place, but is made secondary to worldly ends; to the attainment of wealth, social position, and honors. Even most of our poets and priests, whatever they may say professionally or in their better moments, yet, in the general tenor of their lives, accept the popular standard. The peculiarity of Mr. Thoreau's position is, as indicated both by this book and the other which he has published, "A Week on the Concord and Merrimac Rivers," that he finds another kind of wealth so attractive that he cannot devote his life to the ends which society has in view. However we may speculate about spirit and intellect, it is obvious that our civilization is too exclusively material. In these books we are made acquainted with a life which rests soberly and substantially upon a spiritual basis.

The influence which Mr. Thoreau exerts will not at once spread over a large surface, but it will reach far out into the tide of time, and it will make up in depth for what it wants in extent. He appeals, with all the truly wise, to elements in our nature, which lie far deeper than the sources

*Reprinted from the *Boston Transcript*, 19 October 1854, 1.

of a noisy popularity. There are doubtless already many thoughtful persons here and there, to whom his words are exceedingly precious. This, of course, is the truest outward success, and however convenient, though dangerous, a more abundant pecuniary return for his work might be, none can know better than this writer, that the capacity for entertaining and uttering such thoughts as he gives us is its own and the only adequate reward.

[Review of *Walden*]   "D'A"*

It is an old and well established doctrine, that any man's expression of opinion should be viewed and examined from his own point of vision; that we must judge of his idiosyncrasy of thought, by the light which illumined the mind that recorded it; and not by any greater or lesser brilliancy available to us. Under this rule Mr. Thoreau's volume will fall into the hands of few who can fully appreciate him or assimilate to him; for he has thought and lived and wrought under the sparkle of a moral phosphorescence which illuminates but a small portion of mankind. Not that his speculations and moralizations are in themselves novel in character; not that he has more deeply explored the varied expanse of human nature, its longings and yearnings and dreamings, than many other travellers, some of whom have recorded their explorations, and many more of whom have been silent upon the sights they have beheld. Philosophers of all ages and lands and tongues, have indulged in the same reveries; have been also weighers and gaugers of human pursuits and aspirations. In many a silent, taper lighted chamber in the heart of populous cities, as well as in the depths of the wilderness, have the same sad verdicts been passed upon the busy avocations of our race. It is not necessary to become a hermit, an exile from the companionship of our fellows, to form just such a valuation of their hopes and fears, their efforts and aims, their thoughts and deeds, as the philosopher of Walden Pond. He differs from his brother moralizers simply in this: — they think and speak of mankind as being themselves units of the many, participators in the heritage over which they mourn: — he fondly deems himself emancipated from this thraldom, and looks down upon them as an inferior tribe. He shakes the dust from his shoes as he leaves their thresholds, and goes forth to the green woods, as a temple wherein his greater holiness may dwell uncontaminated. His love for Nature, his sympathy for her wild beauty and contentedness with her society, make him forget that it is only one of her many phases which he views in his sylvan solitude. That the simplicity he adores exists nowhere in

*Reprinted from the *Boston Atlas*, 21 October 1854, 1. I am grateful to Bradley P. Dean for discovering and transcribing this review.

the range of human vision. The huckleberries, which he picked for his food, are more complicated in their structure than any human viands. The shadowy trees, over his lonely hut, are more intricate than any human dwelling. The laws of this wonderful world have more articles than any human code, and rule in the midst of densely aggregated human beings as surely, as beneficently and as ruthlessly as in that little patch of woodland where his philosophy, in its self glorification, sought a temporary sleeping and eating and dreaming place. By leaving the homes of men, he did not merely isolate himself from their meannesses, their sins and life long mistakes; but from their virtues, self-denials and heroism. He did not understand that man's passions, impulses and turbulent desires are one part of the great scheme, of which his woodland abiding place was only another. He left men preying on each other, to watch ants do the same. He left the fond loves which do sometimes bless with their purity the hearts of our misguided race, to note the couplings of brutes. He left the noblest animal in the scale of being, which with all its follies and errors and degradation is still the noblest, to watch the habits of owls and wood-chucks, and imagine that he was in the society most blessed of the great Author, and occupied in pursuits most worthy of our destiny. Our destiny! what is it? Can any one corner of this little sphere, itself minute in the vast universe, afford peculiar light to our groping souls?

In speaking of "Walden," it is impossible not to identify the author with his work. It is a series of observations upon the pursuits of mankind, mingled with descriptions of natural objects. It is the author's autobiography for a year, recording his doings, his thinkings and his human measurements. His doings, as recorded, are the erection of his own dwelling, mostly by himself, partly his acquaintances; and subsequent culture of a little pulse, on which he mainly subsisted, varied by a little fishing and much rambling. His thinking is the indulging of those inexpressible mental sensations which visit all poetic, sensitive natures in the midst of woodland solitudes. The rest, except the descriptive portion, is devoted to moralizations upon the emptiness of human aims and employments. The descriptive portion is terse and graphic. He has a keenly observant relish for all natural scenery, and has painted minutely the changing face of nature in her summer and winter garb. There is a simple, expressive truthfulness in these descriptions, which renders them both interesting and instructive in the highest degree. In spite of his depreciation of human attainments, they exhibit a familiarity with studies which are the legitimate offspring of civilization, and are none the less creditable to him as a student or as a man. No savage, be he ever so much a poet by nature or a savant by practice, could achieve the results which his play-savage, but still civilized intellect has recorded. The lore of bygone ages, written in languages long dead, has furnished this word-warrior with weapons, to use against the very foe which fed and nourished him into his present strength.

The natural enquiry why a young man should leave kindred, and friends, and comfort, to dwell for two years in Concord woods, in a board shanty, and cultivate beans for his sustenance, is answered by the man himself.

"I went to the woods because I wished to live deliberately, to front only the essential facts of life, and see if I could not learn what it had to teach, and not when I came to die, discover than I had not lived. . . . I wanted to live deep and suck out all the marrow of life; to live so sturdily and Spartan-like as to put to rout all that was not life."

Whether he lived as deeply as he desired, or whether he learned out what life has to teach, he does not state, but he quitted his Spartan-life after two years indulgence therein. He relates minutely the story of his house-raising and bean-hoeing, and discloses one great, fatal error, which completely vitiates the experiment. He was no true hermit. He did not bid farewell to human kind and "front only the essential facts of life." He borrowed the cunning tools and manufactured products of civilization, to enable him to endure the wilderness. He did not go unaided and unprovided into the untamed woods, to see life and spend life in its primitive state. He only played savage on the borders of civilization; going back to the quiet town whenever he was unable to supply his civilized wants by his own powers. The war-whoop of a Camanche Indian would have made his heart knock at his ribs in that lonely spot, for all his attempts to exalt and glorify the savage life. Were he indeed in those distant wilds where he sometimes imagined himself, instead of a patch of woodland as safe as his mother's fireside, his romance and self-satisfaction might have fled before the stern unrelenting reality. No, he went back to the village to chat with the people he affects to despise, and spend cosy winter evenings with those who enjoyed the same natural beauties that he did without resigning those unostentatious comforts, which not only had no connexion, but did not in the least conflict with such enjoyments. One glaring mistake throughout the volume, is an apparent conviction that to really and fully relish the sights and sounds of Nature, to adore its spirit through all these noble revelations, it is necessary to shun human kind, and to eat, drink and sleep in the forest depths. As though there is not many and many a dwelling more comfortable than his own erected in the bosom of the woods, and peopled by happy, intelligent men and women, who value their dwelling for its very seclusion, enjoying its charms together.

His descriptions, admirable as they are, are bald in comparison with the glowing word-painting of many lovers of Nature, as devout, and more genial than himself. The sensations he describes are such as have thrilled the hearts of thousands before him. His yearnings to discover that mysterious secret, the end and use of life, have gushed in the bosoms of multitudes who never fancied that the key was hidden in a hermitage. Did he find it there? Did he find that life was truest away from all those dear affections which are given to man for indulgence, as freely as these very longings themselves? Did he fancy that life was only life when shorn of all its attributes? When he had taken the warm, breathing creature, had lopped away its limbs, and cut away, remorselessly, the quivering flesh, and at last reached the throbbing heart; when he had split open that palpitating centre, had he at last found out *what* that life was which animated it? No! he had only thrown from him the very parts for which that heart was made to beat; without which it were worthless.

It is a sorrowful surprise that a constant communion with so much beauty and beneficence was not able to kindle one spark of genial warmth in this would-be savage. Pithy sarcasm, stern judgment, cold condemnation — all these abound in the pages of this volume. The follies and emptiness of men are uncovered with a sweeping hand. There is truth in it; strong, vigorous, nervous truth. But there is not a page, a paragraph giving one sign of liberality, charitableness, kind feeling, generosity, in a word — HEART. The noble deeds, the silent fortitude, the hidden sorrow of mankind, are nowhere recognized. It is difficult to understand that a mother had ever clasped this hermit to her bosom; that a sister had ever imprinted on his lips a tender kiss. The occasional ridiculousness of some of his propositions is only exceeded by the total absence of human affection which they evince. It is scarcely to be credited that any man can have lived thirty years in New England and written a volume treating expressly of human life, which exhibits such an utter dearth of all the kindly, generous feelings of our nature. Could not the warm, budding spring arouse one genial throb in his cynic soul? Could not the instinctive loves of birds and beasts have awakened within him one thought of the purer, loftier, nobler passion accorded to his own race? Did he never people that bare hovel, in imagination, with a loving and beloved wife and blooming children, or did he imagine that to know what life is he must ignore its origin? Did he utterly forget that pain and sickness might have quenched the light of his reason, and drawn a dreadful night over his unsolaced soul? A night in which the meanest of human kind would have beamed at his side like an angel from Heaven! He has much to say to men, and tells them bitter truths; but there is not one recognition of the presence on this earth of woman. There is not a word of that pure, constant, suffering woman's love, beside which his philosophic judgments shrink and shiver in their frigidity. Back to the town, the crowded city, oh, forest philosophers, if the sweet smiles of nature cannot warm within you more than this, the hearts that are better worth your culture than your intellects or your bean fields! No soul is truly expanded by confinement to solitary reverie. It is an old truth that natural scenery does not, of itself, improve the heart or nature. The finest countries in the world are peopled by sanguinary savages. The laborers upon the soil are last to appreciate the glories around them. The loftiest praises ever sung to the majesty and magnificence of nature, have come from the lips of poets whose minds and perceptions were cultivated in the haunts of men.

The Spirit who placed us on this little planet, for his own good purpose, gave us the desire to live in company. Civilization, as it now exists, is merely the culminating point to which this desire, working through the varied channels of human idiosyncrasies, have now attained. We do not all go to the woods and live on pulse, simply because we were not inspired with the desire to do so; and human history does not date back to the time when such was the case. The errors of mankind are simply the creatures of those passions, more or less developed, which are parts of our nature. If it were better that we should be entirely without them, they would never have been given to us. Strong thinkers, skilful anatomists of human impulse, would be better occupied in seeking to assuage the troubles of the body corporate, than in crossing on the other side and railing at it.

Mr. Thoreau's book will be admired by some for its truthful and graphic delineations of natural objects; by others for its just valuations of human pursuits. It is marked by vigorous expression and quaint illustration, though this last sometimes verges into nonsense and puerility. He argues at times with apparent gravity upon topics scarcely worth the consideration of a man seeking to solve the problem of human life. His propositions with regard to dress are certainly unworthy of him. The question may simply be asked, if a man be "fit to worship God" in "patched pantaloons," is he not equally so in whole ones? The preference for clean, well made clothes over dirty, ragged ones, scarcely argues any moral degradation or idle folly in any one. Still, even on this as other topics, he has much truth and sense on his side, so long as he attacks abuse and not use. There is much freshness and vigor in the thoughts strewn through the volume; but it is marred by an affected mannerism belonging to the school which he copies, and by the absence of a genial, truly philosophic, broad-hearted, pervading spirit.

[Review of *Walden*]   Anonymous*

This is a charming volume by a writer who reminds us of Emerson by his philosophy — of the Elizabethan writers by his quaintness and originality — and by his minuteness and acuteness of observation, of Gilbert White, the author of the Natural History of Selborne. Mr. Thoreau lived alone in the woods for two years, a mile from any neighbor, in a house which he had built himself in Concord, Mass., on the shore of Walden

*Reprinted from the *Yankee Blade*, 28 October 1854, 3.

Pond. In the present volume he relates in a lively and sparkling, yet pithy style, his experiences during that period—describing the various natural phenomena, the sights and sounds, as well as the different phases of humanity, that fell under his observation and favoring us with exact statistics of the cost of supporting his hermit life. It is rarely that one finds so much originality and freshness in a modern book—such an entire absence of conventionality and cant—or so much suggestive observation on the philosophy of life. Almost every page abounds in brilliant, and piquant things, which, in spite of the intellectual pride of the author—the intense and occasionally unpleasant egotism with which every line is steeped—lure the reader on with bewitched attention from title-page to finis. Mr. Thoreau has an odd twist in his brains, but, as Hazlitt says of Sir Thomas Browne, they are "all the better for the twist." The best parts of the book, to our mind, are those which treat of Sounds, Solitude, Brute Neighbors, Winter Animals, The Pond in Winter, and Reading; the poorest, the Conclusion, in which he tries to Emersonize, and often "attains" triumphantly to the obscurity which he seems to court.

[Review of *A Week on the Concord and Merrimack Rivers* and *Walden*]

[Lydia Maria Child?]*

These books spring from a depth of thought which will not suffer them to be put by, and are written in a spirit in striking contrast with that which is uppermost in our time and country. Out of the heart of practical, hard-working, progressive New England comes these Oriental utterances. The life exhibited in them teaches us, much more impressively than any number of sermons could, that this Western activity of which we are so proud, these material improvements, this commercial enterprise, this rapid accumulation of wealth, even our external, associated philanthropic action, are very easily overrated. The true glory of the human soul is not to be reached by the most rapid travelling in car or steamboat, by the instant transmission of intelligence however far, by the most speedy accumulation of a fortune, and however efficient measures we may adopt for the reform of the intemperate, the emancipation of the enslaved, &c., it will avail little unless we are ourselves essentially noble enough to inspire those whom we would so benefit with nobleness. External bondage is trifling compared with the bondage of an ignoble soul. Such things are often said, doubtless, in pulpits and elsewhere, but the men who say them are too apt to live just with the crowd, and so their words come more and more to ring with a hollow sound.

*Reprinted from the *National Anti-Slavery Standard*, 16 December 1854, 3.

It is refreshing to find in these books the sentiments of one man whose aim manifestly is to *live*, and not to waste his time upon the externals of living. Educated at Cambridge, in the way called liberal, he seems determined to make a liberal life of it, and not to become the slave of any calling, for the sake of earning a reputable livelihood or of being regarded as a useful member of society. He evidently considers it his first business to become more and more a living, advancing soul, knowing that thus alone (though he desires to think as little as possible about that) can he be, in any proper sense, useful to others. Mr. Thoreau's view of life has been called selfish. His own words, under the head of "Philanthropy" in Walden, are the amplest defence against this charge, to those who can appreciate them. In a deeper sense than we commonly think, charity begins at home. The man who, with any fidelity, obeys his own genius, serves men infinitely more by so doing, becoming an encouragement, a strengthener, a fountain of inspiration to them, than if he were to turn aside from his path and exhaust his energies in striving to meet their superficial needs. As a thing by the way, aside from our proper work, we may seek to remove external obstacles from the path of our neighbours, but no man can help them much who makes that his main business, instead of seeking evermore, with all his energies, to reach the loftiest point which his imagination sets before him, thus adding to the stock of true nobleness in the world.

But suppose all men should pursue Mr. Thoreau's course, it is asked triumphantly, as though, then, we should be sure to go back to barbarism. Let it be considered, in the first place, that no man could pursue his course who was a mere superficial imitator, any more than it would be a real imitation of Christ if all men were to make it their main business to go about preaching the Gospel to each other. Is it progress toward barbarism to simplify one's outward life for the sake of coming closer to Nature and to the realm of ideas? Is it civilization and refinement to be occupied evermore with adding to our material conveniences, comforts and luxuries, to make ourselves not so much living members as dead tools of society, in some bank, shop, office, pulpit or kitchen? If men were to follow in Mr. Thoreau's steps, by being more obedient to their loftiest instincts, there would, indeed, be a falling off in the splendour of our houses, in the richness of our furniture and dress, in the luxury of our tables, but how poor are these things in comparison with the new grandeur and beauty which would appear in the souls of men. What fresh and inspiring conversation should we have, instead of the wearisome gossip which now meets us at every turn. Men toil on, wearing out body or soul, or both, that they may accumulate a needless amount of the externals of living; that they may win the regard of those no wiser than themselves; their natures become warped and hardened to their pursuits; they get fainter and fainter glimpses of the glory of the world, and, by and by, comes into their richly-adorned parlours some wise and beautiful soul, like the writer of these books, who, speaking from the fullness of his inward life, makes their luxuries appear vulgar, showing that, in a direct way, he has obtained the essence of that which his entertainers have been vainly seeking for at such a terrible expense.

It seems remarkable, that these books have received no more adequate notice in our Literary Journals. But the class of scholars are often as blind as others to any new elevation of soul. In Putnam's Magazine, Mr. Thoreau is spoken of as an oddity, as the Yankee Diogenes, as though the really ridiculous oddity were not in us of the "starched shirt-collar" rather than in this devotee of Nature and Thought. Some have praised the originality and profound sympathy with which he views natural objects. We might as well stop with praising Jesus for the happy use he has made of the lilies of the field. The fact of surpassing interest for us is the simple grandeur of Mr. Thoreau's position — a position open to us all, and of which this sympathy with Nature is but a single result. This is seen in the less descriptive, more purely thoughtful passages, such as that upon Friendship in the "Wednesday" of the "Week," and in those upon "Solitude," "What I lived for," and "Higher Laws," in "Walden," as well as in many others in both books. We do not believe that, in the whole course of literature, ancient and modern, so noble a discourse upon Friendship can be produced as that which Mr. Thoreau has given us. It points to a relation, to be sure, which, from the ordinary level of our lives, may seem remote and dreamy. But it is our thirst for, and glimpses of, such things which indicate the greatness of our nature, which give the purest charm and colouring to our lives. The striking peculiarity of Mr. Thoreau's attitude is, that while he is no religionist, and while he is eminently practical in regard to the material economies of life, he yet manifestly feels, through and through, that the loftiest dreams of the imagination are the solidest realities, and so the only foundation for us to build upon, while the affairs in which men are everywhere busying themselves so intensely are comparatively the merest froth and foam.

Town and Rural Humbugs   Anonymous*

When Philip, King of Macedon, had made preparations to march against the Corinthians, the latter, though utterly incapable of coping with that sagacious and powerful monarch, affected to make great efforts at defence with a view to resist him. Diogenes, who took great delight in ridiculing such follies as he was too proud to indulge in himself, or did not happen to have a taste for, began to roll about his tub in a bustling and excited manner, thus deriding the idle hurry and silly show of opposition

*Reprinted from *Knickerbocker Magazine* 45 (March 1855):235–41.

by which the feeble Corinthians were trying to deceive themselves or Philip into a belief that he had something to fear from them.

It is a wonder to a certain Yankee Diogenes, that there are not more tubs rolled about now-a-days; for the world, in his estimation, never contained more bustling, shadow-pursuing Corinthians, than at the present time.

A Concord philosopher, or modern Diogenes, who has an eye of acute penetration in looking out upon the world, discovered so much aimless and foolish bustle, such a disproportion of shams to realities, that his inclination or self-respect would not permit him to participate in them; so he built himself in the woods, on the banks of a pond of pure water — deep enough for drowning purposes if the bean-crop failed — a tub of unambitious proportions, into which he crawled. In this retreat, where he supported animal and intellectual life for more than two years, at a cost of about thirteen (!) dollars per annun, he wrote a book full of interest, containing the most pithy, sharp, and original remarks.

It is a fortunate circumstance for Mr. Thoreau, the name of this eccentric person, that his low estimate of the value of the objects, compared with their cost, for which the world is so assiduously and painfully laboring, should have received, so soon after the publication of his book, such an important, substantial, and practical confirmation in the auto-biography of Barnum. If any thing is calculated to induce a man to see how few beans will support animal life, we think it is a contemplation of the life and career of the great show-man. If there is any thing calculated to reconcile us, not to the career of Barnum, but to whatever laborious drudgery may be necessary to procure good beefsteaks and oysters, with their necessary accompaniments, it is the thought of those inevitable beans, that constituted so large a part of the *crop* of Mr. Thoreau, and that extraordinary compound of corn-meal and water, which he facetiously called bread.

Beyond all question, the two most remarkable books that have been published the last year are the "Auto-biography of Barnum," and "Life in the Woods," by Thoreau. The authors of the two books, in tastes, habits, disposition, and culture are perfect antipodes to each other; and the lessons they inculcate are consequently diametrically opposite. If ever a book required an antidote, it is the auto-biography of Barnum, and we know of no other so well calculated to furnish this antidote as the book of Thoreau's.

If any of the readers of the *Knickerbocker* have so long denied themselves the pleasure of reading "Walden, or Life in the Woods," we will give them a slight account of the book and its author; but we presume the information will be necessary to only very few. Mr. Thoreau is a graduate of Harvard University. He is a bold and original thinker; "he reads much, is a great observer, and looks quite through the deeds of men." "Beware," says Emerson, "when the great God lets loose a thinker on this planet.

Then all things are at risk." Are thinkers so rare that all the moral, social, and political elements of society may be disturbed by the advent of one? The sale Barnum's book has already met with is not, to be sure, suggestive of an overwhelming number of thinkers in the country. Thinkers always have been considered dangerous. Even Caesar, if he could have feared any thing, would have been afraid of that lean Cassius, because

He thinks too much: such men are dangerous.

And why are thinkers dangerous? Because the world is full of "time-honored and venerable" shams, which the words of thinkers are apt to endanger.

After leaving college, Mr. Thoreau doffed the harness which society enjoins that all its members shall wear, in order for them "to get along well," but it galled and chafed in so many places that he threw it off, and took to the woods in Concord. He built a hut there, a mile from any neighbors, that cost him twenty-eight dollars, twelve and a-half cents, and lived there more than two years — eight months of the time at an expense of nearly nine shillings a-month. Before adopting this mode of life, he first tried school-keeping, reporting for a newspaper, and then trading for a livelihood; but after a short trial at each, became persuaded that it was impossible for his genius to lie in either of those channels.

After hesitating for some time as to the advisability of seeking a living by picking huckle-berries, he at last concluded that "the occupation of a day-laborer was the most independent of any, as it required only thirty or forty days in a year, to support one. The laborer's day ends with the going down of the sun, and he is then free to devote himself to his chosen pursuit, independent of his labor; but his employer, who speculates from month to month, has no respite from one end of the year to the other. In short, I am convinced, both by faith and experience, that to maintain one's self on this earth, is not a hardship, but a pastime, if we will live simply and wisely, as the pursuits of the simpler nations are still the sports of the more artificial. It is not necessary that a man should earn his living by the sweat of his brow, unless he sweats easier than it I do."

The establishment in the woods, kept up by the extravagant expenditures we have mentioned before, was the result of these reflections.

If there is any reader of the Knickerbocker — native-born and a Know-Nothing — who needs to be told who P. T. Barnum is, such a person might, without doubt, "hear something to his advantage," by inquiring out and presenting himself before that illustrious individual; for the great show-man has made a good deal of money by exhibiting less extraordinary animals than such a man would be.

It was pretty well understood by physiologists, before the recent experiment of Mr. Thoreau, how little farinaceous food would suffice for the human stomach; and Chatham-street clothiers have a tolerably accurate knowledge of how little poor and cheap raiment will suffice to cover the back, so that his "life in the woods" adds but little to the stock of information scientific men already possessed. But it was not clearly known to what extent the public was gullible until the auto-biography of Barnum fully demonstrated the fact. This renowned individual has shown to a dignified and appreciative public the vulgar machinery used to humbug them, and they (the public) are convulsed with laughter and delight at the exposition. Cuteness is held in such great esteem that the fact of being egregiously cajoled and fooled out of our money is lost sight of in admiration for the shrewdness of the man who can do it. And then there is such an idolatrous worship of the almighty dollar, that the man who accumulates 'a pile' is pretty sure to have the laugh on his side. 'Let him laugh who wins,' says Barnum, and the whole country says amen. It is very evident that shams sometimes 'pay better' pecuniarily than realities, but we doubt if they do in all respects. Although Thoreau 'realized' from his bean-crop one season—a summer's labor—but eight dollars seventy-one and a-half cents, yet it is painful to think what Barnum must have 'realized' from 'Joice Heth' and the 'Woolly Horse.'

If we were obliged to choose between being shut up in 'conventional-ism's air-tight stove," (even if the said stove had all the surroundings of elegance and comforts that wealth could buy,) and a twenty-eight dollar tub in the woods, with a boundless range of freedom in the daily *walk* of life, we should not hesitate a moment in taking the tub, if it were not for a recollection of those horrid beans, and that melancholy mixture of meal and water. Aye, there's the rub, for from that vegetable diet what dreams might come, when we had shuffled off the wherewith to purchase other food, must give us pause. There's the consideration that makes the sorry conventionalisms of society of so long life. We rather bear those ills we have, than fly to others that we know not of. A very reasonable dread of something unpleasant resulting to us from eating beans in great quantities, would be likely to be a consequence of our experience alone, if we happened to be deficient in physiological knowledge. Whatever effects, however, different kinds of diet may have upon different persons, mentally or physically, nothing is more clear than the fact that the diet of Mr. Thoreau did not make him mentally windy. We think, however, between Iranistan, with Joice Heth and the Mermaid for associates, and the tub at Walden, with only Shakespeare for a companion, few probably would be long puzzled in making a choice, though we are constrained to say that the great majority would undoubtedly be on the side of the natural phenom-ena—we mean on the side of Barnum and the other mentioned curiosities. Still, in contemplating a good many of the situations in which Barnum was placed, it is impossible to conceive that any person of a comparatively sensitive nature would not gladly have exchanged places with the man of the woods. (We refer of course to the author of "Walden," and not to the animal known as "the man of the woods." Some perhaps would not have taken pains to make this explanation.)

There is a good deal more virtue in beans than we supposed there was, if they are sufficient to sustain a man in such cheerful spirits as Thoreau appears to have been in when he wrote that book. The spirit oftentimes may be strong when the flesh is weak; but there does not appear to be any evidence of weakness of the flesh in the author of "Walden." We cannot help feeling admiration for the man

> That fortune's buffets and rewards
> Has ta'en with equal thanks:

and since Sylla so coolly massacred so many Roman citizens, there has not been a man who apparently has contemplated his fellow-men with a more cheerful, lofty, and philosophical scorn than the occupant of this Walden tub. If a man can do this upon beans, or in *spite* of them, we shall endeavor to cultivate a respect for that vegetable, which we never could endure.

It was a philosopher, as ancient as Aristotle, we believe, who affirmed that "they most resemble the gods whose wants were fewest." Whether the sentiment is a true one or not, we have no hesitation in saying that the gods we worship will bear a good deal more resemblance to H. D. Thoreau than to P. T. Barnum. We believe it requires a much higher order of intellect to live alone in the woods, than to dance attendance in the museum of a great metropolis upon dead hyenas and boa constrictors, living monkeys and rattle-snakes, giants and dwarfs, artificial mermaids, and natural zanies. There is, however, a good deal of society worse than this.

Of the many good things said by Colton, one of the best, we think, is the following:

"Expense of thought is the rarest prodigality, and to dare to live alone the rarest courage; since there are many who had rather meet their bitterest enemy in the field, than their own hearts in their closet. He that has no resources of mind is more to be pitied than he who is in want of necessaries for the body; and to be obliged to beg our daily happiness from others, bespeaks a more lamentable poverty than that of him who begs his daily bread."

We do not believe there is any danger of proselytes to Mr. Thoreau's mode of life becoming too numerous. We wish we could say the same in regard to Barnum's. We ask the reader to look around among his acquaintances, and see if the number of those whose resources of mind are sufficient to enable them to dispense with much intercourse with others, is not exceedingly small. We know of some such, though they are very few; but their fondness for solitude unfortunately is not associated with any particular admiration for a vegetable diet. It is a melancholy circumstance, and one that has been very bitterly deplored, ever since that indefinite period when "the memory of man runneth not to the contrary," that the accompaniments of poverty should go hand-in-hand with a taste for a solitary life. A hearty appreciation of and love for humble fare, plain clothes, and poor surroundings generally, are what men of genius need to cultivate. "Walden" tends to encourage this cultivation.

The part of Mr. Barnum's life, during which he has become a millionaire, has been spent almost wholly in a crowd. It would be no paradox to say that if the time he has spent as a show-man had been spent in the woods, neither the brilliancy of his imagination nor the vigor and originality of his thoughts would have enabled him to have produced a book that would have created any very great excitement, notwithstanding the extraordinary attributes of that intellect which could conceive the idea of combining nature and art to produce "natural curiosities," and which was shrewd enough to contrive ways and means for drawing quarters and shillings, and for the smallest value received, indiscriminately from residents in the Fifth Avenue and the Five-Points, from the statesman and "the Bowery-boy," from savans, theologians, lawyers, doctors, merchants, and "the rest of mankind," to say nothing about Queen Victoria, the Duke of Wellington, and a large portion of the Eastern continent beside.

Unlike as Barnum and Thoreau are in most every other respect, in one point there is a striking resemblance. Both of them had no idea of laboring very hard with their hands for a living; they were determined to support themselves principally by their wits. The genius of Barnum led him to obtain the meat he fed upon by a skillful combination of nature with art — by eking out the short-comings in the animal creation with ingenious and elaborate manufactures, and then adroitly bringing the singular compounds thus formed to bear upon the credulity of the public. And thus, while he taxed the animal, vegetable, and mineral kingdoms, either separately or combined, to gratify the curiosity of the public, the most valued products of the last-mentioned kingdom flowed in a large and perpetual stream into his pocket. But his expenditures of "brass" in these labors were enormous. Thoreau had no talent for "great combinations." The meat he fed upon evidently would not be that of extraordinary calves or over-grown buffaloes, baked in the paragon cooking-stove of public curiosity; or rather, as he ate no meat, the vegetables he lived upon would not come from the exhibition of India-rubber mermaids, gutta-percha fish, or mammoth squashes. His genius did not lie at all in that direction. On the contrary, he preferred to diminish his wants, instead of resorting to extraordinary schemes to gratify them.

Mr. Thoreau gives a description of a battle fought upon his wood-pile between two armies of ants, that is exceedingly graphic and spirited. We think it surpasses in interest the description of battles fought about Sebastopol, written by the famous correspondent of the London *Times*. Perhaps, however, we are somewhat prejudiced in the matter. The truth is, we have read so much about the war in Europe, that the whole subject has become somewhat tiresome; and this account of the battle of the ants in Concord had so much freshness about it — so much novelty, dignity, and importance, which the battles in Europe cease to possess for us — that we have read it over three or four times with increased interest each time. We regret that the whole account is too long to copy here, but we will give the closing part:[1]. . . .

The more you think of it the less the difference between this fight and those battles about Sebastopol. There appears, however, to have been this advantage in favor of the battle of the ants, there was no "mistake" made in the orders, (that the chronicler could discover,) by which many valuable lives were lost, as in the charge of cavalry at Sebastopol. All the operations of the ants appeared to be systematic and well-timed. This rather goes to show that the commanders of ants are more cautious than the commanders of men, for the reason probably that they hold the lives of their combatants in greater estimation.

The machinery that is used to bring about battles between different nations by "the powers that be," is very much like that Barnum used to divert the public — to divert money from their pockets into his. By adding to the age of his remarkable "nurse" — the vivacious and interesting Joice — in about the same proportion that he increased the age of his juvenile phenomenon, General Thumb, he was guilty of a departure from truth not a whit more extraordinary than the discrepancy between the conversation of the Emperor of all the Russias with the English ambassadors in regard to the health of Turkey, and his actions at the same time. Barnum unquestionably possesses superior diplomatic talents. Talleyrand would have approved them.

We said some little way back that there was one point of resemblance between Barnum and Thoreau. There are half-a-dozen. Both are good-natured, genial, pleasant men. One sneers at and ridicules the pursuits of his contemporaries with the same cheerfulness and good-will that the other cajoles and fleeces them. The rural philosopher measured the length, breadth, and depth of Walden Pond, with the same jovial contentedness that the metropolitan show-man measured the length, breadth, and depth of the public gullibility. Both too are compassionate men. Flashes of pity are occasionally met with in the book of Barnum's, at the extent of the credulity of that public he seemingly so remorselessly wheedled; and Thoreau evinced a good deal of compassion for some of his well-to-do townsmen. His sympathy was a good deal moved in behalf of the farmer that owned "a handsome property," who was driving his oxen in the night to Brighton, through the mud and darkness. Both were artists. He of the wood constructed himself the unpretending edifice he occupied — a representation of which graces the title-page of his book. Barnum's artistic skill was more evinced in constructing such "curiosities" as we have before alluded to. And finally, both were humbugs — one a town and the other a rural humbug.

But both of them have nevertheless made large contributions to the science of human nature. Malherbe, once upon hearing a prose work of great merit extolled, dryly asked if it would *reduce the price of bread!* If "Walden" should be extensively read, we think it would have the effect to reduce somewhat the price of meat, if it did not of bread. At all events it encourages the belief, which in this utilitarian age enough needs encouragement, that there is some other object to live for except "to make money."

In the New England philosophy of life, which so extensively prevails where the moral or intellectual character of a man is more or less determined by his habits of *thrift*, such a book as "Walden" was needed. Extravagant as it is in the notions it promulgates, we think it is nevertheless calculated to do a good deal of good, and we hope it will be widely read. Where it exerts a bad influence upon one person, Barnum's autobiography will upon a hundred.

Notes

1. Omitted is the section quoted from "Brute Neighbors," pp. 229.21–230.29.

[Review of *Walden*]   [George Eliot]*

. . . in a volume called "Walden; or, Life in the Woods" — published last year, but quite interesting enough to make it worth while for us to break our rule by a retrospective notice — we have a bit of pure American life (not the "go a-head" species, but its opposite pole), animated by that energetic, yet calm spirit of innovation, that practical as well as theoretic independence of formulæ, which is peculiar to some of the finer American minds. The writer tell us how he chose, for some years, to be a stoic of the woods; how he built his house; how he earned the necessaries of his simple life by cultivating a bit of ground. He tells his system of diet, his studies, his reflections, and his observations of natural phenomena. These last are not only made by a keen eye, but have their interest enhanced by passing through the medium of a deep poetic sensibility; and, indeed, we feel throughout the book the presence of a refined as well as a hardy mind. People — very wise in their own eyes — who would have every man's life ordered according to a particular pattern, and who are intolerant of every existence the utility of which is not palpable to them, may pooh-pooh Mr. Thoreau and this episode in his history, as unpractical and dreamy. Instead of contesting their opinion ourselves, we will let Mr. Thoreau speak for himself. There is plenty of sturdy sense mingled with his unworldliness.[1] . . .

*Reprinted from *Westminster Review* 65 (January 1856):302–3.

We can only afford one more extract, which, to our minds, has great beauty.[2]. . .

Notes

1. Omitted are the sections quoted from "Where I Lived, and What I Lived For," pp. 90.32–91.15, and from "Economy," pp. 72.18–73.16, 76.15–32, 71.6–16.
2. Omitted are the sections quoted from "Sounds," pp. 111.18–33, 112.11–24.

The Bases of Character   Horace Greeley*

There are those who insist that Society is so radically vicious and corrupt, that we may not hope to meet men and women who satisfy our conceptions of human character as it should be, until our social relations are radically reformed, rationalized, purified. There are those, on the other hand, who insist that Society is now as perfect as it can be, while human nature remains unchanged.

I do not assent fully to either of these statements. I regard Social Reform and Individual improvement not as competitors but as coworkers and mutual helpers. Providence has wisely blended, and man cannot well divorce them. A better Social polity would ensure better men; as better men must ever give the impulse to a better society. Yet my present theme contemplates mainly the principles and the laws of individual or self-culture. And, so far a hurried statement may do justice to so vast a theme, I would lay the bases of a true and generous Mental Training in the following precepts.

I. *Utility is the chief end of life, which no one may innocently disregard.* I choose to commence where too many moralists and even divines are content to close, and some of them a little before they reach this point. I hear that this or that eminent citizen has bequeathed at death, or perhaps given during life, a very handsome donation to some laudable enterprise, and I approve the act. But, before glorifying the donor, I must ask, "Did he fairly and beneficently *earn* this money? Was his life one of active usefulness — of downright industry?" If yea, then his gift is indeed a noble one, and his act should be duly honored.

But if he were one who inherited or suddenly acquired opulence, and thereupon felt himself absolved from all obligation to farther effort — if thenceforth he lived in luxurious indolence or miserly seclusion, then is his

*Reprinted from *The Rose of Sharon: A Religious Souvenir, for MDCCCCLVII*, ed. Mrs. Caroline M. Sawyer (Boston: Abel Tompkins and Sanborn, Carter, and Bazin, 1857), 65–73. Noted at the foot of p. 63 as "Extracted from an unprinted lecture on 'Self Culture.' "

memory unblest and his gift no gift at all. If he gave only the products of others' toil, his bounty is but restitution, and only deserving of praise in that he might have persisted in his wrong to the end, and transmitted the spoil to others equally undeserving. Heaven smiles not on the grudged offerings of Ananias and Sapphira, even to the best of undertakings. I envy not the spiritual shepherds of those who live through years in sumptuous idleness, or any idleness at all, yet fancy themselves good men and Christians. Though the ear of Christendom be gross indeed, it cannot long remain deaf to such glaring inconsistency as theirs.

II. I would gladly impress on every young mind, the truth that *Character creates Opportunity, or renders it unimportant.* I know no more fatal error than prevails almost universally on this point. Aside from that pitiable spectacle exhibited by the multitudes of young men who are daily rushing to our cities — to "get into business," as they say, but really to stake themselves on the chance of finding there some easier means of livelihood, — some more genteel vocation, some shorter road to wealth, than their country homes afford — I perceive among our youth an almost universal expectation, or waiting for, of something different from their present circumstances — some condition more favorable to their advancement or their avarice — something which can only come by working, — never by waiting. It is the canker and blight of our time, this universal jostling for the more advantageous positions — this hanging back in the march of life to steal a ride on the baggage-wagons or in the carriages for the wounded. To do little and receive much, is the ignoble aspiration of the great majority — as cowardly and base as the footman's burning desire to strut his brief hour in his master's habiliments, and give orders instead of obeying them. From every side myriads of youth are turning anxious eyes to the great cities, eager for the expected hour, when they, too, shall have there a foothold. Meantime, the rural valley has no beauty, the lofty mountain no grandeur for them; they loathe the thought of homely labor, and only resort to it as the slave or the convict may do. Of course, Nature rewards no *such* labor with peace and inward joy; they are miserable because they deserve nothing better; useless, because they do not really aspire to usefulness, but only to its rewards. Whether they shall ultimately be punished through the disappointment or the gratification of their wishes, the essential result is the same. Dwarfed in soul by their sordid aims, they live unworthily, and their death makes no void; and if they happen to achieve wealth, and so be buried beneath costly marble, the only enduring product of their lives is the falsehood chiseled on their tombs.

I would say, then, to every youth, "Your place in the world is wherever your Creator has stationed you, provided you can there be useful, until one of wider or higher usefulness shall plainly solicit you. Whenever such shall present itself, accept it thankfully; but do not waste your most precious years in hunting after it. The best preparation for tomorrow's duties is the faithful performance of to-day's; nay, that is the best possible way of seeking nobler opportunities for the morrow. Though it be ditching or herding cattle, he who has done to-day's work cheerfully and well, because it *is* to-day's, and because he scorns to eat the bread of idleness, is on the plain highway to some broader field of usefulness, if such be within the proper scope of his powers!"

III. I think, after this, I need hardly counsel the avoidance of Debt as essential to moral integrity and mental freedom. "The borrower is slave to the lender," not merely in the obvious sense; he has no longer liberty to choose his path in life and manfully pursue it. Debt is one of the most debasing features of our perverted social state—the evidence of a second fall from the landing-place of Adam. And I would say imperatively to the portionless youth who passionately desires an education as the stepping-stone to a profession, "You pay too dearly for the coveted advantages if you consent to go in debt for them. Better be content where you are than incur pecuniary obligations which years will be required to discharge—which many as sanguine as you have carried as a millstone around the neck through life. Do not sell *yourself* even for learning. Plough, team, chop, or do anything to pay your way, and be twice as long acquiring your education, rather than borrow it. Or, better still, adopt and improve upon the example of the young friend of whose course I have elsewhere spoken. This friend found himself at twenty athirst for knowledge, yet without the usual means of assuaging that thirst. He lacked utterly coin and other current values, and, if he had relatives or friends who might have supplied the deficiency by gift or loan, he disdained to barter his independence for their bounty. All he would accept from any man's favor was permission to live on a spot of ground otherwise unused, and convert to his own ends some little of the timber growing thereon—elements, which, in his private thought, were rightfully as much his as those of him whom the law pronounced their exclusive owner, and whom he therefore deferred to as such. Here, by the side of a petty lake, deep in the enshrouding forest, far away from the homes and the haunts of men, he with his own hands built his small but adequate cabin—sufficient to contain his few but choice books, his simple food, his clothing and himself. By its side he planted the patch of corn and other esculents which formed his principal food; for no deadly weapon defiled his peaceful sanctuary, and the gentler denizens of the flood and the forest pursued their sports unharmed and fearless within the shadow of his lodge. There he passed the golden summer and the sterner winter, in thoughtful alternation from book to pen, and thence to the scanty implements of his moderate, invigorating toil; there the few friends who sought found him pensive but not melancholy, modest but not shy; and thence he would emerge at intervals into the seething world without, to fulfil some social obligation, learn the news of the day, procure some book, or earn, by honest, downright labor in the fields of more extensive cultivators, the cost of his plain clothing and the very few additions to his own products that were needed to supply his simple fare. Thus he improved some two or three years, not alone in labor and study, but in unimpeded thought and deep communing with Nature; and when at length he came forth to live and strive with his fellows, I venture to affirm that not many universities had meantime supplied even *one* student with equal opportunities or an education generally comparable to his. His knowledge of Greek and acquaintance with the best remains of the profounder thinkers of antiquity are even now celebrated in no narrow circle; his acquisitions are eminently real and abiding, and he owes no one a farthing. Nay, more, he had learned, as a part of his education, how to live without a wish ungratified on fifty dollars a year—one of the most important acquirements, for which I cannot hear that Professorships have yet been founded in any college but his. I beseech the early attention of trustees and benefactors to this grave deficiency.

And herein is justified our hesitating and qualified regard for what passes current as liberal education. Our Colleges and miscalled Universities do not educate too much, but too little. We object to our prevailing system of collegiate education, not that it is not practical in its ends, for such it certainly endeavors to be—but that it is not catholic—universal. It addresses itself to a few intellectual faculties, instead of dealing with the whole spiritual and physical being. It makes good implements for effecting a particular purpose—scholars, poets, surgeons, lawyers—not vigorous, many-sided, complete Men.

You readily mark the difference between those and men formed in the rough, sturdy school of practical life—Franklin, Boone, Washington. These latter are always at home—always self-possessed—always equal to the emergency—with a faculty for every need and a front for every foe. They are the men who make occasions and create eras in the history of mankind. * * *

[Review of *Walden*]   Anonymous*

Once in a great while come down like manna new words of wisdom and truth. As the blessing falls around us in the evening, we do not distinguish it from the ordinary dew of summer. After the dark hours of night, comes the morning with its sunlight, and we spring from our slothful couch and go out into the fields, and find them covered with elysian food. Walden is crammed full with delicious morsels: rare philosophy, sweet poetry, invaluable facts, suggestive imaginations, strangely charming beauties, gems from the diadem of Queen Nature herself. From this recluse the man of the world may learn experience. Walden is the book

*Reprinted from *Concord Monitor*, 7 June 1862, 53.

to take by one's hand for a companion for your whole summer rambling. When you are snugly ensumed in the shade of a tree at the mountains, or a rock at the sea-shore, open at the chapter on Sounds or Solitude, and read until the delight of the *dolce far niente* has carried you into dreamland too far for any earthly sympathy. Doze awhile, then read again. Walden is the book for the business man to study, for, strange to say, this man who never saw the inside of a counting room, knew more of Economy than the owner of "sails that whiten every sea."

Walden is a book for boys and girls, for men and women, for it is written by a man of heart, mind, and soul. Perhaps you may not break the shell at once with your teeth, but persevere, read it again and again, as the writer has done, and you will surely find the sweet kernal of beauty, knowledge, and truth.

[Review of *Walden*]   Anonymous*

Ten years ago "Walden" came before the public, but owing to unappreciative, if not thoroughly hostile reviews, together with a strong suspicion on our part, of its egotism and eccentricity, it failed to get our attention. It is with some humiliation that we make this confession. But some years later, we chanced to read a portion of an agricultural address by our author on the "Succession of Forest Trees." Here is a man, thought we, who interrogates the squirrels and the trees to some purpose, and who does not deal in hearsay and old clothes; a man who stands wonderfully close to nature; one, in fact, who has a habit of looking into the very atoms of a matter.

Here, at the foot of Mt. Tom, amidst orchards, healthfully remote from the gossip, the bad odors, and the slums of large towns and cities, we have set up our press. Here we take our stand to act as reporters for God and nature, and it is with a good degree of pleasure we call attention to so noteworthy phenomena as "Walden" and its author.

A true life may justly be called a compound motion — a diagonal resulting from two forces, neither of which can be implicitly obeyed nor wholly disobeyed. Do the best we can to express the truth, it often happens that for every *yea* we make, there must be a corresponding *nay*. And so we go on between yea and nay. In all criticism, either of character or of performance, one finds it necessary to bear in mind this dimly outlined philosophy. It is truly wonderful how much of the modern literature, full of Hindooism, pantheism and other paganism, as it is, unconsciously goes to prove the New Testament the best statement and solution of the central

*Reprinted from the *Circular*, 28 March 1864. Text from [Geoffrey Noyes], "Thoreau at the Oneida Community," *Thoreau Society Bulletin*, no. 115 (Spring 1971):3–4.

life questions. We do not wish to make this writing a substitute for "Walden" itself; on the contrary, we intend to induce people to read it; and later, we intend to make our author speak for himself. Therefore, we will speak in general terms. "Walden" is a picturesque and unique continuation of the old battle between the flesh and the spirit. It is a powerful *yea* in favor of the spirit, it is a novel and emphatic *no* to the flesh and fashion. It is the bold and sincere attempt of a young and educated man, who is not a technical Christian, to find the minimum due to his body, and the maximum due to his soul. We hail it as a helper. We do not feel called upon to follow its example, nor to invite others to do so. We may differ from its theology and sociology, but we cannot too heartily commend its philosophy, working so sincerely toward a high, spiritual life, its close and loving adhesion to nature, and its hatred of the conventional and trivial. We shall never hesitate to "speak the praises" of a man, however fractional he may be — in this case our man is a wonderfully perfected fraction — if in behalf of his deep spiritual wants he dares to boldly contradict society and his own body.

Undoubtedly "Walden" is the most original, sincere and unaffected book that has recently issued from the press. Easy and nonchalant in style, still it is densely packed with new thought. It comes to us warm with magnetism and vitality. A strong influence goes with it, which is perhaps hardly equaled by that of Carlyle. We stand in need of such formative books when we are under so much temptation to go to libraries to tell us what to find on the earth and under the water. On a first view one is struck by an apparent simplicity and homeliness of style, but soon all this is transfused into a wonderful beauty. It is a book not only full of nature, but it is nature itself. It is woody, resinous, and strong with ground smells: there are none of the conventional scents of rose, pinks and violets about it, but rather odors of birch, ginseng, and skunk-cabbage. With all its familiarity with nature, it is untainted by the pedantry and literalness of your mere technical men of science.

We shall now let the book speak for itself, and our readers judge for themselves.[1] . . .

Notes

1. Omitted is a long quotation from *Walden*, not in the 1971 reprinting.

Thoreau: A Disparagement   Llewelyn Powys*

To a student of literature, it is interesting to observe how easily, I had almost said how fortuitously, certain men of letters have won that relative immortality which belongs to the craft of writing. In our eagerness to find some criterion, some absolute standard of worth in this difficult trade, we console ourselves with talk about the judgment of posterity, about the continual punctilious process of acceptance and rejection that is undertaken in each succeeding age "by the best minds" and which represents, so we assume, a deep instinct in the human race to preserve that which is of greatest value. There is more in this, however, than meets the eye. As in all human transactions, it is clear that chance or lucky accident plays a large part.

A good case in point is the work of Thoreau which I suspect has been and is today much overrated. Thoreau is cried up as being one of the greatest American writers. In reality, he was an awkward, nervous, self-conscious New Englander who, together with an authentic taste for oriental and classical literature, developed a singular liking for his own home woods. He does not strike me as an original thinker, bolstered up as his thoughts always are by the wisdom of the past. Mysticism, that obstinately recurring form of human self-deception, is, in his case, even more unsatisfactory than usual, while his descriptions of nature that have won such applause are seldom out of the ordinary. I am inclined to think that his reputation owes much to his close association with Emerson, that truly great man, who under so kindly and sedate an exterior possessed so mighty a spirit.

The naivete of Thoreau's mind is incredible. At his best, he is second best. He is too cultured and not cultured enough. It is, in truth, amazing that this provincial pedant, who so strained to be original, should enjoy the distinction he does. "He was as local as a woodchuck," wrote John Burroughs. He observed nature closely but his most original passages are forced. His is a notebook observation, a very different thing from that deep underswell of passionate feeling that distinguishes, for example, the poetry of Walt Whitman when he chants of wild and free life. As I read this dilettante of the bluebird and the bobolink, I constantly find myself becoming impatient. He is too bookish, too literary. To draw direct power out of the ground, out of the smelling, fecund, sweet soil of the earth, it is necessary to lose oneself, it is necessary to lose one's soul to find it. Thoreau never is able to do this. He is always there, the transcendental original of Concord with a lesson to impart. It is impossible for him to feel nature in his lungs, in his navel, in the marrow of his bones. He must always have his journal-book within reach and must be fussing to enter on its pages some

*Reprinted from *Bookman* (New York) 69 (April 1929):163–65.

apothegm or apt description which he knows will later be commended by Emerson or by his less discerning lyceum audiences.

Thoreau plays at loving nature but his authentic background is not really in the cold woods as, for example, was the background of Thomas Bewick or even John Burroughs. We learn that he was extremely deft at making lead pencils. Emerson, always eager to praise his friend, testifies to this: "He could make as good a lead pencil as the English ones". Thoreau certainly used these dainty productions to some purpose, for what a murmur he made about his retreat at Walden Pond!

When we look into the matter there was really little enough "to it." At best it was but a dramatic gesture. The celebrated hut was actually situated on the outskirts of Concord, within a mile and a half of the village, built on Emerson's land — in Emerson's yard, one might almost say. With an axe borrowed from his friend Alcott he constructed his habitation out of boards which had been conveyed to the woods from an Irishman's shanty. It was within sight of the railway and so close to the public highway that the woodland air was continually being impregnated with tobacco smoke from the pipes of wayfarers on the near-by road. Thoreau declares that he "never found the companion that was so companionable as solitude" but actually his house was constantly visited by friends. Indeed, it was fitted with a guest chamber. The undertaking was a form of pedantic play. The hermit himself often spent an evening in the village, returning in the dark, which was to him a great matter. "It is darker in the woods, even on common nights than most suppose." Bookworm that he was, the simplest country occupation fills him with self-conscious satisfaction. He records with pride how he came over the ice "trailing a dead pine tree under each arm to my shed". So little was he acquainted with the lore of the forest that he actually, on one occasion, when he was frying fish during one of his picnics, started a bush-fire which endangered the whole village of Concord!

Much of his writing is sheer affectation. He was asked whether he was not lonely and answered, "no more lonely than the loon on the pond that laughs so loud, or the Walden Pond itself. What company has that lovely lake, I pray. And yet it has not the blue devils, but the blue angels in it, in the azure tint of its waters." He goes for an excursion into Canada. "We styled ourselves Knights of the Umbrella and the Bundle." He was, in truth, a woodsman of the umbrella!

He is never weary of girding at the rich and conventional. "Simplicity, simplicity, simplicity," he exhorts and, then, the next moment can pen a sentence that has upon it the very stamp of finical banality. "The luxuriously rich are not simply kept comfortably warm but unnaturally hot; as I implied before, they are cooked, of course, *a la mode*." Sometimes it is as though he has no conception of what dignity of style means. He will call himself "the self-appointed inspector of snow-storms and rain-storms." "Our whole life is startlingly moral," he writes. "There is never an instant's truce between virtue and vice. Goodness is the only investment that never fails. In the music of the harp which trembles round the world it is the insisting on this which thrills us. The harp is the travelling patterer for the Universe's Insurance Company, recommending its laws, and our little goodness is all the assessment that we pay."

Perhaps it was the unfortunate upshot of his romantic attachment for Miss Ellen Sewall which gave his mind a cramped and crooked turn with regard to that emotion "before which all creation trembles and faints." The girl records that her father "wished me to write immediately in a short explicit and cold manner to Mr. Thoreau" and one wonders if the discouragement of the receipt of this letter did not help to dry up his already somewhat sapless nature. As the years passed Thoreau felt estranged from his indulgent patron, Emerson, and yet how he could have been instructed by that great man!

> Give all to love;
> Obey thy heart;

This back-door hermit has in his mouth all those convenient utterances that are in their very essence contrary to nature. He should have given more attention to the song of the hermit thrush! "Chastity is the flowering of man." "Man flows at once to God when the channel of purity is open." "He is blessed who is assured that the animal is dying out in him day by day, and the divine being established." Could he not have learned better doctrine from his Brooklyn friend, "the greatest democrat the world has ever seen"? We remember his utterance, "The soul is not greater than the body and the body is not greater than the soul." There is no end to Thoreau's Sunday School talk, "If you would avoid uncleanness, and all the sins, work earnestly though it be at cleaning a stable. Nature is hard to be overcome, but she must be overcome." We know now why we hear so much about his brave bean field on that lot of Emerson's which was in the opinion of a local farmer "good for nothing but to raise cheeping squirrels on."

And yet one must not be too captious. One must not depreciate unfairly this bookish philosopher. He does offer a charming picture of himself hoeing his beans, walking with bare feet from end to end of the lines while "green berries deepened their tints by the time I had made another bout." Yes, he is often able by some literary turn to give a freshness to his writing, this man who was "no more lonely than a single mullein or dandelion in a pasture . . . or the first spider in a new house." It is pleasant to think of him walking to Nine-Acre-Corner, or getting his feet wet in Becky Stow's swamp, or exploring some new "all-across-lot route," or gravely meditating how, with thrift, he could support life by using as his habitation "a large box in the railroad six feet long by three wide in which the laborers locked up their tools at night" while earning his daily bread by picking huckleberries.

It is possible from his pages to cull certain passages of wisdom. "This life is a strange dream and I don't believe at all any account men give of it." "There is no more fatal blunderer than he who consumes the greater part of his life getting his living." "The greater part of what my neighbors call good I believe in my soul to be bad, and if I repent of anything it is very likely to be my good behavior." "I wanted to live deep and suck out all the marrow of life." He can also give us glimpses of his life in the woods that have a true beauty, as, for example, when paddling about Walden Pond after dark he would see "perch and shiners, dimpling the surface with their tails in the moonlight." To those of us who love the American countryside, there is a magic in the mere enumeration of the familiar flora, the goldenrod, the St. John's wort, the sumach! And yet, even here, one can be jarred by his method of expression. In his journal we come upon this passage about skunk cabbages. And how discouraging its jocular tone seems when one remembers the sturdy growth of this swamp vegetation which heralds the coming of the spring by thrusting up through the chilled ground mottled, red, curling horns that smell of the arm pits of Pan! "If you are afflicted with melancholy at this season, go to the swamp and see the brave spears of skunk-cabbage buds already advanced toward a new year. Their grave-stones are not bespoken yet. Who shall be sexton to them? Is it the winter of their discontent? Do they seem to have lain down to die, despairing of skunk-cabbagedom? 'Up and at 'em' . . . 'Excelsior' . . . these are their mottoes."

Thoreau was a great reader of books of the ancient tradition, but he was neither a profound thinker nor a great writer, and that is the truth.

Resolution at Walden   Sherman Paul*

I

Walden was published in 1854, eight years before Thoreau died, some seven years after his life in the woods. His journal shows that he had proposed such a "poem" for himself as early as 1841, that its argument would be "the River, the Woods, the Ponds, the Hills, the Fields, the Swamps and Meadows, the Streets and Buildings, and the Villagers. Then Morning, Noon, and Evening, Spring, Summer, Autumn, and Winter, Night, Indian Summer, and the Mountains in the Horizon." Like A Week on the Concord and Merrimack Rivers (1849) — "If one would reflect," Thoreau had written in 1837, "let him embark on some placid stream, and

*Reprinted from Accent 13 (Spring 1953):101–13, by permission of Accent and the author.

float with the current" — *Walden* took a long time maturing, a longer time, because it was more than the stream of his reflections. The *Week* had been written out of joyousness and to memorialize his most perfect excursion in nature. *Walden*, however, was Thoreau's recollected experience, recollected not in tranquillity, but in the years of what he himself called his "decay." Although one need only search the journals to find many of the events of *Walden* freshly put down, *Walden* itself reveals that Thoreau was now looking at these events with more experienced eyes: his long quarrel with society has intervened, his youthful inspiration had become more difficult to summon, the harvest of the *Week* he had hoped to bestow on the public lay in his attic, and, growing older, he was still without a vocation that others would recognize. In *Walden*, at once his victorious hymn to Nature, to her perpetual forces of life, inspiration and renewal, Thoreau defended his vocation by creating its eternal symbol.

The common moral of *Walden* is that of the virtue of simplicity; and simplicity is usually taken on the prudential level of economy with which Thoreau seemingly began the book. In terms of Thoreau's spiritual economy, however, simplicity was more than freedom from the burdens of a mortgaged life: it was an ascetic, a severe discipline, like solitude for Emerson, by which Thoreau concentrated his forces and was able to confront the facts of life without the intervening barriers of society or possessions. For simplicity, Thoreau often substituted poverty, a word which both set him apart from his materialistic neighbors and hallowed his vocation with its religious associations of renunciation and higher dedication. It was the suitable condition for the spiritual crusader: the sign in a land of traders of his profession. But it also signified his inner condition. "By poverty," he said, "*i.e.* simplicity of life and fewness of incidents, I am solidified and crystallized, as a vapor or liquid by cold. It is a singular concentration of strength and energy and flavor. Chastity is perpetual acquaintance with the All. My diffuse and vaporous life becomes as frost leaves and spiculae radiant as gems on the weeds and stubble in a winter morning." Such poverty or purity was a necessity of *his* economy. "You think," he continued, "that I am impoverishing myself by withdrawing from men, but in my solitude I have woven for myself a silken web or *chrysalis*, and, nymph-like, shall ere long burst forth a more perfect creature, fitted for a higher society. By simplicity, commonly called poverty, my life is concentrated and so becomes organized, or a κόσμος [kosmos], which before was inorganic and lumpish."

This was also the hope of his paean to spring in *Walden*, to "pass from the lumpish grub in the earth to the airy and fluttering butterfly." The purpose of his experiment at Walden Pond, begun near the end of his years of undisciplined rapture — Emerson said that the vital heat of the poet begins to ebb at thirty — was to build an organic life as consciously as he built his hut (and his book), and so retain his vital heat. "May I never," he had recorded in his journal, "let the vestal fire go out in my recesses." But there was desperation in his attempt to keep his vital heat, because it was only *vital* (or rather he felt it so) when he was maturing beyond the lumpish, grub-like existence. As well as the advocacy of the organic life which promised renewal and growth, *Walden* for Thoreau filled the immediate need of self-therapy. In the serenity and joy of his art this is often overlooked, but it is there in the journals behind the book. And the greatness of *Walden*, from this perspective at least, is the resolution Thoreau was able to fulfill through art. By creating an organic form he effected his own resolution for rebirth: by conscious endeavor he recaptured, if not the youthful ecstasy of his golden age, a mature serenity.

This serenity, however, is still alert, wakeful, tense. It was a victory of discipline. "That aim in life is highest," Thoreau noted during the composition of *Walden*, "which requires the highest and finest discipline." That aim was highest, that discipline the highest vocation, because the goal and fulfillment of all transcendental callings was purity — a oneness with Nature in which the untarnished mirror of the soul reflected the fullness of being. The cost of doing without conventional life was not too great for Thoreau, considering his desire to "perceive things truly and simply." He believed that "a fatal coarseness is the result of mixing in the trivial affairs of men." And to justify his devotion to purity he wrote *Walden*, a promise of the higher society a man can make when he finds his *natural* center, a record of things and events so simple and fundamental that all lives less courageous and principled are shamed by the *realometer* it provides. Like other masterworks of its time, it has the unique strain of American romanticism: behind its insistent individualism and desire for experience, there is still more earnest conviction of the necessity of virtue.

II

In the concluding pages of *Walden*, Thoreau remarked that "in this part of the world it is considered a ground for complaint if a man's writings admit of more than one interpretation." With his contemporaries, Emerson, Hawthorne, Melville, he wanted the "volatile truth" of his words to "betray the inadequacy of the residual statement." He would have considered *Walden* a failure if it served only to communicate an eccentric's refusal to go along with society, if, taken literally, its spiritual courage was thinned to pap for tired businessmen long since beyond the point of no return. For *Walden* was *his* myth: "A fact truly and absolutely stated," he said, "is taken out of the region of common sense and acquires a mythologic or universal significance." This was the extravagance he sought — this going beyond the bounds. For him, only the fact stated without reference to convention or institution, with only reference to the self which has tasted the world and digested it, which has been "drenched" and "saturated" with truth, is properly humanized — is properly myth. Primarily to immerse himself in truth, to merge himself with the law of Nature, and to humanize this experience by the alchemy of language, Thoreau went to Walden. There, free from external references, he could purify himself and live a sympathetic existence, alive to the currents of being. What he reported, then, would be the experience of the self in its unfolding and exploration of the "not-me." The literal record would merely remain the residual statement — no one knew better the need for concrete fact; but it would also yield a *translated* meaning.

The whole of *Walden* is an experience of the microcosmic and cosmic travels of the self. At Walden Pond, Thoreau wrote, "I have, as it were, my own sun and moon and stars, and a little world all to myself." Thoreau, of course, was a great traveller, if only a saunterer. The profession of traveller appealed to his imagination; it was, he said, the "best symbol of our life." And "Walking" was the best short statement of his way of life, of his journey to the holy land. He yearned, he wrote in 1851, "for one of those old, meandering, dry, uninhabited roads, which lead away from towns. . . ." He wanted to find a place "where you can walk and think with least obstruction, there being nothing to measure progress by; where you can pace when your breast is full, and cherish your moodiness; where you are not in false relations with men. . . ." He wanted "a road where I can travel," where "I can walk, and recover the lost child that I am without any ringing of a bell." The road he wanted led to Walden. There he regained the primal world, and lived the pristine initiation into consciousness over again. "Both place and time were changed," he said in *Walden*, "and I dwelt nearer to those parts of the universe and to those eras in history which had most attracted me."

In this effort to live out of time and space or to live in all times and places, *Walden* immediately suggests Melville's *Moby-Dick*. Melville had written another voyage of the self on which he explored reality, charted the constituents of a chaos, and raised his discovery to the universal level of archetypal experience. He had elaborated the myth of the hunter which Thoreau also employed in the chapter on "Higher Laws." "There is a period in the history of the individual, as of the race," he wrote, "when hunters are the 'best men'. . . ." Hunting, he added, "is oftenest the young man's introduction to the forest [Melville's sea], and the most original part of himself. He goes thither at first as a hunter and fisher, until at last, if he has the seeds of a better life in him, he distinguishes his proper objects. . . ." It was in these "wild" employments of his youth that Thoreau acknowledged his "closest acquaintance with Nature." For Nature revealed herself to the hunter more readily than to "philosophers or poets even, who approach her with expectation" — or, as Melville knew, to the participant and not the observer of life. If Thoreau had long since given up hunting, he still found a sustaining link with the wild in his bean field.

There are obvious differences, of course, in the quality of these travels — each author had his spiritual torment, Melville the need for belief, Thoreau the need for recommunion. But both were projecting the drama of their selves, a drama that in both instances ended in rebirth; and the methods both employed were remarkably similar. Each abstracted himself from the conventional world, established a microcosm by which to test the conventions, and worked at a basic and heroic occupation. For example, the village stands in the same symbolic relation to Thoreau at Walden that the land does to Melville's sea; and it is the occupation in both that supplies the residual statement. In Thoreau's case, it is also a primitive concern with essentials; building his hut, planting, hoeing and harvesting his beans, fishing and naturalizing. And the nature of the occupation gives each its spiritual quality, because whaling (butchery) and colonizing (building from scratch) are projections of different visions of the universe of which only the central similarity remains — the exploration of self.

But this similarity is a sufficient signature for both; one recognizes the existential kinship. At the conclusion of *Walden* Thoreau declared: "Explore thyself . . . Be . . . the Mungo Park, the Lewis and Clark and Frobisher, of your own streams and oceans. . . ." —

" . . . . be
Expert in home-cosmography."

For "there are continents and seas in the moral world to which every man is an isthmus or an inlet, yet unexplored by him, . . . [and] it is easier to sail many thousand miles through cold and storm and cannibals, in a government ship, with five hundred men and boys to assist one, than it is to explore the private sea, the Atlantic and Pacific Ocean of one's being alone." Melville at Pittsfield would have agreed that "herein are demanded the eye and the nerve." But if Melville needed the watery two-thirds of the world and the great whale for this quest, Thoreau, who had the gift of enlarging the small, needed only the pond and its pickerel. And where Melville needed the destructive forces of the sea to mirror himself, Thoreau, who had seen the place of violence in the total economy of nature, needed only the recurrence of the seasons.

III

Walden was Thoreau's quest for a reality he had lost, and for this reason it was a quest for purity. Purity meant a return to the spring (and springtime) of life, to the golden age of his youth and active senses, when the mirror of his self was not clouded by self-consciousness. *Walden*, accordingly, follows the cycle of developing consciousness, a cycle that parallels the change of the seasons. It is a recapitulation of Thoreau's development (and the artistic reason he put the experience of two years into one) — a development from the sensuous, active, external (unconscious *and* out-of-doors) summer of life through the stages of autumnal consciousness and the withdrawal inward to the self-reflection of winter, to the promise of ecstatic rebirth in the spring. It was a matter of purification because Thoreau had reached the winter of decay at the time *Walden* was being revised for the press. With consciousness had come the knowledge of the "reptile" and "sensual" which he knew could not "be wholly expelled." "I fear," he wrote, "that it [the sensual] may enjoy a certain health of its own; that we may be well, yet not pure." For the mind's approach to God, he knew that the severest discipline was necessary; his chapter on "Higher Laws" is concerned almost entirely with the regimen of the appetites because "man flows at once to God when the channel of purity is open." The undeniable sensual energy — the "generative energy" — he had unconsciously enjoyed in the ecstasy of youth, now needed control. "The generative energy," he wrote, "which, when we are loose, dissipates and makes us unclean, when we are continent invigorates and inspires us." He was consciously using instinct for higher ends, seeking chastity by control.

In Walden Pond he saw the image of his purified self — that pristine, eternal self he hoped to possess. In 1853, while he was working on his book, he noted in his journal: "How watchful we must be to keep the crystal well that we were made, clear! — that it be not made turbid by our contact with the world, so that it will not reflect objects." The pond, he recalled, was one of the "oldest scenes stamped on my memory." He had been taken to see it when he was four years old. Now, playing his flute beside its waters, his beans, corn and potatoes replacing the damage of the years, he felt that another aspect was being prepared "for new infant eyes," that "even I have at length helped to clothe that fabulous landscape of my infant dreams. . . ." Later, he recalled his youthful reveries on its waters: "I have spent many an hour, when I was younger, floating over its surface as the zephyr willed . . . dreaming awake. . . ." But time (and woodchoppers) had ravished its shores: "My Muse may be excused," he explained, "if she is silent henceforth. How can you expect the birds to sing when their groves are cut down?" It was the confession of the Apollo who had had to serve Admetus, a confession he made again in "Walking." Visited by fewer thoughts each year, he said that "the grove in our minds is laid waste — sold to feed unnecessary fires of ambition. . . ."

But Thoreau discovered at Walden that even though the groves were cut down, the pond itself remained the same — it "best preserves its purity." "It is itself unchanged," he learns, "the same water my youthful eyes fell on; all the change is in me. . . . It is perennially young. . . ." Catching sight of his eternal self and realizing that the waste of years had only touched his shore, his empirical self, he exclaimed, "Why, here is Walden, the same woodland lake that I discovered so many years ago . . . it is the same liquid joy and happiness to itself and its Maker, ay, and it *may* be to me." The pond, so constant, clear and pure, was truly the *Walled in* pond, the undefiled soul of which the Thoreau-in-decay said, "I am its stony shore. . . ."

If Thoreau spent his youth drifting with the inspiring zephyrs on

Walden's surface, he now plumbed its depths, angled for its pickerel and its bottom. For it was the purpose of *Walden* to find bottom, to affirm reality; and the reality Thoreau discovered in the soul and in the whole economy of Nature he found at the bottom of the pond. What renewed his faith was the sign of the never-dying, all-promising generative force which he symbolized when he wrote: ". . . a bright green weed is brought up on anchors even in midwinter." The hope of a renewed life, rhapsodized in the concluding chapters of *Walden* and there symbolized in the hardy blade of grass—the green flame of life—, was the assurance he now had that "there is nothing inorganic."

And by sounding the bottom Thoreau also discovered the law of the universe and of the intellect that made possible his organic participation in the process of renewal and provided him the guarantee of its expression in natural objects. "The regularity of the bottom and its conformity to the shores and the range of the neighboring hills were so perfect," he wrote, "that a distant promontory betrayed itself in the soundings quite across the pond, and its direction could be determined by observing the opposite shore." He found, too, that the intersection of the lines of greatest length and breadth coincided with the point of greatest depth; and he suggested that this physical law might be applied to ethics. "Draw lines through the length and breadth of the aggregate of a man's particular daily behaviors and waves of life into his coves and inlets, and where they intersect will be the height or depth of his character. Perhaps we need only to know how his shores tend and his adjacent country or circumstances, to infer his depth and concealed bottom." *Walden* was just such an account of Thoreau's moral topography, and if the lines were drawn, the pond itself would be his center. For wasn't the eternal self, like the pond, " 'God's Drop' "?

The search for the bottom was conscious exploration. Here, and in the passages on fishing for pickerel and chasing the loon, Thoreau was not a naturalist but a natural historian of the intellect, using the natural facts as symbols for his quest for inspiration and thought. In "Brute Neighbors" he had asked, "Why do precisely these objects which we behold make a world?" And he had answered that "they are all beasts of burden . . . made to carry some portion of our thoughts." The natural world merely reflects ourselves. Having overcome his doubts of this central article of transcendental faith by assuring himself of the regularity of Walden's depth—that the hidden reality corresponded to its visible shores, that "Heaven is under our feet as well as over our heads"—he could trust once more his own projection of mood and thought to be reflected in its proper and corresponding object. He had noted in his journal that the poet "sees a flower or other object, and it is beautiful or affecting to him because it is a symbol of his thought, and what he indistinctly feels or perceives is matured in some other organization. The objects I behold correspond to my mood." His concern with the pond and the seasons, then, was symbolic of his soul's preoccupation. "Our moulting season . . . must be the crisis in our lives," he said; and like the loon he retired to a solitary pond to spend it. There, like the caterpillar—to use another symbol—, "by an internal industry and expansion" he cast off his "wormy coat."

IV

Thoreau went to Walden to become an unaccommodated man, to shed his lendings and to find his naked and sufficient self. Of this, the pond was the symbol. He also went to clothe himself in response to his inner needs. Building an organic life was again a conscious endeavor which was chastened by the necessity of maintaining his vital heat—the heat of body and spirit; for his purpose was not to return to nature, but to combine "the hardiness of . . . savages with the intellectualness of the civilized man." "The civilized man," he said, "is a more experienced and wiser savage," meaning, of course, that the instinctive life was most rewarding when channeled by intellectual principles. "What was *enthusiasm* in the young man," he wrote during the crisis of his life, "must become *temperament* in the mature man." The woodchopper, the animal man, must be educated to consciousness, and still retain his innocence. Properly seen in the total economy of Nature the once freely taken gift of inspiration must be earned by perceiving the law of Nature, by the tragic awareness that inspiration, like its source, has its seasons. The villagers, Thoreau wrote indignantly, "instead of going to the pond to bathe or drink, are thinking to bring its waters, which should be as sacred as the Ganges at least, to the village in a pipe, to wash their dishes with! —to earn their Walden by the turning of a cock or drawing of a plug!" The spiritual soldier had learned that after laying siege to Nature, only passivity would bring victory.

Thoreau earned his Walden by awaiting the return of spring, by sharing the organic process. Of this his hut and his bean-field became the symbols. The latter, as we have seen, helped to renew the aspect of the pond; as the work of the active self, it was rightly an alteration of the shore. And the pond, as the pure, eternal self—the "perfect forest mirror"—, was the calm surface on which these purifying activities were reflected. Thoreau labored in his bean-field because he took seriously Emerson's injunction to action in *The American Scholar*. He knew that the higher ends of the activity of the empirical self were self-consciousness, that the eternal self, the passive center, only acquired consciousness by observing the empirical self at work on the circumference. He recognized "a certain doubleness by which I can stand as remote from myself as from another." "However intense my experience," he wrote, "I am conscious of the presence of and criticism of a part of me, which, as it were, is not part of me, but spectator, sharing no experience, but taking note of it. . . ." The reward of activity, the result of this drama of selves, was self-reflection, insight. "All perception of truth is the detection of an analogy,"

Thoreau noted in the journal; "we reason from our hands to our head." And so through the labor of the hands, even to the point of drudgery, he was "determined to know beans." He did not need the beans for food but for sympathy with Nature; he needed to work them because, as he said, "They attached me to the earth, and so I got strength like Antaeus." His fields were also symbolic of his attempt to link the wild and the cultivated. And the "immeasurable crop" his devoted hoeing yielded came from the penetration of the earth's crust—a knowledge of the depths similar in significance to Melville's descent to the unwarped primal world. "I disturbed," Thoreau wrote, "the ashes of unchronicled nations who in primeval times lived under these heavens. . . ." In his bean-field beside Walden he was not serving Admetus, for he had found a way to delve beneath the "established order on the surface."

The prudential value of this labor came to $16.94, but the spiritual value was the realization that the Massachusetts soil could sustain the seeds of virtue—that in Thoreau's case at least, the seed had not lost its vitality and that the harvest of his example might be "a new generation of men." Later on, in the chapter on "Former Inhabitants," he again disturbed the surface by delving into the past, comparing his life at Walden to the defeated lives of its previous occupants. Here, Thoreau expressed his desire for the higher society, the ideal community in which he could wholly participate and which he hoped he was beginning. "Again, perhaps, Nature will try," he wrote, "with me for the first settler. . . . I am not aware that any man has ever built on the spot which I occupy." Like Joyce's Finnegan, he was to be the father of cities, not those reared on ancient sites, but cities growing out of the union with the earth. Looking back to Concord from the distances of past and future, Thoreau felt that *Walden* was not so much his quarrel with society, but an expiation. "Through our recovered innocence," he confessed, "we discern the innocence of our neighbors." He was willing to share his regeneration, for above the constant interplay of Walden and village, there hovered a vision of an ideal village that transcended both. In the radical sense of the word, Thoreau, who had given up the wilder pursuit of hunting for farming, was a civilizer.

When he came to build his hut—the container of his vital heat—Thoreau used second-hand materials and borrowed tools and showed his dependence on civilization. He did not abandon collective wisdom: his intention was to practice philosophy, to come directly at a conduct of life, that is, to simplify, or experience the solid satisfaction of knowing immediately the materials that made his life. He scrupulously accounts for these materials, he tells their history—where he got the boards, who used them and under what conditions. And James Collins' life in the shanty is implicitly contrasted with Thoreau's, especially in Thoreau's remark that he purified the boards by bleaching and warping them in the sun. He also acknowledged his debt for tools. He did not push his economy too far, to the verge of self-sufficiency that some believe necessary to a defense of *Walden* as social gospel. He said — and this is the only way of repaying one's social indebtedness — that he sharpened the tools by use. In a similar way, he applied the funded wisdom of man to his experiment on life. Individualist that he was, he often confirmed his experience by the experience of others: he made his use of the classics and scriptures, Indian lore and colonial history, pay their way. He was starting from scratch, but he knew that the materials were old.

The building of the hut is so thoroughly described because on the symbolic level it is the description of the building of the body for his soul. A generation that was read in Swedenborg might have been expected to see this correspondence. "It would be worth the while," Thoreau suggested, "to build still more deliberately than I did, considering, for instance, what foundation a door, a window, a cellar, a garret, have in the nature of man, and perchance never raising any superstructure until we found a better reason for it than our temporal necessities even." He was speaking the language of functionalism that Swedenborgianism had popularized; and after listing his previous shelters, he remarked that "this frame, so slightly clad, was a sort of crystallization around me, and reacted on the builder."

Thoreau built his hut as he needed it, to meet the progressing seasons of developing consciousness, a development which was as organic as the seasons. He subscribed to Emerson's use of the cycle of day and night as the symbol of the ebb and flow of inspiration and extended it to the seasons: "The day is an epitome of the year. The night is the winter, the morning and evenings are spring and fall, and the noon is the summer." In this way he also followed Emerson's "history" of consciousness. "The Greek," Emerson wrote, "was the age of observation; the Middle Age, that of fact and thought; ours, that of reflection and ideas." In *Walden*, Thoreau's development began in the summer, the season of the senses and of delicious out-of-door life. This was the period when he was in sympathetic communion with Nature, refreshed by the tonic of wildness. The chapters on "Sounds" and "Solitude" belong to this period, during which he enjoyed the atmospheric presence of Nature so essential to his inspiration. And the hut, which he began in the spring and first occupied at this time, was merely a frame through which Nature readily passed.

When the "north wind had already begun to cool the pond," Thoreau said that he first began to "inhabit my house." During the autumn season of harvest and preparation for winter, he lathed and plastered; and finally as winter approached he built his fireplace and chimney, "the most vital part of the house. . . ." By the fireside, in the period of reflection and inner life, he lingered most, communing with his self.[1] It was the time of soul-searching, when he cut through the pond's ice and saw that "its bright sanded floor [was] the same as in the summer"; and before the ice broke up he surveyed its bottom. Even in this desolate season Thoreau looked for all the signs of spring's organic promise, and in the representative anecdote of his despair, he told of Nature's sustaining power: "After a still winter night I awoke with the impression that some question had been put to me, which I had been endeavoring in vain to answer in my sleep, as what— how—when—where? But there was dawning Nature, in whom all creatures live, looking in at my broad windows with serene and satisfied face, and no questions on *her* lips. I awoke to an answered question, to Nature and daylight." Even in the winter of his discontent, "Nature seemed to him to say " 'Forward' " and he could calmly await the inevitable golden age of spring.

V

Rebirth came with spring. In one of the best sustained analogies in transcendental writing, the chapter "Spring," Thoreau reported ecstatically the translation of the frozen sand and clay of the railroad cut into the thawing streams of life. Looking at the sand foliage—the work of an hour—he said that "I am affected as if . . . I stood in the laboratory of the Artist who made the world and me. . . ." The Artist of the world, like Thoreau and like Goethe whom he had in mind, labored "with the idea inwardly" and its correspondence, its flowering, was the leaf. Everywhere Thoreau perceived this symbol of creation, and in ascending forms from the sand, the animal body, the feathers and wings of birds, to the "airy" butterfly. "Thus it seemed," he wrote, "that this one hillside illustrated the principle of all the operations of Nature. The Maker of this earth but patented a leaf." And the moral Thoreau drew from this illustration was the central law of his life, for it was the law of renewal: "This earth is not a mere fragment of dead history, stratum upon stratum like the leaves of a book, to be studied by geologists and antiquarians chiefly, but living poetry like the leaves of a tree, which precede flowers and fruit, — not a fossil earth, but a living earth; compared with whose great central life all animal and vegetable life is merely parasitic. Its throes will heave our exuviae from their graves." And furthermore the law applied to man and the higher society: ". . . the institutions upon it [the earth] are plastic like clay in the hands of the potter."

For Thoreau, who had found that the law of his life was the law of Life, these perceptions were the stuff of ecstasy. Reveling in the sound of the first sparrow, Thoreau wrote, "What at such a time are histories, chronologies, traditions, and all written revelations?" The spring had brought forth "the symbol of perpetual youth," the grass-blade; human life, having died down to its root, now put forth "its green blade to eternity." Walden Pond had begun to melt—"Walden was dead and is alive again." The change in the flowing sand, from excremental to spiritual, had also been accomplished in him by the discipline of purity: "The change from storm and winter to serene and mild weather, from dark and sluggish hours to bright and elastic ones." Like the dawning of inspiration this

"memorable crisis" was "seemingly instantaneous at last." "Suddenly,"
Thoreau recorded that change, "an influx of light filled my house, though
evening was at hand, and the clouds of winter still overhung it, and the
eaves were dripping with sleety rain. I looked out of the window, and lo!
where yesterday was cold grey ice there lay the transparent pond already
calm and full of hope as in a summer evening, reflecting a summer evening
sky in its bosom, though none was visible overhead, as if it had intelligence
with some remote horizon. I heard a robin in the distance, the first I had
heard for many a thousand years, methought, whose note I shall not
forget for many a thousand more, — the same sweet and powerful song as
of yore. . . . So I came in, and shut the door, and passed my first spring
night in the woods."

With the coming of spring had come "the creation of Cosmos out of
Chaos and the realization of the Golden Age." And with his renewal had
come the vindication of his life of purity. He had recorded what he felt was
nowhere recorded, "a simple and irrepressible satisfaction with the gift of
life. . . ." He had suggested what the eye of the partridge symbolized to
him, not merely "the purity of infancy, but a wisdom clarified by
experience." He had recounted the experience of his purification so well
that even the reader who accepts only the residual statement feels purified.
"I do not say," he wisely wrote at the end of *Walden*, "that John or
Jonathan will realize all this [the perfect summer life]; but such is the
character of that morrow which mere lapse of time can never make to
dawn." To affirm this eternal present, to restore, as he said in "The
Service," the original of which Nature is the reflection, he fashioned
Walden as he himself lived, after the example of the artist of the city of
Kouroo. This parable unlocks the largest meaning of the book. The artist
of Kouroo "was disposed to strive after perfection," Thoreau wrote; and
striving, he lived in the eternity of inspiration which made the passing of
dynasties, even eras, an illusion. In fashioning his staff, merely by minding
his destiny and his art, he had made a new world "with full and fair
proportions." The result, Thoreau knew, could not be "other than wonderful," because "the material was pure, and his art was pure. . . ."

Notes

1. Hawthorne in "Peter Goldthwaite's Treasure" and Melville in "I and My Chimney"
also made imaginative use of the house and the chimney.

On the Organic Structure
of *Walden*

Lauriat Lane, Jr.*

The organic form, on the other hand, is innate; it shapes as it develops itself from within, and the fullness of its development is one and the same with the perfection of its outward form.[1]

To speak of the organic form of *Walden* is hardly novel or startling, but to pursue more closely some of the phrase's implications for our response to the work may still be worth while. We may start with Coleridge's statement, whose relevance to Thoreau and to *Walden* has already been well established, especially by Fred W. Lorch and F. O. Matthiessen.[2] In his discussion of "Coleridge's Mechanical Fancy and Organic Imagination" M. H. Abrams finds five propositions characteristic of the organic theory: "(1) The plant originates in a seed. . . . (2) The plant *grows*. . . . (3) Growing, the plant assimilates to its own substance the alien and diverse elements of earth, air, light, and water. . . . (4) The plant evolves spontaneously from an internal source of energy . . . and organizes itself into its proper form. . . . (5) The achieved structure of a plant is an organic unity."[3] Of these propositions, (4) and (5) apply to the completed work of art, the first reflecting Coleridge's term, "innate," the second his emphasis on "fullness of development."

In his section "*Walden*: Craftsmanship vs. Technique" Matthiessen demonstrates the book's innate form, how it "develops itself from within," and concludes that Thoreau has mastered "the right order of the thing to be made, the right revelation of the material" (p. 175). But the scope of Matthiessen's total argument does not allow him to explore fully the meaning of the term organic form for *Walden*. The truly organic form not only fulfills the inner needs of the material to be expressed, but fulfills it with a complexity and even multiplicity not attained by more artificial or conventional forms. *Walden* demonstrates its organic nature by its multiple form; to examine this multiple form more closely is to come to see *Walden*'s greatness as a complex yet integrated work of art.

Walden also exemplifies Professor Abrams's first three propositions. We may find the seeds of the book in Thoreau's early attachment to the pond and in the fact that his resolution to live by it was expressed years before he could carry it out. We may see the book's growth not only in the materials in the Journals but in the seven versions of the manuscript analyzed in J. Lyndon Shanley's *The Making of Walden* (1957). And we may see, in even the most summary light of *Walden*'s sources, what "alien and diverse elements" Thoreau has assimilated.

We may consider the organic or multiple form of the completed work

*Reprinted from *College English* 21 (January 1960):195–202, by permission of the publisher. © 1960 by the National Council of Teachers of English.

of art — of the *Walden* that most general readers, who may have read neither the Journals nor Professor Shanley's reconstruction, know — as texture and structure. Considering each of these in turn, we will find the complexity and multiplicity of organic form. We will find not a form but a set of forms, all of them innate in Coleridge's sense, and all of them merging to produce the one final form, the work itself.

The texture of *Walden*, usually considered under the general heading of Thoreau's style, has been treated at some length by various commentators. Krutch, Cook, and Matthiessen especially have discussed Thoreau's choice of words and the shape of his sentences, the basic elements of style.[4] His characteristic richness of allusion has been universally noted, especially by those studies which deal with his sources,[5] although the precise rhetorical purpose and force of this richness have yet to be defined. And critics have begun to explore, though they have hardly exhausted, the symbolic complexity of Thoreau's use of such recurring images and metaphors as sound, light, water, morning, the sun, the stars, and others.[6] This texture of style, allusion, and symbol, with the range and force it gives Thoreau's style and the demands it makes on the reader's whole sensibility, clearly grows organically out of and fulfills Thoreau's wish to wake his neighbors and readers up to how they were leading their lives and how they should lead them. Clearly, too, it does support the structure of *Walden* by providing what Lorch calls "a centrality of mood" (p. 292). But the real structure of *Walden*, that "harmonious relation of parts to the whole and of the whole to its parts" which Lorch, in the same passage, says *Walden* and *A Week on the Concord and Merrimac Rivers* lack, lies elsewhere.

This real structure has been recognized by critics since Lorch but has not been fully analyzed. Matthiessen wishes more to prove that such a structure exists than to examine it in any detail, confining his analysis to noting the relation and transitions between the individual sections and noting the seasonal-pattern, Thoreau's "poem of the seasons or myth of the year" (p. 169). Krutch finds only that "the structural units are topical, the whole is actually an exposition rather than a narrative" (p. 95); Cook, that "there is a sense of compositional effect . . . a harmony of the separate objects in a total effect . . . a sense of the essential beauty of nature when realized as a composition" (p. 210). Only Shanley considers at any length the presence in *Walden* of a set of structural patterns, which he calls chronicle, topical essay, and persuasive argument, and shows by a survey of the contents of the book both how these three patterns alternate and combine and how Thoreau revised and developed *Walden* to establish them more firmly (pp. 76–82).[7]

One cause of the unwillingness of some critics to recognize or admit that *Walden* has any real structure was undoubtedly Thoreau's own unwillingness to make things easy for the reader, his reluctance to have *Walden* require anything less than what he said all good reading should require, "the steady intention almost of the whole life." We can see this reluctance in so slight a matter as *Walden*'s lack of chapter numbers. The casual reader may choose to take this lack as Thoreau's confession that the book is fragmentary, a mere collection of essays on several topics grouped around a central subject. But the athletic reader, to borrow Thoreau's phrase, may see in the lack of numbers a hint, even a challenge, to ignore mere mechanical sequence and seek for some more elaborate and meaningful pattern of movement or movements. He will find them even on a first reading, but even more as he comes to feel on repeated readings the total shape and complexity of the structure of the book.

First, *Walden* takes on, from Thoreau's arrangement of its sections, what we may call absolute form. That is to say, this arrangement has an overall shape and symmetry mainly separate from the specific content and function of each individual section. After a long introduction, these sections gather themselves, for various purposes, in two groups roughly balanced around a longer central section, "The Ponds." Each group anchors in a section especially essential to the point and purpose of the whole book, the first taking its start with "Where I Lived and What I Lived For," the second coming to rest in *Walden*'s "Conclusion." Whether we find this form analogous to the arching, multipathed rainbow, in whose "very abutment" Thoreau once stood, to "one arch at least over the darker gulf of ignorance which surrounds us," or to the pure parabola of mathematics, clearly the form does give a basic aesthetic satisfaction. And this form, with its hint of forward movement and of changing direction, to this extent mirrors *Walden*'s central purpose.

Second, *Walden* has narrative movement. It takes the reader through a sequence in time, and although Thoreau often moves outside the limits of his two years and two months at the pond and at the same time, for convenience and economy and for symbolic purposes, condenses the two years into one, he retains a basic, linear, chronological pattern. He sometimes expresses this pattern by alluding to the season, sometimes by citing the month and even at critical points the date. Thus, in spite of the obviously topical arrangement of the first half of the book and the obvious typicality of many of the activities Thoreau narrates, the basic chronology remains in force and gives a second, vital shape to the book, vital because it reaffirms our faith in that healthy, deliberate progress of time organic to the world of nature but too often accelerated by man in his world beyond all due proportion. Thoreau finds this organic time embodied everywhere in nature, and on this time, as we shall see, he bases his myth of spiritual rebirth.

Third, in *Walden* Thoreau is obviously trying not only to narrate the story of his sojourn at the pond but to present to the reader a body of information about the two worlds of man and of nature, information both useful and meaningful. Thus, the sections of the book are so arranged as to give us facts in the right expository order, for important expository purposes.

What makes "Economy" over twice as long as any other section of *Walden* is, more than anything else, its special expository purpose. In this, his opening, introductory section, Thoreau has to put forth much crucial information. The basic facts of his stay at the pond, many details about his way of life there that he will later treat more expansively and suggestively, information about his previous existence, practical advice on how to go about building a cabin — all this and more Thoreau gives to the reader, to inform him and thereby to equip him to read further in *Walden*. Some of this information, no doubt, Thoreau intended ironically, to answer those pertinent impertinent questions asked him by his more literal-minded neighbors. He has assumed some of his circumstantiality to suit the circumstantial minds of his questioners. But his "statistics," as he says, do, "as they have a certain completeness, have a certain value also." For they give *Walden*, from the beginning, the actuality needed to make it a true reading of life, a grounding in expository detail to keep it from being, as some captious critics might complain, mere prophecy, mere poetry.

"Where I Lived and What I Lived For" is one of the three pivotal sections of *Walden*, the other two being, as we have already seen, "The Ponds" and "Conclusion." Thus its expository purpose, less vital to its force as literature than its rhetorical and mythic ones, is submerged within them. Yet Thoreau does, in the short opening part of the section, remind us with the story of his past farm-hunting of some of the more literal terms of his decision, characteristically complicated by his final "possession" of each purchase. In the body of the section, in spite of the dominant note of rhetorical challenge and of preparation for mythic adventure, he does complete his factual background and begins, in some small ways, to expose his central subject, to "burrow" for "reality."

The sections between "Where I Lived and What I Lived For" and "The Ponds" deal with six specific topics, each important for our literal understanding of *Walden*. They tell us Thoreau's main activities at Walden and the principles behind them. Now that we are fully aware of Thoreau's basic situation, these sections extend our knowledge in six important directions. "The Ponds" completes Thoreau's exposition of his typical summer world and expands our information about the ponds into other seasons and other years, thereby preparing us for the later sections. These later sections, between "The Ponds" and "Conclusion," develop in several ways from the first half of the book. They take every chance offered by *Walden*'s narrative movement to treat again such earlier topics as Thoreau's habits, his walks, his visitors, his animal neighbors, and even co-tenants, and the ever-present, ever-changing pond: all of them in the new context of the different seasons, especially winter; some of them, as in "Brute Neighbors," with an intenser focus gained from greater familiarity.

Some topics, such as "Former Inhabitants," are properly taken up now because the special circumstances of winter life justify them. In all these ways, in short, *Walden* shows its expository order.

To turn to *Walden's* fourth and fifth patterns of movement, the rhetorical and the mythic, is to change modes of expression radically. For narrative and exposition of essentially factual and autobiographical matter, no matter how well ordered, belong to assertive, nonfictional prose; but rhetorical appeals and the creation of myth belong to imaginative prose. To put it another way, factual narrative and exposition direct us centrifugally toward real experience; rhetoric and myth direct us centripetally toward literary experience.[8] *Walden's* ordered narrative and expository movement we see and accept; to *Walden's* ordered rhetorical and mythic movement we react and respond.

As literary expression, moreover, *Walden's* rhetoric and myth, as we shall see, relate closely to each other, far more closely than they relate to the expository and narrative patterns, or to the absolute form. They are almost two ways of looking at the same literary effect: one, the myth, the content of *Walden's* meaning; one, the rhetoric, the means by which the verbal images, symbols, and gestures of the myth come to the reader. Yet both rhetoric and myth also grow organically out of the absolute form of *Walden's* most basic shape and out of the progressive yet cyclical movement of its narrative and the literal, factual matter of its exposition.

In "Economy" Thoreau catches our attention rhetorically by humbly stating that it is our curiosity he answers, that he speaks at our request and not his own insistence. He disarms us, too, by confessing freely and frankly his egotism and egoism. He appeals not to our dreams and impracticalities, he says, but to something much more stable, to our business sense, our economy. Thereby, as well as by the immediate and continuing appeal and challenge of his style itself, he at once gains a hold on our thoughts and feelings. Next, given this hold, he begins to vex us with problems. Much of the autobiography in "Economy" challenges us by its novelty and by the ambiguous tone in which Thoreau presents it. Moreover, by treating so fully his own four necessities — Food, Shelter, Clothing, and Fuel — he not only queries our ordering of our material life but attacks our materiality itself as false and unreal, thereby bringing us, though we may not yet realize it, already face to face with one of *Walden's* essential meanings. Finally, by his apparent digression on philanthropy, Thoreau anticipates a fundamental objection to his whole way of life and to *Walden* and answers it before it can harm his purpose.

Walden sets forth not one but two myths — of entry into nature and of rebirth through nature. In "Economy" Thoreau tells how he first entered the world of nature and hints of the rebirth to come. Not only is Thoreau's initial move to the side of Walden Pond an essential step, but as he discusses how men should order their lives, he supports his myth by praising the natural against the artificial whenever possible. In his use of images of growth and of moulting and shedding and in his short description of the spring during which he built his cabin, a single paragraph that looks forward to *Walden's* climax, Thoreau foreshadows his myth of rebirth and regeneration, which he and the reader can only re-enact after they have become as fully a part of nature as possible. At the same time, through such symbolic details as the materials for his cabin, Thoreau warns us that both myths are myth and not reality, that man must compromise and make adjustments, that he can commit himself to nature emotionally and even spiritually but never wholly.

"Where I Lived and What I Lived For" sets the pattern for *Walden's* rhetorical and mythic movement. Thoreau recalls and reaffirms the challenging epigraph of the title-page and more bluntly than elsewhere affirms his own position and comments critically on that of his readers — their desire for "news," what "sleepers" they are. And as he describes his own "morning" life, Thoreau establishes his two myths, of uniting with nature and through that union being spiritually reborn.

Not only do the six sections between "Where I Lived and What I Lived For" and "The Ponds," as we saw, extend our knowledge in important directions, but by having various dialectic relations, both singly and in groups, to each other and to our own ideas, they further challenge and disturb our thinking. For example, taken as a group the first three, the activities of the private life, in their fullness and richness contrast sharply with the second three, the activities of the public life. Taken in pairs, "Reading" contrasts with "Sounds," "Solitude" with "Visitors," and "The Bean-Field" with "The Village," always significantly. Furthermore, not only does each of them invariably upset our own thoughts on its subject, but each has a special rhetorical function. "Reading," for example, shows how to give ourselves to *Walden*; "Solitude" under what conditions best to do so; and the ending of "The Village," when Thoreau cries out that "wherever a man goes, men will pursue and paw him with their dirty institutions," shows to what a desperate strait we have come, thereby completes our mental and spiritual derangement, and makes us eager for the reassurance of "The Ponds."

Through these six essays, moreover, Thoreau brings his myth of entry into nature ever closer to its fulfillment in "The Ponds." The first three draw us more and more into nature from the world of man; in the second three, the point of view has reversed, and we are now within nature, looking back at the world of man from a further and further remove. As our involvement in the world of nature increases, so do Thoreau's promises and prophecies of the natural cycle of rebirth and renewal. The image of the silent and secret growth of summer recurs, and climaxes in "The Bean-Field" in Thoreau's own parable of the sower and the seed. At the end of "Solitude," Thoreau invokes and hymns the climactic images of the two myths of *Walden* by calling for a "draught of undiluted morning air" from that Hebe of whom he says, "wherever she came it was spring."

"The Ponds" is the central, crucial, pivotal section of *Walden*. Its length suggests this; its contents confirm it. In reading "The Ponds" we feel *Walden*'s five patterned movements even more intensely than elsewhere in the book. As we have seen, "The Ponds" is the keystone of the arch of *Walden*'s absolute form. Also, it marks a major stage in *Walden*'s narrative movement, and it reflects that movement in little, displaying within itself Thoreau's double chronology of compression into one year and extension far beyond two. It completes the first half of *Walden*'s exposition and makes an important transition to the second half. It does more than this, however. By inviting us to think poetically and imaginatively, rather than logically and dialectically, it frees us from the challenge and controversy of the first half of the book and admits us into Thoreau's innermost, most secret confidence as the earliest sections never seemed to do. Finally, as we respond poetically and imaginatively to "The Ponds," we are immersed as fully in the world of nature as we are ever to be, thereby completing Thoreau's first myth, and are symbolically baptized and purified and thereby made ready to re-enact Thoreau's second myth, of seasonal change, with him. Symbolically, too, "The Ponds" tells us, in our seasonal renewal, to shun the muddy, impure shallows, to seek the clear, deep, solitary life, a life cleansed by regular change, and reflecting heaven.

Thus, after "The Ponds," not only have the context and content of Thoreau's exposition changed, but the tone of his rhetorical appeal as well. He has subtly adopted a new manner to suit the second half of his and the reader's journey together. Often he seems more generous and less demanding, for he and the reader are now one in purpose, and we share his thoughts rather than being tested by them. At times, even—"Higher Laws" for example—he now dares admit to personal crotchets and whims that humanize his ideals without marring them. In the winter sections, his tone grows quieter and more private yet, as if, forced by Thoreau's isolation to abandon his actual presence, we have retreated within his mind and there listen to his symbolic telling and enacting of his myth of spiritual sleep or death followed by the miraculous rebirth or reawakening of spring, at which time the tone of the rhetoric passes out of revery, and rises swiftly to affirmation and exultation.

This myth of rebirth, long promised, and made manifest in these final sections, is *Walden*'s most important literary statement. To trace this myth, by responding poetically and imaginatively to the formal, narrative, expository, and especially the rhetorical movement of the second half of *Walden*, is to read *Walden* fully as a work of literature. Now that we have entered fully into nature by way of the first half of *Walden*, now that our imaginations are stimulated and symbolically consecrated by "The Ponds," we are ready to do this.

Thoreau begins his myth with the opening section of "Baker Farm," his religious communion with and consecration by nature. After thus affirming his priesthood, Thoreau offers the example of John Field the

Irishman, which must be read as a parable of the need of all Thoreau's readers for *talaria* for their "wading webbed bog-trotting feet" rather than as Thoreau's serious solution to Concord's Irish problem — although, characteristically, Thoreau's "poetic" recommendations seem more realistic on second glance than does John Field's present reality. Through this parable Thoreau asserts the need for spiritual regeneration, for moral rebirth. In "Higher Laws," just as bathing in the pond cleansed more than physically, so does the gradual renunciation of a mere physical tasting of and feeding on natural life lead to a further betterment not just physical but moral, not just of the body but of the imagination, a betterment by laws "higher" in several senses. And at the end, Thoreau offers a second, reinforcing parable, this time of John Farmer, who heard the flute of Pan-Thoreau leading him "to let his mind descend into his body and redeem it."

With "Brute Neighbors" come, as the fulfillment of Thoreau's refusal to prey any longer on natural life, what are for most readers the richest and most intimate moments of his life in nature, each of them a further source of moral education and a rite of communion. By such episodes, and especially by the mysterious and intensely empathetic final encounter with the loon and the god of the loon, the mind is fed with matter for it in turn to feed on during the long winter quiescence before rebirth in spring. Now, too, it is the fall days of October in *Walden's* narrative movement, and we feel the center of interest turn in toward the silence and night and death of winter.

The winter sections, from "House-Warming" through "The Pond in Winter," prepare directly and symbolically for Thoreau's "Spring" and for the reader's. To trace their symbolism in detail would make an explication as long as *Walden* itself, and for the aware reader *Walden* is its own explication. But the main patterns can be noted. The fires of "House-Warming" burn "both within my house and within my breast" to keep the cabined spirit alive through the symbolic death of winter, a death whose meaning is only intensified by our knowing how easily "a little colder Friday or greater snow" could turn symbol to reality. This winter death and the promise of spring parallel the real deaths (and failures) of *Walden's* "Former Inhabitants" and the spring lilacs growing out of the abandoned cellars of Breed, Col. Quoil, and the rest. Thoreau's "Winter Visitors" are those best suited for such a time of isolation and renewal, farmer, poet, philosopher, and, above all, "the Visitor who never comes." The quiet discussion of "Winter Animals" not only reminds us of the life also continuing around Thoreau but at the same time marks the low point of the mythic cycle, of the curve of lessening and then resurging moral and spiritual intensity. "The Pond in Winter," the last and most important of the winter sections, reasserts and reaffirms, within the context of winter's stasis and with all the difference this implies, the poetic and imaginative demands of *Walden's* pivotal "The Ponds"; it shows once again "that this pond was made deep and pure for a symbol"; and it ends with parallel visions of the coming of spring to Walden and of Thoreau's symbolic meeting with "the servant of the Brahmin, priest of Brahma and Vishnu and Indra," a meeting which expands into a vision of universal purification and consecration.

With "Spring," in style, image, allusion, and theme the most insistently symbolic of all *Walden*'s sections, the myth is fulfilled, the rite is enacted. "Walden was dead and is alive again," and so likewise is the soul of man on that symbolic "spring morning" that fuses *Walden*'s two dominant images into a moment of forgiveness and renewal.

Walden's "Conclusion" is, as we have seen, the further abutment of the arch of formal structure. Apart from this, it is, as suits its purpose, no real conclusion at all but rather, to re-phrase another literary moralist, a conclusion in which everything is begun, in short, the near abutment of an even higher and firmer arch. For although Thoreau does end his narrative, he makes us even more aware that he has gone on to live "several more lives." His exposition suddenly shows us "new continents and worlds" and makes clear that *Walden* has always been not a program but a parable, not a way of life but only one man's way of leading life rightly. By his rhetoric he once more challenges us, this time hopefully and affirmatively, to put foundations under our castles in the air, and leaves us on a rising note. Finally, by such images as the sea journey and such stories as that of the artist of Kouroo, Thoreau suggests new myths through which we may inform our lives, and by others, such as the fable of the "strong and beautiful bug" or the image of the sun that is but a "morning star," he reillumines *Walden*'s main literary statement.

To sum up, *Walden* has organic structure—a patterned movement that is formal, narrative, expository, rhetorical, and above all, mythic. The careful and responding reader of *Walden* feels these patterns of movement, at places some more intensely than others, at crucial places all united as one, working together to further Thoreau's intent to revive and re-form his reader's mind. *Walden*'s straight narrative chronology carries the reader naturally from one stage of exposition to the next: moving in time, he grows in knowledge. And as *Walden*, rhetorically heightened and imaginatively ordered and intensified, becomes literature, narrative in turn becomes ritual, and knowledge revelation; and the sum of these becomes myth, the ultimate literary experience, still contained within the arch of absolute form. Thus, when the reader has finished *Walden*, for the first time or the fiftieth, he has moved with Thoreau through this fivefold organic structure. He has expected and had his expectations fulfilled. He has traveled much in *Walden*.

Notes

1. *Coleridge's Shakespeare Criticism*, ed. Thomas M. Raysor (1930), I, 224.

2. "Thoreau and the Organic Principle in Poetry," *PMLA*, LIII (1939), 286–302; "The Organic Principle," *American Renaissance* (1941), Ch. IV.

3. *The Mirror and the Lamp* (1953), pp. 171–174.

4. Joseph Wood Krutch, *Henry David Thoreau* (1948), pp. 263–275; Reginald L. Cook, *Passage to Walden* (1949), pp. 212–231; *American Renaissance*, pp. 83–99.

5. See especially Edith Seybold, *Thoreau: The Quest and the Classics* (1951), and Joseph Jones, *Index to Walden* (1955).

6. For sound see Sherman Paul, "The Wise Silence: Sound as Agency of Correspondence in Thoreau," *NEQ*, XII (1949), 511–527; for spring and morning see John C. Broderick, "Imagery in *Walden*," *University of Texas Studies in English*, XXXIII (1954), 80–89; for sun and natural rebirth see Stanley Edgar Hyman, "Henry Thoreau in Our Time," *Atlantic Monthly*, CLXXVIII (November 1946), 137–146, reprinted in *Thoreau: A Century of Criticism*, ed. Walter Harding (1954).

7. In "Resolution at Walden," *Accent*, XII (1953), 101–113, and in *The Shores of America* (1958), pp. 293–353 (published after this article was written), Sherman Paul writes of spiritual autobiography and literary self-expression more than of artistic structure and effect, and writes more from Thoreau's point of view than from the reader's, but his discussion of Thoreau's "fable of the renewal of life" (p. 293) is detailed, thorough, and suggestive.

8. For this distinction I am indebted to Northrop Frye's *Anatomy of Criticism* (1957), pp. 73–74. I should also like to acknowledge several helpful suggestions by Stephen E. Whicher.

The Movement of Thoreau's Prose   John C. Broderick*

Our voyaging is only great-circle sailing.

Walden

Our expeditions are but tours, and come round again at evening to the old hearth-side from which we set out. Half the walk is but retracing our steps.

"Walking"

Although Henry David Thoreau clearly aimed such barbs as these at the unadventurous sojourner in life, the quotations fairly describe the pattern of his own walks, the history of his life, and even — I venture to suggest — the patterns of his most characteristic prose and the structure of some of his controlling ideas.

*Reprinted from *American Literature* 33 (May 1961):133–42, by permission of Duke University Press. © 1961 by Duke University Press.

I

A geometric design of the life of Thoreau would run to loops and curlicues. Concord was home base for a series of forays into the larger, more or less alien world. These began as practical *ad hoc* ventures: a pencil-selling trip to New York, interim teaching in Canton, Massachusetts, the four-year Harvard enterprise itself, designed to fit him for the great world and thus perhaps to disqualify him for Concord. That Henry—and not his brother John—should have been the beneficiary of family sacrifices is curious, and Thoreau himself is reported to have said that his education was not worth its cost. Whatever the family hopes and whatever his own evaluation, Harvard did not entirely "take" with Thoreau. During his freshman year, he walked home from Cambridge, the last two miles in his stocking feet. And when at the end of four years he returned to Concord, better shod and clutching the diploma a misinformed posterity has sought to deny him, he was—though he may not have realized it then—home to stay.

He may not have realized it, for the young graduate busily set out his trotlines for employment, and one who knew him well said that he would have gone to Alexandria, Virginia, to teach "if accepted." Nevertheless, there soon appeared a nagging, if only partly conscious, reluctance to leave his native town for more than a short excursion. Shortly before he left college Mrs. Thoreau had advised her son to "roam abroad to seek your fortune." His eyes filled with tears, but his sister Helen kissed him and spoke comfortingly, "No, Henry. You shall not go. You shall stay at home and live with us."[1] And so he did. His longest subsequent absence from Concord occurred in 1843 during his perfunctory and unhappy assault on the literary capital of New York at the urging of his patron, Emerson. It was conspicuously unsuccessful, and perhaps made Thoreau the readier the next year to decline a friend's invitation to visit Europe.

The outings made memorable for literature had begun in 1839 when Henry and John Thoreau spent a week on the Concord and Merrimac rivers. Others followed: to Wachusett, to Cape Cod, to Maine, to Canada, most memorably to Walden Pond. The river voyage initiated the pulsations of departure and return prominent especially in the years after Walden. Thoreau made the excursions of the 1850's with his eye on the periodical market, no doubt, but an excursion to Maine was an excursion merely, defined by return to Concord, whereas the ambitious venture to Staten Island had threatened to become linear, not circular. Concord, "the most estimable place in all the world," was his locus of value, periodic departures from which were followed by symmetrical returns.

The Concord he loved was, of course, not the tiny village but the spacious "town." When the restless 1840's ended with the failure of his first book, Thoreau settled into a routine of daily existence, the high moment of which was the afternoon walk to Conantum, to White Pond, to

Walden. "Set out at 3 P.M. for Nine-Acre Corner Bridge *via* Hubbard's Bridge and Conantum, returning *via* Dashing Brook, rear of Baker's, and railroad at 6:30 P.M."[2] So goes a representative passage in Thoreau's *Journal*, the literary monument of the normal life of the 1850's. Excursions outside the township supplied the travel books; daily excursions within it supplied the *Journal*. It is said that the amount of his daily writing in his *Journal* was equivalent to the length of his daily walk.

As for the longer excursions, only at Walden and on the rivers did Thoreau achieve ideal rapport between physical and spiritual. The river voyage was mental as well as literal, but, as study of Thoreau's revisions has shown, speculation was rooted in the sheer hard facts of the 1839 voyage. At Walden Thoreau soared because he first came "to know beans." The walk or the successful excursion was thus the factual grounding, the means of spiritual release, and often the literary symbol for their fusion.

II

Thoreau's writings, like *Leaves of Grass*, are full of movement, are on the go. The "walk" supplies structural thread for "Walking," "A Walk to Wachusett," "A Winter Walk," and *Cape Cod*. The extended walk or "journey" serves for *The Maine Woods, A Week on the Concord and Merrimack Rivers*, a "water walk" with occasional scrambling along the bank. Even "Civil Disobedience" records what its author calls "a long journey," the result of "traveling into a far country," and the dislocations of life arraigned in "Slavery in Massachusetts" symbolically culminate in this: "The remembrance of my country spoils my walk." (The surprisingly optimistic conclusion of the latter essay is occasioned by a white water-lily, "the emblem of purity," discovered on a walk.) *Walden* itself might be regarded as a year-long walk, for as in his daily walk Thoreau moved away from the mundane world of the village toward one of heightened awareness and potentiality, only to return spiritually reinvigorated, so *Walden* records an adventuring on life which structurally starts from and returns to the world of quiet desperation.

Thoreau has rarely received credit for such compositional excellence in large matters. James Russell Lowell spoke of his inability to sustain a work "to the serene balance of completeness" while praising his "exquisite mechanical skill" in the sentence or the paragraph.[3] The distinction has remained viable, despite considerable recent interest in Thoreau's structures. His writing is still likely to be described by friendly critics as a "mosaic" or "montage." One of the best, while comparing the writing to "an Indian's quiet tread, covering ground, making distance," nonetheless considers Thoreau "essentially an aphorist whose unit of writing was the epigrammatic sentence."[4] Thoreau's best paragraphs, however, do not depend entirely on "the personality of the writer" for their unity. Instead, they move as Thoreau did and as his books do — from the mundane known to the transcendent knowable and back again. By various stylistic means he involves the reader in an intense spiritual experience, only to set him down again in the world from which he has been removed, presumably with more abundant resources for living.

A fairly simple example of such writing is the first paragraph of *Walden*:

> When I wrote the following pages, or rather the bulk of them, I lived alone, in the woods, a mile from any neighbor, in a house which I had built myself, on the shore of Walden Pond, in Concord, Massachusetts, and earned my living by the labor of my hands only. I lived there two years and two months. At present I am a sojourner in civilized life again.[5]

The paragraph begins deceptively, especially since the disarming qualification, "or rather the bulk of them," suggests a characteristic fastidiousness about fact which authenticates *Walden* as a whole. But the remainder of the first sentence comprises a series of short phrasal units, all but one of which ("in Concord, Massachusetts") puts the "I" at greater and greater remoteness from the world of the ordinary reader, removed by solitude, by locality, by personal construction of his dwelling, and by activity — manual labor. The last two sentences of the paragraph mark the return. The second sentence suggests that the distancing experience had temporal limits (a suggestion implicit in the first three words of the paragraph; we have also been reassured by "Concord, Massachusetts"). The last sentence "places" the "I," but there is ambiguity in the word "sojourner," suggesting that his return may be only temporary, that like Melville's Bulkington he may soon ship on another voyage, that he has not passively renewed ordinary obligations. The paragraph, in short, is a miniature of *Walden* as a whole.

In its "out-and-back" movement the paragraph is typical, but in its simplicity of means it is less so. Many of Thoreau's paragraphs have the same movement but employ more complicated devices. Such paragraphs often begin with deceptively simple, largely monosyllabic utterances which are succeeded by poetic, allusive, metaphorical enrichment before the return. But the closing sentence — often humorous — serves two functions: it completes the release, but it also recalls the journey just completed. Meanwhile, during the journey Thoreau has kept his reader aware of starting point and destination. Puns, irony, quirky quotations and allusions, careful etymologies — these are a few of his devices to relieve some of the tension of the journey and forecast release from its spiritual intensity.

The most concentrated example of such writing may be an amusing, rather trivial paragraph near the end of "Economy" in *Walden*:

> Not long since I was present at the auction of a deacon's effects, for his life had not been ineffectual: —

"The evil that men do lives after them."
As usual, a great proportion was trumpery which had begun to
accumulate in his father's day. Among the rest was a dried tapeworm.
And now, after lying half a century in his garret and other dust holes,
these things were not burned; instead of a *bonfire*, or purifying
destruction of them, there was an *auction*, or increasing of them. The
neighbors eagerly collected to view them, bought them all, and carefully transported them to their garrets and dust holes, to lie there till
their estates are settled, when they will start again. When a man dies he
kicks the dust.[6]

The spiritual exhortation of the paragraph is slight, emerging chiefly from
the negative examples of "desperation" concerning furnishings. But almost
all the devices are here: the pun ("ineffectual"), the familiar quotation
eccentrically used, the etymologically exact play on *auction* and *bonfire*.
The sheer ingenuity of these words and phrases prompts a double
response, in which amusement softens the ardors of the better life and
actually secures these ardors a hearing. But the most effective sentence is
the last, in which the familiar folk remark cuts two ways. Its familiarity is
reassuring (even the low-keyed demands of this paragraph are ultimately
impracticable). But its metaphoric aptness ("dust" is a favorite term of
Thoreau's for what is wrong with life) sets up reverberations which echo
the demands for a life of sanity and principle, even at the moment of
release from absolute insistence upon it.

One of the most justly famous passages in *Walden* is that sublime
apologia for life in the woods.

I went to the woods because I wished to live deliberately, to front
only the essential facts of life, and see if I could not learn what it had to
teach, and not, when I came to die, discover that I had not lived. I did
not wish to live what was not life, living is so dear; nor did I wish to
practise resignation, unless it was quite necessary. I wanted to live deep
and suck out all the marrow of life, to live so sturdily and Spartanlike as
to put to rout all that was not life, to cut a broad swath and shave close,
to drive life into a corner, and reduce it to its lowest terms, and, if it
proved to be mean, why then to get the whole and genuine meanness of
it, and publish its meanness to the world; or if it were sublime, to know
it by experience, and be able to give a true account of it in my next
excursion. For most men, it appears to me, are in a strange uncertainty
about it, whether it is of the devil or of God, and have *somewhat hastily*
concluded that it is the chief end of man here to "glorify God and enjoy
him forever."[7]

An intense paragraph like this provides little comfort for the man
unwilling to accept the most strenuous demands of the moral life; but
there is some. The first sentence, like its author, begins deliberately, then
mounts and mounts — to an ironic climax. The ultimate distinction of the
idealist between "life" and "not life" is nonetheless presented in a verbally

playful way. The slightly humorous qualifications of the next sentence ("living is so dear" and "unless it was quite necessary") provide additional momentary relief before we are confronted with that remarkable series of metaphors for life at its best. We have passed Conantum and Nine-Acre Corner now; we are at Walden itself. The language which records the author's fronting of life at "its lowest terms" (really the highest) has forced the reader to a similar fronting. The excitement, the challenge, the appeal are almost unbearable. But we cannot live at Walden forever. To perpetuate such godlike moments would require transfiguration of the human condition. Mercifully, the author initiates a return by the parallel qualifications, "if it proved to be . . . or if it were. . . ." The jocularity of "my next excursion" distances both author and reader from the epiphany only recently shared. The joke continues with the powerful extravagance of the next sentence (ironically balanced by the modest "it appears to me"), but the last words of the paragraph are "glorify God and enjoy him forever," words almost meaningless in their reassuring familiarity. The sojourner through this paragraph, however, has had a glimpse of the glory itself, and for him life (and the stale quotation) can never be exactly the same as before he entered the woods.

The long paragraph following this one in *Walden* reveals other stylistic means of departure and safe return: playful allusions to classical myth and fable (ants and men, pygmies and cranes) and the straight-faced drollery connected with the extended pun on "sleepers." Between these is the almost strident recommendation of "simplicity." In such a passage as that on simplicity, Thoreau loses some of the aesthetic detachment which he elsewhere maintains, but his functional stylistic devices enable the reader, at least, to enter and leave the paragraph with profit and without embarrassment. The companion passage in "Conclusion" in *Walden* ("I left the woods . . ." and the paragraph following) has roughly the same movement, out and back, culminating: "If you have built castles in the air, your work need not be lost; that is where they should be. Now put the foundations under them." Here we emerge almost with a blueprint for approximating in ordinary life the glimpsed reality in art of Romantic idealism.

And there are similar passages: such familiar paragraphs in *Walden* as those beginning "The mass of men lead lives of quiet desperation" ("Economy") and "With thinking we may be beside ourselves in a sane sense" ("Solitude"); that in *A Week* beginning "The New Testament is an invaluable book" ("Sunday"); the paragraph in "Walking" from which the epigraph is taken; and others. Thoreau's highly charged polemical writing ("Civil Disobedience," "Slavery in Massachusetts," and "A Plea for Captain John Brown"), on the other hand, has many paragraphs in which the author provides a journey without a return, working instead toward a more conventional climax. And, needless to say, a great many paragraphs do not reveal this kind of movement at all. But a surprising amount of Thoreau's best remembered and most effective writing through analysis displays its stylistic kinship to the well-loved walk.

Walden as a whole has recently surrendered its dynamic structural secret, in which the movement of the book is associated with the rhythm of the seasons. Still obscure, however, is the nature of some subordinate "movements," embracing several chapters. For example, after explaining where "I" lived and what "I" lived for, Thoreau treats first "Reading," an activity closely associated with civilized life, moves next to "Sounds," many of which still remind him of the village but which progressively and inexorably lead him (and us) further and further into the intense, distancing experience available in "Solitude," which culminates in the account of mystical visits from "the old settler and original proprietor," God himself. An almost too startling return from this high moment begins in the next chapter, "Visitors," the first paragraph of which incongruously, we almost feel *irreverently*, associates the saintly hero of *Walden* with a "bar-room." And the return is completed two chapters later in "The Village," a momentary return (the shortest chapter in *Walden*) before renewing the memorable journey.

At the very center of *Walden* is a troublesome but important chapter called "Higher Laws," which re-echoes some of the objectionable stridency of earlier passages. It nevertheless clearly contains a very intense spiritual exhortation in which fishing is associated with the primitive or wild and the renunciation of animal food with the spiritual or higher nature. The next chapter, "Brute Neighbors," commences with a comic, ironic dialogue between Poet and Hermit, in which the hermit must choose between going "to heaven or a-fishing." He eventually casts for the latter, sure that there "never is but one opportunity of a kind." Astute readers have recognized here some kind of descent, but this particular descent is merely one more example of the Thoreauvian "return" since the ironic dialogue is a comic version of the dualism so stridently insisted on in "Higher Laws." The function of the irony of self-disparagement here and elsewhere is to relax the tensions of the earlier chapter and enable the reader to return, chastened and invigorated but not left in the air of the inhuman abstraction of an impossible dualism.

It is of some interest that these two patterned side trips off the main itinerary of *Walden* cannot be discovered in the first prospectus, the earliest version of the book as reconstructed by J. Lyndon Shanley.[8] That first version lacks also "Conclusion" and thus lacks the ultimate return from Walden with its poignant admission: "I do not say that John or Jonathan will realize all this." In fact, almost none of the specimen passages cited above appear in the "first" *Walden*. Their absence suggests that whatever else Thoreau did with his masterpiece between 1847 and 1854, he discovered the possibilities of a pulsating, dynamic style which would engage the reader, secure his willing suspension of inertia, and involve him in a series of literary journeys seemingly of the greatest import, but not journeys without end.

In style as well as structure, in language as well as idea, then, Thoreau recapitulates the archetypal Romantic theme of rebirth. His significant contribution to the theme is his recognition that the moment of spiritual rebirth is not infinite, that the walk cannot be prolonged indefinitely, that return is inevitable. To death and re-birth, he adds re-entry. In a way, readers of Thoreau have always sensed this characteristic, seeking, however, to define it in philosophical or ethical terms, "the poet-naturalist," for example. But Thoreau, we must remember, is a literary artist, whose service to philosophy and ethics is to provide a fresh literary experience of perhaps old ideas and values. At its best his writing renews the vitality of a life of principle by providing the reader vicarious participation in a compelling version. His rhetorically extreme and seemingly intransigent claims for such a life, however, carry their own ironic qualification and thus make it available as ideal reality, if not as normal actuality.

Thoreau the man had his forbidding rigidities and intransigencies, of course, and Thoreau the almost priggish letter-writer even more. Such static intransigency does pop up now and then in the writing on "simplicity" or "Higher Laws" and occasionally threatens to dominate an entire work, "Life Without Principle," but only rarely. More often the wit, the humor, the irony render Romantic idealism accessible as a guide to life at its best rather than a monstrous abstraction existentially, perhaps, worthless.

The companions of Henry Thoreau's literary walks achieve a concrete experience of Romantic idealism, perhaps ultimately inaccessible in any other way. The dynamism of Thoreau's best writing takes us momentarily out of ourselves to that heaven-approaching plane from which the world of normality is seen and judged. We are reluctant to depart and, once there, perhaps more reluctant to return. The movement of Thoreau's probe enables us to do both and thus extract the maximum benefit from both the going and the coming back.

Notes

1. The anecdote is told by William Ellery Channing in *Thoreau the Poet-Naturalist* (Boston, 1902), p. 18.

2. Henry David Thoreau, *Writings*, Walden Ed. (Boston and New York, 1906), VIII, 307.

3. James Russell Lowell, *Writings*, Riverside Ed. (Boston and New York, 1892), I, 370.

4. Reginald L. Cook, *Passage to Walden* (Boston, 1949), pp. 220–225.

5. *Writings*, II, 3.

6. *Writings*, II, 75.

7. *Writings*, II, 100–101.

8. *The Making of Walden* (Chicago, 1957).

Five Ways of Looking at *Walden*   Walter Harding*

Although *Walden* was not exactly a roaring success when it was published in 1854 — it took five years to sell out the first edition of only two thousand copies — it has become, in the century since, one of the all-time best sellers of American literature. It has been issued in more than one hundred and fifty different editions — with a number of these editions having sold more than half a million copies each. At this moment it is in print in at least twenty-four different editions in this country alone as well as in English language editions in England, India, and Japan and in translations into French, Spanish, Portuguese, Italian, German, Dutch, Norwegian, Finnish, Swedish, Danish, Czechoslovakian, Japanese, and Sanskrit. What are the causes of this phenomenal popularity?

For the past twenty-one years I have had the good fortune to be the secretary of the Thoreau Society — one of the most unpredictable groups of individualists that has ever united itself around a common enthusiasm. It is the only literary society I know of where the professional teachers of literature are vastly outnumbered by the non-professionals. Among the regular attenders of our annual meetings are a stockbroker, a retired letter carrier, a clergyman, an outspoken atheist, an entomologist, an ornithologist, a music teacher, an archeologist, a poet, a publishing company executive, a printer, a druggist, a socialist organizer, a hardware store owner, a church organist, the author of a book entitled *Why Work?* (each year he gets permission from the local police to sleep on the front porch of the Concord High School), a telephone company executive, a novelist, a conservationist, an exponent of subsistence farming, a woman who announces that she "covers the culture front in Brooklyn," a professional mountain climber, a crime expert — the list could go on almost indefinitely. What is even more interesting is that when these people have been asked to state why they are sufficiently interested in Thoreau to make the annual journey to Concord — and some of our most regular attenders come from as far away as Quebec, Illinois, North Carolina, and Texas — it is very rarely that two give the same reason. They are interested in his natural history, his politics, his economics, his prose style, his anarchism, his theology, and so on. The most phenomenal facet of Thoreau's appeal —

*Reprinted from the *Massachusetts Review* 4 (Autumn 1962):149–62, by permission of the *Massachusetts Review*. © 1963 by The Massachusetts Review, Inc.

and the appeal of his masterpiece, *Walden* — is its tremendous breadth. *Walden* is read, not for just one reason, but for many.

To most people, I suppose, *Walden* is a nature book. Certainly back at the time of its appearance it was almost universally considered to be a book about natural history, and some of Thoreau's contemporaries were annoyed that he allowed anything but nature to have a part in the book. The lengthy opening chapter on "Economy," they fussed, was a waste of time and should be skipped by the average reader. They also suggested the reader skip over such philosophical chapters as "Where I Lived and What I Lived For," "Higher Laws" and "Conclusion." When Thoreau wrote about ants or loons or muskrats or pickerel or squirrels or snow or ice, they argued, he was superb. But, unfortunately, he was all too ready to go off into transcendental nonsense comprehensible only to such "tedious arch-angels" as Amos Bronson Alcott or to such radical corrupters of idealistic American youth as Ralph Waldo Emerson. But on the birds, the bees, the flowers, and the weather Thoreau could write — and did write superbly. The late 19th Century anthologies of American literature, when Thoreau is included, almost invariably print "The Battle of the Ants" from the "Brute Neighbors" chapter of *Walden* or "The Pond in Winter."

I am not at all trying to belittle Thoreau as a nature writer. I am simply stating that that was his first and widest appeal — and in fact, still is. In the second-hand book stores of our country the dealers more often than not categorize him as a nature writer rather than as a literary figure or a philosopher.

It has been claimed — and I think quite rightfully — that he invented the natural history essay — and certainly his writings are the standard by which all nature writers since his time have been judged. He has successfully avoided the traps so many nature writers fall into of being too cute, too sentimental, too technical, or just plain dull. He never indulges in the pathetic fallacy of attributing human characteristics to the lower classes of animals. Yet neither does he write down to them. He accepts them for what they are and writes about them on their own terms. He writes about them with wit and humor — but the humor is as often at the expense of himself and his fellow man as at the expense of the animal. Take for example that passage near the end of his chapter on "Brute Neighbors" in which he talks about his checker game with the loon on Walden Pond:

> As I was paddling along the north shore one very calm October afternoon, for such days especially they settle on to the lakes, like the milkweed down, having looked in vain over the pond for a loon, suddenly one, sailing out from shore toward the middle a few rods in front of me, set up his wild laugh and betrayed himself. I pursued with a paddle and he dived again, but I miscalculated the direction he would take, and we were fifty rods apart when he came to the surface this time, for I had helped to widen the interval; and again he laughed long and loud, and with more reason than before. He manoeuvered so

cunningly that I could not get within half a dozen rods of him. Each time, when he came to the surface, turning his head this way and that he coolly surveyed the water and the land, and apparently chose his course so that he might come up where there was the widest expanse of water and at the greatest distance from the boat. It was surprising how quickly he made up his mind and put his resolve into execution. He led me at once to the widest part of the pond, and could not be driven from it. While he was thinking one thing in his brain, I was endeavoring to divine his thought in mine. It was a pretty game, played on the smooth surface of the pond, a man against a loon. Suddenly your adversary's checker disappears beneath the board, and the problem is to place yours nearest to where his will appear again. Sometimes he would come up unexpectedly on the opposite side of me, having apparently passed directly under the boat. . . . Once or twice I saw a ripple where he approached the surface, just put his head out to reconnoitre, and instantly dived again. I found that it was as well for me to rest on my oars and wait his reappearing as to endeavor to calculate where he would rise; for again and again, when I was straining my eyes over the surface one way, I would suddenly be startled by his unearthly laugh behind me. But why, after displaying so much cunning, did he invariably betray himself the moment he came up by that loud laugh? Did not his white breast enough betray him? He was indeed a silly loon, I thought. I could commonly hear the plash of the water when he came up, and so also detected him. But after an hour he seemed as fresh as ever, dived as willingly, and swam yet further than at first.

But so much for Thoreau as a nature writer.

A second appeal of *Walden* is as a do-it-yourself guide to the simple life. I think it highly significant that the first real surge of interest in Thoreau in the twentieth century came during the depression years of the nineteen-thirties when large masses of people — indeed almost all of us — were required willy-nilly by the press of circumstances to adopt the simple life. We had no choice in the matter, but Thoreau was one of the very few authors who not only made this simple life bearable — he even made it appealing. A friend of mine said to me back in the thirties, "You know, Thoreau is the only author you can read without a nickel in your pocket and not be insulted."

What is perhaps more phenomenal than his appeal during the depression years is the fact that in our present era of super-materialism and status-seeking he still continues to make the simple life appealing. Now I am not one who advocates that we all, literally, go out and find our own Walden Ponds, build our own cabins, and ignore civilization. It was only through a profound misunderstanding of the book *Walden* that the idea that such an abandonment of civilization was Thoreau's aim ever got into circulation. He was very careful to say in the first chapter of *Walden*:

> I would not have any one adopt *my* mode of living on any account; for,
> beside that before he has fairly learned it I may have found out another

for myself, I desire that there may be as many different persons in the world as possible; but I would have each one be very careful to find out and pursue *his own way*, and not his father's or his mother's or his neighbor's instead.

He himself lived at Walden only two of the forty-four years of his life — roughly about four per cent of his life. He went to Walden Pond to live because he had a specific purpose in mind — the writing of a book that he had found he did not have time to write if he spent his time keeping up with the proverbial Joneses. And when he had finished writing that book (incidentally that book was not *Walden* but its predecessor, *A Week on the Concord and Merrimack Rivers*), he left the pond as freely and as happily as he had gone there.

Thoreau's philosophy of the simple life does not advocate the abandonment of civilized life or a return to the jungle. He simply points out that modern life is so complex that it is impossible for each one of us to embrace all of it. We must of necessity be selective. But unfortunately our standards of selection tend to be imposed upon us by the society we live in rather than based on our own personal interests and desires. We live not our own lives but the lives imposed on us by those who surround us. We keep up with the Joneses instead of ourselves. And when we come to die, we discover that we have not lived. How many of us will be able to say as Thoreau did on his death-bed:

> I *suppose* that I have not many months to live; but, of course, I know nothing about it. I may add that I am enjoying existence as much as ever, and regret nothing.

"And regret nothing." Those are the key words. Are we able to say that honestly of our own lives? Thoreau, when he went to Walden Pond, said that "he wished to live deliberately, to front only the essential facts of life." And because he determined what was the essence of life — not for his parents, nor for his neighbors — but for himself, he was able to say at the end of his life that he regretted nothing.

How then does one get at the essence of life? All of *Walden* is devoted to answering that question. But perhaps we can find it epitomized in a brief quotation from his chapter entitled "Where I Lived and What I Lived For":

> Our life is frittered away by detail. An honest man has hardly need to count more than his ten fingers, or in extreme cases he may add his ten toes, and lump the rest. Simplicity, simplicity, simplicity! I say, let your affairs be as two or three, and not a hundred or a thousand; instead of a million count half a dozen, and keep your accounts on your thumbnail. In the midst of this chopping sea of civilized life, such are the clouds and storms and quicksands and thousand-and-one items to be allowed for, that a man has to live, if he would not founder and go to the bottom and not make his port at all, by dead reckoning, and he must be

a great calculator indeed who succeeds. Simplify, simplify. Instead of three meals a day, if it be necessary eat but one; instead of a hundred dishes, five; and reduce other things in proportion.

Let us spend one day as deliberately as Nature, and not be thrown off the track by every nutshell and mosquito's wing that falls on the rails. Let us rise early and fast, or break fast, gently and without perturbation; let company come and let company go, let the bells ring and the children cry, — determined to make a day of it. . . . Why should we knock under and go with the stream? . . . Let us settle ourselves, and work and wedge our feet downward through the mud and slush of opinion, and prejudice, and tradition, and delusion, and appearance, that alluvion which covers the globe, through Paris and London, through New York and Boston and Concord, through Church and State, through poetry and philosophy and religion, till we come to a hard bottom and rocks in place, which we can call reality, and say, This is, and no mistake; and then begin, having a point d'appui, below freshet and frost and fire, a place where you might found a wall or a state, or set a lamp-post safely, or perhaps a gauge, not a Nilometer, but a Realometer, that future ages might know how deep a freshet of shams and appearances had gathered from time to time. . . . Be it life or death, we crave only reality. If we are really dying, let us hear the rattle in our throats and feel cold in the extremities; if we are alive, let us go about our business.

A third facet of *Walden* is its satirical criticism of modern life and living. Strangely enough this is one side of Thoreau that is sometimes misunderstood by the reader. Some take everything Thoreau says literally and seriously, ignoring the fact that the book's epigraph reads:

I do not propose to write an ode to dejection, but to brag as lustily as chanticleer in the morning, standing on his roost, if only to wake my neighbors up.

Even as astute a critic as James Russell Lowell made the rather astounding statement that Thoreau had no sense of humor. And if one does not see Thoreau's humor, he can be assured that he is missing — or worse, misreading a major portion of *Walden*.

A large portion of *Walden* cannot — or at least should not — be read literally. Throeau had a rollicking, witty sense of humor and used it extensively throughout the pages of his masterpiece. He used just about every humorous literary device on record — puns, hyperbole, slapstick, mockery, parody, burlesque, and so on. And just about every one of these devices was used with satirical intent. It is true that now and then he gets off a pun just for the pun's sake — such as that worst — or best — of all puns in the chapter on "The Ponds" where he speaks of the patient but unlucky fishermen at Walden Pond being members of the ancient sect of "Coenobites." (At least one scholarly edition of *Walden* points out in a footnote that a Coenobite is "a member of a religious community," and ignores the pun about the fishermen—"See, no bites.") But such pure puns—if I may call them "pure"—are comparatively rare. Most of Thoreau's humor, as I have said, is directed at the foibles of contemporary society—and is not only directed at them, but hits with a wallop.

Unfortunately humor is almost impossible to demonstrate by excerpts. One of its essentials is that it be seen in context, for it is often its very context that makes it humorous. But let me try a few samples:

> The head monkey at Paris puts on a traveller's cap, and all the monkeys in America do the same.

> One farmer says to me, "You cannot live on vegetable food solely, for it furnishes nothing to make bones with"; and so he religiously devotes a part of his day to supplying his system with the raw material of bones; walking all the while he talks behind his oxen, which, with vegetable-made bones, jerk him and his lumbering plow along in spite of every obstacle.

> I observed that the vitals of the village were the grocery, the bar-room, the post-office, and the bank; and, as a necessary part of the machinery, they kept a bell, a big gun, and a fire-engine, at convenient places; and the houses were so arranged as to make the most of mankind, in lanes and fronting one another, so that every traveller had to run the gauntlet, and every man, woman, and child might get a lick at him. Of course, those who were stationed nearest to the head of the line, where they could most see and be seen, and have the first blow at him, paid the highest prices for their places; and the few straggling inhabitants in the outskirts, where long gaps in the line began to occur, and the traveller could get over walls or turn aside into cow-paths, and so escape, paid a very slight ground or window tax.

> If I should only give a few pulls at the parish bell-rope, as for a fire, that is, without setting the bell, there is hardly a man on his farm in the outskirts of Concord, notwithstanding that press of engagements which was his excuse so many times this morning, nor a boy, nor a woman, I might almost say, but would forsake all and follow that sound, not mainly to save property from the flames, but, if we will confess the truth, much more to see it burn.

> We are eager to tunnel under the Atlantic and bring the Old World some weeks nearer to the New; but perchance the first news that will leak through into the broad, flapping American ear will be that the Princess Adelaide has the whooping cough.

If excerpting humor is dangerous, analyzing humor is even more so. Humor should stand on its own two legs—or it will fall flat on its face. But I wish to point out once again that Thoreau's humor is not used for its own sake. It is satirical humor and aimed at the reform of existing institutions and customs that Thoreau feels need the reform. And although we laugh at it—or with it—down deep underneath we realize there is often more validity to Thoreau's suggested reforms than to the customs of the society in which we live.

A fourth approach to *Walden* is the belletristic. From a purely technical standpoint, *Walden* is good writing and is worth examining as such. It has been frequently—and quite rightfully—said that Thoreau wrote the first modern American prose. One has only to compare a passage from *Walden* with one from almost any one of its contemporaries to see the difference. It was the vogue at the time to be abstract, circumlocutory, periphrastic, euphemistic, and euphuistic. *Walden* in contrast is clear, concrete, precise, and to the point. Emerson made the point a century ago when he said:

> In reading Henry Thoreau's journal [and the same can be said of *Walden*], I am very sensible of the vigour of his constitution. That oaken strength which I noted whenever he walked, or worked, or surveyed wood-lots, the same unhesitating hand with which a field-labourer accosts a piece of work, which I should shun as a waste of strength, Henry shows in his literary task. He has muscle, and ventures on and performs feats which I am forced to decline. In reading him, I find the same thought, the same spirit that is in me, but he takes a step beyond, and illustrates by excellent images that which I should have conveyed in a sleepy generality. 'Tis as if I went into a gymnasium, and saw youths leap, climb, and swing with a force unapproachable,—though their feats are only continuations of my initial grapplings and jumps.

Walden, like Thoreau's cabin, is tightly constructed. Each sentence, each paragraph, and each chapter is in its carefully chosen niche and cannot be moved or removed without severe damage to the artistry of the whole. The basic unifying device of the book is the year. Although Thoreau spent two years, two months, and two days at Walden Pond, in writing the book he compressed his adventures into the cycle of one year. *Walden* opens with the cutting down of the pine trees in March and the construction of the cabin through the spring. In summer he moves into the cabin and tends his beanfield. In the autumn he builds his fireplace and warms his house. In the winter he observes his neighbors—human, animal, and inanimate. Then with the breaking up of the ice on the pond and the renascence of spring he brings his book to a close. One of the most interesting facets of Lyndon Shanley's *The Making of Walden* is his revelation of how carefully Thoreau reworked and transposed his sentences to better carry out this theme of the cycle of the year.

Each individual chapter in the book has its set place in the book as a whole. There is a careful alternation of the spiritual and the mundane ("Higher Laws" is followed by "Brute Neighbors"), the practical and the philosophical ("Economy" is followed by "Where I Lived and What I Lived For"), the human and the animal ("Winter Visitors" is followed by "Winter Animals"). Adjacent chapters are tied together by contrast (as

"Solitude" and "Visitors"), by chronology (as "The Pond in Winter" and "Spring"), or by carefully worded connective phrases (as after "Reading" he begins "Sounds" with: "But while we are confined to books . . ." Or after "The Bean-Field" he begins "The Village" with: "After hoeing . . ."). And the three major expository chapters ("Economy," "Higher Laws," and "Conclusion") are placed strategically at the beginning, middle, and end of the book.

Within the individual chapters the details of construction are just as carefully worked out. In "The Ponds" he starts with Walden and then takes a southwestern sweep (his favorite direction for hiking according to his essay on "Walking") across Concord from Flint's Pond to Goose Pond to Fairhaven Bay, to White Pond. In "Former Inhabitants; and Winter Visitors," he starts with the residents of the days of the Revolution, works up through the most recent resident of the area—Hugh Quoil, who died the first autumn Thoreau was at the pond—and ends with those who visited him throughout his stay at the pond. Similar patterns can be worked out for each chapter.

Carefulness of construction continues into the individual paragraph. Although the average reader is not usually aware of it, Thoreau's paragraphs are unusually long. Walden contains only 423 paragraphs, an average of only slightly more than one page in the typical edition. But so carefully developed are they that one does not ordinarily notice their length. Their structure is so varied that there is little point in attempting to pick out typical examples. However, one of his favorite devices is at least worth mentioning—his use of the climax ending. Notice how frequently the final sentence in his paragraphs not only neatly sums up the paragraph as a whole, but usually carries it one step beyond, with an added thrust if the paragraph is satirical, with a broader concept if the paragraph is philosophical. Just as with his chapters, many of Thoreau's paragraphs are independent essays in themselves and can stand alone. But they cannot be moved from their specific niche within the book as a whole without damage to its structure.

Thoreau's sentences too are often unusually long. It takes very little search to find one half a page in length and more than one runs on for a full page and more. But again so carefully constructed are they that the average reader has no difficulty with their syntax and is hardly aware of their complexity. Let me take just one serpentine example from "House-Warming":

> I sometimes dream of a larger and more populous house, standing in a golden age, of enduring materials, and without gingerbread work, which shall still consist of only one room, a vast, rude, substantial, primitive hall, without ceiling or plastering, with bare rafters and purlins supporting a sort of lower heaven over one's head,—useful to keep off rain and snow, where the king and queen posts stand out to receive your homage, when you have done reverence to the prostrate

Saturn of an older dynasty on stepping over the sill; a cavernous house, wherein you must reach up a torch upon a pole to see the roof; where some may live in the fireplace, some in the recess of a window, and some on settles, some at one end of the hall, some at another, and some aloft on rafters with the spiders, if they choose; a house which you have got into when you have opened the outside door, and the ceremony is over; where the weary traveler may wash, and eat, and converse, and sleep, without further journey; such a shelter as you would be glad to reach in a tempestuous night, containing all the essentials of a house, and nothing for housekeeping; where you can see all the treasures of the house at one view, and everything hangs upon its peg that a man should use; at once kitchen, pantry, parlor, chamber, storehouse, and garret; where you can see so necessary a thing as a barrel or a ladder, so convenient a thing as a cupboard, and hear the pot boil, and pay your respects to the fire that cooks your dinner, and the oven that bakes your bread, and the necessary furniture and utensils are the chief ornament where the washing is not put out, nor the fire, nor the mistress, and perhaps you are sometimes requested to move from off the trapdoor, when the cook would descend into the cellar, and so learn whether the ground is solid or hollow beneath without stamping.

Three hundred and fifty-one words — and yet I doubt if any attentive student has any difficulty with its meaning. I do not, however, want to give the impression that all of Thoreau's sentences are grammatical leviathans. There are sentences in *Walden* only five words in length. One extreme is as frequent as the other and the majority are of more moderate length. Thoreau understood fully the necessity of variety in sentence structure and length. The point is that he could handle the sentence well no matter what its length.

Perhaps the most noticeable characteristic of Thoreau's word choice is the size of his vocabulary. *Walden* is guaranteed to send the conscientious student to the dictionary. In a random sampling we find such words as *integument, umbrageous, deliquium, aliment, fluviatile,* and *periplus.* Yet Thoreau cannot be termed ostentatious in his word-use. He simply searches for and uses the best possible word for each situation.

A second characteristic is his allusiveness. On a typical page he may echo a Biblical phrase, quote from a metaphysical poet, translate a few words from an ancient classic, make an allusion to a Greek god, cite an authority on early American history, and toss in a metaphor from a Hindu "Bible." It is true that he is usually careful to make his allusions in such a way that knowledge of the work alluded to is not essential to an understanding of Thoreau's meaning. But the serious reader has his curiosity aroused and wants his questions answered. To satisfy my own curiosity I once took a list of more than fifty different types of figures of speech — allusions, metaphors, rhetorical questions, alliteration, analogy, puns, epanorthosis, parables, similes, meiosis, anti-strophe, oxymoron, epizeuxis, anaphora, litotes, anti-thesis, portmanteau words, metonomy, contrast, personification, epistrophe, synecdoche, irony, apostrophe, hyperbole, and so on — and with no difficulty at all found excellent examples of each one in *Walden*. There is hardly a trick of the trade that Thoreau does not make use of. I think it significant that one of the most recent editions of *Walden* — one in fact published just this past year — is aimed for use as a textbook in college classes in rhetoric and grammar.

A fifth level on which to read *Walden* is the spiritual level. And I would not be exaggerating in the least to say that *Walden* has become veritably a bible — a guidebook to the higher life — for many, many people. In his chapter on "Reading," Thoreau says, "How many a man has dated a new era in his life from the reading of a book!" And *Walden* has been just such a book for many people. I spoke earlier of the fact that many of Thoreau's contemporaries went out of their way to skip over such chapters as "Economy," "Where I Lived, and What I Lived For," "Higher Laws," and "Conclusion." Ironically it is just those chapters which are most essential to *Walden* as a spiritual guidebook. And it is interesting to note that our contemporary anthologies of American literature are tending to print excerpts from those chapters rather than from the natural history chapters that I spoke of earlier.

It is a major thesis of *Walden* that the time has come for a spiritual rebirth — a renewal and rededication of our lives to higher things. It is true that we have progressed a long way from the status of the caveman. But our progress has been for the most part material rather than spiritual. We have improved our means, but not our ends. We can unquestionably travel faster than our ancestors, but we continue to waste our time in trivial pursuits when we get there. We have cut down on the number of hours of labor required to keep ourselves alive, but we have not learned what to do with the time thus saved. We devote the major part of our national energy to devising new means of blowing up the rest of the world and ignore attempts to make better men of ourselves.

Thoreau could hardly be called orthodox from a religious standpoint (or, as a matter of fact, from any standpoint at all), but it is significant to note that one of his favorite texts was "What shall it profit a man if he gain the whole world but lose his own soul?" And *Walden*, on its highest level is a guide to the saving of your own soul, to a spiritual rebirth.

As many recent critics, from F. O. Matthiessen onward, have pointed out, the most frequently recurring symbol in *Walden* from the beginning of the book to the very end is the symbol of rebirth and renewal. The book as a whole, as I have said, is based on the cycle of the seasons ending with the renewal of the earth and its life with the coming of spring. The chapter on "Sounds" follows the same pattern for the day, beginning with the sounds of morning, continuing on through the afternoon, the evening, and the night, and ending with the renewal of the world from its sleep with the crowing of the cock in the morning. Thoreau speaks of the purification ceremonies of the Indians and of the Mexicans. He tells us of the strange and wonderful insect that was reborn out of the apple-tree table after sixty years of dormancy. The very closing words of the book are a promise of a newer and better life that can be achieved if we but strive for it:

> I do not say that John or Jonathan will realize all this; but such is the character of that morrow which mere lapse of time can never make to dawn. The light which puts out our eyes is darkness to us. Only that day dawns to which we are awake. There is more day to dawn. The sun is but a morning star.

How can we approach, how can we achieve such a life? We will find one answer in "Higher Laws":

> If one listens to the faintest but constant suggestions of his genius, which are certainly true, he sees not to what extremes, or even insanity, it may lead him; and yet that way, as he grows more resolute and faithful, his road lies. The faintest assured objection which one healthy man feels will at length prevail over the arguments and customs of mankind. No man ever followed his genius till it misled him. Though the result were bodily weakness, yet perhaps no one can say that the consequences are to be regretted, for these were a life in conformity to higher principles. If the day and the night are such that you greet them with joy, and life emits a fragrance like flowers and sweet-scented herbs, is more elastic, more starry, more immortal, — that is your success. All nature is your congratulation, and you have cause momentarily to bless yourself.

And the second is from his "Conclusion":

> I learned this, at least, by my experiment: that if one advances confidently in the direction of his dreams, and endeavors to live the life which he has imagined, he will meet with a success unexpected in common hours. He will put some things behind, will pass an invisible boundary; new, universal, and more liberal laws will begin to establish themselves around and within him; or the old laws be expanded, and interpreted in his favor in a more liberal sense, and he will live with the license of a higher order of beings. In proportion as he simplifies his life, the laws of the universe will appear less complex, and solitude will not be solitude, nor poverty poverty, nor weakness weakness. If you have built castles in the air, your work need not be lost; that is where they should be. Now put the foundations under them.

Thoreau is sometimes dismissed as a misanthrope or a skulker, one who devoted himself to carping and criticism. But note that when *Walden* is approached on this spiritual level, it is not negative, it is positive. Thoreau is not so much complaining about the way things are but rather showing the way things might be. He is firmly convinced that the sun *is* but a morning star.

I have approached *Walden* from five different angles. But I have by no means exhausted the number of such approaches. *Walden* can and does mean all things to all men. Therein lies its very strength. It has been tested by time and not found wanting. In its first hundred years it has grown, not diminished in stature. I have no fear as to its being lost sight of in one more century — or two — or three — or four. It will endure.

The Extra-vagant Maneuver: Paradox in *Walden*

Joseph J. Moldenhauer*

I fear chiefly lest my expression may not be extra-vagant *enough, may not wander far enough beyond the narrow limits of my daily experience, so as to be adequate to the truth of which I have been convinced.* Extra- vagance! *it depends on how you are yarded. . . . I desire to speak somewhere without bounds; like a man in a waking moment, to men in their waking moments; for I am convinced that I cannot exaggerate enough even to lay the foundation of a true expression.*[1]

I

The idiosyncrasies of Thoreau's personality and opinions are so absorbing that "paradox" has always been a key term in Thoreau scholar- ship. Critic of government and relentless reporter of tortoises, Platonic dreamer and statistician of tree rings, Transcendental friend who calls for "pure hate" to underprop his love,[2] Thoreau invites description as para- doxical, enigmatic, or even perverse. But as Joseph Wood Krutch main- tains, "to unite without incongruity things ordinarily thought of as incongruous *is* the phenomenon called Thoreau."[3] In *Walden* this propen- sity toward the resolved contradiction may be observed in full flower. Here Thoreau talks only of himself, yet "brag[s] for humanity." Self-isolated in a spot as remote, he says, as Cassiopeia's Chair, he strolls to the village "every day or two." Renouncing materialism for a poetic and mystic life, he proudly reports his own prudential efficiency, and documents his "economic" success with balance sheets. Bewailing the limitations of science, he painstakingly measures the depth of the pond and counts the bubbles in its ice.

The dominant stylistic feature of *Walden* is paradox — paradox in such quantity and of such significance that we are reminded of the works of Donne, Sir Thomas Browne, and other English metaphysical writers. Thoreau's paradoxical assertion — for instance, "Much is published, but little printed" — seems self-contradictory and opposed to reason. As a poetic device it has intimate connections with metaphor, because it remains an absurdity only so long as we take the terms exclusively in their

*Reprinted from the *Graduate Journal* (University of Texas at Austin) 6 (Winter 1964): 132–46, with the author's revisions, by permission of the *Graduate Journal*.

conventional discursive senses. The stumbling block disappears when we realize that Thoreau has shifted a meaning, has constructed a trope or a play on words. The pun, that highly compressed form of comparison in which two or more logically disparate meanings are forced to share the same phonemic unit, lends itself admirably to Thoreau's purpose and underlies many of his paradoxes, including the example cited above. The peculiar impact of the paradox lies in our recognition that an expected meaning has been dislocated by another, remaining within our field of vision but somewhat out of focus. We are given, in Kenneth Burke's splendid phrase, a "perspective by incongruity."

The user of paradox thus defines or declares by indirection, frustrating "rational" expectations about language. Shortly before the publication of *Walden*, another New England Transcendentalist, the theologian Horace Bushnell, affirmed the usefulness of the device, declaring that "we never come so near to a truly well rounded view of any truth, as when it is offered paradoxically; that is, under contradictions; that is, when under two or more dictions, which, when taken as dictions, are contrary to one another."[4] In *Walden*, Thoreau wants to convey truths of the most unconventional sort—to bring other minds into proximity and agreement with his own attitudes and beliefs. He employs paradox not only for its galvanic effect in persuasion (i.e., as a verbal shock-treatment which reorients the audience), but for the special precision of statement it affords.

At the outset of Thoreau's literary career, his friend Emerson criticized the "*mannerism*" of "A Winter Walk," objecting most strenuously to the oxymorons: "for example, to call a cold place sultry, a solitude public, a wilderness *domestic.* . . ."[5] And we are not astonished to find that Thoreau himself deprecated the very instrument he used so skillfully. When he set down in the *Journal* a list of his "faults," the first item was "Paradoxes,—saying just the opposite,—a style which may be imitated."[6] On another occasion he complained that a companion, probably Ellery Channing, "tempts me to certain licenses of speech. . . . He asks for a paradox, an eccentric statement, and too often I give it to him."[7] But in spite of these warnings and hesitations (which, incidentally, are echoed in the reservations of some of his most sympathetic later critics), Thoreau did not abandon the paradoxical style. Richard Whately, the author of his college rhetoric text, had acknowledged, though rather reluctantly, the value of the device in argumentation. Thoreau's seventeenth-century reading illustrated its rich literary possibilities. Most important, his ironic sensibility embraced paradox. Thoreau wisely followed what he called the crooked bent of his genius and practiced a rhetoric appropriate to his aims.

These aims were in part determined by the character of Transcendental thinking, with its emphasis upon the perception of a spiritual reality behind the surfaces of things. Nature for the Transcendentalist was an expression of the divine mind; its phenomena, when rightly seen, revealed moral truths. By means of proper perception, said Emerson, "man has access to the entire mind of the Creator," and "is himself the creator" of his own world.[8] The pure, healthy, and self-reliant man, whose mind is in harmony with the Over-Soul, continually discerns the miraculous in the common. But for the timid or degraded man, whose eyes are clouded by convention, nature will appear a "ruin or . . . blank." Idealism is the Transcendentalist's necessary premise: it assures him that things conform to thoughts. By way of demonstration, Emerson tells his uninitiated reader to look through his legs at an inverted landscape. Thoreau was sufficiently tough-minded, and sufficiently interested in the details of natural phenomena, to resist the systematic translation of nature into ideas and moral precepts which Emersonian theory implied. He placed as much emphasis upon the "shams and delusions" which hinder men from "seeing" nature as upon the spiritual meanings of individual natural objects. But he always believed that to recognize one's relations with nature is the basis of moral insight; and he was convinced that the obstacles to this wisdom were removed by the simplification of life. Strip away the artificial, Thoreau tells the "desperate" man, and you will be able to read nature's language. Reality, the "secret of things," lurks under appearances, waiting to be seen. Describing his conversations with the French-Canadian woodchopper, Thoreau says he tried to "maneuver" him "to take the spiritual view of things."[9]

The language of *Walden* is, in a very immediate sense, strategic. The problem Thoreau faced there—and to some extent in all his writings—was to create in his audience the "waking moments" in which they could appreciate "the truth of which [he had] been convinced." In other words, he tries to wrench into line with his own the reader's attitudes toward the self, toward society, toward nature, and toward God. He "translates" the reader, raising him out of his conventional frame of reference into a higher one, in which extreme truths become intelligible. To these ends Thoreau employs a rhetoric of powerful exaggeration, antithesis, and incongruity. Habitually aware of the "common sense," the dulled perception that desperate life produces, he could turn the world of his audience upside-down by rhetorical means. He explores new resources of meaning in their "rotten diction" and challenges ingrained habits of thought and action with ennobling alternatives: "Read not the Times," he exhorts in "Life Without Principle." "Read the Eternities."[10] With all the features of his characteristic extravagance—hyperbole, wordplay, paradox, mock-heroics, loaded questions, and the ironic manipulation of cliché, proverb, and allusion—Thoreau urges new perspectives upon his reader. These rhetorical distortions or dislocations, rather than Transcendental doctrines *per se*, are Thoreau's means of waking his neighbors up. They exasperate, provoke, tease, and cajole; they are the chanticleer's call to intellectual morning; they make *Walden*, in the words of John Burroughs, "the most delicious piece of brag in literature."[11]

II

Walden is not, of course, merely a sophisticated sermon. It is the story of an experiment; a narrative; a fable. In 1851, with his "life in the woods" four years behind him and the book which would celebrate that experience, which would give it a permanent artistic and moral focus, still far from finished, Thoreau wrote, "My facts shall be falsehoods to the common sense. I would so state facts that they shall be significant, shall be myths or mythologic."[12] Even the most hortatory sections of the book are grounded in this "mythology" or significant fiction. I hope to demonstrate that paradox is apposite to the literary design of *Walden*: its themes, symbols, characters, and plot.

As a number of literary theorists have maintained, we can to some extent isolate "a fictional hero with a fictional audience" in any literary work.[13] The "I" of *Walden*, Thoreau as its narrator and hero, is a deliberately created verbal personality. This dramatized Thoreau should not be confused in critical analysis with the surveyor and pencil-maker of Concord: the *persona* stands in the same relation to the man as *Walden* — the symbolic gesture, the imaginative re-creation — stands to the literal fact of the Walden adventure. The narrator is a man of various moods and rhetorical stances, among them the severe moralist, the genial companion, the bemused "hermit," and the whimsical trickster who regards his experiment as a sly joke on solid citizens. The mellowest of all his moods is the one we find, for instance, in "Baker Farm," "Brute Neighbors," and "House-Warming," where he pokes fun at his own zeal as an idealist and reformer. In all his roles he conveys a sense of his uniqueness, the separateness of his vision from that of his townsmen.

The "fictional audience" of *Walden* likewise requires our attention. In defining it I take a hint from Burke, who in "Antony in Behalf of the Play" distinguishes between the play-mob and the spectator-mob as audiences for the oration in *Julius Caesar*. The reader of *Walden*, like Shakespeare's spectator, adopts a double perspective, weighing the speaker's statements both in terms of the fictional circumstance and in terms of their relevance to his own experience. I would distinguish a range of response *within* the dramatic context of *Walden* from an external or critical response. The reader in part projects himself into the role of a hypothetical "listener," whom the narrator addresses directly; and in part he stands at a remove, overhearing this address. Psychologically, we are "beside ourselves in a sane sense,"[14] both spectators who respond to *Walden* as an aesthetic entity and vicarious participants in the verbal action. As spectators, or what I will call "readers," we are sympathetic toward the witty and engaging narrator. As projected participants, or what I will term "audience," we must imagine ourselves committed to the prejudices and shortsightedness which the narrator reproves, and subject to the full tone of the address.

The rhetoric of *Walden*, reflecting in some measure the lecture origins of the early drafts, assumes an initially hostile audience. Thoreau sets up this role for us by characterizing, in the first third of "Economy," a mixed group of silent listeners who are suspicious of the speaking voice. He would address "poor students," "the mass of men who are discontented," and "that seemingly wealthy, but most terribly impoverished class of all, who have accumulated dross." In addition Thoreau creates individual characters who express attitudes to be refuted by the narrator, and who serve as foils for his wit. These are stylized figures, briefly but deftly sketched, who heckle or complain or interrogate. Their function is overtly to articulate the implicit doubts of the audience. "A certain class of unbelievers," "some inveterate cavillers," "housewives . . . and elderly people," "my tailoress," "the hard-featured farmer," "a factory-owner" — such lightly delineated types register their protests against Thoreau's farming techniques, his lack of charity, his conclusions about the pond's depth, his manner of making bread, and even the cleanliness of his bed linen. Their objections tend to be "impertinent," despite Thoreau's disclaimer early in "Economy," to the lower as well as the higher aspects of the experiment. He answers these animadversions with every form of wit: puns, irony, redefinition, paradoxes, twisted proverbs, overstatements, Biblical allusions (cited by a "heathen" to shame the Christian audience), and gymnastic leaps between the figurative and the literal. It is in this context of debate, of challenge and rejoinder, of provocation and rebuttal and exhortation, that the language of *Walden* must be understood. Thoreau's rhetoric is a direct consequence of the way he locates himself as a narrator with respect to a hostile fictional audience. The dramatic status of the speaker and his hearers accounts for the extraordinary "audibility" of *Walden* as well as for the aesthetic distance between author and reader.

Our bifurcation into spectator and participant is most intense in the hortatory and satirical passages. In the latter role, we are incredulous, shocked, and subject to the direct persuasive techniques of the argument. As spectator, on the other hand, we applaud Thoreau's rhetorical devastation of the premises of his fictional audience, and, if we find the instructive and polemical statements in *Walden* meaningful, as we most certainly can, we recognize that they are contained by the literary structure, and that they must, as statements about life, be understood first within that context. Even the reader who conforms to the type of the fictional audience, and who brings to *Walden* a full-blown set of prejudices against Thoreauvian "economy," does not stay long to quarrel with the narrator. The force of Thoreau's ridicule encourages him to quit the stage. For the participant, *Walden* is "an invitation to life's dance";[15] the sympathetic reader dances with Thoreau from the start.

Thoreau's paradoxes are also congenial to the "comic" themes and narrative movement of *Walden*. Using the distinctions of Northrop Frye, we can consider comedy one of the four "mythoi" or recurrent patterns of plot development which may appear in any genre. The "mythos of spring" or comic plot is typified by a rising movement, "from a society controlled by habit, ritual bondage, arbitrary law and the older characters to a society controlled by youths and pragmatic freedom . . . a movement from illusion to reality."[16] Frye's generalization may call to mind a passage in "Conclusion" where Thoreau proclaims the joys of the "awakened" man: "new, universal, and more liberal laws will begin to establish themselves around and within him; or the old laws be expanded, and interpreted in his favor in a more liberal sense, and he will live with the license of a higher order of beings." On the human level, *Walden*'s narrator performs this ascent. On the level of nature, the green life of spring and summer must rise from old winter's bondage, repeating the hero's own movement and prefiguring the spiritual transformation of his audience, "man in the larva state."

Following a traditional comic pattern, Thoreau represents in *Walden* two worlds: the narrator's private paradise and the social wasteland he has abandoned. Each of these polar worlds has its basic character type and body of symbols. The narrator is the *Eiron*, the virtuous or witty character whose actions are directed toward the establishment of an ideal order. The audience and hecklers, who take for granted "what are deemed 'the most sacred laws of society,' "[17] serve as the *Alazon* or impostor. This comic type is a braggart, misanthrope, or other mean-spirited figure, usually an older man, who resists the hero's efforts to establish harmony but who is often welcomed into the ideal order when the hero succeeds. The narrator of *Walden*, both clever and good, withdraws from a society of "skinflint[s]" to a greenwood world at the pond. His pastoral sanctuary is represented in images of moisture, freedom, health, the waking state, fertility, and birth. The society he leaves behind is described in images of dust, imprisonment, disease, blindness, lethargy, and death. Upon these symbolic materials Thoreau builds many of his paradoxes. In his verbal attacks upon the old society, whose "idle and musty virtues" he finds as ridiculous as its vices, the narrator assumes a satirical or denunciatory pose. When he records his simple *vita nuova*, that is, in the idyllic passages, his tone becomes meditative or ecstatic.

III

But it is, after all, to the dusty world or wasteland that *Walden*'s fictional audience belongs. Despite their dissatisfactions, they are committed to this life and its values, and blind to the practical as well as the spiritual advantages of the experiment. The narrator, far from being a misanthropic skulker, wishes to communicate his experience of a more harmonious and noble life. His language serves this end: the first rhetorical function of paradox is to make the audience entertain a crucial doubt. Do they value houses? Thoreau calls them prisons, almshouses, coffins, and family tombs. Farming? It is digging one's own grave. Equipment and livestock? Herds are the keepers of men, not men of herds; and men are "the tools of their tools." Traditional knowledge and a Harvard education? Thoreau describes them as impediments to wisdom. Financial security, or "something [laid up] against a sick day," is the cause of sickness in the man who works for it. Fine and fashionable clothing is a form of decoration more barbaric than tattooing, which is only "skin-deep." The landlord's sumptuous furnishings are really "traps" (an elaborate pun) which hold the holder captive. The railroad, marvel of the industrial age, is a means of transportation ultimately slower than going afoot. Religion, Thoreau tells his pious audience, is a "cursing of God" and distrust of themselves. "Good business," the bulwark of their culture, is the quickest way to the devil. In short, says Thoreau, "the greater part of what my neighbors call good I believe in my soul to be bad, and if I repent of anything, it is very likely to be my good behavior. What demon possessed me that I behaved so well?" These paradoxes, often executed with brilliant humor, jostle and tumble the listener's perspective. To be sure, the narrator is a self-acknowledged eccentric — but he is not a lunatic. Thoreau makes sense in his own terms, and the fictional audience no longer can in theirs.

At the same time as he makes nonsense of the audience's vocabulary with satirical paradoxes, Thoreau appropriates some of its key terms to describe the special values of his life in the woods. For example, though he despises commerce he would conduct a profitable "trade" with the "Celestial Empire." In this second body of rhetorical devices Thoreau again exploits polarities of symbol and idea, and not without irony. But these paradoxes differ sharply in their function from the satirical ones. They attach to the hero's world, to nature and simplified action, the deep connotations of worth which social involvements and material comforts evoke for the desperate man. Thoreau astounds and disarms the audience when he calls his experiment a "business" and renders his accounts to the half- and quarter-penny. By means of this appropriately inappropriate language he announces the incompatibility of his livelihood and his neighbor's, and simultaneously suggests interesting resemblances. Thoreau's enterprise, like the businessman's, requires risks, demands perseverance, and holds out the lure of rewards. The statistical passages of "Economy" and "The Bean-Field" are equivocal. On the one hand, they prove the narrator's ability to beat the thrifty Yankee at his own game; on the other, they parody the Yankee's obsessions with finance. Thoreau's argument that a man achieves success in proportion as he reduces his worldly needs is likewise paradoxical, a queer analogue to the commercial theory of increasing profits by lowering costs. He reinforces this unconventional economic principle by declaring that the simple life is to be carefully cultivated and jealously preserved: "Give me the poverty that enjoys true wealth." Similarly he contrasts the rich harvest which a poet reaps from a farm with the *relatively* worthless cash crop, and is eager to acquire the Hollowell place before its owner destroys it with "improvements." I would also include in this category of paradoxes Thoreau's constant reference to fish, berries, and other common natural objects in the language of coins, precious gems, and rare metals; his praise of the humble simpleton as an exalted sage; his assertion that the woods and ponds are religious sanctuaries; and his description of his labors as pastimes and his solitude as companionable. Some related statements carry the mystical overtones of the New Testament: "Not till we are lost, in other words, not till we have lost the world, do we begin to find ourselves." "Walden was dead and is alive again." All these apparent contradictions support Thoreau's triumphant subjectivism in *Walden*, his running proclamation that "The universe constantly and obediently answers to our conceptions."[18] The highest and most sincere conception yields the noblest life.

By nature a dialectical instrument, the paradox is thus stylistically integral to this severely dialectical work. Viewed generally, the two large groups of paradoxes reflect the comic structure of *Walden* and its two major themes: the futility of the desperate life and the rewards of enlightened simplicity. With the paradoxes of the first or satirical group, Thoreau declares that his listener's goods are evils, his freedom slavery, and his life a death. Those of the second group, corresponding rhetorically to the recurrent symbolism of metamorphosis, affirm that the values of the natural and Transcendental life arise from what the audience would deprecate as valueless. In these paradoxes, the beautiful is contained in the ugly, the truly precious in the seemingly trivial, and the springs of life in the apparently dead.

As *Walden* progresses the proportion of the first to the second kind gradually changes. The rhetoric of the early chapters is very largely one of trenchant denunciation, directed against the desperate life. That of the later chapters is predominantly serene, playful, and rapturous. Thoreau creates the impression of a growing concord between himself and his audience by allowing the caustic ironies and repudiations of "Economy" to shift by degrees to the affirmations of "Spring" and "Conclusion." Thoreau the outsider becomes Thoreau the magnanimous insider, around whom reasonable men and those who love life may gather. Rhetorically and thematically, as the book proceeds, the attack becomes the dance.

IV

One of the numerous extended passages in *Walden* which is dominated by oxymoron and which leads itself to close rhetorical analysis is the following, from "Where I Lived and What I Lived For":

We do not ride on the railroad; it rides upon us. Did you ever think what those sleepers are that underlie the railroad? Each one is a man, an Irishman, or a Yankee man. The rails are laid on them, and they are covered with sand, and the cars run smoothly over them. They are sound sleepers, I assure you. And every few years a new lot is laid down and run over; so that, if some have the pleasure of riding on a rail, others have the misfortune to be ridden upon. And when they run over a man that is walking in his sleep, a supernumerary sleeper in the wrong position, and wake him up, they suddenly stop the cars, and make a hue and cry about it, as if this were an exception. I am glad to know that it takes a gang of men for every five miles to keep the sleepers down and level in their beds . . . for this is a sign that they may sometime get up again.

In developing his initial paradox and the thesis of the passage, "We do not ride on the railroad; it rides upon us," Thoreau relies heavily upon a pun, for "sleepers" refers simultaneously to the railroad ties and to the benighted laborers who lay them. The repetitions in the short third sentence—"man . . . Irishman . . . Yankee man"—vigorously connect the miserable workers with the more fortunate riders of the cars; they are all in the human family. The train rides on mankind in the sense that a *man* would degrade his life in the railroad enterprise, working on the tracks all day for a pittance. His life is a form of death; symbolically he has been buried, like the wooden sleepers which he himself has covered with sand. He may stay "buried" or "asleep" for many years, perhaps as long as the wooden ties, the "sound sleepers," remain solid and unrotted. When Thoreau remarks, "if some have the pleasure of riding on a rail, others have the misfortune to be ridden upon," he ironically suggests a brutal insouciance on the part of those wealthy enough to travel over an extension of the track, laid by new workers. But in terms of the opening statement, the travelers share the misfortune of being ridden upon; they are to an extent themselves "sleepers" or unenlightened men. The occasional sleep-walker struck by the train is very likely an exhausted laborer, walking on the track in the mental and moral stupor typical of his way of life. Thoreau calls him a "supernumerary sleeper," equating once more the literal block of wood with the wooden man who places it. But "in the wrong position" involves a new paradox: instead of walking stupidly and sleepily on the track—preserving a merely physical uprightness—he should perhaps have wholly abandoned himself to his futile labor and lain down with the ties. Nevertheless, his calamity excites a "hue and cry." In terms of the railroad's "economy" he should have been at the same time a sleeper and not a sleeper. To be struck and run over by the train, or literally to assume the position of the wooden sleepers in man's last and permanent sleep, is to be withdrawn from the fruitless life of track-laying, or to be "awakened." For if the laborer's life is *figuratively* a death and a sleep, his *actual* death, the end of that existence, would be a birth or a waking. Finally, Thoreau sees in the restlessness of the ties, their tendency to shift in the roadbed, an intimation that the very workmen who keep the sleepers down and level may awaken to the dawn of their own moral day, and rise.

V

The principle of paradox likewise controls individual chapters, such as "Higher Laws," and fully developed arguments such as the discussion of philanthropy in the first chapter. It can also be discovered in the juxtaposed rhythms of rise and fall, ascent and descent, primitivism and transcendence which pervade the imagery and action of the book. In this last connection we might briefly note that the Transcendental distinction between what "*is*" and what "*appears to be*" is reflected in the recurrent contrasting of surface and subsurface phenomena. When the narrator chases the diving loon, or fishes for pouts at night, he acts out his pursuit of higher truth. Common sense will provide only superficial catches; the earnest truth-seeker, the "hunter and fisher of men," must search beneath appearances and within himself. The pond in its most consistent symbolic role is the self, the beholder's own profound nature. Here, as elsewhere, Thoreau ascends by descending: on dark nights his fishing line is lost in the black water below, and his line of thought wanders to "vast and cosmogonal themes in other spheres." The bite of the pout links him to nature again, and as the fish comes wriggling upward, the mind pins down an intuition to a perceived fact. "Thus I caught two fishes as it were with one hook." Legislators prescribe the number of fish-hooks to be permitted at Walden, "but they know nothing about the hook of hooks with which to angle for the pond itself, impaling the legislature for a bait." Thoreau, however, has mastered this fishing lore; he sacrifices social institutions in the quest for himself, for reality. In a similar paradox, Thoreau admits that "Snipes and woodcocks . . . may afford rare sport; but I trust it would be nobler game to shoot one's self."

"Conclusion," which is richer in paradoxes than any other chapter, announces the grand prospects of the awakened life: "In proportion as [a man] simplifies his life, the laws of the universe will appear less complex, and solitude will not be solitude, nor poverty poverty, nor weakness weakness." The chapter reaches its climax in two dramatized paradoxes, fables of metamorphosis. In the first, the timeless artist of Kouroo, like the liberated human spirit Thoreau is celebrating, creates a new and glorious world around himself. The second fable, more humble in its materials but not less marvelous in its import, is the anecdote of a bug which gnaws its way out of an old table, emerging from "society's most trivial and handselled furniture" to enjoy a beautiful and winged life after a long death. "Morning," Thoreau had declared earlier, "is when I am awake and there is a dawn in me." To an audience now capable of sharing his ecstatic vision, his wonder at the infinite possibilities open to the self, he makes his final appeal in the heightened language of paradox: "Only that day dawns to which we are awake. There is more day to dawn. The sun is but a morning star."

Notes

1. *The Writings of Henry David Thoreau*, Walden Edition, 20 vols. (Boston, 1906), II (*Walden*), 357.

2. *Ibid.*, I, 305. See Perry Miller, *Consciousness in Concord* (Boston, 1958), pp. 80–103, for a full examination of the paradoxes in Transcendental friendship.

3. Joseph Wood Krutch, *Henry David Thoreau* (New York, 1948), p. 286.

4. Horace Bushnell, *God in Christ: Three Discourses . . . with a Preliminary Dissertation on Language* (Hartford, 1849), p. 55; cited in Charles Feidelson, Jr., *Symbolism and American Literature* (Chicago, 1953), p. 156.

5. Walter Harding and Carl Bode, eds., *The Correspondence of Henry David Thoreau* (New York, 1958), p. 137; RWE to HDT, Sept. 18, 1843.

6. Thoreau, XIII, 7, n.

7. *Ibid.*, XII, 165.

8. *The Complete Works of Ralph Waldo Emerson*, Centenary Edition, 12 vols. (Boston, 1903), I, 64.

9. Thoreau, II, 166.

10. *Ibid.*, IV, 475.

11. Burroughs, "Henry D. Thoreau," *Indoor Studies* (Boston, 1895), p. 29.

12. Thoreau, IX, 99.

13. Northrop Frye, *Anatomy of Criticism* (Princeton, 1957), p. 53. See also W. K. Wimsatt, Jr., *The Verbal Icon* (Lexington, Ky., 1954), p. xv; John Crowe Ransom, *The World's Body* (New York, 1938), p. 247 ff; René Wellek, "Closing Statement," *Style in Language*, ed. Thomas A. Sebeok (New York, 1960), p. 414.

14. Thoreau, II, 149.

15. E. B. White, "Walden—1954," *Yale Review*, XLIV (1954), 13. White does not distinguish between reader and fictional audience.

16. Frye, p. 169.

17. Thoreau, II, 355.

18. *Ibid.*, II, 108.

The Functional Satire of
Thoreau's Hermit and Poet   Robert R. Hodges*

Readers of Thoreau's *Walden* have never been comfortable with the dialogue between Hermit and Poet at the beginning of "Brute Neighbors," the twelfth chapter. They agree that it functions as a transition from the

*Reprinted from *Satire Newsletter* 8 (Spring 1971):105–8, by permission of *Satire Newsletter*.

transcendental heights of "Higher Laws," the previous chapter, to the relaxed observation of nature which follows immediately, and one critic points out that the Hermit's dilemma, whether to go to heaven or to go fishing, indicates the two realms.[1] But the "comic" or "whimsical" or "mock-pastoral" tone they discern, as well as the dramatic form, stimulate uneasy and inadequate explanations. Although some of them agree that the tone helps effect the transition, none of them says how it works.

Sherman Paul finds the humor "self-protective," and the whole dialogue a "sportive" treatment of serious concerns that brings the narrative back to its "summer level — and this seems the only excuse for the dialogue."[2] But the dialogue does not need an "excuse." Its humor does not provide a self-protective defense mechanism for an uncharacteristically anxious Henry Thoreau. And the entire passage accomplishes more than a mere shift in mood. Another critic, Charles Anderson, dismisses the dramatic form: "It is a departure only in mode being cast in play form for emphasis."[3] But we cannot separate form from content so easily, and Thoreau chose the dramatic form not for a purpose so general as "emphasis" but because it communicates an important aspect of his meaning. Thomas Blanding finds the bookish style of the passage a meaningful imitation of the dialogues in *The Compleat Angler*. Such literary reminiscence functions transitionally, "reinforcing Walton's observation that angling is a 'contemplative man's recreation.' "[4] The style is certainly not typical of Thoreau, but is the reader really expected to recall so specific a phrase of Walton's in order to make sense of the passage? None of these explanations is much more satisfactory than the uneasy, if oft-cited comment of Thomas Shanley: "He used the comic interlude . . . probably because he felt the need of some such descent from the level of 'Higher Laws.' "[5] Again we find the critic transferring his own anxiety about the purpose of the dialogue to Thoreau.

Clearly we need an explanation of the dialogue which shows how its comic or whimsical tone, its dramatic form, the element of literary imitation or parody, and its ideas function as a transition from the austere spirituality of "Higher Laws" to the descriptions of nature in the rest of "Brute Neighbors." All these aspects of the passage cohere, I believe, when we read it as satire. Thoreau's satire functions not to dramatize his half-conversion to spiritual laws nor his backsliding from them[6] but to make clear the perils of taking their strictures too rigidly and severely. In a broader sense the dialogue satirizes in the characters of both Hermit and Poet the dangers of self-conscious transcendentalism. Those who imitate its outward forms, Thoreau suggests, experience a complete divorce of the realms of both nature and spirit, the objective world and the inner man, and degrade both to barren verbalism. Both of the characters lower nature to the practical and predatory — no more than Emerson's commodity — and the principal character, the Hermit, cannot even deal with it competently on that level. Furthermore, he dissipates the realm of spirit into overly conceptualized pretention or fraud, where deception of others leads to self-deception.

The rest of the chapter, as most critics have pointed out, unites the two realms authentically. So rudely sundered and degraded in the dramatic dialogue, nature and spirit become progressively reconciled through a series of increasingly sophisticated literary techniques. In describing the mice and the birds, Thoreau first joins the two realms through an expository prose made up of accurate observation, comment, and metaphor. In the battle of the ants, he more elaborately connects the two in the mock-heroic literary mode. Although the description of dogs and cats returns to the expository prose of the initial description, it makes an effective contrast with the symbolic narrative that concludes the chapter. In recounting the chase game with the loon, Thoreau infuses his narrative of direct participation in nature with subtle suggestions of both the operation of imagination[7] and otherworldly contact.[8] This climactic union of man and nature stands out because it represents a triumph over the literary and thematic sterility of the dialogue between Hermit and Poet.

Thoreau uses the dramatic form because its obvious conventions express the artificiality of a willed transcendental pose. Both the carefully labelled Poet and Hermit are frauds, self-conscious esthetes and philosophers, appropriately presented through the dramatic conventions of a fixed scene, soliloquy, and stilted language. It begins with the Hermit alone, not inwardly content nor meditating, but anxiously concerned about what the "world" is doing and disturbed that in three hours he has heard no diverting sound from it.[9] But as soon as he hears, or thinks he hears, the farmer's noon horn, his mind begins to work smoothly. Imagining the dinner served to the hands, he smugly considers his own superiority to the world with its noise and its housekeeping. Clearly, his retired life subsists on a continuous self-righteous contrasting of himself to conventional society, not on any inner conviction. The approach of the Poet is then signaled by these stagey lines: "Hark, I hear a rustling of leaves," two guesses at the origin of the sound to cover the off-stage approach, and then, in mock terror, "It comes on apace, my sumachs and sweetbriers tremble." Finally the Poet appears in view, and the Hermit struggles to recognize him, "Eh, Mr. Poet, is it you?" One cannot miss the calculated sequence. The Hermit's first question reveals his unending concern with externals. "How do you like the world to-day?"

The Poet, when he speaks, turns out to be as pretentious as the Hermit. He parades his esthetic sensitivity and his European travels. First carefully placing the beauty of the clouds in relation to "old paintings" and "foreign lands," he finally gives them the stamp of approval of the picturesque, "a true Mediterranean sky" such as he had seen "off the coast of Spain." His esthetic credentials established, he abruptly gets down to business with an invitation to go fishing. But even this must be carefully sanctioned as "the true industry for poets." The Hermit, like a tempted sinner in a melodrama, replies, "I cannot resist," justifying himself none the less by saying his "brown bread will soon be gone." Brown bread, Thoreau noted in the previous chapter, was the abstemious diet of the self-styled Puritan which might be eaten, he further said, with "as gross an appetite as ever an alderman to his turtle."[10] But lest he appear too eager, the Hermit carefully adds with unconvincing reasonableness, "I will go with you gladly soon, but I am just concluding a serious meditation. I think that I am near the end of it. Leave me alone, then, for a while." An unlikely claim in view of his previous obsession with what the world was doing. This need for solitude to finish a meditation is merely a trick to maneuver the Poet into digging for worms for both of them as is the ingenious argument meant to show the thrill of digging for worms for the unconventional mind. "The sport of digging the bait is nearly equal to that of catching the fish, when one's appetite is not too keen; and this you may have all to yourself to-day." The sentence burlesques Thoreau's characteristic paradoxical thinking and suggests that it merely excuses idleness.

The Hermit alone illustrates that deceiving others leads to self-deception, for he soliloquizes on the problem of inducing his meditational mood again. He begins, "Let me see; where was I?" as though meditation were an ordinary mental process of association or logic. "Methinks I was nearly in this frame of mind; the world lay about at this angle." The angle recalls Emerson's famous advice in "Nature" that by looking through his legs a man can alter his prospects and take a fresh look at things. But the Hermit's angle is unsuccessful, and he gets no closer to "being resolved into the essence of things." Nevertheless, he attempts by another means to find the path of his thoughts. "I will just try these three sentences of Con-fut-see; they may fetch that state about again." Failing again he moralizes in a fussy memorandum; "Mem. There never is but one opportunity of a kind."

The Poet returns unexpectedly with a large number of fat worms. This casts serious doubt on the Hermit's knowledge of nature, for he had asserted confidently, "Angle-worms are rarely to be met with in these parts, where the soil was never fattened with manure; the race is nearly extinct." Clearly the Hermit is as incompetent in the world of nature as he is fraudulent in the world of the spirit.

The episode concludes with the Hermit's archaic sounding invitation, "Shall we to the Concord?" Thoreau has chosen the river rather than the pond at hand as a final suggestion of the meaning of the passage. In "The Ponds" he had expressed horror that a little digging would make Walden Pond flow into the Concord River "to waste its sweetness in the Ocean Wave."[11] Clearly in *Walden* the river symbolizes something lesser than the pond. Thus the false Hermit of the dialogue must begin his quest at some distance from the pond, "reserved and austere like a hermit in the woods."[12] Only after a process of reconciliation can the narrative return for the climactic union of man and nature on the waters of the pond.

The dialogue of Hermit and Poet has dramatized a state of spiritual emptiness and fraud, an unhappy possibility of following literally Thoreau's Higher Laws, a state that the rest of the chapter overcomes. By the conclusion the reader understands the rich paradox of the title, but only because the opening dialogue has forced him first to experience the sterile antipathy between the exploitable realm of the brutes and the pretentious spirituality of the humane realm of neighbors.

Notes

1. Charles Anderson, *The Magic Circle of Walden* (New York, 1968), p. 182. See also Melvin Lyon, "Walden Pond as a Symbol," *PMLA*, 82 (May 1967), 299.

2. Sherman Paul, *The Shores of America* (Urbana, Illinois, 1958), p. 340.

3. Anderson, p. 179.

4. Thomas Blanding, "Walton and Walden," *Thoreau Society Bulletin*, 107 (Spring 1969), p. 3.

5. J. Lyndon Shanley, *The Making of Walden* (Chicago, 1957), p. 80. Walter Harding quotes this sentence as an interpretive note on the dialogue in *The Varorium Walden* (New York, 1962), p. 304. Thomas Blanding quotes the same sentences with agreement.

6. After a study of the Huntington Library MS of *Walden*, Paul suggests: "The dialogue did the work of the transitional sentence he omitted: 'But practically I was only half converted to my own arguments, for I still found myself fishing at rare intervals.' " And Paul notes the moral of the incident: ". . . the obvious breach in discipline destroyed the hermit's 'budding ecstasy' " (p. 340).

7. *Ibid.*, pp. 340–41.

8. Anderson, pp. 195–96. For a thorough analysis of Thoreau's varieties of imaginative treatment of natural fact in this chapter see Anderson, pp. 182–98.

9. *Walden*, Norton Critical Edition, ed. Owen Thomas (New York, 1966), p. 148. Since the passage I am concerned with is only two pages long, I will not cite further page references. Quotations from elsewhere in *Walden* are from this edition.

10. *Ibid.*, p. 145.

11. *Ibid.*, p. 130.

12. *Ibid.*

Reflections in Walden Pond: Thoreau's Optics
Richard J. Schneider*

Henry David Thoreau's friend, William Ellery Channing, liked to point out the analogy between mental reflection and optical reflection by a pun on Newton's second axiom of optics: "The angle of incid*ents* should be equal to the angle of reflection."[1] Thoreau recorded this pun in his journal and seems to have been both amused and impressed by its

*Reprinted from *ESQ: A Journal of the American Renaissance* 21 (2d Quarter 1975):65–75, by permission of the author.

relevance to his own artistic method. He too was interested in the relationship between mental and optical reflection. His journals and published books and essays frequently record his observations of such optical phenomena as mirages, optical illusions, and, most frequently, water reflections. These observations, an important part of Thoreau's artistic method, have been almost completely ignored by his readers.[2] Therefore, it is the purpose of this paper to explore the significance of Thoreau's interest in optics to his life and writing.

A first step is to recognize that Thoreau's interest in optics was part of his lifelong attempt to resolve for himself the basic epistemological problem with which many of the nineteenth-century Romantic writers grappled, the problem of whether the subject (perceiver) or the object was more important to man's acquisition of knowledge and recognition of truth. As Perry Miller states, it was the problem of "striking and maintaining the delicate balance between object and mental reflection, of fact and truth, of minute observation and generalized concept,"[3] the conflict, that is, between the vague concepts of idealism and empiricism, with their respective champions popularly considered to be Kant and Locke. Thoreau's struggle with the problem led him from one side to the other and back again, from Emersonian idealism and Oriental mysticism, emphasizing subjective perception, to scientific empiricism emphasizing objective perception.

Yet neither seems to have satisfied Thoreau, and his writing is filled with contradictory statements about them. Although he explored both approaches thoroughly, ultimately he attempted to steer a middle course between them. He saw that neither the subject nor the object alone could contain the truth of a perception, because both were undeniably real and necessary to the perceptual experience. He believed that the true point of interest had to be somewhere between subject and object, as he explains in this criticism of both scientists and philosophers:

> I think that the man of science makes this mistake, and the mass of mankind along with him: that you should coolly give your chief attention to the phenomenon which excites you as something independent on you, and not as it is related to you. . . . It is the subject of the vision, the truth alone, that concerns me. The philosopher for whom rainbows, etc., can be explained away never saw them. With regard to such objects, I find that it is not they themselves (with which the men of science deal) that concern me; the point of interest is somewhere *between* me and them (i.e. the objects). (XVI, 164–165)

The truth was not entirely in either the perceiver or the object, but in the relation between them: "I know that the thing that really concerns me is not there, but in my relation to that. That is a mere reflecting surface" (XVI, 164).

Much of Thoreau's time on his daily walking excursions was spent in trying to discover a way to capture that intangible and apparently invisible "relation" between himself and the reflecting surfaces of nature's objects. Nature was the only worthwhile area for a sustained search for the truth. Thoreau could not sit smugly waiting for God to reveal it to him; nor could he study his fellow men, because they had long ago denied the spiritual truth within them. Only in establishing and fully understanding his relation to nature could he hope to see the truth about his own place in the universe. So he opened his senses in as many ways as possible to that relationship.

The goal of all of Thoreau's physical discipline—early rising from bed, bathing in ponds and rivers, maintaining (sometimes) a natural diet, and exercising his senses whenever possible—was "making to yourself a perfect body" (XIV, 44) and "the free use and command of all . . . faculties, and equal development" (VIII, 160). In moments when his body seemed to be "all sentient," that equal development seemed possible. But most of the time some of his senses seemed more valuable than others. Taste and touch, for instance, were severely limited by the need to have the object near to the perceiver, thus eliminating the intervening space which contained the most valuable part of the perception—the relation between the subject and object. Thoreau felt that when he was close enough to taste or touch something he was too close to perceive it as a whole, to see the reflections from its surfaces. The senses of smell and hearing were less limited, however. For Thoreau, the scents of nature and of men revealed their spiritual and moral essences, so he paid close attention to the messages his nose detected. Hearing too was important, and Thoreau was particularly alert for moments when he could hear beyond nature's louder sounds to the faint sound of his "distant drummer," the sound of the rhythmical workings of the universe.[4] For Thoreau, such music was "God's voice, the divine breath audible" (VII, 154).

But both scents and sounds had an elusive quality which limited the poet's ability to seek them out actively. That elusiveness was part of their charm, because Thoreau was always conscious that there was more to know, that "I never saw to the end, nor heard to the end; but the best part was unseen and unheard" (VII, 321). But that very elusiveness made thorough investigation almost impossible. Scents and sounds were like the vague idealism of youth, "we merely receive an impulse in the proper direction. To suppose that this is equivalent to having travelled the road or obeyed the impulse faithfully throughout a lifetime, is absurd" (XVI, 202). To pursue nature's impulses actively throughout a lifetime required the guidance of the fifth sense, sight.

Thoreau was seldom as ecstatic as Emerson about the sense of sight and did not attempt to become a "transparent eyeball." But he was more able than Emerson to put into practice Emerson's ideas about the importance of observing nature. It was Thoreau whom Hawthorne described as "a keen and delicate observer of nature—a genuine observer — which, I suspect, is almost as rare a character as even an original poet."[5] Thoreau himself recognized quite early the practical superiority of the eye over the other senses. In his journal for 1840, he pays this tribute to the eye:

> The eye does the least drudgery of any of the senses. It oftenest escapes to a higher employment — The rest serve, and escort, and defend it — I attach some superiority even priority to this sense. It is the oldest servant in the soul's household. . . . In circumspection double — in fidelity single — it serves truth always, and carries no false news. Of five castes it is the Brahmin — it converses with the heavens. How man serves this sense more than any — when he builds a house he does not forget to put a window in the wall.[6]

In 1841 he again emphasizes the importance of the eye: "How much virtue there is in simply seeing. . . . We are as much as we see" (VII, 248). For Thoreau, the eye was in some ways man's most godlike feature: "When God made man, he reserved some parts and some rights to himself. The eye has many qualities which belong to God more than man" (VII, 331).

It was upon the godlike sense of sight that Thoreau based his sustained search for the truth of his relationship to God and to nature. His goal was to be a poet-seer, a seer both in the sense of one who sees and understands fully the natural world around him and in the sense of one who sees into the spiritual world beyond the limitations of most men's vision. As a poet, he would try to communicate his visions, both physical and spiritual, to his readers in an effort to wake them up, open their eyes, and make them seers also. As he asks his readers in *Walden*, "Will you be a reader, a student merely, or a seer? Read your fate, see what is before you, and walk on into futurity" (II, 123).

What Thoreau needed in order to sustain his effort to be a seer was a method of observing nature which would allow the senses to remain alert, put them in the best position for perceiving nature's truths, and keep them from becoming either too subjective or too objective. To maintain the balance between subjective and objective observation, Thoreau adopted the technique of sauntering — going "*à la Sainte Terre*, to the Holy Land" (V, 205). It involved several specific and simultaneous ways of walking and observing. First, he avoided walking directly to his destination on his daily excursions. Instead, he proceeded "as a river does, meanderingly" (XI, 531). He allowed himself to meander wherever the immediate relationship between nature and his senses led him. To go straight to his destination permitted only subjective seeing. He would know too well where he was going and what he could expect on the way. But to meander allowed for surprises which could include both subjective and objective perception.

Sauntering also involved the development of what he called paradoxically "relaxed attention," a concentration on the business at hand combined with a willingness to be distracted by fresh perceptions. As he says in his journal, "The man who is bent upon his work is frequently in the best attitude to observe what is irrelevant to his work, (Mem. Wordsworth's observations on relaxed attention)" (IX, 123). Finally, sauntering required the eye in particular to maintain this relaxed attention: "I must let my senses wander as my thoughts, my eyes see without looking. Carlyle said that how to observe was to look, but I say that it is rather to see, and the more you look the less you will observe. . . . What I need is not to look at all, but a true sauntering of the eye" (X, 351). To look at nature directly was to be merely a scientist, an objective collector of mere facts; but a discreet sidelong glance at nature allowed the seer's subjectivity (his previous knowledge and expectation) to complement the objective report gathered by the senses: "Man cannot afford to be a naturalist, to look at Nature directly, but only with the side of his eye. He must look through and beyond her. To look at her is fatal as to look at the head of Medusa" (XI, 45). Such a side view kept the subjective part of perception from becoming mere prejudice and left the senses free to detect and report new facts or new views of old facts.

The problem of subjective versus objective observation also involved the problem of physical point of view. Having discovered an interesting object, what was the best position from which to observe it? At times Thoreau felt that it was best to probe nature's objects as closely as possible, for "Nature will bear the closest inspection" (V, 107). At other times he felt that "You cannot see anything until you are clear of it" (XVII, 273) and that his main interest should be "in an indistinct prospect, a distant view, a mere suggestion often" (XV, 495). Close observation tended to place too much emphasis on the object itself, while distant views tended to be too subjective, to encourage idealization at the expense of actuality, and to "overlook" things. He sometimes found it frustrating to be "placed . . . with eyes between a microscopic and a telescopic world" (XII, 133). But he realized that it was necessary physically and intellectually to try both extremes and to remember that "There are innumerable avenues to a perception of the truth. . . . It is not in vain that the mind turns aside this way or that: follow its leading; apply it whither it inclines. Probe the universe in a myriad points. . . . He is a wise man and experienced who has taken many views" (VIII, 457). The seer needed to explore the limits of his world, but unlike most men he did not want to stay "always on the limits." Thoreau recognized that he needed continually to return from those myriad points of view to a balanced, intermediate point of view. Writing of Homer, he says, "The poet does not leap, even in imagination, from Asia to Greece through mid-air, neglectful of the fair sea and still fairer land beneath him, but jogs on humanly observant over the intervening segment of a sphere" (VII, 33). Thoreau was always conscious of man's mediate position between heaven and earth, and as a seer he was ultimately interested in mid-points, whether between telescopic and microscopic distances or between subject and object. After exploring the extremes of his world, he felt that it was crucial to return always to a balanced middle position.

Despite his overriding concern with disciplining his own mind and senses at the perceiver's end of the perception, Thoreau felt that nature too was actively involved in the communication between itself and man. The object was not merely passive. Thoreau seems to have believed that every natural object, animate and inanimate, was a living spiritual entity; thus each object had some quality which, like man's soul, was intangible. If man had thoughts which expressed the essence of his soul, each natural object also had its own elusive but distinct emanation which expressed its spiritual essence: "The ultimate expression or fruit of any created thing is a fine effluence which only the most ingenuous worshipper perceives at a reverent distance from its surface even. The cause and effect are equally evanescent and intangible, and the former must be investigated in the same spirit and with the same reverence with which the latter is perceived. . . . Only that intellect makes any progress toward conceiving of the essence which at the same time perceives the effluence" (XVIII, 23). Whether they were revealed to the senses or remained undetected, these effluences were means by which nature actively communicated with men. One day, for instance, Thoreau noticed that "There is a fine effluence surrounding the wood, as if the sap had begun to stir and you could detect it a mile off. . . . Such is the genialness of nature that the trees appear to have put out feelers by which our senses apprehend them more tenderly" (XVIII, 32). Another time he says of a tall aspen that attracted his attention by its yellow top, "It is as if it recognized me too, and gladly, coming halfway to meet me" (XVII, 268). So in addition to the Emersonian theory of symbolic correspondence between natural fact and spiritual truth, Thoreau was interested in what might be called "co-respondence," the mutual and active response of man to nature and of nature to man. Thoreau liked to think of himself as "Nature's brother," but the problem with the co-respondence between these brothers was that nature's effluences were too seldom available to man's senses. He needed to discover some way of objectifying the relationship between nature's effluences and man's senses.

To a limited extent, both man and nature were already trying to move closer to the truth between them. Thoreau believed that although man's senses are intimately connected to his thoughts, the source of his subjectivity, they are also partially independent of them. He says of the eye that it "revolves on an independent pivot which we can no more control than our own will" (VII, 166). At the other end of perception, an object's effluence existed at a "reverent distance" from the object itself. But there were obviously other components of perception that helped to bridge the gap between subject and object. Perhaps the key to the relationship was in those other components.

In visual perception, the most obvious other component was light.

Indeed, light itself could sometimes be the most interesting part of perception, as in this passage from the journal: "When sometimes the pure light that attends the setting sun falls on the trees and houses, the light itself is the phenomenon, and no single object is so distinct to our admiration as the light itself" (VII, 447). Light was interesting to Thoreau because of its traditional symbolic associations with God and truth. In an early essay, "Paradise (To Be) Regained," he says, "The light of the sun is but the shadow of love. 'The souls of men loving and fearing God,' says Raleigh, 'receive influence from that divine light itself, whereof the sun's clarity, and that of the stars is by Plato called but a shadow. . . . Light is the shadow of God's brightness, who is the light of light' " (IV, 304). But it was equally important as a natural phenomenon. As Charles Feidelson, Jr., suggests, for Thoreau such a symbol was "not a 'literal' fact with a 'figurative' meaning, since Thoreau has left no room for this traditional distinction. It is a radically symbolic fact of both nature and thought, body and mind."[7] Light was important on both a spiritual and a natural level, because the two levels could not be separated.

Sometimes, of course, Thoreau spoke of light primarily in its spiritual connotations. Because it reminded him of his own similar experience, Thoreau was interested in a passage from Benvenuto Cellini's memoirs in which Cellini describes the seemingly miraculous appearance of a halo of light above his head. Thoreau says, "This reminds me of the halo around my shadow which I notice from the causeway in the morning . . . as if, in the case of a man of an excitable imagination, this were basis enough for his superstition" (VIII, 495). The halo seemed to Thoreau to suggest a close relationship between man and God. At other times light seemed to be important as a moral symbol. He says, for instance, that "Light is somewhat almost moral. The most intense — as the fixed stars and our own sun — has an unquestionable preeminence among the elements" (VII, 451). Years later, when he noticed an "incredibly intense and pure white light" in the woods, he recorded in his journal that the light was "a glory in which only the just deserved to live" (XVI, 133).

Before Thoreau could fully understand the spiritual and moral implications of light, however, he first needed to understand its physical laws. Thus when he observed the first rays of sunlight one morning, he asked himself, "Why these rays? What is it divides the light of the sun? Is it thus divided by distant inequalities in the surface of the earth, behind which the other parts are concealed, and since the morning atmosphere is clearer they do not reach so far?" (VIII, 502). Occasionally Thoreau could answer such questions about light with his basic knowledge of Newtonian optics acquired at Harvard.[8] When he noticed a "celestial light on all the land" after a rainstorm, he came to this solution: "We were in the westernmost edge of the shower at the moment the sun was setting; and its rays shone through the cloud and the falling rain. We were, in fact, in a rainbow and it was here its arch rested on the earth" (VIII, 382–383). But more often his own knowledge of optics was insufficient to explain the elusive phenomena of light; so he made it one of his lifelong interests to increase his understanding of light.

His study was complicated by the presence of still other elements through which light had to pass between the subject and the object. The influence of the air was crucial in visual perception, because the air was God's universal paint which gave color to the world: "I wish to see the earth through the medium of much air or heaven, for there is no paint like the air" (VIII, 496). Like light, it was both literally and figuratively an expression of God's artistry; it was both "the heavens" and "Heaven." He could say that in a double sense "Heaven intervenes between me and the object" (VIII, 187). Air was not only a natural muse, an "inspirer," but the agent of co-respondence, the medium which made possible and which colored all of the other elements of visual perception. It altered the light which passed through it, it altered the effluence of light refracted and reflected by a natural object, and it altered the seer's perception of that object.

Thoreau's limited understanding of optics convinced him that air altered according to its opacity the light that passed through it. He believed, for instance, that blue was the color of light seen through a minimum of opacity: "Light, I should say, was white; the absence of it, black. . . . hold up to it the least opaque body, such as air, and you get blue. Hence you may say that blue is light seen through a veil" (XVIII, 78). Blue was of particular interest to Thoreau because of this minimum alteration of light. Thoreau believed that pure light, like the face of the Old Testament God, was too brilliant to be viewed directly. Light, the natural expression of Thoreau's transcendent God, could only be seen when filtered, refracted, or reflected by the air. Thus blue, with its supposed minimum opacity, was for Thoreau the color most directly expressive of God which could be endured and viewed by man's limited capacity for vision. The color blue was an expression of the immediate presence of God in the natural world. When he noticed "little azures" in the crannies of snowdrifts, he remarked that "I see the heaven hiding in nooks and crevices in the snow" (IX, 180). When he noticed a blue tint in his own shadow in the snow, he commented that "It suggests that there may be something divine, something celestial, in me" (XIII, 178). The air, with its ability to tint light blue, convinced Thoreau that "Heaven is the outside of the earth everywhere."

The air also had an effect on both the subject and the object. It could either cheer or depress the seer (the subject) and thereby affect both what he expected to see and his perception of what he did see: "The influences which make for one walk more than another, and one day more than another, are much more ethereal than terrestrial. It is the quality of the air much more than the quality of the ground that concerns the walker, — cheers or depresses him" (VIII, 339). Thus Thoreau's detailed journal records of the weather were an integral part of his attempt to understand the process of poetic perception. As he writes in his journal for 1855, "In a journal it is important in a few words to describe the weather, or character of the day, as it affects our feelings. That which is so important at the time cannot be unimportant to remember" (XII, 171). Again, in 1860, he says of the weather that "It makes a material difference whether it is foul or fair, affecting surely our mood and thoughts" (XIX, 106).

At other times the air seemed to affect the object more than the subject. It sometimes seemed to alter the appearance of objects. Thoreau observed, for instance, that "the trunks and branches of trees" were "different colors at different times and in different lights and weather, — in sun, rain, and in the night" (IX, 279). It also sometimes could reveal objects usually hidden from the seer. One day, for instance, Thoreau was surprised to find himself in the midst of many "fine gossamer cobwebs" and asked himself, "What is the peculiar condition of the atmosphere, to call forth this activity? If there were so sunshine, I should never find out that they existed, I should not know that I was bursting a myriad barriers" (IX, 87). At still other times, air seemed to idealize objects by giving them "ideal remoteness and perfection" even though they might be quite near (I, 45).

Such was the effect of air that the truth of a visual perception often seemed to be more in the distortion or illusion caused by the intervening atmosphere than in the actual substance being viewed. Thoreau's interest in such illusions is particularly strong in *Cape Cod*. In "The Sea and the Desert," for instance, he describes approaching a chain of shallow pools on the beach-desert and finding that "they appeared inclined at a slight but decided angle to the horizon, though they were plainly and broadly connected with one another, and there was not the least ripple to suggest a current. . . . They appeared to lie by magic on the side of the vale, like a mirror left in a slanting position. It was a very pretty mirage for a Provincetown desert, but not amounting to what, in Sanscrit, is called 'the thirst of the gazelle' " (IV, 191). Then, saying that "this was not the only mirage which I saw on the Cape," he goes on to describe other mirages which he saw or heard about. Earlier, in "The Highland Light," he reports an illusory sunrise seen by the lighthouse keeper. One morning the keeper was amazed to discover that the sun was already two-thirds above the horizon twenty minutes before it was scheduled to rise, and "it remained at that height for about fifteen minutes by the clock, and then rose as usual, and nothing else extraordinary happened during that day" (IV, 173). The truth of that illusion for Thoreau was that "he certainly must be a son of Aurora to whom the sun looms, when there are so many millions to whom it *glooms* rather, or who never see it till an hour *after* it has risen. But it behooves us old stagers to keep our lamps trimmed and burning to the last, and not trust to the sun's looming" (IV, 174). Still another illusion which frequently impressed Thoreau was the rainbow. To him it was God's face and expressed the full glory of God's immanence in the natural world. All such mirages were somehow visible expressions, though elusive and impermanent ones, of the relation among object, light, air, and perceiver.

A more permanent expression was available in another element, water. Water, like air, was thoroughly transparent and mediate: "A single glass of Walden's water held up to the light is as colorless as an equal quantity of air" (II, 197). Water too was an agent of co-respondence, because light often passed through it before bringing an image to the seer's eye. Like the air, it modified the light, and that modification could be seen in the reflections of natural objects in the water, reflections which appeared every day and which could be studied at any time.

Thoreau studied reflections frequently and was interested in how they were created. For many years he seems to have accepted the common view that reflections are exactly reversed images of substantial objects. Their charm for him was that they seemed to show the other invisible half of the substantial object and make it whole: "These answering reflections — shadow to substance — impress the voyager with a sense of harmony and symmetry, as when you fold a blotted paper and produce a regular figure, — a dualism which nature loves. What you commonly see is but half" (IX, 51). But later he became convinced that reflections were not merely reversed repetitions of actual objects. He disagreed, for instance, with Ruskin's definition of a reflection: "I think that Ruskin is wrong about reflections in his 'Elements of Drawing,' page 181. He says the reflection is merely the substance 'reversed' or 'topsy-turvy,' and adds, 'Whatever you can see from the place in which you stand, of the solid objects so reversed under the water, you will see in the reflection, always in the true perspective of the solid objects so reversed' " (XVI, 210). Thoreau's own experience with reflections was somewhat different: "I perceive that more or other things are seen in the reflection than in the substance. As I look now over the pond westward, I see in substance the now bare outline of Fair Haven Hill a mile beyond, but in the reflection I see not this, only the tops of some pines, which stand close to the shore but are invisible against the dark hill beyond, and these are indefinitely prolonged into points of shadow" (XV, 172–173). In another journal entry he elaborates on this apparent originality of reflections:

> I perceive that the reflection of the hillside seen from an opposite hill is not so broad as the hillside itself appears, owing to the different angle at which it is seen. The reflection exhibits such an aspect of the hill, *apparently*, as you would get if your eye were placed at that part of the surface of the pond where the reflection seems to be. In this instance, too, then, Nature avoids repeating herself. Not even reflections in still water are like their substances as seen by us. This too accounts for my seeing portions of the sky through the trees in reflections often when none appear in the substance. . . . The reflection is never a true copy or

repetition of its substance, but a new composition, and this may be the source of its novelty and attractiveness, and of this nature, too, may be the charm of an echo. I doubt if you can ever get Nature to repeat herself exactly. (XVI, 96–97)

A reflection, then, was something new between the perceiver and the object — something which was neither the object itself nor solely the seer's interpretation of it. It appeared to be a unique visible expression of the relationship between the seer's senses and the object's effluence.

Thoreau was intrigued by this apparent novelty of reflections, and he was curious about how it occurred. At times the novelty seemed to be simply in the reflection's intensification of color: "The sky in the reflection . . . at Hubbard's Bath is more green than in reality, and also darker blue" (XIX, 95). At other times the novelty seemed to be in the distortion or exaggeration of the form of an object. One day in Spring, he observed this reflection in a flooded meadow: "A wall which ran down to the water on the hillside, without any remarkable curve in it, was exaggerated by the reflection into the half of an ellipse. The meadow was expanded to a large lake, the shoreline being referred to the sides of the hills reflected in it" (XIII, 310). Such a reflection also suggested that water, like air, could magnify and idealize objects. At still other times, the novelty of a reflection was in its ability to reveal details and colors which were not otherwise visible to the seer. On a wintry day, for instance, he observed a sunset reflected in a river and found that "the colors in the reflection were different from those in the sky. The sky was dark clouds with coppery or dun-colored under sides. In the water were dun-colored clouds with bluish-green patches" (X, 461). On a "sober, moist day" in Spring, he noticed a "circle round the sun, which I can only see in the reflection in the water" (XIII, 281). Such observations suggested to him that "We see things in the reflection which we do not see in the substance" (X, 338).

Perhaps the most spiritually significant peculiarity of water reflections, however, was that "a field of water betrays the spirit that is in the air" (II, 209). The water could bring, both literally (by reflecting the sky's blue color) and figuratively, heaven down to earth. It could show the seer that heaven is not distant but immediately present below as well as above us: "These reflections suggest that the sky underlies the hills as well as overlies them, and in another sense than in appearance" (IX, 100). Even the smallest puddles could reveal heaven on earth: "It is not merely a few favored lakes or pools that reflect the trees and skies, but the obscurest pond . . . does the same" (IX, 100). This ability of water to reflect the sky proved to Thoreau "how intimate heaven is with earth" and that water was in some way an earthly extension of heaven — "the grossest part of heaven" (VIII, 438). Water was important because, as Thoreau says, "it multiplies the heavens" (X, 21).

By multiplying the heavens and thus conveying more light to the seer than his eye could detect directly, a reflection also beautified the scene it reflected. For Thoreau (as for Emerson) light was the source of visual beauty, and it sometimes seemed that the beauty increased as the light increased. Upon seeing that an object reflected in water seemed "fairer than the substance," Thoreau speculated, "Is it not that we let much more light into our eyes, — which in the usual position are shaded by the brows . . . in the case of reflections by having the sky placed under our feet? i.e. in both cases we see terrestrial objects with the sky or heavens for a background or field. Accordingly, they are not dark and terrene, but lit and elysian" (XII, 17). By revealing the "elysian" quality of the substance it reflected, a reflection idealized natural objects and showed Thoreau that the ideal and "substance" were inseparably connected. So Thoreau studied reflections because they could present previously known truths from a new point of view, reveal new truths, and idealize all truths. They could be essential tools for the seer in his main task, detecting the relationship between subject and object and between heaven and earth.

The precise process by which reflections achieved their unique effects was more difficult for Thoreau to discover, however. Newton's axioms were insufficient to explain these watery idealizations. If Ruskin was indeed wrong about reflections merely reversing the image of the substances they reflected, then what was their relationship to those substances and to the seer himself? One of the answers which Thoreau considered was that a reflection is the view the seer would get if he could put himself at the point on the water where the reflection occurred: "Looking from the Cliffs, the sun being as before invisible, I saw far more light in the reflected sky in the neighborhood of the sun than I could see in the heavens from my position and it occurred to me that the reason was that there was reflected to me from the river the view I should have got if I had stood there on the water in a more favorable position" (XIII, 237). But further questioning and observation eventually suggested to him that the solution was not quite that simple. For instance, upon observing a hillside reflected in White Pond, he asked himself,

Is the reflection of a hillside . . . such an aspect of it as can be obtained by the eye directed to the hill itself from any single point of view? It plainly is not such a view as the eye would get looking upward from the immediate base of the hill or water's edge, for there the first rank of bushes on the lower part of the hill would conceal the upper. The reflection of the top appears to be such a view of it as I should get with my eye at the water's edge above the edge of the reflection; but would the lower part of the hill also appear from this point as it does in the reflection? (XVI, 97)

His answer to this last question was an uncertain "no," and he began to suspect that a reflection was not a view which the seer could ever get directly on his own from any single point of view.

This suspicion was the reason for his curiosity about multiple reflections. He read with great interest, for instance, Elisha Kane's description of a triple reflection of an iceberg in Baffin's Bay (see XII, 139–140). Such multiple reflections must have suggested to Thoreau his conclusion that "In the reflection you have an infinite number of eyes to see for you and report the aspect of things each from its point of view" (XVII, 213). A reflection could give the seer not just one additional view of an object, but many simultaneous views, each point on the reflection containing a slightly different viewpoint. By looking at a reflection, the seer could quite literally be in more than one place at a time. He could view things subjectively from his own point of view and at the same time objectively through the many viewpoints relayed to him by the reflection.

Thus Thoreau's interest in optics and in water reflections in particular revealed three truths to him which could be applied to his own task as a poet-seer. One was that reflections could enable him to "probe the universe in a myriad points" by making many points of view available to him simultaneously. Another was that reflections could be an invaluable aid to the seer by mediating between the subject and object and by making visible the relationship among all of the components of the visual process — the subject, the object, the light, the air, and the water. A third was that a reflection is not simply a reproduction but a new and unique creation of the water. He saw it as an original creation, "a permanent picture to be seen there, a permanent piece of idealism" (IX, 100). The poet-seer too needed to observe the world from a myriad viewpoints, reveal the relationship between himself and that world, and form a new poetic creation out of his understanding of that relationship.

Because of his recognition of the similarities between water reflections and the poet — similarities which he had begun to recognize even before writing *Walden* but which he did not fully understand until late in his life — Thoreau consistently describes bodies of water as mirrors. Of Walden Pond he says, "It is a mirror which no stone can crack, whose quicksilver will never wear off, whose gilding Nature continually repairs; no storms, no dust can dim its surface ever fresh; — a mirror in which all impurity presented to it sinks, swept and dusted by the sun's hazy brush — this the light dust-cloth, — which retains no breath that is breathed on it, but sends its own to float as clouds high above its surface, and be reflected in its bosom still" (II, 209). In both "A Winter Walk" and his "Ur" journal, Thoreau refers to a lake as "a mirror in the breast of nature" (V, 174; Ur, 185), and he frequently describes rivers as mirrors — the Assabet river in winter, for instance, looked like a "polished silver mirror" (XIII, 82).

Thoreau's concept of water as a mirror was closely related to his concept of the eye of the poet-seer. Several times he uses mirror and eye metaphors almost interchangeably to describe Walden Pond. In his "Ur" journal, for instance, he says of the pond, "It is the earth's liquid eye — it is blue or grey, or black as I choose my time. In the night it is my more than forty foot reflector" (Ur, 185). The revised version of this passage which appears in "A Winter Walk" makes the comparison between the mirror and the eye even more direct: "In summer it [the pond] is the earth's liquid eye; a mirror in the breast of nature" (V, 174). Just as the mirror of the pond received the images of light reflected to it by an object, modified that image in the medium of its water, and then in turn reflected a new idealized image to the seer, so the poet's eye also functioned as a mirror which received images reflected to it by an object, idealized that image in the medium of the poet's mind, and reflected it in turn onto the pages of his writing. This centrality of the pond in visual perception and, by analogy, in Thoreau's own creative processes is undoubtedly his reason for placing his chapter "The Ponds" at the center of *Walden*.

Also like the mirror of the pond, which could not be muddied by impurities, the poet's eye needed to be kept unmuddied by social influences and by the subjective prejudices of his own mind. As Thoreau warns himself in his journal, "How watchful we must be to keep the crystal well that we were made, clear! — that it be not made turbid by our contact with the world, so that it will not reflect objects" (XI, 453). It was for this reason that all of the preparation for walking (the early rising, the bathing, the natural diet) and the special techniques of observation (sauntering and looking with the side of the eye) were so important. Only a clear and unmuddied eye could see the truth of reflections: "We notice that it required a separate intention of the eye, a more free and abstracted vision, to see the reflected trees and the sky, than to see the river bottom merely; and so are there manifold visions in the direction of every object, and even the most opaque reflect the heavens from their surface" (I, 47–48). The poet's eye needed to be clearer than that of other men, because "most men . . . walk along a river's bank, or paddle along its stream, without seeing the reflections. Their minds are not abstracted enough from the surface, from surfaces generally. It is only a reflecting mind that sees reflections" (XVI, 156–157). The poet's eye needed to be clearer than even nature's mirrors, because the poet's task was more complex: "The poet must bring to Nature the smooth mirror in which she is to be reflected. He must be something superior to her, something more than natural. He must furnish equanimity" (XI, 183–184).

If he could maintain such a clear eye, the poet-seer would see that nature was not a "chamber of mirrors" which merely reflected the seer's image back to him; it was a chamber of mirrors that reflected the truth of the relationship among God (as expressed by light), nature, and the seer. It was that truth that he needed to preserve as a "permanent piece of idealism" in his own writing. Thoreau's interest in optics was not merely the hobby-horse of an amateur scientist. It was a key element in his attempt to yoke idealism and empiricism, poetry and science, and in his attempt to understand his relationship to God, to nature, and to his own role as a poet.

Most of Thoreau's observations of phenomena of light are to be found in his journal, and some of his conclusions about water reflections appear quite late in the journal, well after his books and major essays had been written. His interest in water reflections in particular seems to have begun early in his career but to have increased noticeably toward the end of his life. Yet even in *Walden* Thoreau felt the importance of the reflections in Walden Pond and their relation to him. He says in *Walden*, for instance, that "A lake is the landscape's most beautiful and expressive feature. It is the earth's eye; looking into which the beholder measures the depth of his own nature" (II, 206–207). In the mirror of Walden Pond, Thoreau saw an analogy for his own role as poet-seer. Both the seer and the ponds of the Concord woods were poets in their ability to capture the relationship between subject and object and between heaven and earth, and both could reveal the new and beautiful truth that it contained. Like God, nature and man too were creators and revealers of truth. The poet's role was to help other men to see that relationship so that they too could quit their lives of quiet desperation and become creative reflectors of truth themselves.

Nathaniel Hawthorne, Thoreau's neighbor in Concord for a brief time, once recorded in his own notebook that "I am half convinced that the reflection is indeed the reality—the real thing which Nature imperfectly images to our grosser sense."[9] Thoreau, however, was more than convinced that the reality of man's relation to nature and to God could be seen in the reflections in Walden Pond.

Notes

1. Channing's pun is recorded in *The Writings of Henry David Thoreau.* "Walden" edition, ed. Bradford Torrey (Boston: Houghton Mifflin, 1906), X, 421. Unless otherwise indicated, all quotations are from this edition and will be indicated parenthetically by volume and page number in the text. The volume numbers are as follows: I—*A Week on the Concord and Merrimack Rivers*, II—*Walden*, III—*The Maine Woods*, IV—*Cape Cod and Miscellaneous Essays*, and V—*Excursions and Poems*. Volume VI contains Thoreau's letters, and volumes VII–XX contain his journal. All emphases within quotations are Thoreau's.

2. For two brief discussions of Thoreau's interest in water reflections, see Laurence Stapleton, "Introduction," *H. D. Thoreau: A Writer's Journal* (New York: Dover Publications, 1960), pp. xiv–xvi, and Charles Anderson, *The Magic Circle of Walden* (New York: Holt, Rinehart, and Winston, 1968), pp. 119–120.

3. "Thoreau in the Context of International Romanticism," *New England Quarterly*, 34 (1961), 150.

4. See Sherman Paul, "The Wise Silence," *New England Quarterly*, 22 (1949), 513–514.

5. *The Complete Writings of Nathaniel Hawthorne*, Manse ed. (Boston: Houghton Mifflin, 1900), XVIII, 403.

6. This passage is from Thoreau's "Ur" journal, published by Perry Miller in *Consciousness in Concord* (Boston: Houghton Mifflin, 1958), pp. 165–166. Subsequent quotations will be indicated parenthentically in the text by the word "Ur" and page number.

7. *Symbolism in American Literature* (Chicago: Univ. of Chicago Press, 1966), p. 141.

8. Thoreau's college textbook of optics was J. Farrar's *Experimental Treatise on Optics*.

See Kenneth Walter Cameron, *Thoreau's Harvard Years* (Hartford: Transcendental Books, 1966), Part I, p. 17.

9. Hawthorne, *The Complete Writings*, XVIII, 410. For more about Hawthorne's interest in reflections, see Hawthorne's "The Old Manse" and Malcolm Cowley, "Hawthorne in the Looking Glass," *Sewanee Review*, 56 (1948), 545–563.

The Transcendental Georgic in *Walden*
James S. Tillman*

The description of the farming experiment in *Walden* that Leo Marx characterizes as a manifestation of Thoreau's Transcendental pastoralism[1] can also be understood as an appropriation of another established ideal from classical country life literature. For Thoreau's didactic account of his farming experiences (especially in "The Bean-field"), his allusions to classical agricultural works, and his use of a husbandman persona create a Transcendental version of the georgic. Although Thoreau is too familiar with impious and immoral Concord farmers ever to endorse the farmer's life as the most virtuous and blessed life in the manner of classical georgics, he can still find the georgic ideal appealing enough to teach his own ironic version of true husbandry with some respectful adaptations of ancient georgic themes.

Most students of American literature are familiar with the farmer heroes of Crèvecoeur and Jefferson, as well as with the less idealistic rustic heroes of Frost and Faulkner, but (according to Leo Marx and John Lynen[2] in particular) these heroes, along with Thoreau's persona in *Walden*, are generally associated with the pastoral ideal, rather than with the distinct classical and English tradition of the georgic.[3] Though the pastoral and georgic often overlap, even in classical works, the two genres usually provide quite different images of the good life.[4] For instance, country life in the pastoral is essentially characterized by *otium*, pleasure, and the enjoyment of poetry and contemplation, whereas georgic country life is characterized by labor, painstaking forethought, and respect for science and common sense. While the pastoral is commonly a dramatic preoccupation with self-indulgent love, friendship, and poetry, the georgic provides an objective science of farming with a fairly realistic presentation of the self-sacrificing labors and pious duties imposed by the social and economic responsibilities of country life. If truly profound pastorals rarely present their golden-age worlds of ease and pleasure without threatening tragic possibilities surrounding them, the best georgics rarely present their realistic accounts of country arts and piety without assurances that such

*Reprinted from *ESQ: A Journal of the American Renaissance* 21 (3rd Quarter 1975): 137–41.

pragmatic labors will be blessed with some vestiges of golden-age ease and pleasure in the end. Thoreau's description of his experience at Walden Pond obviously partakes of both of these classical ideals at different times without finally being fully explained by either one, but he seems particularly responsive to the georgic ideal whenever he makes his own labors and piety an exemplum of true husbandry.

With typical georgic pride Thoreau boasts in the first sentence of *Walden* that he earned his living at the pond by the labor of his own hands, and with a typical georgic exhortative tone he makes both his first chapter on the necessity of "Economy" and his principal account of his bean farm in "The Bean-field" a handbook of instructions for the farmer who wishes to recover the georgic hero's piety. Though these instructions only rarely descend to the pragmatic science of farming taught by most georgics, Thoreau's wry transformation of the chief concern of the georgic from the culture of crops to the culture of piety and even of the self is not wholly inconsistent with georgic tradition. Georgics have usually been prompted by strong motives for ethical reform anyway: Hesiod's *Works and Days* is full of moral maxims; Virgil's *Georgics*, written during a time of civil turmoil, is pervaded with a nostalgic longing for the ancient piety and industry of the husbandman; and the prose georgic works of Cato, Varro, and Columella—that Thoreau seems particularly to have admired[5]—uphold the noble virtues of the farmer against the corrupting vices of Rome. Thoreau's exhortative presentation of his own economically restrained life, expressive of a piety toward nature, as well as a concern for moral self-culture, is true to the spirit of these earlier celebrations of the moral superiority of the farmer's life.

Yet in "The Bean-field," when Thoreau actually describes his farming experiences, his georgic inclinations at times seem at odds with his more deeply seated love of wild nature and with his Romantic notion that the only truly blessed life existed before man fell[6] to the economic necessity of cultivation. Since in modern times man has degenerated even more, Thoreau creates an impression of modern cultivation and cultivators as being incapable of the piety for nature so often associated with them in classical georgics (pp. 46–47, 144–145). Even the proud economist—the regenerated georgic hero—of Walden Pond seems reluctant about his enterprise at times, perhaps because he suspects that its materialistic bent will inevitably corrupt him a bit, but, more likely, because he simply cannot bear the loss of even one wild field. Hence his account of his successful venture in beans is laced with ambivalent comments that at times threaten to make the whole narration a parody of the georgic, rather than an attempt to recover the combination of piety and realistic economy that Thoreau apparently admired in ancient farming literature. He begins his success story, for example, not with a triumphant celebration of the cultivated field, but with a nostalgic glimpse of its beauty before cultivation, when it grew "sweet wild fruits and pleasant flowers" (p. 137). And he seems most delighted, not with his harvest, but with his "half-cultivated field," full of beans "cheerfully returning to their wild and primitive state" (p. 139). He seems no more at ease in his role as the ideal cultivator. As he hoes his field, he can fancy himself the *"agricola laboriosus,"* the "home-staying" (p. 138) laborer, contrasting, in typical georgic form,[7] with the idle villagers at their ease in their gigs as they pass by on the nearby highway, as well as with the noisy militia enjoying their "gala" day at Concord (p. 140). Yet Thoreau cannot exploit these contrasts for all of their potential as exempla of the georgic virtues of labor and self-discipline, because he, too, is idle in his own way. After all, he can conclude, just a couple of paragraphs later, that he took up farming mostly as a "rare amusement" that he feared would become a "dissipation" if continued too long (p. 142). And he can only claim for hoeing, in contrast to easy traveling in gigs, that it is not the "worst form of idleness" (p. 138).

In spite of this ambivalence about cultivation and cultivators, however, Thoreau never forsakes the georgic spirit altogether in "The Bean-field." He mocks his own cultivated field, not because he is contemptuous of agriculture, but because he knows that in God's world, which is all "equally cultivated like a garden" (p. 145), man's planting of one crop in a field must inevitably displace another of God's "crops" that might very well have been more beneficial in the long run. Similarly, he represents his own role of husbandman as a kind of idleness and amusement, not to criticize an ancient occupation, but to praise it. For the hoer enjoys an "inexhaustible entertainment" (p. 140) afforded by his country labors; he knows pleasures — such as the music of his hoe tinkling against the stones and the sight of the night-hawk circling overhead — that far surpass the pleasures of the traveller in his gig or of the soldiers parading their warlike spirit. This version of the georgic may be unconventional in its reverence for wild nature and in its wry manner of portraying the husbandman's happy life, but it still has a recognizable connection to georgic tradition. Where ancient georgics usually made cultivation methods their chief concern and the piety and moral fiber of the farmer a secondary, or even just an implicit, concern, Thoreau simply reverses the emphasis. Hence, at the end of "The Bean-field," he relegates his pragmatic methods and economic results to a couple of short paragraphs of details (p. 143), while promoting the moral and religious "profits" (p. 145) of his experience to a central place. Indeed, to Thoreau with his extreme love of piety, the only "true husbandman" becomes the man who relinquishes "all claim to the produce of his fields . . . sacrificing in his mind not only his first but his last fruits also" (p. 145). Though such a georgic writer as Cato, whose highly pragmatic *De Re Rustica* Thoreau takes as his "Cultivator" (p. 84), would no doubt have been somewhat puzzled by his student's extraordinary emphasis upon the piety of the "true husbandman," he would still have conceded — like most georgic writers — that piety must indeed be the supreme virtue of husbandmen.

This extreme version of the pious "true husbandman" appears elsewhere in *Walden* as a foil to that least pious of all characters in Thoreau's work — the Concord farmer. In the beginning of "Where I Lived and What I Lived For," for instance, Thoreau recounts his imaginary life as a husbandman of farms that he considered as possible homes, including the Hollowell Farm that he even tried to buy. He farms these places though, not by actually breaking ground and planting crops like the typical Concord farmer, but by imagining how he would care for the land and by harvesting an "abundant crop" (p. 84) of wild beauty. Hence he claims with characteristic irony that he was most anxious to buy the Hollowell farm before the owner made "any more of his improvements" that might ruin the "crop" that he found on the place (p. 84). Similarly, in "Economy," he appears as the "true husbandman" who looks after the "wild stock of the town, which give a faithful herdsman a good deal of trouble by leaping fences" and who waters rare, wild plants that might otherwise have withered during droughts (p. 36). There is even a hint of his georgic ethos in his appearance as a fisherman in "Baker Farm." He creates an effective contrast there between his own day of profitable and enjoyable fishing for his livelihood and John Field's toilsome, unproductive life as a farm laborer. "I tried to help him with my experience," Thoreau relates, "telling him that he was one of my nearest neighbors, and that I too, who came a-fishing here, and looked like a loafer, was getting my living like himself" (p. 174).

Each of these labors of true husbandry exemplifies a similar kind of piety for God's "crops" as that which Thoreau practices in "The Bean-field," but this time without any references to such typical, pragmatic labors as hoeing to remind us of the classical true husbandman. Once again, then, this kind of pious husbandry may seem far indeed from Cato's more worldly emphasis, but Thoreau's point is that his piety is at least closer to Cato's than that of any Concord farmer. And, in fact, as long as Thoreau's chief competitor for the role of the pious georgic hero is the Concord farmer, then he is assured of our deepest sympathies, for the Concord farmer, at least as Thoreau depicts him in *Walden*, is a victim of a debased georgic pragmatism that is ultimately impious and even self-destructive. As Thoreau explains in "Economy," the very means employed by the farmer have come to overshadow his ends: "The farmer is endeavoring to solve the problem of a livelihood by a formula more complicated than the problem itself. To get his shoestrings he speculates in herds of cattle" (p. 46). Inevitably, such inflation of the value of the means of subsistence subordinates moral development to economics and substitutes material gain for spiritual wealth: "We have adopted Christianity merely as an improved method of *agri*-culture. . . . When I think of acquiring for myself one of our luxurious dwellings, I am deterred, for, so to speak, the country is not yet adapted to *human* culture, and we are still forced to cut our *spiritual bread* far thinner than our forefathers did their wheaten" (pp. 50–51).

It is this tendency of farmers to show more concern for material security, even extravagance, than for spiritual development that Thoreau finds so irksome about men like John Field. Perhaps his most characteristic statement of his frustration comes in "Baker Farm," after an unsuccessful attempt to educate Field in a more intelligent form of husbandry. "I should be glad if all the meadows on the earth were left in a wild state," he concludes unhappily (p. 174), "if that were the consequence of men's beginning to redeem themselves." What Thoreau deplores here, as well as in "Economy," is not agriculture itself, but an undiscriminating worship of the ideals that have always supported agriculture. His portrayal of Concord farmers creates a consistent critique in *Walden* of two kinds of false worship: the worship of labor as a redemptive value without sufficient regard for the possible sacrifice of the laborer's moral development, and the worship of the ownership of property without sufficient regard for the possible sacrifice of the owner's personal piety and freedom. Where John Field, in particular, represents the unredeemed laborer, those farmers in "Economy" who become "tools of their tools" (pp. 49, 26) and property of their property (pp. 26, 47) most vividly represent the slaves of ownership. In contrast, the fisherman of "Baker Farm," who appears to be loafing more than laboring, and the "portionless" man of "Economy," who knows it is enough to "subdue and cultivate a few cubic feet of flesh" (p. 26), are, ironically, the best exemplars of intelligent husbandry.

Later, Thoreau turns in his chapter on "The Ponds" to the "poor farmer" as yet another of his ironic georgic heroes, inspired this time not so much by the pitiful idolatry of Concord farmers, as by the willful impiety and immorality of the worst of them — John Flint. At first Thoreau merely deplores the fact that a beautiful pond has become known by the name of its impious owner who "would have drained it and sold it for the mud at its bottom" if he could. But, then, he makes of Flint a symbol of all that model farmers have become:

> I respect not his labors, his farm where every thing has its price; who would carry the landscape, who would carry his God, to market, if he could get any thing for him; who goes to market *for* his god as it is; on whose farm nothing grows free, whose fields bear no crops, whose meadows no flowers, whose trees no fruits, but dollars; who loves not the beauty of his fruits, whose fruits are not ripe for him till they are turned to dollars. (p. 168)

These impious labors are coupled with an immoral use of men:

> A model farm! where the house stands like a fungus in a muckheap, chambers for men, horses, oxen, and swine, cleansed and uncleansed, all contiguous to one another! Stocked with men! . . . Under a high

state of cultivation, being manured with the hearts and brains of men! As if you were to raise your potatoes in the church-yard! Such is a model farm. (p. 168)

Although this bitter critique provides its own implicit hints about what must be done to redeem the farmer's life from such a degeneration, Thoreau also provides an explicit statement of his preferences: "Give me the poverty that enjoys true wealth. Farmers are respectable and interesting to me in proportion as they are poor . . ." (p. 168).

Much of the power of Thoreau's georgic in *Walden* can be attributed to its ironic revelation that one must turn to poor farmers, apparent loafers, portionless self-cultivators—in short, social outcasts—in order to find the respect for morality and regard for piety that used to be epitomized by most farmers. Thoreau's heroes are all paradoxical georgic figures: they must be poor in order to enjoy true wealth; they must sacrifice all their crops in their minds in order to make a true harvest; and they must curtail the cultivation of their property in order to cultivate properly themselves. In comparison with these paradoxical figures, Thoreau's *"agricola"* in "The Bean-field" seems fairly sensible and only mildly paradoxical, but still the whole instruction in husbandry in *Walden* is, finally, as much concerned with mocking false husbandry as it is with teaching true husbandry.

It would be a mistake, however, to assume that this critique of modern farming in *Walden* shows such repugnance for farming itself and for georgic values that it leads Thoreau to embrace instead a pastoral country life with its ease, pleasure, poetry, and contemplation. Certainly, there are signs of the pastoral ideal in Thoreau's life as the "true husbandman" (especially when he seems to enjoy all the pleasures of country life while bearing few of its responsibilities), but Thoreau does still think of himself as a husbandman who has a "harvest" (p. 182) to gather from God's "cultivated garden," and he is still interested enough in the georgic ideal to allude to it as his inspiration during his description of his experimental bean farm. More importantly, more of Thoreau's experience described in *Walden* is essentially a moral and pious labor in the spirit of the georgic husbandman, even if it may appear to his own society to be merely loafing and even if its fruits are almost always intangible. Finally, a recognition of Thoreau's half-ironic, half-serious appropriation of the georgic ethos makes us more sensitive to his significant contribution to the modern georgic tradition created by such recent husbandman heroes as Robert Frost's personae in his mowing poems,[8] Aldo Leopold's ecological "farmer" persona in his *Sand County Almanac* (1948), and Wendell Berry's "Mad Farmer" in his *Farming: A Handbook* (1967).

Notes

1. *The Machine in the Garden: Technology and the Pastoral Ideal in America* (New York: Oxford Univ. Press, 1964), pp. 255–259.

2. *The Pastoral Art of Robert Frost* (New Haven: Yale Univ. Press, 1960).

3. See Dwight Durling's *Georgic Tradition in English Poetry* (New York: Columbia Univ. Press, 1935); John Chalker's *The English Georgic: A Study in the Development of a Form* (Baltimore: Johns Hopkins Press, 1969); and Maren-Sofie Rostvig's *The Happy Man: Studies in the Metamorphoses of a Classical Ideal*, 2nd ed., 2 vols. (New York: Humanities Press, 1962).

4. For distinctions between pastoral and georgic, see Joseph Addison, "Essay on Virgil's Georgics" (1967) in *Eighteenth-Century Critical Essays*, ed. Scott Elledge, 1 (Ithaca: Cornell Univ. Press, 1961), 2; Marie Loretto Lilly, *The Georgic: A Contribution to the Study of the Vergilian Type of Didactic Poetry*, Studies in English Philology, No. 6 (Baltimore: Johns Hopkins Press, 1919), pp. 19–47; John R. Cooper, *The Art of the Compleat Angler* (Durham, N.C.: Duke Univ. Press, 1968), pp. 59–60; Rostvig, I, 46–47; Thomas J. Rosenmeyer, *The Green Cabinet: Theocritus and the European Lyric* (Berkeley: Univ. of California Press, 1969), pp. 20–29; and Harold E. Toliver, *Pastoral Forms and Attitudes* (Berkeley: Univ. of California Press, 1971), pp. 340–352.

5. Edith Seybold, *Thoreau: The Quest and the Classics* (New Haven: Yale Univ. Press, 1951), pp. 16, 70–71, 75–78.

6. *The Varorium Walden*, ed. Walter Harding (New York: Twayne Publishers, Inc., 1962), pp. 49–50, 69. Future references to this edition are cited in my text.

7. See Virgil's *Georgics*, II, 11. 458–541. The bulk of Rostvig's first chapter on "Sources and Arguments" (I, 16–47) provides the best introduction to this motif in georgics.

8. Harold Toliver analyzes the "tension" in Frost's poetry between georgic and pastoral, pp. 340–360, especially 340–345.

Walden's False Bottoms   Walter Benn Michaels*

Walden has traditionally been regarded as both a simple and a difficult text, simple in that readers have achieved a remarkable unanimity in identifying the values Thoreau is understood to urge upon them, difficult in that they have been persistently perplexed and occasionally even annoyed by the form his exhortations take. Thoreau's Aunt Maria (the one who bailed him out of jail in the poll tax controversy) understood this as a problem in intellectual history and blamed it all on the Transcendental *Zeitgeist*: "I do love to hear things called by their right names," she said, "and these *Transcendentalists* do so transmogrophy . . . their words and pervert common sense that I have no patience with them."[1] Thoreau's Transcendentalist mentor, Emerson, found, naturally enough, another explanation, blaming instead what he called Henry's "old

*Reprinted from *Glyph* 1 (1977):132–49, by permission of Johns Hopkins University Press.

fault of unlimited contradiction. The trick of his rhetoric is soon learned: it consists in substituting for the obvious word and thought its diametrical antagonist. . . . It makes me," he concluded, "nervous and wretched to read it."[2] That old fault of contradiction is in one sense the subject of this essay, so is wretchedness and especially nervousness, so, in some degree, are the strategies readers have devised for feeling neither wretched nor nervous.

The primary strategy, it seems to me, has been to follow a policy of benign neglect in regard to the question of what *Walden* means; thus, as Charles Anderson noted some ten years ago, critics have concerned themselves largely with "style," agreeing from the start that the book's distinction lies "more in its manner than its matter."[3] Anderson was referring mainly to the tradition of essentially formalist studies ushered in by F. O. Matthiessen's monumental *American Renaissance* in 1941, in which Thoreau is assimilated to the American tradition of the "native craftsman," and *Walden* itself is compared to the "artifacts of the cabinet maker, the potter and the founder."[4] Anderson himself has no real quarrel with this procedure; his chief complaint is that Matthiessen's successors have not taken their enterprise seriously enough. The concern with *Walden*'s style, he says, "has not usually been pursued beyond a general eulogy. Perhaps it is through language that all the seemingly disparate subjects of this book are integrated into wholeness." "Why not try an entirely new approach," he suggests, "and read *Walden* as a poem?"[5]

From our present perspective, of course, it is hard to see how reading *Walden* "as a poem" constitutes an entirely new approach; it seems, if anything, a refinement of the old approaches, a way of continuing to bracket the question of *Walden*'s meaning in at least two different ways. The first is by introducing a distinction between form and content which simultaneously focuses attention on the question of form and reduces content to little more than a banality, typically, in the case of *Walden*, a statement to the effect that the book is fundamentally "a fable of the renewal of life."[6] But from this first move follows a second, more interesting and more pervasive: the preoccupation with *Walden*'s formal qualities turns out to involve a more than tacit collaboration with the assumption that *Walden*'s meaning (what Anderson might call its content and what Stanley Cavell will explicitly call its "doctrine") is in a certain sense simple and univocal. The assertion implicit in this approach is that to examine the form of any literary "artifact" (in fact, even to define the artifact) is precisely to identify its essential unity, thus the continuity between Matthiessen's concern with *Walden*'s "structural wholeness" and Anderson's project of showing how well "integrated" the book is. Where nineteenth-century critics tended to regard *Walden* as an anthology of spectacular fragments and to explain it in terms of the brilliant but disordered personality of its author (his "critical power," writes James Russell Lowell, was "from want of continuity of mind, very limited and inadequate"),[7] more recent criticism, by focusing directly on the art of *Walden*, has tended to emphasize the rhetorical power of its "paradoxes," finding elegant formal patterns in what were once thought to be mere haphazard blunders. Thus, in accepting unity and coherence not simply as *desiderata* but as the characteristic identifying marks of the work of art, these critics have begun by answering the question I should like to begin by asking, the question of *Walden's* contradictions.

Thoreau himself might well have been skeptical of some of the claims made on behalf of *Walden's* aesthetic integrity. He imagined himself addressing "poor students," leading "mean and sneaking lives," "lying, flattering, voting."[8] "The best works of art," he said, "are the expression of man's struggle to free himself from this condition, but the effect of our art is merely to make this low state comfortable and that higher state to be forgotten" (p. 25). In this context, what we might begin to see emerging as the central problem of reading *Walden* is the persistence of our own attempts to identify and understand its unity, to dispel our nervousness by resolving or at least containing the contradictions which create it. It is just this temptation, Thoreau seems to suggest, which must be refused. And in this respect, the naïve perspective of someone like Lowell, who saw in Thoreau the absolute lack of any "artistic mastery" and in his works the total absence of any "mutual relation" between one part and another, may still be of some provisional use, not as a point of view to be reclaimed but as a reminder that resolution need not be inevitable, that we need not read to make ourselves more comfortable.

One way to begin nurturing discomfort is to focus on some of the tasks Thoreau set himself as part of his program for living a life of what he called "epic integrity." There were, of course, a good many of them, mostly along the lines of his own advice to the unhappily symbolic farmer John Field—"Grow wild according to thy nature," Thoreau urged him, "Rise free from care before the dawn. Let the noon find thee by other lakes and the night overtake thee everywhere at home" (p. 138). Some other projects, however, were conceived in less hortatory terms and the possibility of their completion was more explicitly imaginable. "To find the bottom of Walden Pond and what inlet and outlet it might have,"[9] worked its way eventually out of Thoreau's *Journal* and into a central position in the experiment of *Walden* itself. What gave this quest a certain piquancy were the rumours that the pond had no bottom, that, as some said, "it reached quite through to the other side of the globe." "These many stories about the bottom, or rather no bottom, of this Pond," had, Thoreau said, "no foundation for themselves." In fact, the pond was "exactly one hundred and two feet deep," his own "soundings" proved it. This is, he admits, "a remarkable depth for so small an area; yet not an inch of it can be spared by the imagination. What if all ponds were shallow? Would it not react on the minds of men? While men believe in the infinite some ponds will be thought to be bottomless" (p. 189).

If Thoreau's final position on bottoms seems to come out a little blurred here, this has an interest of its own which may be worth pursuing. On the one hand, the passage seems to be asserting that a belief in the potential bottomlessness of ponds is a Bad Thing. The villagers predisposed in this direction who set out to measure Walden with a fifty-six-pound weight and a wagon load of rope were already entrapped by their own delusions, for "while the fifty-six was resting by the way," Thoreau says, "they were paying out the rope in the vain attempt to fathom their truly immeasurable capacity for marvellousness" (p. 189). On the other hand, it isn't enough that the pond is revealed to have a "tight bottom," or even that it turns out symbolically "deep and pure"; it must be imagined bottomless to encourage men's belief in the "infinite." Thus, the passage introduces two not entirely complementary sets of dichotomies. In the first, the virtues of a pond with a "tight bottom" are contrasted with the folly of believing in bottomless ponds. But then the terms shift: the tight bottom metamorphoses into the merely "shallow" and the bottomless becomes the "infinite." The hierarchies are inverted here: on the one hand, a "tight bottom" is clearly preferable to delusory bottomlessness, on the other hand, the merely "shallow" is clearly not so good as the symbolically suggestive "infinite." Finally, the narrator is thankful that the pond was made deep, but "deep" is a little ambiguous: is he glad that the pond is *only* deep so that tough-minded men like himself can sound it and discover its hard bottom, or is he glad that the pond is so deep that it deceives men into thinking of it as bottomless and so leads them into meditations on the infinite? This second explanation seems more convincing, but then the account of the experiment seems to end with a gesture which undermines the logic according to which it was undertaken in the first place.

Sounding the depths of the pond, however, is by no means the only experimental excavation in *Walden*. There is perhaps a better-known passage near the end of the chapter called "Where I Lived and What I Lived For" which helps to clarify what is at stake in the whole bottom-hunting enterprise. "Let us settle ourselves," Thoreau says, "and work and wedge our feet downward through the mud and slush of opinion, and prejudice, and tradition, and delusion, and appearance . . . through church and state, through poetry and philosophy and religion, till we come to a hard bottom and rocks in place which we can call *reality*, and say This is, and no mistake; and then begin, having a *point d'appui* . . . a place where you might found a wall or a state" (p. 66). Measurement here is irrelevant — the issue is solidity, not depth, and the metaphysical status of hard bottoms seems a good deal less problematic. They are real, and "Be it life or death," Thoreau says, "we crave only reality." It is only when we have put ourselves in touch with such a *point d'appui* that we really begin to lead our lives and not be led by them, and the analogy with the *Walden* experiment itself is obvious — it becomes a kind of ontological scavenger-hunt — the prize is reality.

But there is at least one more hard bottom story which unhappily complicates things again. It comes several hundred pages later in the "Conclusion," and tucked in as it is between the flashier and more portentous parables of the artist from Kouroo and of the "strong and beautiful bug," it has been more or less ignored by critics. "It affords me no satisfaction to commence to spring an arch before I have got a solid foundation," Thoreau begins in the now familiar rhetoric of the moral imperative to get to the bottom of things. "Let us not play at kittly-benders," he says, "There is a solid bottom everywhere." But now the story proper gets underway and things begin to go a little haywire. "We read that the traveller asked the boy if the swamp before him had a hard bottom. The boy replied that it had. But presently the traveller's horse sank in up to the girths, and he observed to the boy, "I thought you said that this bog had a hard bottom.' 'So it has,' answered the latter, 'but you have not got half way to it yet.' " And "so it is with the bogs and quicksands of society," Thoreau piously concludes, "but he is an old boy that knows it" (p. 219).

This puts the earlier story in a somewhat different light, I think, and for several reasons. For one thing, the tone is so different; the exalted rhetoric of the evangelist has been replaced by the fireside manner of the teller of tall tales. But more fundamentally, although the theme of the two stories has remained the same — the explorer in search of the solid foundation — the point has been rather dramatically changed. The exhortation has become a warning. The exemplary figure of the heroic traveller, "tied to his mast like Ulysses," Thoreau says, who accepts no substitutes in his quest for the real, has been replaced by the equally exemplary but much less heroic figure of the suppositious traveller drowned in his own pretension. In the first version, Thoreau recognized death as a possibility, but it was a suitably heroic one: "If you stand right fronting and face to face to a fact," he wrote in a justly famous passage, "you will see the sun glimmer on both its surfaces, as if it were a cimeter, and feel its sweet edge dividing you through the heart and marrow, and so you will happily conclude your mortal career" (p. 66). The vanishing traveller of the "conclusion" knows no such happy ending, when he hits the hard bottom he will just be dead, his only claim to immortality his skill in the art of sinking, dispiritedly, in prose.

The juxtaposition of these three passages does not in itself prove anything very startling but it does suggest what may be a useful line of inquiry. What, after all, is at stake in the search for a solid bottom? Why is the concept or the project of foundation so central to *Walden* and at the same time so problematic? At least a preliminary answer would seem justified in focusing on the almost Cartesian process of peeling away until we reach that point of ontological certainty where we can say "This is, and no mistake." The peeling away is itself a kind of questioning: what justification do we have for our opinions, for our traditions? What authorizes church and state, poetry, philosophy, religion? The *point d'appui* has been reached only when we have asked all the questions we know how to ask and so at last have the sense of an answer we are unable ourselves to give. "After a still winter night," Thoreau says, "I awoke with the impression that some question had been put to me, which I had been endeavouring in vain to answer in my sleep, as what — how — when — where? But there was dawning Nature in whom all creatures live . . . and no question on *her* lips. I awoke to an answered question, to Nature. . ." (p. 187). The *point d'appui* then, is a place we locate by asking questions. We know that we've found it when one of our questions is answered. The name we give to this place is Nature. The search for the solid bottom is a search for justification in Nature, wedging our way through "appearance," that is to say human institutions, like church and state and philosophy, until we hit what is real, that is, natural, and not human.

That nature in its purest form should exclude humanity is perhaps a somewhat peculiar doctrine, and one which runs counter to much of what Thoreau often says, and to much of what we think about him and his enterprise. But the logic and the desires which generate this conception are made clear in *Civil Disobedience* when Thoreau attacks the "statesmen and legislators" who, "standing so completely within the institution, never distinctly and nakedly behold it" (p. 241). In an essay called "What Is Authority?" Hannah Arendt has described what she calls "the dichotomy between seeing truth in solitude and remoteness and being caught in the relationships and relativities of human affairs" as "authoritative for the (Western) tradition of political thought,"[10] and it is precisely this privilege of distance and detachment to which Thoreau seems to be appealing in *Civil Disobedience*. He goes on, however, to diagnose more specifically what is wrong with the legislators: "They speak of moving society, but have no resting-place without it." Webster, for instance, "never goes behind government and so cannot speak with authority about it." The appeal here is to the example of Archimedes — "Give me a place to stand and I will move the earth" — and the suggestion in *Walden* is that nature must be much more than a place of retreat. She is a "resting-place" only in the sense of the *"point d'appui,"* the place to stand, and she is an authoritative *point d'appui* only insofar as she is truly "behind," first, separate, and other. Thus, through most of *Walden*, when Thoreau is addressing himself to the problems of his search for a *cogito*, a political and philosophical hard bottom, the human and the natural are conceived as standing in implicit opposition to each other. Nature has a kind of literal authority precisely because she is not one of men's institutions. She serves as the location of values which are real insofar as they are not human creations. She is exemplary. "If we would restore mankind," Thoreau says, "let us first be as simple and as well as Nature ourselves" (p. 53). The force of this conception is expressed most directly, perhaps, in the short essay "Slavery in Massachusetts," written to protest the state's cooperation with the Fugitive Slave Law of 1850. The image of Nature here is a white water-lily, an emblem, like Walden Pond itself, of "purity." "It suggests what kind of laws have prevailed longest," Thoreau writes, ". . . and that there is virtue even in man, too, who is fitted to perceive and love it."[11] And, he goes on to say, "It reminds me that Nature has been partner to no Missouri Compromise. I scent no compromise in the fragrance of the water-lily." The point again is that it is Nature's independence which makes her exemplary, which, from this standpoint, justifies the retreat to Walden and authorizes the hope that something of real value may be found and hence founded there.

But this conception of nature, as attractive and useful as it is, turns out to be in some ways a misleading one. In "Slavery in Massachusetts," the encomium on the lily is preceded by a brief excursion in search of solace to "one of our ponds" (it might as well be Walden). But there is no solace to be found there. "We walk to lakes to see our serenity reflected in them," Thoreau says, "when we are not serene we go not to them."[12] For "what signifies the beauty of nature when men are base?" If the water-lily is a symbol of nature free and clear, sufficient unto itself, the pond in its role as reflector symbolizes a nature implicated in human affairs. It fails as a source of consolation because, unlike the water-lily, it participates in the world of Missouri Compromises and Fugitive Slave Laws. And this vision of nature compromised finds a significant position in *Walden* as well. In the chapter called "Sounds," Thoreau devotes the beginning of one paragraph to a sound he claims he never heard, the sound of the cock crowing. This is no doubt a kind of back-handed reference to his own declaration at the beginning of the book: "I do not propose to write an ode to dejection, but to brag as lustily as chanticleer in the morning . . . if only to wake my neighbors up" (p. 1). The writing of *Walden* makes up for the absent cock-crow. But he goes on to speak of the cock as a "once wild Indian pheasant" and to wonder if it could ever be "naturalized without being domesticated" (pp. 85–86). Here *Walden*'s customary opposition between nature and civilization turns into an opposition between wilderness and civilization, and nature ("naturalized") appears as a third term, at one remove from "wild" and in constant danger of being domesticated and so rendered useless. Furthermore, this danger appears most pronounced at a moment which has been defined as that of writing, the cock-crow. The dismay at seeing only one's face reflected in the pond repeats itself here for a moment as the text imagines itself as a once wild voice now tamed and defused.

These two accounts suggest, then, the kind of problem that is being defined. The attraction of Nature as a bottom line is precisely its otherness — "Nature puts no question and answers none which we mortals ask" (p. 187) — and touching bottom is thus (paradoxically) a moment of recognition; we see what "really is" and our relation to it is basically one of appreciation (and perhaps emulation). The paradox, of course, is our ability to recognize something which is defined precisely by its strangeness to us, a difficulty Thoreau urges upon us when he insists that "Nature has no human inhabitant who appreciates her" (p. 134), and that "she flourishes most alone." But, as I have said, this aloneness is the chief guarantee of authenticity—when we have reached the bottom, we know at least that what we are seeing is not just ourselves. And yet this is also what is most problematic in the symbolic character of Walden Pond itself; looking into it, we find ourselves sounding the depths of our own "nature," and so the reflection makes a mockery of our enterprise. "For his genius to be effective," one critic has written, Thoreau recognized that he "had to slough off his civilized self and regain his natural self,"[13] and this seems innocuous enough. But the cosmological continuity which would authorize a notion like the "natural self" is exactly what is being questioned here. For us to recognize ourselves in Nature, Nature must be no longer herself, no longer the *point d'appui* we were looking for when we started.

But even if Nature proves inadequate as a final category, an absolute, *Walden's* response is not to repudiate the notion of intrinsic value. The pond remains a precious stone, "too pure," he says, to have "a market value" (p. 134), and so it provides at least a symbolic alternative to the commercial values of the first chapter, "Economy." "Economy" has usually been read as a witty and bitter attack on materialism, perhaps undertaken, as Charles Anderson has suggested,[14] in response to Mill's *Political Economy* and/or Marx's *Manifesto* (both published in 1848), motivated, in any event, by a New Testament perception: "Men labor under a mistake. . . . They are employed . . . laying up treasures which moth and rust will corrupt and thieves break through and steal" (p. 3). But it isn't simply a mistake in emphasis—too much on the material and not enough on the spiritual—that Thoreau is concerned with here, for the focal point of "Economy's" attack is not wealth *per se* but "exchange," the principle of the marketplace. Thus, he questions not merely the value of material goods but the process through which the values are determined; "trade curses everything it handles," he says, "and though you trade in messages from heaven, the whole curse of trade attaches to the business" (p. 47). In some degree this can be explained as a nineteenth-century expression of a long-standing ideological debate between the political conceptions of virtue and commerce, which depended in turn upon an opposition between what J.G.A. Pocock has called "real, inheritable, and, so to speak, natural property in land,"[15] and property understood to have only what Pocock calls a "symbolic value, expressed in coin or in credit." One of the phenomena Pocock describes is the persistence with which various social groups attempted to convince themselves that their credit economies were "based on the exchange of real goods and the perception of real values." Failing this, he says, "the individual could exist, even in his own sight, only at the fluctuating value imposed upon him by his fellows."[16]

Thoreau was obviously one of those unconvinced and unhappy about it. Not only did he repudiate what he perceived as false methods of determining value, not only did he rail against the maintenance of a standing army and even reject at times the validity of the entire concept of representative government (all these, as Pocock depicts them, classical political positions); he also attacked real, so-called natural property as well, and precisely at the point which was intended to provide its justification, its inheritability. "I see young men," he says at the very beginning of *Walden*, "my townsmen, whose misfortune it is to have inherited farms, houses . . . for these are more easily acquired than got rid of" (p. 2). Here he blurs the customary distinction between real or natural and symbolic or artificial property, insisting that all property is artificial and so exposing laws of inheritance as mere fictions of continuity, designed to naturalize values which in themselves are purely arbitrary.

This points toward a rather peculiar dilemma — Thoreau's doggedly ascetic insistence on distinguishing natural values from artificial ones leads him to reject the tokens of natural value which his society provides, and so the category of the natural becomes an empty one. But this doesn't mean that the natural / arbitrary distinction breaks down. Quite the contrary: the more difficult that it becomes to identify natural principles, the more privilege attaches to a position which can be defined only in theoretical opposition to the conventional or institutional. The "resting-place without" society that Thoreau speaks of in *Civil Disobedience* now turns out to be located neither in nature nor in culture but in that empty space he sometimes calls "wilderness." This is perhaps what he means when he describes himself once as a "soujourner in civilized life" and another time as a "sojourner in nature." To be a sojourner everywhere is by one account (Thoreau's own in "Walking") to be "at home everywhere." In *Walden*, however, this vision of man at home in the world is undermined by the Prophetic voice which proclaims it. He denounces his contemporaries who "no longer camp as for a night but have settled down on earth and forgotten heaven" by comparing them unfavorably to the primitive nomads who "dwelt . . . in a tent in this world" (p. 25), thus invoking one of the oldest of western topoi, the moral authority of the already atavistic Hebrew nomads, the Rechabites, relating the commandments of their father to the prophet Jeremiah: "Neither shall ye build house, nor sow seed, nor plant vineyard, nor have any: but all your days ye shall dwell in tents; that ye may live many days in the land where ye be strangers" (*Jeremiah* 35:7). The Rechabites were at home nowhere, not everywhere. Jeremiah cites them as exemplars not of a healthy rusticity but of a deep-seated and devout alienation which understands every experience except that of Yahweh as empty and meaningless.[17] Thus, to be, like Thoreau, a self-appointed stranger in the land is to repudiate the values of a domesticated pastoral by recognizing the need for a resting-place beyond culture and nature both, and to accept the figurative necessity of living always in one's tent is to recognize the impossibility of ever actually locating that resting-place.

Another way to deal with this search for authority is to imagine it emanating not only from a place but from a time. In *Walden*, the notion of foundation brings these two categories uneasily together. The solid bottom is a place where you might "found a wall or a state," but the foundation of a state is perhaps more appropriately conceived as a time— July 4, for example, the day Thoreau says he moved to the woods. This constitutes an appeal to the authority of precedent which would justify also the exemplary claims *Walden* makes on behalf of itself. The precedent has force as the record of a previous "experiment," and since "No way of thinking or doing, however ancient, can be trusted without proof" (p. 5), the "experiment" of *Walden* can apparently be understood as an attempt to repeat the results originally achieved by the Founding Fathers. But the scientific term "experiment," precisely because it relies on the notion of repeatability, that is, on an unchanging natural order, turns out to work much less well in the historical context of human events. "Here is life," Thoreau says, "an experiment to a great extent untried by me; but it does not avail me that they have tried it" (p. 5). This now is a peculiar kind of empiricism which stresses not only the primacy of experience but its unrepeatability, its uniqueness. (What good is *Walden* if not as a precedent?) The revolutionary appeal to foundation as a new beginning seems to be incompatible with the empiricist notion of foundation as the experience of an immediate but principled (i.e., repeatable) reality. The historical and the scientific ideas of foundation are clearly at odds here, and Thoreau seems to recognize this when he speaks of his desire "to anticipate not the sunrise and the dawn merely, but if possible Nature herself," that is, to achieve a priority which belongs to the historical but not the natural world. Coleridge had written some twenty years before that "No natural thing or act can be called an originate" since "the moment we assume an origin in nature, a true beginning, that moment we rise above nature."[18] Thoreau speaks of coming before rather than rising above, but the sense of incompatibility is the same. Once again the desire for the solid bottom is made clear, but the attempt to locate it or specify its characteristics involves the writer in a tangle of contradictions.

What I have tried to describe thus far is a series of relationships in the text of *Walden*—between nature and culture, the finite and the infinite, and (still to come) literal and figurative language—each of which is imagined at all times hierarchically, that is, the terms don't simply coexist, one is always thought of as more basic or more important than the other. The catch is that the hierarchies are always breaking down. Sometimes nature is the ground which authorizes culture, sometimes it is merely another of culture's creations. Sometimes the search for a hard bottom is presented as the central activity of a moral life, sometimes that same search will only make a Keystone-cop martyr out of the searcher. These unresolved contradictions are, I think, what makes us nervous reading *Walden*, and the urge to resolve them seems to me a major motivating factor in most *Walden* criticism. Early, more or less explicitly biographical criticism tended to understand the inconsistencies as personal ones, stemming, in Lowell's words, from Thoreau's "want of continuity of mind." But as the history of literary criticism began to deflect its attention from authors to texts, this type of explanation naturally began to seem unsatisfactory. Allusions to Thoreau's psychological instability were now replaced by references to *Walden*'s "literary design," and paradox, hitherto understood as a more or less technical device, was now seen to lie near the very center of *Walden*'s "literariness." In one essay, by Joseph Moldenhauer,[19] Thoreau's techniques are seen in easy analogy to those of Sir Thomas Browne, Donne, and the other English Metaphysicals, and generally the "presentation of truth through paradox" is identified as Thoreau's characteristic goal, although sometimes the truth is mythical, sometimes psychological, sometimes a little of both. In any event, the formalist demand that the text be understood as a unified whole (mechanical or organic) is normative; what Moldenhauer calls the "heightened language of paradox" is seen as shocking the reader into new perceptions of ancient truths.

More recently, the question of *Walden*'s hierarchies has been raised again by Stanley Cavell in a new and interesting way. Cavell recounts what he calls the "low myth of the reader" in *Walden*. "It may be thought of," he says, as a one-sentence fabliau:

> The writer has been describing the early spring days in which he went down to the woods to cut down timber for his intended house; he depicts himself carrying along his dinner of bread and butter wrapped in a newspaper which while he was resting he read. A little later, he says: "In those days when my hands were much employed, I read but little, but the least scraps of paper which lay on the ground . . . afforded me as much entertainment, in fact answered the same purpose as the *Iliad*."
>
> If you do not know what reading can be, you might as well use the pages of the *Iliad* for the purpose for which newspaper is used after a meal in the woods. If, however, you are prepared to read, then a fragment of newspaper, discovered words, are sufficient promptings . . . The events in a newspaper, our current lives are epic, and point morals, if we know how to interpret them.[20]

The moral of this interpretation, as I understand it, is that just as the hierarchical relation between nature and culture is uncertain and problematic, so there is no necessary hierarchy among texts — a Baltimore *Morning Sun* is as good as an *Iliad* if you know how to read it. But it is interesting that one of the passages Cavell elsewhere refers to (from *Walden*'s chapter on "Reading") is concerned precisely to specify a hierarchy of texts. "I kept Homer's *Iliad* on my table through the summer,"

Thoreau writes, "though I looked at his page only now and then. . . . Yet I sustained myself by the prospect of such reading in the future. I read one or two shallow books of travel in the intervals of my work, till that employment made me ashamed of myself, and I asked where it was then that *I* lived" (p. 67). The contrast here is between the epic and the travelogue, and for Thoreau the latter was a particularly vexing genre. "I would fain say something, not so much concerning the Chinese and Sandwich Islanders as you who read these pages, who are said to live in New England" (p. 2), he proclaims in *Walden*'s first chapter, and in its last chapter he renounces any "exploration" beyond one's "private sea, the Atlantic and Pacific Ocean of one's being alone" (p. 212). In his personal life, too, he shied away from voyages; until his last years, he never got any farther from Concord than Staten Island, and it took only several youthful weeks on that barbaric shore to send him scurrying for home. But he was at the same time inordinately fond of travel books; one scholar's account has him reading a certifiable minimum of 172 of them,[21] and as any reader of *Walden* knows, these accounts make frequent appearances there. In fact, in "Economy," no sooner has Thoreau announced his intention to ignore the lure of Oriental exoticisms than he plunges into a series of stories about the miraculous exploits of certain heroic "Bramins." *Walden* is, in fact, chock full of the wisdom of the mysterious East. The epics which Thoreau opposes to "shallow books of travel" are, in almost the same breath, described as "books which circulate around the world," that is, they are themselves travelling books.

All this serves mainly to reinforce Cavell's point; judging by subject matter at least, epics and travelogues turn out to look pretty much the same — the significant distinctions must then be not so much in the books themselves as in the way we read them. And along these lines, Thoreau suggests in "Reading" another, perhaps more pertinent way of distinguishing between the two genres: travel books are "shallow," epics presumably are not, which is to say that in reading epics, we must be prepared to conjecture "a larger sense than common use permits" (pp. 67–68). The mark of the epic is thus that it can be, indeed must be, read figuratively, whereas the travel book lends itself only to a shallow or literal reading. Thoreau goes on to imagine the contrast between classical literature and what he calls a "cheap, contemporary literature" (p. 68) as a contrast between the eloquence of the writer who "speaks to the intellect and heart of mankind, to all in any age who can *understand* him" and the lesser eloquence of the orator who "yields to the inspiration of a transient occasion, and speaks to the mob before him, to those who can *hear* him" (p. 69). Thus the opposition between the epic and travelogue has modulated into an opposition between the figurative and the literal and then between the written and the oral. In each case, the first term of the opposition is privileged, and if we turn again to the attempt to sound the depths of Walden Pond, we can see that these are all values of what I have called 'bottomlessness.' A shallow pond would be like a shallow book, that is, a travel book, one meant to be read literally. *Walden* is written "deep and pure for a symbol."

But this pattern of valorization, although convincing, is by no means ubiquitous or final. The chapter on "Reading" is followed by one called "Sounds," which systematically reconsiders the categories already introduced and which reasserts the values of the hard bottom. Here the written word is contrasted unfavorably with the magical "noise" of nature. The 'intimacy' and 'universality' for which Thoreau had praised it in the first chapter are now metamorphosed into 'confinement' and a new kind of 'provincialism.' But not only is the hierarchical relation between the written and the oral inverted, so is what we have seen to be the corresponding relation between the figurative and the literal. What in the chapter on "Reading" was seen to be the greatest virtue of the classic texts, their susceptibility to interpretation, to the conjecturing of a larger sense "too significant," Thoreau says, "to be heard by the ear," a sense which "we must be born again to speak" (p. 68), all this is set aside in favor of the "one articulation of Nature" (p. 83), the "language which all things and events speak without metaphor" (p. 75). In "Sounds," Nature's voice is known precisely because it resists interpretation. The polysemous becomes perverse; the models of communication are the Puri Indians who, having only one word for yesterday, today, and tomorrow, "express the variety of meaning by pointing backward for yesterday, forward for tomorrow, and overhead for the passing day" (p. 75). Where the classic texts were distinguished by their underdetermined quality — since the language they were written in was "dead," their "sense" was generated only by the reader's own interpretive "wisdom," "valor," and "generosity" — nature's language in "Sounds," the song of the birds, the stirring of the trees, is eminently alive and, as the example of the Indians shows, correspondingly overdetermined. Theirs is a system of words modified only by gestures and so devised that they will allow only a single meaning. No room is left for the reader's conjectures; the goal is rather a kind of indigenous and monosyllabic literalism, so many words for so many things by the shores of Gitcheegoomee. This means, of course, that the values of bottomlessness are all drained away. The deep is replaced by the shallow, the symbolic by the actual — what we need now, Thoreau says, are "tales of real life, high and low, and founded on fact" (p. 81).

This particular set of inversions helps us to relocate, I think, the problem of reading *Walden*, which we have already defined as the problem of resolving, or at least containing, its contradictions, of establishing a certain unity. Critics like Lowell domesticated the contradictions by understanding them as personal ones; to point out Thoreau's (no doubt lamentable) inconsistencies was not, after all, to accuse him of schizophrenia — the parts where he seemed to forget himself or ignore what he had said before were evidence only of certain lapses of attention. The formalists, turning their attention from the author to the text, transformed Thoreau's faults into *Walden*'s virtues; theirs was already the language of paradox, apparent inconsistencies pointing toward final literary (i.e., not necessarily logical) truths. Now Cavell takes this process of resolution, of replacement, as far, in one direction, as it can go; the unity which was claimed first for the personality of the author, then for the formal structure of the text itself, now devolves upon us the reader. *Walden*'s contradictions are resolved, he says, "if you know how to interpret them." The reader who knows how, it turns out, can discern in *Walden* "a revelation in which the paradoxes and ambiguities of its doctrine achieve a visionary union."[22] And more recent writers like Lawrence Buell have extended this principle to others among the Transcendentalists. "Emerson's contribution," Buell writes, "is to show through his paradoxical style the inoperability of doctrine, to force the auditor to read him figuratively, as he believes that scriptures should be read."[23]

But Cavell's position has its own peculiarity, for while it recognizes and even insists upon the difficulty of maintaining hierarchies in the text of *Walden*, it goes on simply to reinscribe those hierarchies in *Walden*'s readers. Knowing how to read for Cavell and for Buell is knowing how to read figuratively, and this is one of the things, Cavell says, that *Walden* teaches us. Thus the coherence that the formalists understood as the defining characteristic of the text becomes instead the defining characteristic of the reader, and the unity which was once claimed for the object itself is now claimed for the reader's experience of it. But, as we have just seen, the power of figurative reading is not the only thing *Walden* teaches us; it also urges upon us the necessity of reading literally, not so much in addition to reading figuratively as *instead of* reading figuratively. In the movement from "Reading" to "Sounds," the figurative and the literal do not coexist, they are not seen as complementary; rather the arguments Thoreau gives in support of the one take the form of attacks on the other. If, following Thoreau's guide, we conceive the literal as a meaning available to us without interpretation (i.e., the unmediated language of nature) and the figurative as a meaning generated by our own interpretive "wisdom," we find that the very act of reading commits us to a choice, not simply between different meanings, but between different stances toward reality, different versions of the self. Thus books must inevitably be "read as deliberately and reservedly as they were written" because to read *is* to deliberate, to consider and decide. "Our whole life is startlingly moral," Thoreau says, "There is never an instant's truce between virtue and vice" (p. 145). This is a call to action in the most direct sense, and the action it imagines is reading, conceived as an explicitly moral activity. Elsewhere he writes, "it appears as if men had deliberately chosen the common mode of living because they preferred it to others. Yet they honestly think there is no choice left" (p. 5). Thoreau's concern in *Walden* is, of course, to show us that we do have choices left and, by breaking down hierarchies into contradictory alternatives, to insist upon our making them. But this breakdown, which creates the opportunity, or rather the necessity for choosing, serves at the same time to undermine the rationale we might give for any particular choice. If there is no hierarchy of values, what authority can we appeal to in accounting for our decisions? What makes one choice better than another?

This is what the search for a solid bottom is all about, a location for authority, a ground upon which we can make a decision. *Walden* insists upon the necessity for such a search at the same time that it dramatizes the theoretical impossibility of succeeding in it. In this sense, the category of the bottomless is like the category of the natural, final but empty, and when Cavell urges upon us the desirability of a figurative reading, he is just removing the hard bottom from the text and relocating it in the reader. The concept remains equally problematic, our choices equally unmotivated. The result is what has been described in a different context, precisely and pejoratively, as "literary anarchy,"[24] a complaint which serves, like Emerson's attack of nerves, as a record of the response *Walden* seems to me to demand. In a political context, of course, the question of authority is an old one. Thoreau raises it himself in *Civil Disobedience*. "One would think," he writes, "that a deliberate and practical denial of its authority was the only offence never contemplated by a government" (p. 231). The form this denial takes in *Civil Disobedience* is "action from principle—the perception and the performance of right," but the perception of right is exactly what *Walden* makes most equivocal, and the possibility of action from principle is exactly what *Walden* denies, since the principles it identifies are always competing ones and hence inevitably inadequate as guidelines.

To be a citizen or to be a reader of *Walden* is to participate always in an act of foundation or interpretation which is inevitably arbitrary—there is as much to be said against it as there is for it. The role of the citizen / reader then, as Thoreau said in *Civil Disobedience*, is "essentially revolutionary," it "changes things and relations . . . and does not consist wholly with anything that was." But not only is it revolutionary, it is divisive: it "divides states and churches, it divides families," it even "divides the *individual*," that is, it divides the reader himself—he is repeatedly confronted with interpretive decisions which call into question both his notion of the coherence of the text and of himself. In *Civil Disobedience*, however, as in most of the explicitly political texts, Thoreau professes no difficulty in locating and identifying legitimate principles of action. It is only in *Walden* itself that the principle of uncertainty is built in. "Let us not play at kittlybenders," he wrote in *Walden*'s "Conclusion," "There is a solid bottom everywhere." Kittlybenders is a children's game; it involves running or skating on thin ice as quickly as you can so that you don't fall through. If the ice breaks, of course, you're liable to find the solid bottom and so, like the traveller in the story, "conclude your mortal career." The traveller is an image of the writer and, as we can now see, of the reader too. *Walden*, as it has been all along, is a book. To read it, as Thoreau suggested some hundred pages earlier, you "lie at your length on ice only an inch thick, like a skater insect on the surface of the water, and study the bottom at your leisure" (p. 163). But, he goes on to say, "the ice itself is the object of most interest." To read *Walden*, then, is precisely to play at kittlybenders, to run the simultaneous risks of touching and not touching bottom. If our reading claims to find a solid bottom, it can only do so according to principles which the text has both authorized and repudiated; thus we run the risk of drowning in our own certainties. If it doesn't, if we embrace the idea of bottomlessness and the interest of the ice itself, we've failed *Walden*'s first test, the acceptance of our moral responsibility as deliberate readers. It's heads I win, tails you lose. No wonder the game makes us nervous.

Notes

1. Quoted in H. S. Canby, *Thoreau* (Boston: Houghton Mifflin, 1939), p. 243.

2. Quoted in Charles R. Anderson, *The Magic Circle of Walden* (New York: Holt, Rinehart, and Winston, 1968), p. 55.

3. Anderson, *The Magic Circle of Walden*, p. 14.

4. F. O. Matthiessen, *American Renaissance* (New York: Oxford University Press, 1968), p. 172.

5. Anderson, *The Magic Circle of Walden*, p. 14.

6. This particular quotation is from Sherman Paul, *The Shores of America* (Urbana: University of Illinois Press, 1958, 1972), p. 293, but the sentiment is almost unanimous, and it is perhaps a little misleading to single out Paul, whose book is probably the single most important work of Thoreau scholarship and whose assumptions are in many ways different from those of Matthiessen, Moldenhauer, Broderick, Anderson, *et al.*

7. James Russell Lowell, "Thoreau," reprinted in *Walden and Civil Disobedience*, ed. Owen Thomas (New York: W. W. Norton, 1966), p. 4. All future references to *Walden* are to this edition and are included in parentheses in the text.

8. H. D. Thoreau, *Journal*, eds. Bradford Torrey and Francis H. Allen (New York: Dover, 1962), p. 127, entry 435.

9. Hannah Arendt, *Between Past and Future* (New York: Viking, 1961), p. 115.

10. H. D. Thoreau, "Slavery in Massachusetts," reprinted in *Thoreau: The Major Essays*, ed. with an introduction by Jeffrey L. Duncan (New York: E. P. Dutton, 1972), p. 144.

11. Ibid.

12. Melvin E. Lyon, "Walden Pond as Symbol," *PMLA* 82 (1967): 289.

13. Anderson, *The Magic Circle of Walden*, p. 19.

14. J. G. A. Pocock, *The Machiavellian Moment* (Princeton: Princeton University Press, 1975), p. 463.

15. Ibid., p. 464.

16. On this point, see Herbert N. Scheidau, *Sacred Discontent*, forthcoming from Louisiana State University Press.

17. Quoted in Geoffrey Hartman, *The Fate of Reading* (Chicago: University of Chicago Press, 1975), p. 259.

18. Joseph J. Moldenhauer, "Paradox in *Walden*," in *Twentieth Century Interpretations of Walden*, ed. with an introduction by Richard Rutland (Englewood Cliffs, N.J.: Prentice-Hall, 1968), p. 73–84.

19. Stanley Cavell, *The Senses of Walden* (New York: Viking, 1972), p. 67.

20. John Aldrich Christie, *Thoreau as World Traveller* (New York: Columbia University Press, 1965), p. 44.

21. Cavell, *The Senses of Walden*, p. 109.

22. Lawrence Buell, *Literary Transcendentalism* (Ithaca: Cornell University Press, 1973), pp. 118–19.

23. Charles Feidelson, Jr., *Symbolism and American Literature* (Chicago:University of Chicago Press, 1953, 1966), p. 149. Feidelson is actually discussing Emerson's own "literary doctrines."

The Psychological Rhetoric
of *Walden*
Richard H. Dillman*

I

Henry David Thoreau's rhetoric in *Walden* — his most rhetorically effective work — is more than the expression of his personality or the logical extension of his naturalist activities. It reflects the tradition of psychological rhetoric that began in 1776, with the birth of the nation, when George Campbell published his *Philosophy of Rhetoric*. When Thoreau encountered this tradition, it was influential in England, Scotland, and New England, partially supplanting the neo-classical rhetoric typified by John Ward's *System of Oratory*, a five-canon classical rhetoric, and Hugh Blair's *Lectures on Rhetoric and Belles Lettres*, which was still tied to concepts of ornament, symmetrical discourse, and the periodic sentence form.

Derived in part from classical rhetoric, psychological rhetoric was founded on the eighteenth-century "science of human nature." Its practitioners attempted to analyze an audience's reactions to discourse strategies by applying a theory of mental psychology derived from David Hume's notion of the lively idea[1] and from the philosophy generated by the Aberdeen Philosophical Society, led by the associationist philosophers Thomas Reid and Dugald Stewart. Psychological rhetoric represented an important shift in the direction of rhetorical theory. It was, in effect, a

*Reprinted from *ESQ: A Journal of the American Renaissance* 25 (2d Quarter 1979):79–91, by permission of the author.

"new rhetoric" based on the most current theories of psychology and communication. It codified many practices of the seventeenth-century Anti-Ciceronians, including Bacon and Raleigh, and, most importantly, it presented an "organic" analysis of style that undercut the Ciceronian notion of style as ornament—the idea that thoughts can be dressed in a variety of outfits depending on the occasion—and suggested that the subject matter should govern the manner of expression.

This "new rhetoric" first appeared at Harvard University in 1832, two years before Thoreau entered the university and eleven years after Emerson graduated, when Edward Tyrell Channing, the Boylston Professor of Rhetoric and Oratory, adopted Richard Whately's *Elements of Rhetoric* (1828) as the sole rhetoric text. In 1837, he added Campbell's *Philosophy of Rhetoric*. These two books presented the theory of psychological rhetoric in its philosophical and practical forms—Campbell's, an exploration of the psychological basis of perception and persuasion, laying the theoretical basis, and Whately's, which often paraphrased Campbell, developing its practical applications.[2]

Psychological rhetoric was also supplemented at Harvard by Dugald Stewart's *Elements of the Philosophy of the Human Mind*, a treatise that Thoreau studied in his junior year (1835–36) in Francis Bowen's course in Intellectual Philosophy.[3] Although presented as philosophy, Stewart's discussions of wit, principles of association, lively ideas, and the advantages of sensual diction all can be found in Campbell's *Philosophy*.[4]

Channing taught the elements of this tradition, both written and oral, in Thoreau's sophomore, junior, and senior years (1834–37). Channing's lectures, articles, notes, and reports to the Harvard administration all reveal a preference for psychological rhetoric,[5] and his *Lectures Read to the Seniors in Harvard College* lean heavily on Campbell's philosophy and Whately's practical analysis. The required text for Thoreau's sophomore rhetoric course was Whately's *Elements of Rhetoric*, which Emerson later examined him on.[6] Both Thoreau and Emerson owned Whately's text as well as Stewart's *Elements of the Philosophy of the Human Mind*.[7] Although Emerson's rhetorical training at Harvard was based on Blair's *Lectures on Rhetoric and Belles Lettres*, it is reasonable to conclude that he discussed psychological rhetoric with Thoreau during the years of their close association.

Thus Thoreau could scarcely avoid the influence of psychological rhetoric. As R. W. B. Lewis rightly points out, Channing introduced Thoreau to a rhetoric that was well suited to the intellectual climate of his day.[8] Instead of emphasizing the old style training in sermon form and political discourse that was common, for example, when John Quincy Adams held the Boylston Professorship (1806–09),[9] Channing applied Campbell and Whately to any mode of discourse in order to extend the scope of rhetoric to "all communication by language," claiming that "the written book, the novel, the history, the fable, and the acted play" all use similar principles of persuasion.[10]

Channing's rhetoric course, then, was based on the belief that rhetoric includes all skills fundamental to communication. When he assumed the Boylston Professorship, he integrated the study of grammar and logic into the rhetoric course, thus emphasizing the trivium at a time when the classroom study of literature was increasing in popularity. At times, for example, he supplemented his rhetoric texts with Whately's *Elements of Logic*.[11] Channing was also a rigorous critic of themes. In conference with individual students, he was often severe, sometimes sarcastic, occasionally encouraging.[12] The surviving record of his theme assignments indicates that he required his students to write most often in the persuasive and expository modes of discourse, and that he preferred topics that required students to write on problems connected with their personal or political lives. At times, intending to enlarge his students' understanding of psychological rhetoric, he assigned such topics as "Discuss Campbell's view of good usage in literature" and "Select passages from orations illustrating Whately on persuasion."[13]

The development of this "new rhetoric" coincided with the growth of the Romantic movement. Some of its characteristics — flexible approaches to form, the absence of rigidly prescribed rules, the rejection of artificial ornament, and an emphasis on clear language grounded as much as possible on sensory phenomena — parallel the Romantic reaction against artistic rigidity and prescribed form. Psychological rhetoric represented a new direction in the movement of American rhetorical theory, just as Transcendentalism signaled a new direction in American philosophy and literature.

To understand fully the rhetorical strategies that Thoreau skillfully used in *Walden*, one must examine the theory articulated by Campbell and extended by Whately. Although I do not agree with Lawrence Buell's view that *Walden*, originally presented in part as a lecture, is strongly indebted to the sermon form and the Unitarian preaching tradition,[14] he correctly seeks the roots of Thoreau's rhetoric in religious discourse. Whately's rhetoric was designed for theological disputation to help the Christian apologist defend his position against an increasingly skeptical world. It offered tools of argument and persuasion suited to defending *a priori* "truth" and producing lively descriptive writing. It was a rhetoric useful for defending a metaphysical view of life to non-believers instead of one designed to present "received truth" to the faithful. It had little to do with the discovery of truth but instead offered strategies through which a skeptical audience could be persuaded to believe, or at least to consider, pre-conceived "truth." Thoreau used these strategies to present his unconventional views and unusual metaphysics. In *Walden*, Thoreau probably used psychological rhetoric more singularly than Whately, Campbell, or

Channing ever anticipated, applying their principles to his own specific rhetorical situation in which he strove to persuade an unsympathetic, if not hostile, audience to re-evaluate its culture and life.

II

The argumentative strategies of psychological rhetoric are reflected in *Walden*, particularly in the first two chapters, "Economy" and "Where I Lived and What I Lived For." Richard Whately, for instance, recommended using paradox — one of Thoreau's major devices — and analyzed its operation. He defined an argumentative paradox as an idea contrary to received opinion that could shock an audience, and he suggested that such paradoxes be used to introduce arguments. They would, he reasoned, encourage speakers to concentrate on the improbability of the unconventional notions.[15] Thoreau often used such paradoxes as shock tactics to provoke and prod his conventional Yankee audience.[16] His retreat to the pond is paradoxical in this sense, as are his assertions in "Economy" that his fellow citizens were "doing penance in a thousand remarkable ways" and that his townsmen had the misfortune of inheriting "farms, houses, cattle, and farming tools."[17]

Most of Thoreau's paradoxes are also stylistic, seemingly self-contradictory statements, yet containing a basis of truth that reconciles apparent contradictions. Commenting on this kind of paradox in the *Philosophy of Rhetoric*, George Campbell explained that paradox, as a form of wit, agreeably surprised an audience because it juxtaposed ideas in unusual ways, presented an uncommon point of view, and required hearers to reconcile contradictions and find similarities in apparently heterogeneous ideas.[18] Dugald Stewart echoed Campbell's notion of paradox in his *Elements of the Philosophy of the Human Mind*, observing that "contrariety" is one of the most important principles of association and an aid to effective communication. He reasoned that a speaker's fine control over the association of contradictory ideas could both surprise and entertain an audience. Thoreau's paradoxes, like the following, are intended to disrupt conventional thinking: "The better part of the man is soon ploughed into the soil for compost" (p. 5); "But lo! men have become the tools of their tools" (p. 37); or "I have learned that the swiftest traveler is he that goes afoot" (p. 53), and "When a man dies he kicks the dust!" (p. 68). They are, in effect, dissociative, dividing the reader's usual thought patterns in unanticipated ways.

Thoreau also followed Whately's analysis of ethical appeal in developing the persona of *Walden*. Whately explained that a successful ethical appeal depended on the projection of a character of good sense, good principle, and good will in terms of the audience's concerns and values. The speaker had to convince his listeners that he thinks, at least in some ways, as they do (p. 207). In order to change an audience's opinions, a speaker had to, in Kenneth Burke's terms, "yield to that audience's opinion" in some respects.[19] This notion of ethical appeal, derived from Aristotle, depended on the speaker's analysis of the psychology of his audience — of its attitudes, concerns, and thought patterns. Similarly, Thoreau works to convince his audience that he thought as they did in some ways. He carefully presents himself as a man of good will, first by assuring his readers that he intends to help them improve their lot (p. 16), and second "by appearing to be of the same party." He also disavows any radical designs for overthrowing the status quo, admitting that he is "not interested in the success or failure of the present economical and social arrangements" (p. 56). Carefully projecting himself as a man with a sense of humor, he pokes fun at his own reputation for eccentricity, as when he claims he was "self-appointed inspector of snow storms and rain storms" (p. 18) and when he admits that he "dearly" loves to talk (p. 82). In describing his view of agriculture, he also refers to his reputation as an eccentric; "for I was not anchored to a house or farm, but could follow the bent of my genius, which is a very crooked one, every moment" (p. 56).

Thoreau also meticulously presents himself as a man of good principle as described by Whately, who felt that a speaker should act as an advocate for his principles (p. 218). As Channing expressed it, a speaker had to convince his audience that his "life is steadily influenced by the sentiments he is trying to impress on them, — that he is willing to abide by principle at any hazard, and give his opinions and professions the full authority of his actions."[20] By supporting his arguments with factually-based details, Thoreau convincingly establishes his integrity. He advocates self-reliance and then describes how he built his house and grew his own food (pp. 40–58, 161–164); and he advocates heightened sensitivity to nature's unity and then presents his own search for it. He also quotes and paraphrases the Bible to illustrate his familiarity with it and to help identify his persona with some of the religious values held by his conventional audience (p. 32).

Thoreau's projection of his persona as a man of good sense is more complex. Whately equated good sense with a speaker's intellectual qualifications, specifically discussing audience in terms of political economy — one of Thoreau's main concerns. He explained that a speaker could legitimately appeal to "the experience of practical men" instead of to the opinions of theorists (pp. 162–163). Although Thoreau went beyond political economy to spiritual economy, he used imagery and language that his frugal Yankee audience would appreciate. He adopted the stance of a shrewd Yankee, a man of practical business sense, in order to persuade his readers to accept his ideas and vicariously participate in his experience. At the same time, his persona ironically parodies his neighbors in that Thoreau sought a non-material, spiritual profit. His calculation of income and expenses in balance-sheet form (pp. 59–60) suggests an accountant's scrupulous attention to detail, and his vocabulary of commerce projects the image of a shrewd capitalist—a self-reliant, many-talented business man who was captain, owner, underwriter, accountant, and superintendent of his Walden venture. Thoreau, at any rate, saw Walden Pond as a "good place for business" (p. 21).

Thoreau uses three modes of argument derived from Whately's theory: analogy, identification of inconsistencies, and indirect persuasion. In applying the concept of burden of proof to argument, Whately reasoned that the "pre-occupation of the ground" (p. 74) was held by defenders of existing institutions. The burden of proof lay with anyone arguing against the prevailing opinion. In attacking existing institutions, Thoreau assumes this burden and an aggressive rhetorical stance.

According to Whately, an analogy is a "resemblance of ratios," in which the parts stand in similar relations to something else, yet are dissimilar to each other (p. 56). They are useful as illustrations for supporting propositions and are based on the associative principle of resemblance, discussed by Campbell, that helps the mind link ideas easily. Thoreau, who as Channing's student analyzed Whately's concept of analogy, and who later declared in his *Journal* that "all perception of truth is the detection of an analogy,"[21] used many analogies in the first two argumentative chapters of *Walden*. In "Economy," he requires readers to follow his reasoning process and identify patterns of resemblance. To illustrate the frenzied activity of his peers, for example, he compares their doings to the torture of the Brahmins; and the Brahmins' prodigious efforts to meet their religious requirements resemble the crazed scramble of Thoreau's fellow citizens to meet their social and economic goals. Also based on analogy is his depiction of the Walden experiment as a business venture in which his persona stands in the same relationship to his enterprise—as owner, underwriter, and balance-sheet accountant—as a business manager bears to his business. Comparisons in the remaining chapters are usually metaphorical, often presenting Thoreau's narrative perspective.

Although Whately accepted some forms of inconsistency, such as accommodating one's opinion to changing circumstances, he felt that the charge of inconsistency was the most powerful method of refuting an opponent. Thoreau often makes this charge in the first two chapters of *Walden*, even setting up vaguely delineated straw men whose inconsistencies he can expose. Early in "Economy," he observes that his audience is concerned with Negro slavery yet ignores the subtle slavery to their economic customs: "It is hard to have a southern overseer; it is worse to have a northern one" (p. 7). He points out the farmer who criticizes Thoreau's vegetarian diet yet walks all day behind his oxen with their vegetable-made bones (p. 90), and those who feed their animals with grain grown on their farms, only to buy flour at greater cost (p. 63). He also finds inconsistencies in his contemporaries' partial attempts at reform. Philanthropists, for example, a group that Thoreau intensely disliked, help the poor with external and material aid yet ignore problems of character and spirit (p. 74), and New Englanders care more about the decoration of their houses than the quality of their lives (p. 38). Thoreau portrays his contemporaries as viewing reality in a fragmented, divided way, unable to see the transcendental unity that he would have them see.

Finally, Thoreau's argumentative technique reflects Whately's theory of indirect persuasion, a combination of argument and exhortation, in a variation of the traditional view of exhortation. Whately advised a speaker to avoid direct exhortation as too obvious to be effective, and instead to present material so as to hold his audience's attention. An author must copiously amplify his views to give his readers time to form "vivid and distinct ideas" (p. 134). Wherever possible, he should present a lively series of images and ideas that would require readers to meditate on the subject (p. 124). In about one quarter of the paragraphs in *Walden's* first two chapters, Thoreau employs this pattern of persuasion, often following sections of propositional argument with longer sections of expanded illustration embodying the essence of prior argument. For example, to support his contention that his peers are their own slave drivers, Thoreau urges his readers to "Look at the teamster on the highway, wending to market, by day or night; does any divinity stir within him? His highest duty to fodder and water his horses! What is his destiny to him compared with the shipping interests? Does not he drive for Squire Make-a-stir? How godlike, how immortal, is he? See how he cowers and sneaks, how vaguely all the day he fears, not being immortal nor divine, but the slave and prisoner of his own opinion of himself, a fame won by his own deeds" (p. 7). While each detail illustrates the teamster's dehumanizing activities, the series of questions facilitates the reader's participation and requires tacit response. The full potential of indirect persuasion is evident in Thoreau's description of the Brahmins:

> What I have heard of Brahmins sitting exposed to four fires and looking in the face of the sun; or hanging suspended, with their heads downward, over flames; or looking at the heavens over their shoulders "until it becomes impossible for them to resume their natural position, while from the twist of the neck nothing but liquids can pass into the stomach;" or dwelling, chained for life, at the foot of a tree; or measuring with their bodies, like caterpillars, the breadth of vast empires; or standing on one leg on the tops of pillars, — even these forms of conscious penance are hardly more incredible and astonishing than the scenes which I daily witness. (pp. 4–5)

The concrete examples detain the reader, forcing him to consider Thoreau's viewpoint, and the pattern of loosely connected phrases and clauses modifying the main clause retards the pace of the prose, so that the reader can consider separately each unit of amplification.

III

The design of Thoreau's sentences also reflects psychological rhetoric. Thoreau used three patterns of sentence organization which the psychological rhetoricians analyzed and recommended — terse, aphoristic sentences; cumulative ones; and rhetorical questions. Campbell and Whately favored brief, compact sentences that expressed ideas forcefully, comparing their effect to the intensification of light rays filtered through a magnifying glass: "the narrower the compass of words is, wherein the thought is comprised," they claimed, "the more energetic is the expression" (Whately, p. 210; Campbell, pp. 333–334). In addition, both restricted the use of terse sentences to argumentative and persuasive discourse, holding that brevity is better suited to writing than to oratory and inappropriate to descriptive and pathetic writing. Whately also advocated a style that suggests much without details. A concise statement or proverb, he explained, which often saves a long explanation, will imply more than is said and will "serve the purpose of a mathematical diagram, which though itself an individual, serves as a representative of a class" (p. 222). In his *Journal* of 1851, Thoreau also calls for "a suggestive style" that relies on sentences "which suggest as many things and are as durable as Roman aqueducts," and he extolled sentences that were "concentrated and nutty" (II, 418), claiming that natural forms are untranslatable aphorisms (I, 380): "A well-built sentence, in the rapidity and force with which it works, may be compared to a modern corn-planter, which furrows out, drops the seed, and covers it up with one movement" (I, 219). Most of his compressed sentences are aphorisms that either sum up arguments or are themselves arguments. Usually placed strategically, they are intended to carry forcefully Thoreau's unconventional views. Most, like the following, are quotable, the type of sentence Thoreau claimed would stick in his "crop" (II, 54): "The mass of men lead lives of quiet desperation" (p. 8); "To be awake is to be alive" (p. 90); and "The day is an epitome of the year" (p. 301). He used aphoristic sentences most commonly in argumentative chapters like "Economy" and "Where I Lived and What I Lived For" and in philosophical chapters like "Reading," "Solitude," and "Higher Laws," where they often embody the core of his thinking.

Thoreau also used proverbs often in *Walden*, a device Whately likened to ready-made medicinal formulas, that serve "as equipment for living."[22] Thoreau strategically employed them, sometimes in altered form, to address members of a proverb-oriented society with a traditional mode of expression, thus helping ingratiate himself with his audience. Typical examples are "A living dog is better than a dead lion" (pp. 325–26) and "Men say that a stitch in time saves nine, and so they take a thousand stitches to-day to save nine to-morrow" (p. 93). In "Sounds," for instance, Thoreau varied Franklin's "Early to bed . . ."[23] when he asked "Who would not be early to rise, and rise earlier and earlier every successive day of his life, till he became unspeakably healthy, wealthy, and wise?" (p. 127). As Kenneth Lynn points out, Thoreau ironically undercut his audience with its own weapon.[24] Such proverbs indeed serve as medicine, as prescriptions intended to cure Thoreau's audience of the "disease of materialism."

Thoreau's use of cumulative sentences also reflects Whately's advice about expanding basic ideas. Whately recommended repetition as an aid to perspicuity, advising writers to repeat ideas in different forms, allowing variations to expand the sense and retain the reader's attention (p. 171). What has been expressed literally, he claimed, may be repeated in metaphorical terms; the antecedent and consequent of the parts of a contrast may be transposed, or several different points may be presented in varied order (p. 172). "Often repeated blows" (p. 211) would enhance the energy of a sentence. Basing his notion of sentence modifiers on the process of casual speaking, Whately explained that speakers vary their mode of expression until their listeners fully comprehend the meaning (p. 223). An author's most important idea will naturally be expressed first, and the parts of an effective sentence will be discrete and thus easily comprehended. In describing Walden Pond, Thoreau typically used cumulative sentences like this that reflect Whately's ideas on amplifying basic ideas: "We must be refreshed by the sight of inexhaustible vigor, vast and Titanic features, the sea-coast with its wrecks, the wilderness with its living and its decaying trees, the thunder cloud, and the rain which lasts weeks and produces freshets" (p. 318). The additions amplify the notion of "inexhaustible vigor" on different levels of generality, and Thoreau seems to follow Whately's advice to repeat ideas in diverse form because each detail is a concrete variation of the central idea.

This informal pattern, which creates the impression of artlessness, of thinking while writing or speaking, is well-suited to the colloquial tone of *Walden*. It suggests a lack of pretense, "an unstudied air" (p. 236), an organic approach to style, and ultimately a rejection of artificial ornament common in the well-formed periodic sentence that Thoreau disliked (*Journal*, I, 313). Thoreau uses cumulative sentences most often in descriptive and narrative chapters like "The Pond in Winter," "Winter Animals," "Former Inhabitants and Winter Visitors," and infrequently in argumentative and philosophical chapters. In most of these sentences, which run from thirty to fifty words, a main clause contains the central thought, with additions and sensuous detail probing and amplifying its implications. A typical cumulative sentence describes the fish in Walden Pond: "Paddling gently to one of these places, I was surprised to find myself surrounded by myriads of small perch, about five inches long, of a rich bronze color in the green water, sporting there and constantly rising to the surface and dimpling it, sometimes leaving bubbles on it" (p. 189). The additions expand the sense, making the idea of the main clause more concrete and vivid.

Thoreau often uses rhetorical questions, a third pattern that Whately recommended. Rhetorical questions, Whately believed, forcibly call the audience's attention to major points and make a personal appeal to each reader either to assent to the proposition advocated or to supply a reasonable objection. Such questions also apply persuasive pressure on an audience and carry an "air of triumphant defiance of an opponent to refute the argument if he can" (p. 242). Thoreau uses rhetorical questions most commonly in "Economy," "Reading," and "Conclusion," all persuasive chapters, and often, though with less intensity, in "The Bean-Field" and "Solitude." They rarely occur in his most descriptive chapters in which he attempts to involve his readers in the Walden experience rather than to persuade them directly to accept his unconventional views. Thoreau evidently found the rhetorical question less suited to his descriptive objectives than to emphasizing important facets of his philosophy and challenging his readers. The following passage from "Economy" illustrates the persuasive pressure he often placed on his readers: "The success of great scholars and thinkers is commonly a courtier-like success, not kingly, not manly. They make shift to live merely by conformity, practically as their fathers did, and are in no sense the progenitors of a nobler race of men. But why do men degenerate ever? What makes families run out? What is the nature of the luxury which enervates and destroys nations? Are we sure that there is none of it in our own lives? The philosopher is in advance of his age even in the outward form of his life" (p. 15). Five questions prod the reader to respond and thereby participate in the argument. His first three questions each include an implicit suppressed idea that Thoreau tries to slip by his readers. To answer them, the reader must accept the hidden premises that men continually degenerate, families run out, and luxury enervates and destroys nations. The final question also contains an implicit conclusion — philosophers can maintain their vital heat by better methods than can other men. Thoreau, reflecting Whately's advice, embedded some of the premises and even the conclusions of his argument in rhetorical questions.

IV

The sensory quality of Thoreau's prose in *Walden* also reflects the language theory of psychological rhetoric. George Campbell developed a theory of word choice and figurative language that was transmitted to Thoreau through the Harvard rhetoric program and Whately's text. Based on Campbell's notion of vivacious language, this theory stresses three types of mental perceptions — sensations, ideas of memory, and ideas of imagination — with the mind differentiating between them according to their relative degrees of vivacity. Sensations are accompanied by high degrees of vivacity; ideas of imagination by the least degrees. And vivacity attracts attention, arouses emotions, and is largely responsible for belief because sensations possessing high levels of vivacity command assent (Campbell, pp. 73–74, 81). A skilled writer can make abstractions lively and compelling by developing them with sensory details and thus infusing them with the power of sense impressions. Energy, furthermore, can be transferred from lively ideas of sense to languid ideas of memory. Essentially, Campbell's advice for using lively language can be reduced to four maxims later adopted by Whately: (1) use the less for the more general; (2) stress the most interesting circumstances of a subject; (3) use sensory details for intellectual ideas; and (4) use things animate for things lifeless (Campbell, pp. 299–310).

Like the psychological rhetoricians, Thoreau favors concrete language, as comments in his *Journal* reveal. He avoids "wooden or lifeless words, such words as 'humanitary,' which have a paralysis in their tails" (X, 225). A writer is blessed, he says, "who has most use of nature as raw material for tropes and symbols with which to describe his life" (V, 136). In another *Journal* entry, he claims that the "roots of letters [words] are things. Natural objects and phenomena are the original symbols or types, which express our thoughts and feelings, yet American scholars, having little or no root in the soil, commonly strive with all their might to confine themselves to the imported symbol alone" (XII, 389).

To create a graphic sense of his life at the pond, Thoreau uses sensory, concrete language throughout *Walden*, especially in the descriptive and narrative chapters and, to a lesser degree, in the argumentative and philosophical ones like "Higher Laws" and "Reading." In the narrative and descriptive chapters, like "Sounds," "Visitors," "The Village," and "The Ponds," Thoreau poetically and imagistically re-creates the Walden scene, providing rich sensory description that serves a rhetorical purpose. His concrete details help his readers vicariously enter his experiment to see and hear Walden as he did.

On the surface, Thoreau's use of sensory details may appear to reflect John Locke's theory of persuasion, as Joel Porte has argued, claiming that "the other transcendentalists were unknowingly harboring a Lockean in their midst."[25] But Thoreau's practice is probably more complex, incorporating ideas of Campbell, Whately, and even Hume. In his rhetoric, in fact, Thoreau often begins sequences with general ideas, then supports and amplifies them with sensory details. But a Lockean theory of perception requires the opposite intellectual movement, with sense data imprinted on the mind before ideas are formulated. In his cumulative sentences and larger units of discourse that illustrate Whately's theory of indirect persuasion, Thoreau begins with preconceived ideas, usually supporting *a priori* ideas with examples and thus following a deductive movement. Although Thoreau derives some of his ideas empirically, he often presents them deductively.

George Campbell based his theory of language choice upon the notion of the lively idea, which he developed most fully in his analysis of figurative language. This theory was transmitted through Whately and Channing to Thoreau and appears most frequently in his use of three figures—metaphor, personification, and synecdoche. Campbell's theory of figurative language goes beyond the classical view held by Channing's predecessors in the Boylston Professorship. For instance, John Quincy Adams, who held the Rhetoric Chair from 1806 to 1809, limited the use of figurative language to making communication clear and distinct and presented figures as little more than tropes using words in senses different from their original meanings.[26] Campbell, in contrast, developed a psychological theory of figures based on his concept of mental psychology. A writer should use sensory-based vehicles precisely because they are an effective means of persuasion. Campbell believed that, because discourse deals almost exclusively with ideas of imagination, one of the best ways to enhance them is to tie them to the natural world through sensory details. Accordingly, he emphasized sensation as a result of his understanding of the elements of perception, while Adams, in his *Lectures on Rhetoric and Oratory*, was unconcerned with the psychology of comprehending figures or with the sensory basis of figurative language.[27]

Whately, who believed that metaphor was grounded in the associative principle of resemblance, required that "vivacious" metaphors employ "sensible objects" to illustrate abstractions. Essentially, Campbell's and Whately's notion of metaphor depended on two factors: the expression of an abstraction by a sensory object and the principle of resemblance. The second principle, also central to Aristotle's *Rhetoric*,[28] is one of Campbell's principles of association, along with contiguity and causation. Resemblance in metaphors—the identification of similarities between items being compared—acts as a bridge between ideas, a transmitter of vivacity from the livelier sensory vehicle to the more languid ideas of imagination or memory embodied in the tenor. The resemblance should rarely, Whately explained, be stated explicitly because readers are often gratified by catching the similarities and thus using their associative ability (p. 191). According to this theory, metaphors grounded in sensory detail derive their persuasive power from attention-getting sensory vehicles. Adams' theory, in contrast, ignored sensation and was based on five simple principles: (1) the figurative and literal objects should resemble each other; (2) metaphors should be briefly emphasized; (3) they should not be drawn from "mean or disgusting subjects"; (4) they should not be crowded together; and (5) they should be chosen for their appropriateness to either oratory or poetry.[29]

Thoreau often uses sensory metaphors in *Walden* to carry his themes and involve his readers in his poetic world. Emerson recognized this tendency in describing the "cardinal fact" about Thoreau as the way he could regard "the material world as a means and a symbol."[30] Thoreau used concrete, familiar objects as the vehicles for most of his metaphors. In one of his most poetic images, for example, he compared time to a clear stream: "Time is but the stream I go a-fishing in. I drink at it; but while I drink I see the sandy bottom and detect how shallow it is. Its thin current slides away, but eternity remains" (p. 98). His metaphors often embody his arguments and carry his themes. For instance, in "The Ponds," Thoreau explores the meaning of Walden Pond in sensory, metaphorical terms, calling it the "earth's eye" looking into which the beholder measures "the depth of his own nature" (p. 186) and, later, describing the pond as "a perfect forest mirror" (p. 188). In an extended personification in "Spring," Thoreau expresses the theme of renewal by comparing the thawing pond to a waking man (p. 301), and in "Conclusion" the artist of Kouroo becomes a metaphor for the spirit of craftsmanship in life and work, presenting an antidote to alienation and a model for full involvement in life (p. 327). Thoreau's metaphors help define his abstractions, particularly his themes, and they amplify his less accessible ideas.

Synecdoche, the second major figure for Campbell and Whately, is also an important rhetorical device in *Walden*. Campbell claimed that synecdoche contributed to vivacity and depended on distinguishing "the most interesting circumstance of a situation" (p. 301). For the psychological rhetoricians, in synecdoche "a part is made to represent the whole, the abstract to suggest the concrete" (Campbell, p. 301). Whately explained that synecdoche—a vehicle for using specific terms—adds to the energy of the expression without risking misinterpretation. In a more recent analysis, Kenneth Burke argues that synecdoche is the most basic figure; the "noblest synecdoche, the prototype for all lesser usages, is found in metaphysical doctrines proclaiming the identity of 'microcosm' and 'macrocosm.' In such doctrines, where the individual is treated as a replica of the universe, and vice versa, we have the ideal synecdoche, since microcosm is related to macrocosm as part to whole, and either the whole can represent the part or the part can represent the whole."[31]

Thoreau frequently uses the microcosm-macrocosm relationship in *Walden* to develop important themes in his descriptive chapters. Powerful sequences in "The Ponds," "The Pond in Winter," "Spring," and "Conclusion" are built around this trope, which again requires the reader to use the associative principle of resemblance. Thoreau expected his readers to move inductively from the concrete to the general by following the development of extended synecdoches. His concrete vehicles—microcosms—of his synecdoche usually represent larger concepts and are often richly sensuous, graphic images. In "Solitude," Walden is portrayed as Thoreau's "little world" all to himself (p. 130), and the self is presented as a microcosm of the cosmos (p. 322). The cycle of the seasons, which governs the structure of *Walden*, represents the larger rhythms of the universe, and the concrete movement of the seasons through the year comes to represent the movement of all life: growth, fruition, old-age, and, if possible, resurrection. The cycle of the day, in turn, is a synecdoche for that of the year: "The phenomena of the year take place every day in a pond on a small scale" (p. 311). The narrative progression thus follows a synecdoche pattern that moves Thoreau's audience beyond themselves to larger, sometimes more spiritual themes.

Walden Pond, as well, is presented as a microcosm in "The Ponds." It is "a type of the purest waters"; it is " 'God's Drop' " (p. 194), and it can be synecdochically reduced to a small portion in Thoreau's hand that suggests the larger pond and the principles of nature (p. 193). The fisherman's pail, which one looks into "as into a summer pond," embodies the macrocosm of Walden, which, in progression, embodies the principles of nature (pp. 283–284). The Walden pickerel, moreover, are "small Waldens in the animal kingdom, Waldenses" (p. 284).

The two most extensive synecdoche passages are the battle of the ants and the melting of the sandbank. The first is a microcosm for human war, perhaps even for economic competition — ideas intensified when Thoreau places a few combatants under a magnifying glass (pp. 230–231). Again in his description of the melting sandbank, he suggests cosmic themes. A mass of muddy sand, resembling foliage, oozes excrementally from the sandbank until it resembles a vegetable leaf, with its network of veins and lobes — "the fingers of the leaf" — that flow in many directions (p. 308). The patterns of the melting sandbank represents "the principle of all the operations of Nature" (p. 308). The growth of the leaf, following the expanding network of veins, becomes the synecdoche for all organic growth. This passage, which embodies the important theme of renewal, is exhortative, urging readers to emerge from the spiritual "winter" and renew themselves because they, like the sandbank or leaf, also embody organic principles.

The psychological rhetoricians' theory of concrete and figurative language seems ideally suited to Thoreau's persuasive objectives in *Walden*. The sensory metaphors, synecdoches, and images help draw readers into his imaginative world until they see it from the narrator's perspective. This same language theory is also well suited to the Transcendentalist theory of language as Emerson expressed it in "Nature" (1836), his earliest influential essay. Maintaining that "Nature is the vehicle of thought," Emerson listed three principles of language:

1. Words are signs of natural facts.
2. Particular natural facts are symbols of particular spiritual facts.
3. Nature is the symbol of spirit.[32]

Thoreau's synecdochic patterning produces vivacious writing and also provides a rhetorical vehicle for this notion of correspondence. The microcosms of the Walden pickerel, the battle of the ants, and the melting sandbank all represent spiritual facts, and *spiritual*, as the Transcendentalists used it in this context, may be roughly translated as universal or cosmic. "Spiritual facts" are always larger and more abstract than "natural facts."

Campbell's and Whately's theory of lively synecdoche and metaphor provides a rhetoric that is well suited to the philosophy of correspondence. Their theory of sensory and concrete language is appropriate, as well, to Thoreau's emphasis on nature. Thoreau created "lively ideas" from sensory ideas, which he, in turn, derived from the natural world. "Vivacity" derives in part from the living quality of objects, and nature imagery is a requisite for creating a vivacious style—a major emphasis of psychological rhetoric.

Psychological rhetoric, in general, was suited to the conditions of American writers, faced with new materials to be shaped on their own terms, because it offered effective rhetorical strategies in a non-prescriptive way and stood against rigid laws of discourse, artificial form, and pretense. It offered Thoreau, a rebel against artificial living and art who claimed that rhetorical ornament distracts the mind,[33] a rhetoric amenable to his needs grounded in a theory of human nature and individual perception. Its tenet that subject matter should govern form parallels his belief that matter should govern the manner of expression. Psychological rhetoric, moreover, offered Thoreau strategies well-suited to expressing the new Transcendental philosophy and to describing the American natural environment in sensory terms. Associative techniques, such as analogy and sensory-based metaphors and synecdoches, help Thoreau's audience view nature in Transcendental terms by presenting nature's underlying unity— the deeper layer of coherence. The rhetoric of *Walden* reflects the operation of many of these strategies, illustrating their potential effectiveness. In *Walden*, the major strategies of psychological rhetoric depart from the vacuum of theory and move to a shifting, dynamic rhetorical situation.

Notes

1. Lloyd Bitzer, "Hume's Philosophy in George Campbell's *Philosophy of Rhetoric,*" *Philosophy and Rhetoric*, 2 (1969), 141.

2. *Seventh Annual Report of the President of Harvard University to the Overseers of the State of the Institution for the Academical Year 1831-32* (Cambridge: E. W. Metcalf, 1933), pp. vi-vii. Also see Dorothy Anderson, "Channing's Definition of Rhetoric," *Speech Monographs*, 14 (1947), 81-86, for a discussion of Channing's use of these texts. Although Thoreau's critics have discussed his Harvard studies, they have not linked his rhetorical strategies to the tradition of psychological rhetoric. Christian Gruber, in "The Education of Henry David Thoreau: Harvard, 1833-37," Diss. Princeton Univ., 1953, pp. 200-270, analyzes Channing's teaching of composition and Thoreau's college essays, overlooking the relationship between Thoreau's rhetoric studies and his published writing. Nowhere does Gruber, who seems unfamiliar with rhetorical traditions, connect Whately to Campbell and psychological rhetoric. More concerned with logic than with rhetoric, Gruber discusses the possible influence of Whately's *Elements of Logic* on Thoreau's "Civil Disobedience." Another critic, Annette Woodlief, in "The Influence of Theories of Rhetoric on Thoreau," *Thoreau Quarterly Journal*, 7 (1975), 13-20, attempts to gauge the influence of various rhetoricians on Thoreau, including Cicero and Aristotle, but is unfamiliar with psychological rhetoric, with the character of the Harvard rhetoric program during Thoreau's college years,

and with Whately's indebtedness to Campbell. She draws few firm conclusions and claims that Thoreau may have weighed some of Whately's suggestions.

3. *Thirteenth Annual Report of the President of Harvard University to the Overseers on the State of the Institution for the Academic Year 1836–37* (Cambridge: Folsom, Wells, and Thurston, 1939), p. v.

4. For passages in Stewart paralleling Campbell's rhetoric, see *Elements of the Philosophy of the Human Mind* (Boston: Little, Brown, and Co., 1854), I, 252–78.

5. Anderson, p. 81.

6. Kenneth Walter Cameron, *Thoreau's Harvard Years* (Hartford: Transcendental Books, 1966), p. 15.

7. Walter Harding's *Thoreau's Library* (Charlottesville: Univ. of Virginia Press, 1957), pp. 90, 98; and *Emerson's Library* (Charlottesville: Univ. of Virginia Press, 1967), pp. 258–297.

8. *The American Adam* (Chicago: Univ. of Chicago Press, 1955), p. 82. Raymond Adams, "Thoreau's Literary Apprenticeship," *Studies in Philology*, 29 (1932), 623, claims, without presenting any evidence, that Thoreau's rhetoric studies under Channing were insignificant; and Wendell Glick, "Three New Early Manuscripts by Thoreau," *Huntington Library Quarterly* 15 (1951–52), 50, also unfamiliar with psychological rhetoric, asserts somewhat shortsightedly that "Thoreau achieved greatness by shedding the very precepts which he [Channing] had striven so assiduously to inculcate."

9. Ronald Reid, "The Boylston Professorship of Rhetoric and Oratory – 1806–1904," *Quarterly Journal of Speech*, 45 (1959), 239–244.

10. Edward T. Channing, *Lectures Read to the Seniors in Harvard College*, ed. Dorothy Anderson and Waldo Braden (Carbondale: Southern Illinois Univ. Press, 1968), p. 33.

11. Anderson, pp. 83–86.

12. Anderson and Braden, eds., Channing's *Lectures*, p. xxiii.

13. Dorothy Anderson, "Edward T. Channing's Teaching of Rhetoric," *Speech Monographs*, 16 (1949), 78.

14. *Literary Transcendentalism: Style and Vision in the American Renaissance* (Ithaca: Cornell Univ. Press, 1973), pp. 103–104.

15. *Elements of Rhetoric* (Cambridge: Brown, Shattuck, and Co., 1832), p. 114. Subsequent references are to this, the edition Thoreau owned, unless otherwise noted. Throughout this essay, I use the words speaker and writer interchangeably when discussing Campbell's and Whately's specific recommendations. The psychological rhetoricians, while often concerned with writing, directed their books to orators, and Channing applied theories of public speaking and debate to composition. During the American Renaissance, oratory was, to an extent that we have lost sight of, the basis for the forms of writing.

16. Joseph Moldenhauer, "Paradox in *Walden*," in *Twentieth Century Interpretations of Walden*, ed. Richard Ruland (Englewood Cliffs, N.J.: Prentice-Hall, 1968), p. 83. Moldenhauer views paradox as Thoreau's major argumentative strategy.

17. Henry David Thoreau, *The Illustrated Walden*, ed. J. Lyndon Shanley (Princeton: Princeton Univ. Press, 1973), pp. 4–5. Subsequent references to *Walden* are to this, the new standard edition.

18. *The Philosophy of Rhetoric*, ed. Lloyd Bitzer (Carbondale: Southern Illinois University Press, 1963), pp. 8–10. Subsequent references to Campbell's theory are to this edition.

19. *A Rhetoric of Motives* (Berkeley: Univ. of California Press, 1969), pp. 55–56.

20. Channing, p. 23.

21. *The Journal of Henry David Thoreau*, ed. Francis H. Allen and Bradford Torrey

(1906; rpt. New York: Dover Publications, 1962), II, 463. Subsequent references to the *Journal* are from this fourteen-volume edition.

22. *The Elements of Rhetoric*, ed. Douglas Ehninger (Carbondale: Southern Illinois Univ. Press, 1963), pp. 393–394. Whately's analysis of proverbs first appeared in a later edition of *Elements* than the 1832 edition that Thoreau owned. See Kenneth Burke, *The Philosophy of Literary Form* (Berkeley: Univ. of California Press, 1967), pp. 293–294, for a discussion of proverbs as "equipment for living." For a technical discussion of Thoreau's use of proverbs, see Joseph Moldenhauer's "The Proverbs in *Walden*," *Journal of American Folklore*, 80 (1967), 151–159.

23. Benjamin Franklin, "The Way to Wealth," in *The Autobiography of Benjamin Franklin and Selections from His Writings*, ed. Henry Steele Commager (New York: Random House, 1944), p. 218.

24. "Henry David Thoreau," in *Major Writers of America* (New York: Harcourt, Brace, and World, 1962), I, 598.

25. *Emerson and Thoreau: Transcendentalists in Conflict* (Middletown, Conn.: Wesleyan Univ. Press, 1966), pp. 138, 140.

26. *Lectures on Rhetoric and Oratory*, intro. J. Jeffrey Auer and Jerold L. Bannings (1810; rpt. New York: Russell and Russell, 1962), II, 289, 308. John Quincy Adams was the first Boylston Professor of Rhetoric and Oratory and firmly in the classical tradition. His lectures were a mixture of instruction on composition, delivery, rhetorical criticism, and the history of rhetorical theory. In 1809, Adams was succeeded in the Professorship by Joseph McKean, who also followed the classical rhetorical tradition. See Reid, pp. 239–257, for the history of the Boylston Professorship.

27. Adams did not address the problem of audience psychology in his *Lectures*; instead he analyzed figures from the writer's point of view, explaining how to compose them and use them with decorum. His treatment of figurative language includes a catalogue of types of figures, numerous examples from classical literature, and "rules" for employing figures. He discusses the "beauty" of various tropes and advises the speaker or writer to find similarities between the elements of their metaphors. Moreover, he limited his discussion of the sensory basis of much figurative language to this vague comment: "But figurative speech is subject in some sort to the dominion of the senses and the laws of matter," p. 283. See pp. 249–327 for his treatment of figurative language.

28. *Rhetoric and Poetics*, trans. W. Rhys Roberts and Ingram Bywater (New York: Modern Library, 1954), pp. 191–192. Resemblance is, of course, crucial to Aristotle's theory of metaphor.

29. Adams, pp. 326–327.

30. *The Complete Works of Ralph Waldo Emerson* (Boston: Houghton Mifflin Company, 1903), X, 464.

31. *A Grammar of Motives* (Berkeley: Univ. of California Press, 1969), pp. 507–508.

32. *Emerson's* Nature: *Origin, Growth, Meaning*, ed. Merton M. Sealts, Jr., and Alfred R. Ferguson, 2nd ed. enl. (Carbondale & Edwardsville: Southern Illinois Univ. Press; London & Amsterdam: Feffer & Simons, Inc., 1979), ch. IV, 15.

33. "The Simple Style," in F. B. Sanborn, *The Life of Henry David Thoreau* (Boston: Houghton Mifflin Company, 1917), pp. 90–91).

Delving and Diving for Truth: Breaking Through to Bottom in Thoreau's *Walden*

Joseph Allen Boone*

One of Thoreau's overriding purposes in writing *Walden* involves his effort to educate his audience in the "deep" art of living; consequently, the reader is continually made aware of the difference between the conventional life that merely skims the surface of existence and the fully-experienced life that fathoms its depths. Throughout *Walden* this theme is insinuated by a pattern of kinetic imagery suggestive of penetrating or breaking through surfaces in order to near the greater reality beneath. In his unique and idiosyncratic fashion, Thoreau reverses the concept of ascendent movement generally associated with Transcendentalism by stressing that the searcher must dig, delve, mine, and burrow toward truth. Not only does the earth become a metaphor for the material reality through which truth-seekers must break, but bodies of water, those emblematic mirrors of the heavens, serve as markers dividing perceived reality, or life on the top, from the unseen substratum that may be fathomed, fished after, or gauged with patience. In a key passage Thoreau identifies the inability to penetrate surfaces as the cause of the "mean" lives of his New England neighbors: "our vision does not penetrate the surface of things. We think that that *is* which *appears* to be" (p. 96).[1] Consequently the convolutions of his very writing style — a freely cavorting mixture of image, incidental reference, and anecdote — become for the reader a lesson in how to dip beneath the surface of the literal or the apparent in order to "get at the inside at last" (p. 322). And it is particularly the cumulative effect of the infrequently examined yet pervasive references to probing earth and water that triggers the reader's insight into Thoreau's metaphoric quest for meaning.[2]

Of course, as Walter Benn Michaels has warned, critics should beware of reducing *Walden*'s aesthetic enterprise to one all-encompassing pattern that implies a single meaning;[3] just as the text contains many levels of meaning, it contains them through a variety of methods. Indeed, the conglomeration of action, imagery, and figurative statement having to do with penetration provides a particularly instructive example of Thoreau's multiple methods. For instance, he at times quite consciously imbues natural action with symbolic intention — as when he compares digging up stumps for firewood to mining for "gold, deep [in] the earth" (p. 252). In other instances the literal action — such as the trope of fishing — becomes metaphoric only through incremental reference and holds differing resonances depending on the context. Thoreau's language can also be purely

*Reprinted from *ESQ: A Journal of the American Renaissance* 27 (3d Quarter 1981): 135–46, by permission of the author.

figurative, drawing upon phraseology that has been used descriptively elsewhere to present key actions that now function solely on a metaphoric level; thus he can speak matter-of-factly of wedging one's feet downward through the earth or using the head as an organ for burrowing, knowing of course that we will understand his terms figuratively. What would sometimes appear to be unconnected imagery, furthermore, often achieves relation through juxtaposition and proximity; it becomes the responsibility of the reader tunnelling beneath the surface of Thoreau's prose to assimilate the rapid-fire transformations that occur within clustered series of metaphors. One such strategic grouping occurs at the end of chapter 2, "Where I Lived, and What I Lived For." Because its sustained catalogue of seemingly diffuse imagery provides an apt introduction to Thoreau's methods and intentions, I will begin by reviewing this short passage and then proceed to a more specific analysis of groupings of breakthrough imagery, particularly the land and water references, that interweave their patterns throughout the text.

In unfolding his general philosophy of life at the end of "Where I Lived, and What I Lived For," Thoreau begins with a typically transcendental affirmation of the nature of reality and moves to a series of chameleon-like images that describe ways of apprehending that reality. The keynote is sounded in the theoretical distinction between appearance and reality with which Thoreau opens the sequence: the "Shams and delusions" of complacent lives are nothing in comparison to the "permanent and absolute existence" of the laws underlying "the surface of things" (pp. 95–96). Nor is truth as remote as most men deem, since the eternal spirit perpetually emanates throughout nature "in the present moment" (p. 97). Having delivered this philosophical statement of belief, Thoreau proceeds to create illustrative metaphoric analogies. First, he depicts reality as the underlying foundation or bedrock to be reached by *downward* rather than ascendent movement; our feet become the instrument breaking through the accumulation of unwanted "mud and slush":

> Let us settle ourselves and . . . wedge our feet downward through the mud and slush of opinion, and prejudice, and tradition, and delusion, and appearance, that alluvion which covers the globe . . . till we come to a hard bottom and rocks in place, which we can call *reality*, and say, This is, and no mistake. . . . (pp. 97–98)

Reality, the reader learns, lies not only behind or beyond (the more conventional literary conceit), but in this case, beneath the "alluvion."[4] Moving from this definition of reality to our common need to face the truth, Thoreau now compares facts — agents of truth — to the cutting edges of a sword or "cimeter," an instrument which penetrates to "the heart and marrow" of the "reality" that we crave (p. 93); like the preceding image of the feet pushing toward the "hard bottom and rocks in place," the sword enables us to get beyond the surface to the pulse of life.

Shifting to fishing as a metaphor for life, Thoreau begins his next paragraph with the analogy, "Time is but the stream I go a-fishing in" (p. 98). Through the sliding current of the surface, one perceives the "sandy bottom," another configuration of the unchanging truth that Thoreau envisions underlying all transient or superficial life, for the "thin current glides away, but eternity remains" (p. 98). The action of fishing becomes emblematic of the attempt to attain — or perceive transparently — this eternity or truth, for the implied fishing line breaks through the metaphoric stream of time just as the feet have been depicted as moving downward and the cimeter as piercing inward through barriers. As his train of thought skips from the metaphor of fishing for universal principles to his wish for greater intuitive knowledge, Thoreau recalls the image of the sword: "The intellect is a cleaver; it discerns and rifts its way into the secret of things" (p. 98). Next, the primacy of the thought process as true activity ("My head is hands and feet") opens onto yet another grouping of linked metaphoric expressions of penetrating surface reality in search of the deeper truth:

> My instinct tells me that my head is an organ for burrowing, as some creatures use their snout and fore-paws, and with it I would mine and burrow my way through these hills. I think that the richest vein is somewhere hereabouts; so by the divining rod and thin rising vapors I judge; and here I begin to mine. (p. 98)

In this passage the image of the speaker burrowing underground like a woodland creature becomes an act of mining after gold or divining an underground spring; be it gold or water, the concealed "richest vein" (analogous to "the secret of things" toward which the blade "rifts its way") represents the precious treasure which Thoreau hopes his experience at the pond will help *dis*cover by *un*covering.

The remarkable compilation of imagery concluding Thoreau's statement of "Where I Lived, and What I Lived For" thus moves from a theoretical statement of the need to break through to truth, to representations of the solid bottom that is reality, the cimeter that divides, the fishing line that by sinking connects us with the stars, the cleaver that rifts, and, finally, the mental capacity that burrows and mines its way toward greater knowledge. The concentrated quality of the prose advances Thoreau's account of how "to live deep" (p. 91), his purported aim, as a major theme, while the rapid metamorphoses of imagery alert the reader to Thoreau's manipulation of the figurative levels of language.

Walden's proliferating imagery of breakthrough or penetration may be most usefully categorized into those references having to do with the earth, in which getting below ground in some form represents the effort to uncover truth, and those having to do with water, particularly Walden Pond, in which fathoming its depths becomes a measure of what Charles Anderson has called "the buried life of the soul" (p. 37). Of the earth-associated references, the action of digging is predominant; it is first introduced in the instance of housebuilding discussed in chapter 1, for housebuilding, it turns out, necessitates the digging of a firm, worthy foundation. This essential fact has been obscured by the superfluities of contemporary architecture, and Thoreau propagandizes for the principle of simplification running throughout "Economy" when he hyperbolically imagines the floor of the ornate but badly constructed house giving way under the feet of the unaware visitor, letting him fall "through into the cellar, to some solid and honest though earthy foundation" (p. 38). This is indeed a *felix culpa*, if ever there were one for Thoreau, for the foundation of any house, *rooted* in earth, interests him more than the visible structure: it is the source, the essential principle, supporting the whole.

In short, Thoreau finds in the construction of a house a metaphor for his conception of the cosmos, wherein the unseen and constant spirit, like the solid foundation, supports the visible reality. And in the building of his own home at the pond, he discovers a way of rooting himself more closely to the natural universe and the eternal principles it exemplifies. The fact that the original settlers of Concord "burrow[ed] themselves in the earth for their first shelter" (p. 38) is also important to Thoreau because it establishes a precedent for living naturally; imitating nature — that is, the woodland animals who burrow for shelter — will sufficiently satisfy our most rudimentary needs. Thus, when ready to dig his own cellar, Thoreau chooses a site where "a woodchuck had formerly dug his burrow" (p. 44), and he emphasizes the fact that his shelter is merely an organic extension of the original woodchuck's natural habitat: "The house is still but a sort of porch at the entrance of a burrow" (p. 45). Nature has preceded his own effort, guiding yet reminding him of humanity's secondary place in the history of the natural universe.[5]

The idea of digging below ground to lay the unseen but fundamental foundation not only calls to mind the nature of the universe, but also reminds Thoreau of the relationship between the individual's body and soul. A truly functional dwelling, in Thoreau's viewpoint, exists as a manifestation of its "indweller." Therefore, the shelter with which one surrounds oneself resembles the body that encloses one's indwelling soul. Later, when Thoreau speaks of the human need to live close to "the perennial source of our life," he identifies such a location as "the place where a wise man will dig his cellar" (p. 132); in this statement, the reference to cellar-digging has become a metaphoric definition of the search for the self's essential core, the soul or "perennial source." Thus, the architectural principle Thoreau espouses — that buildings express "a core of truth, a necessity" (p. 46) — mirrors both his general assumptions about the spiritual reality that underlies appearances and his specific conception of the individual human life of body and soul. The aim of digging the cellar has become that of unearthing the foundation upon which an inner sanctum, a shelter for the self and for the soul, may be constructed.[6] Once the approaching winter drives Thoreau to take shelter in his "snug harbor" (p. 169) or "shell" (p. 249), he is warmed by the "bright fire both within my house and within my breast" (p. 249) — one more example of the correspondence between dwelling and indweller.

The literal hearth fire is kept going by fuel supplied by yet another act of digging, for Thoreau warms himself by burning pine roots which he mines out of the ground: "With axe and shovel you explore this mine, and follow the marrowy store, yellow as beef tallow, or as if you had struck on a vein of gold, deep into the earth" (p. 252). The precious "gold" recalls the treasure Thoreau wishes to find at the end of chapter 2 where he also employs the mining metaphor. By depicting the "marrowy store" as gold, Thoreau makes the fuel a symbol of the soul's elemental purity and value, while retaining its firewood connotations as the burning spirit that warms and animates man. Again, the descriptive action of mining, penetrating the earth, leads to the symbolic uncovering of a source vital to humanity's well-being.[7]

Besides digging up roots for fuel, another practical ground-breaking task to which Thoreau applies himself is that of hoeing his bean-field. But in chapter 7, the literal action quickly becomes a meditative exercise which yields a transcendent, spiritual crop. Previously, Thoreau has expressed the doctrine that man has "rooted" himself firmly in the earth so "that he may rise in the same proportion into the heavens above" (p. 15), and now the beans become Thoreau's personal anchor to the world of organic process: "They attached me to the earth, and so I got strength like Antaeus" (p. 55).[8] By implication, such rootedness is important because the radicle breaks through the earth toward the foundation or bedrock that is the source of being. Consequently, Thoreau's determination "to know beans" forms part of his larger search to know himself by knowing his own origin, and the lesson in rootedness imparted by his husbandry — more important than any tangible yield — leads him to the optimistic conclusion at the end of the chapter, "How, then, can our harvest fail?" (p. 166).

Thoreau's desire for rootedness is given further metaphoric expression in those hyperbolic passages which describe his feet sinking downward through the earth's alluvion to "a hard bottom and rocks in place," the first of which occurs, as noted, in the passage ending chapter 2. The motif recurs in the penultimate passages of Walden's "Conclusion." Here Thoreau metaphorically pictures the magnetic power that truth holds for him by listing a series of verbs that describe a gravitational pull downward: "I love to weigh, to settle, to gravitate toward that which most strongly and rightfully attracts me; — not hang by the beam of the scale and try to weigh less . . . but take the case that is" (p. 330). The immediate textual consequence of this description of sinking movement is a moment of figurative breakthrough signalled by the epiphanic announcement, "There is a solid bottom everywhere" (p. 330). This simulated "discovery" of bedrock, as in chapter 2, becomes Thoreau's means of illustrating the Transcendentalist concept of the Oversoul—although the term "Undersoul" might better suit his revisionist configuration.

In the next paragraph, a vignette unfolds that gives a humorous slant to the whole metaphoric pattern. In this tall-tale, a traveller's horse sinks "up to the girths" in a swamp identified as "the bogs and quicksands of society." When the traveller complains to the boy who has assured him that the swamp has a "hard bottom," the boy fires off the reply, " 'So it has . . . but you have not got half way to it yet' " (p. 330). One has to *work* at the task of discovery, Thoreau intimates, at the same time that his own effort at Walden is meant to assure us that the reward exists.[9] It is again significant that Thoreau figures his representation of the truth underlying existence as something substantial—"*solid* bottom everywhere"—for the idea ties in with his doctrine that the "Builder of the universe" (p. 329) is not merely an abstraction. Rather, because God's spirit interpenetrates the nature of all life, the Creator is in a sense also tangible, a solid foundation. This motif of digging beneath the surface of earth appears a final time as Thoreau admonishes his readers, "We are acquainted with a mere pellicle of the globe on which we live. Most have not delved six feet beneath the surface" (p. 332). Thus, as Thoreau approaches the end of his account of self-discovery, he continues to call for the penetrating vision that will help separate surface and reality, the conventional and individualistic life.

Throughout *Walden* Thoreau establishes a counterbalancing principle related to, but different than, this action of delving beneath the earth's surface. On one hand, man digs to find truth, but simultaneously, truth is rising to the surface of its own accord because its spirit permeates all creation. This organic shaping principle often appears in conjunction with the digging metaphor. For example, the action of having "burrowed" into the earth like the woodchuck to lay the foundations of his shelter leads Thoreau to the following observation: "What of architectural beauty I now see, I know has gradually grown from within outward, out of the necessities and character of the indweller, who is the only builder—out of some unconscious truthfulness. . ." (p. 47). The statement applies to human character as much as to architectural beauty; we are shaped by our essential personality, which in turn makes us the only true creator of the plans of our lives—to such an extent that "The universe constantly and obediently answers to our conceptions" (p. 97). The idea that the inward essence will eventually work its way outward also finds expression in the hoeing of the beanfield, "making the earth say beans instead of grass" (p. 157). And the incipient forms of organic life that Thoreau imaginatively perceives in the thawing clay of the "Spring" chapter illustrate that Nature is always " 'in full blast' within" (p. 308). It is precisely because the earth "labors with the idea inwardly" that it "expresses itself outwardly in leaves" (p. 306). *Walden* concludes with an analogous image, where truth emerges despite our complacency with "an established order on the

surface" (p. 332). For the closing vignette of the seventeen-year locust—
which leads to the prophetic query, "Who knows what . . . will next come
out of the ground?" (p. 332)—attests to Thoreau's hope that the inner life
of the soul may awaken and rise in human nature at last.

The emergence of truth, however, most often remains dependent on
our willingness to delve more deeply into human nature. This movement
to "get at the inside" (p. 322) also involves a whole set of images having to
do with bodies of water. Ponds, springs, and wells all share the common
characteristic of being conduits which pierce through the earth to its core;
the language of the crucial "The Ponds" chapter continually conflates
these three types of water passageways. Walden becomes "my well ready
dug" (p. 183), an inverted hill shaped by the mythic ancient settler, God,
who has used his divining rod to locate the site for a well. "It is a clear and
deep green well," Thoreau elaborates, "a perennial spring in the midst of
pine and oak woods, without any visible inlet or outlet" (p. 175). If
actually a spring, the pond would then be, as a source fed solely from the
earth's interior, an origin of pure life. As Melvin Lyon demonstrates in his
well-known analysis of the pond's symbolic values, Walden as such
becomes an image of the eternal springing up in nature, as well as in the
soul of man—that is to say, "the most perfect image of God on Earth."[10]
The "original" quality of this "perennial spring" is next stressed in an
Edenic reference to the pond as a "gem of the first water" (p. 179), which
emphasizes the untainted and precious nature of man's inner spirit. The
Edenic analogy continues as Walden's bubbling underground spring is
described in fountain terminology (p. 188) that evokes Milton's depiction
of the fountain of life in *Paradise Lost*. Walden, if not always figured as
the source itself, becomes a way to apprehension of universal truth.

Thoreau's most common pastime involving the pond—fishing—
becomes analogous to those other actions—digging, mining, burrowing—
which represent attempts at penetrating the surface of things. The chapter
"Higher Laws" suggests that fishing helps the young person find "the most
original part of himself," those "seeds of a better life" located within (pp.
212–213). For the adult Thoreau, fishing, like hoeing the bean-field, must
evolve into a meditative exercise to be meaningful: his fishing line becomes
for him an instrument as vital as his spade, shovel, or knife in linking him
to the interior reality of things.[11] In this action-turned-metaphor at the
end of chapter 2, Thoreau fishes in "the stream of time" in order to
apprehend the real, unchanging order of existence symbolized by the
eternally "sandy bottom" (p. 98). The later account of his actual midnight
fishing expeditions epitomizes this sense of connection with the real order.
The faint jerks on the line "link you to Nature again," Thoreau observes,
and he personally feels "anchored in forty feet of water . . . and communi-
cating by a long flaxen line with nocturnal fishes . . . [and] now and then
feeling a slight vibration along it, indicative of some life prowling about its
extremity" (p. 175). This almost mystic experience mirrors man's unseen

but intuited connection to God, for what Thoreau feels is his own soul's connection to that Oversoul from which he was created. The fish which are the ostensible goal of fishing, here pictured as "some life prowling" about the bottom, are later incorporated into the metaphoric patterning when Thoreau describes the "dazzling and transcendent beauty" of winter pickerel. Likening them to precious stones ("the pearls, the animalized *nuclei* or crystals of the Walden water"), Thoreau transforms "this great gold and emerald fish" (p. 285) into yet another emblem of the spiritual treasure that awaits the fisher of life.[12]

Although Thoreau himself needs the actual aid of his "long flaxen line" to "communicate" with the "extremities" of pond life, he can vicariously participate in the diving activity that brings the loon into contact with life at the bottom. The loon personifies Thoreau's indefatigable effort to live deeply, as it repeatedly plunges beneath the pond's smooth surface: "So long-winded was he and so unweariable, that when he had swum farthest he would immediately plunge again, nevertheless; and then no wit could divine where in the deep pond, beneath the smooth surface, he might be speeding his way like a fish, for he had time and ability to visit the bottom of the pond in its deepest part" (p. 235). This passage brims over with the metaphoric language Thoreau has repeatedly used to describe the endeavor to penetrate surfaces and gain knowledge of the deeps. Ironically, the loon betters man in his attempt, its laughter mocking the human failure to plumb the soul's depths. At the end of this episode, Thoreau shifts without warning from his "game" with the loon to a description of ducks "cunningly" holding to the center of the pond. This juxtaposition converts the kinetic image of diving to the static one of the truth contained at the center of existence. In their separate ways, these natural creatures embody lives attuned to the higher laws of nature.

The knowledge Thoreau wishes to gain about Walden's bottom parallels the truths he is learning about his own interior depths. As the poem included in chapter 14 illustrates, the "deepest resort" of the pond "Lies high in my thought" (p. 193). And the instrument by which one breaks through the "stony shore" of the external self is *in*-sight: "Direct your eye right inward," Thoreau instructs in another poem appearing in the last chapter, "and you'll find / A thousand regions in your mind" (p. 320). Walden Pond is also compared to an eye, hence a passageway to the interior of the self: "It is earth's eye; looking into which the beholder measures the depth of his own nature" (p. 186). Thus, looking into Walden, he sees into the spirit that animates all life as he simultaneously gains insight into himself. The metaphoric "eye" — both as pond and as the individual's inward organ of perception — becomes one more means of penetration, the object of which (in one of Thoreau's word-plays) is the "I," the subjective center of the narrative from its opening.[13]

The significance that accrues to Thoreau's fathoming of Walden for its reputed "long lost bottom" (p. 285) in "The Pond in Winter" builds upon ideas found in the "The Ponds" chapter. The sounding line resembles the fishing line in its function of plumbing the depths. Because the pond is ice-covered ("the illusive medium" of ice is an apt concretization of the metaphoric surface to be penetrated), Thoreau must first break "open a window under my feet" (p. 283). No new knowledge will be gained by remaining on the icy surface and making vain observations about what lies beneath without taking the effort to solve the problem by breaking through the ice: "It is remarkable," Thoreau comments, "how long men will believe in the bottomless of a pond without taking the trouble to sound it" (p. 285). As a consequence of his assertive action, he *finds* the bottom and thus, symbolically, affirms his belief that life is not without foundation. In a sermon-like peroration, he declares to the reader: "But I can assure my readers that Walden has a reasonably tight bottom at a not unreasonable, though at an unusual, depth. *I fathomed it easily. . .*" (pp. 285–287; my emphasis). Thoreau's "finding" Walden's bottom — like the references to the "hard bottom and rocks in place" (p. 98) and "a solid bottom everywhere" (p. 330) — is an explicit attempt to give solidity to the otherwise abstract motion of the transcendent source of life.[14]

The analogy between literally fishing in the pond or fathoming its depths and undergoing a spiritual search is enhanced by a frequent concurrence of upward and downward movement, such as I have noted in regard to the land references. Often the water of Walden is figured as sky, a mirrored reflection of the heavens; therefore, although truth is most frequently depicted as an underground stratum or inner core toward which the searcher plunges, the consequent mental action is often that of soaring or rising in transcendent ecstasy. Hence a seeming paradox exists in the final lines of the poem in "The Ponds": "And its deepest resort / Lies high in my thought" (p. 193). Similarly, when Thoreau identifies time as the stream in which he fishes, he continues, "I would drink deeper; fish in the sky whose bottom is pebbly with stars" (p. 98), and thus the limitless expanse of the heavens and the "bottom" of the stream become one. The midnight fishing episode also conflates the fishing action with "vast and cosmogonal" thoughts: "It seemed as if I might next cast my line upward into the air, as well as downward into this element, which was scarcely more dense. Thus I caught two fishes as it were with one hook" (p. 175). As Thoreau realizes when he axes the "windows" into the ice-covered lake in winter, stooping to drink at this fount, "Heaven is under our feet as well as over our heads" (p. 283). Consistently, this kinetic action of breaking through water, as through earth, opens the way to a transcendental perception of the unmoving truth.

Although land and water references provide the readiest sites, as it were, for delving beneath surfaces, the imagery of penetration extends to even the most commonplace actions of the narrative. A look at some examples illuminates Thoreau's method of creating significance through repetition in differing contexts. The act of nailing, for example, is latent with symbolic meaning. In chapter 13 Thoreau speaks of the satisfaction of "send[ing] home each nail with a single blow of the hammer" (p. 245); in his conclusion, he immediately turns from the passage declaring "solid bottom everywhere" to hammering as an illustration: "Give me a hammer, and let me feel for the furring. . . . Drive a nail home and clinch it so faithfully that you can wake up in the night and think of your work with satisfaction." As usual the metaphor quickly reaches universal dimension — "Every nail driven should be as another rivet in the machine of the universe" — and leads into an outright declaration of the aim of the search: "give me truth" (p. 330).

Splitting wood is also an energetic action that Thoreau imbues with a similar metaphoric meaning. Commenting on John Field's mean and moiling life, Thoreau surmises that the Irishman has not the skill "to split its [life's] massive columns with any fine entering wedge" (p. 206). In other words, Fields cannot penetrate to the core of life's potential meaning because his own life is neither as keen nor as hardy as "the fine entering wedge." Thoreau employs the splitting metaphor to praise the "wild men" who come to Walden in the winter to fish. He compares their instinctive life in nature to the dabblings of the self-conscious naturalist: "His life itself passes deeper in Nature than the studies of the naturalist [can] penetrate . . . . the former lays open logs to their core with his axe . . . Such a man has some right to fish, and I love to see Nature carried out in him" (pp. 283–284). The actions of fishing and "barking trees" coalesce in this passage to illustrate a type of life that succeeds in attaining meaning.

Incisive as the axe, the knife recurs as an instrument of penetration throughout *Walden*, and both suggest the violence sometimes needed to break from convention. One particularly recalls the slicing edge of the cimeter-like facts and the metaphor of the intellect as a cleaver which "discerns and rifts its way into the secret of things" (p. 98) in the compilation of imagery ending chapter 2. Such knowledge, incidentally, divides us "through the heart and marrow" (p. 98), and marrow — contained within the bone and the source of the blood that pulses through the heart — is another of Thoreau's synonyms for the sought-after goal. As he says in his famous enunciation of purpose, "I wanted to live deep and suck out all the marrow of life" (p. 91), and it is "life near the bone" that is "sweetest" (p. 329). Through such examples, Thoreau makes his images support each other in a profuse, overlapping patterning so extensive that the imagery of penetration begins to influence the reader's perception of the less conscious vocabulary of the narrative. Phraseology such as "to strike to the root at once. . ." (p. 65), intended as a humorous rejoinder, unconsciously reinforces the total metaphor: striking below the surface has become *the* experience of *Walden* through and through.

At the very beginning of "Economy," Thoreau lists among those implements necessary for life "a knife, an axe, a spade" (p. 14). To these items might be added a hammer, hoe, divining rod, fishing pole, and sounding line for a basic catalogue of those instruments whose daily use inspired Thoreau to employ them as images expressive of his stance toward life.[15] For him the purpose of the Walden venture has been that of living deeply; the purpose of retrospectively recording his experiences has been that of helping his readers liberate themselves from the limits of the commonplace and lives of surface convenience. This freedom is gained by *insight* into the organic unity underlying material objects, a perception which expands one's conception of reality. The patterns of images having to do with penetrating surfaces — most frequently, getting below ground or fathoming the depths of water — aid in the educative process; but the metaphoric movement downward or within implies the question of what one breaks through to. The goal is figured variously, but the representations of the solid bottom, the vein of gold, the pickerel, and like images all form part of a movement back toward a source, an origin, and a Unity. The "secret of things" (p. 98), the "perennial source of our life" (p. 133), is variously identifiable as Truth, Reality, or "the workman whose work we are" — each a synonym for the Oversoul, the unifying spirit which interpenetrates the whole of life (just as Thoreau's images interpenetrate the whole of the text) and makes Nature its emblem. All these configurations of the goal toward which Thoreau's resolve to live the deep life leads are inseparable from the self, the "I" voice, which stands at the subjective center of *Walden*'s explorations. A bedrock of truth and reality is to be found not only in the outer world, but also in the inner world of self. For any search after the universal principles governing life (and the Oversoul is such a concept) inevitably becomes a personal quest for the origin of being that sparks one's own soul.

One can measure the affirmative quality of *Walden*'s message by setting it against Emerson's use of a similar set of images in the "Experience" essay. Thoreau's mentor poignantly expresses an inability to find the solid bottom that Thoreau confidently asserts is everywhere: "Gladly we would anchor, but the anchorage is quicksand." Emerson couples this inability with his recognition that "We live amid surfaces," an evaluation of society with which Thoreau concurs. But whereas Emerson ruefully acknowledges that for most people "the true art of life is to skate well"[16] on them, Thoreau eagerly plunges into the depths beneath. Largely because his philosophy is rooted, as his images evince, in the physical world and is thus less abstractly ideal than Emerson's, Thoreau writes *Walden* as a testament to the search for hard, solid bottom that makes of life a constant quest, a perpetual awakening, and a pervasive reality.

Notes

1. *Walden*, ed. J. Lyndon Shanley (Princeton: Princeton Univ. Press, 1971), p. 96; hereafter cited in the text.

2. Stanly Cavell briefly examines downward movement in *The Senses of Walden* (New

York: Viking Press, 1972) and his comments, though concise, are informative. Citing the fact that Thoreau goes "*down* to the woods" in chapter 8, Cavell continues, "And downward is the direction he invites us in" (see pp. 69, 70). Two critics whose studies of Thoreau focus on circularity in *Walden* also take note of linear imagery but downplay the descending movement: in *Central Still: Circle and Sphere in Thoreau's Prose* (The Hague: Mouton, 1975), Richard Tuerk talks about descent as a means to ascent, by which humanity finally frees itself from all roots; in *The Magic Circle of Walden* (New York: Holt, Rinehart and Winston, 1968), Charles Anderson associates vertical movements with Thoreau's final "leap" out of the "magic circle" that Walden inscribes. In contrast to my interpretation of the crucial significance of downward motion, see David Mason Greene, *Frail Duration: A Key to Symbolic Structure in Walden* (San Diego: San Diego State College Press, 1966), who discusses the vertical imagery as an indication that growth for Thoreau occurs only as *upward* movement.

Most recently and most relevantly, Walter Benn Michaels in "*Walden's* False Bottoms," *Glyph 1: Johns Hopkins Textual Studies* (Baltimore and London: Johns Hopkins Univ. Press, 1977) concludes that Thoreau's search for foundation is a search for "a location in authority, a ground upon which we can make a decision" (p. 147), that is countered by its own ontological premises; thus, in the opening stages of his argument he cites three of the most prominent "bottom" passages to show that the value assigned to "bottomlessness" as a symbol of infinity contradicts the immediately preceding assertion of the pond's "solid bottom." (For my differing interpretation of this "contradiction," see n. 14). As an example of deconstructionist methodology, Michaels' essay serves the highly useful general function of exposing the ambivalences of any philosophical credo which at once posits a "return to Nature" and a non-materialist apprehension of the "unchanging Real," and certainly Thoreau's personal feelings about his relation to the primitive and abstract realms fluctuate. But Michaels' specific identifications of contradictory stances at war within *Walden's* language often do severe injustice to the intentions of Thoreau's metaphoric method: in this regard Michaels almost seems to commit the error of those univocalist critics he dislikes (see n. 3) by imposing on the text oppositional pairings and hierarchical assignments of value which do not exist for Thoreau. For example, in examining only three "bottom" passages rather than the larger complex of imagery of which they are a part, Michaels ends up concentrating on the significance of "bottom" itself, whereas the pervasive downward motion implied in the metaphoric associations of penetration suggests that Thoreau's major concern lies in the *process*, in the quality of the search itself. Furthermore, by failing to take note of the poetics underlying Thoreau's metaphoric method, Michaels overlooks the fluidity by which images are allowed to undergo transformation, to appear in differing lights, and to interpenetrate each others' field of meaning. What often appears inherently contradictory to Michaels thus exists for Thoreau as a purposive methodology for creating multiple avenues to vision.

3. One of Michaels' foremost contributions is to debunk those univocal readings of *Walden* in which a formalist concern with presenting a totally coherent text — one with an "essential unity" or integrated "wholeness" — leads to "simple" meaning (p. 133).

4. It is interesting to note the evolution of the swamp image in Thoreau's prose; as a potentially nourishing environment, one that, in the words of David L. James, "Movement and Growth in 'Walking,'" *Thoreau Journal Quarterly*, 5, No. 3, (July 15, 1972), pp. 16–21, "manifests [Thoreau's] progress toward the bedrock of nature."

5. As Anderson points out in regard to another reference to burrowing, "The way must be through nature, though the goal is heaven" (p. 37).

6. The longevity of cellars, in contrast to the superstructure, is also emphasized: "long after the superstructure has disappeared posterity remarks its dent in the earth" (pp. 44–45). Later, in the chapter about "Former Inhabitants," Thoreau finds visible evidence of this fact as he visits the remnants of previous habitations built in the woods: "Now only a dent in the earth marks the site of these dwellings. . . . These cellar dents, like deserted fox burrows, old

holes, are all that is left where once were the stir and bustle of human life. . ." (p. 263). Interestingly, Thoreau also notes the deserted wells, whose symbolic value I will later address, which resemble the cellar holes: "Sometimes the well dent is visible, where once a spring oozed. . . . What a sorrowful act must that be, — the covering up of wells!" (p. 263); one is reminded of the forty cellar holes dotting the landscape of Frost's "Directive."

7. Compare this metaphoric rendering of mining to a description of *actual* mining for gold in the essay, "Life without Principle," *Reform Papers*, ed. Wendell Glick (Princeton, N.J.: Princeton Univ. Press, 1973), which Thoreau cites as an example of foolish labor. Such effort is mining for the wrong source, for he wonders, "why *I* might not sink a shaft down to gold within me, and work that mine" (p. 164).

8. In Greek mythology, Antaeus was a fabulous wrestler who retained his strength as long as he remained rooted to the earth. He was also the son of Poseidon, god of the sea, and Gaea, goddess of earth. His strength is thus a product of both land and sea, and his rootedness provides the link to both these sources of power.

9. For Michaels this tall-tale of getting bogged down without reaching bottom "unhappily complicates" and controverts the immediately preceding 'discovery' of solid bottom. The fact that the "tone is so different" and that the quester, previously an exemplary hero, has been replaced by a "suppositious traveller drowned in his own pretension" are signs of Thoreau's uneasy attitude toward the possibility of finding foundation: "The exhortation has become a warning" (p. 136). But as my analysis of Thoreau's stylistic methods has begun to demonstrate, such categorical conclusions cannot be assigned to Thoreau's shifting approaches to an idea. Rather than pessimistically warning us that we are all doomed to drowning in slush (or, as Michaels puts it, of "sinking, dispiritedly, in prose"), Thoreau's point is that it takes *effort* to be a true quester; the purpose of the tall-tale (recasting this message in a comic form) is to provide a droll comment on the laziness of those who take "bottom" for granted, those who expect life to be an easy venture. The dual perspectives emerging from these passages — straightforward declaration followed by anecdote — complement rather than contradict each other and clarify rather than cloud the overall metaphoric endeavor.

10. "Walden Pond as Symbol," *PMLA*, 82 (1957), 291.

11. Of course Thoreau goes on to reject both hunting and fishing, as well as the animalistic eating of flesh, as "primitive" or "wild" stages in the ever-developing "embryo man" whose dual nature is the subject matter of "Higher Laws." Thus, returning to the earth is not an absolute rejection of civilized life or thought, nor is Thoreau's intellectual unease with the precarious balance of the natural and primitive any rejection of the mind's need to "redeem" the body and "respect" the physical by the downward movement of "descend[ing] into" it (p. 222).

12. For an explanation of the genesis of the concentrated symbolic value of these pickerel, see Gordon V. Boudreau's "Thoreau and Richard C. Trench: Conjectures on the Pickerel Passage of *Walden*," *ESQ*, 20 (1974), 117–124.

13. Thoreau's method here reminds one of Kenneth Burke's analysis of the Emersonian mode of transcendence in "I, Eye, Ay — Emerson's Early Essay on 'Nature': Thoughts on the Machinery of Transcendance," *Sewanee Review*, 74 (1966), 875–895.

14. Having shown the myth of Walden's unfathomableness to be the result of inexpert explorers, Thoreau now feels free to change the connotations of bottomlessness from the negative idea of uncertainty and vagueness to the positive concept of infinity: "This is a remarkable depth [he says of the pond] . . . yet not one inch of it can be spared by the imagination. Would it not react on the minds of men? I am thankful that this pond was thought to be bottomless" (p. 287). In terms of the imagination, the mind of man is indeed bottomless, and with good cause, for it is this sense of limitlessness that stimulates the impulse toward freedom and the potential for discovery. Thoreau amplifies this idea in *Walden's* last chapter: "At the same time that we are in earnest to explore and learn all things, we require

that all things be mysterious and unexplorable . . . unfathomed by us because unfathomable" (pp. 317–318).

These successive descriptions of "a reasonably tight bottom" and "bottomlessness" form the basis of Michaels' initial assault on Thoreau's search for foundation. The two examples introduce, in Michaels' view, "not entirely complementary sets of dichotomies" in which the virtue of a tight bottom "metamorphoses into the merely 'shallow' " while the initial idea of "bottomlessness . . . [as] a Bad Thing" turns into "the symbolically suggestive 'infinite' "; and hence he concludes that "the account of the experiment [to fathom the pond] seems to end with a gesture which undermines the logic according to which it is undertaken in the first place" (p. 135). This reading, however, reduces what for Thoreau are metaphoric connotations into literal statements of value. For *both* of these adjacent descriptions the symbolic *action* of penetrating, the *process* of reaching for bottom, *retains* its positive meaning. Thus, taking the pond's bottomlessness for granted is "folly" in the first instance because it inspires the continual act of searching. Conversely, the locating of bottom in the first description is "positive" because it indicates someone has exerted the effort; the idea that a shallow bottom, because easily discernible, would obviate the need to search gives it its "negative" connotation in the second example. Taken as metaphors, the associations of "bottom" thus seem to shift with admirable — rather than undermining — logic.

15. This example of Thoreau's use of catalogue rhethoric forms a corollary to the argument advanced by Lawrence Buell in "Transcendentalist Catalogue Rhetoric: Vision versus Form," *American Literature*, 40 (1968), 325–339, which demonstrates the technique at work in the verse of Whitman and the prose of Emerson.

16. The Emerson quotations are taken from *The Complete Works of Ralph Waldo Emerson*, ed. Edward Waldo Emerson (Boston: Houghton Mifflin, 1903), III, 55, 59.

Walden and the "Curse of Trade"   Michael T. Gilmore*

I

Among the many paradoxes of *Walden* perhaps none is more ironic than the fact that this modernist text — modernist in its celebration of private consciousness, its aestheticizing of experience, its demands upon the reader — starts out as a denunciation of modernity. It is inspired by the agrarian ideals of the past, yet in making a metaphor of those ideals it fails as a rejoinder to the nineteenth century and creates as many problems as it lays to rest. Personal and historical disappointment determines the shape of Thoreau's masterpiece. In important ways it is a defeated text. Though Thoreau begins with the conviction that literature can change the world, the aesthetic strategies he adopts to accomplish political objectives involve him in a series of withdrawals from history; in each case the ahistorical

*Reprinted from Michael T. Gilmore, *American Romanticism and the Marketplace* (Chicago: University of Chicago Press, 1985), 35–51, by permission of the University of Chicago Press and the author.

maneuver disables the political and is compromised by the very historical moment it seeks to repudiate.

This is not to deny *Walden*'s greatness, but rather to emphasize the cost of Thoreau's achievement and to begin to specify its limits. No reader of the book can fail to notice the exultant tone of the "Conclusion"; the impression it leaves is of an author who has made good on his promise not to write "an ode to dejection" (p. 84).[1] But one might say, in another paradox, that *Walden*'s triumphant success is precisely what constitutes its defeat. For underlying that triumph is a forsaking of civic aspirations for an exclusive concern with "the art of living well" (in Emerson's phrase about his former disciple).[2] And to say this is to suggest that *Walden* is a book at odds with its own beliefs; it is to point out Thoreau's complicity in the ideological universe he abhors.

II

At the heart of Thoreau's dissent from modernity is a profound hostility to the process of exchange, to what he calls the "curse of trade" (p. 70). He pictures a contemporary Concord where everyone is implicated in the market, and he mounts a critique of that society as antithetical to independence, to identity, and to life itself. His antimarket attitude, though it has similarities to pastoralism,[3] is more properly understood as a nineteenth-century revision of the agrarian or civic humanist tradition. Civic humanists regarded the economic autonomy of the individual as the basis for his membership in the polis. The self-sufficient owner of the soil, in their view, was the ideal citizen because he relied on his own property and exertions for his livelihood and was virtually immune to compromising pressures. Commercial enterprise, in contrast, endangered liberty because it fostered dependence on others and, by legitimating the pursuit of private interest, undermined devotion to the common good. Jeffersonian agrarianism, the American development of this tradition, retained its antimarket bias and its stress on freedom from the wills of others. In Jefferson's own formulation from the *Notes on the State of Virginia*, commerce is productive of subservience, and the independent husbandman uniquely capable of civic virtue.[4]

Thoreau, writing some sixty years after Jefferson, shows a similar antipathy to exchange but entertains no illusions about either the present-day husbandman or the benefits conferred by real property. Several pages into *Walden* appears his well-known indictment of the various forms of ingratiation and venality practiced by his neighbors in order to make money — an indictment that applies to the farmer as much as to the tradesman.

> It is very evident what mean and sneaking lives many of you live, . . . always promising to pay, promising to pay, tomorrow, and dying to-day, insolvent; seeking to curry favor to get custom, by how

many modes, only not state-prison offences; lying, flattering, voting [cf. Thoreau's attacks on democracy in "Civil Disobedience"], contracting yourselves into a nutshell of civility, or dilating into an atmosphere of thin and vaporous generosity, that you may persuade your neighbor to let you make his shoes, or his hat, or his coat, or import his groceries for him. [Pp. 6–7]

Thoreau's position in this passage is directly opposed to the laissez-faire ideology gaining in popularity among his contemporaries. He sees the marketplace not as a discipline in self-reliance, an arena where the man of enterprise can prove his worth, but rather as a site of humiliation where the seller has to court and conciliate potential buyers to gain their custom. The interactions of exchange, in his view, breed not independence but servility. Nor, insists Thoreau, does nineteenth-century agriculture offer an exemption from the abasements and dependencies of the exchange process. The land has become an investment like any other and the farmer a willing participant in the marketplace. The husbandmen of Concord, immortalized by Emerson for their stand "by the rude bridge that arched the flood," are now "serfs of the soil" who spend their lives "buying and selling" and have forgotten the meaning of self-reliance (pp. 5, 208). Thoreau envisions them, in a celebrated image, "creeping down the road of life," each pushing before him "a barn seventy-five feet by forty . . . and one hundred acres of land, tillage, mowing, pasture, and wood-lot!" (p. 5).

For Thoreau, commercial agriculture has an impact on the physical world which is just as devastating as its effect on the farmer. In the chapter "The Ponds" he describes an agricultural entrepreneur named Flint for whom nature exists solely as commodity. Indeed, on Flint's farm the use value of natural objects has been consumed by their exchange value; their abstract character as potential money has completely obliterated their "sensuous" reality (to use a favorite adjective of Marx's in this connection) as fruits and vegetables. The result is an impoverishment of the thing, an alteration of its very nature. "I respect not his labors," Thoreau writes of Flint,

his farm where every thing has its price; who would carry the landscape, who would carry his God, to market, if he could get any thing for him; . . . on whose farm nothing grows free, whose fields bear no crops, whose meadows no flowers, whose trees no fruits, but dollars; who loves not the beauty of his fruits, whose fruits are not ripe for him till they are turned to dollars. [P. 196]

A companion chapter, "The Pond in Winter," shows this destruction of nature actually coming to pass through the speculations of "a gentleman farmer" who carries the landscape off to market. Wanting "to cover each one of his dollars with another," the farmer has hired a crew of laborers to strip Walden of its ice. Thoreau treats the entire operation as though the ice-cutters were "busy husbandmen" engaged in skimming the land: "They went to work at once, ploughing, harrowing, rolling, furrowing . . . [and] suddenly began to hook up the virgin mould itself, with a peculiar jerk, clear down to the sand, or rather the water, . . . all the *terra firma* there was, and haul it away on sleds" (pp. 294–95).

As Thoreau's denunciation of Flint makes clear, his quarrel with the marketplace is in large measure ontological. He sees the exchange process as emptying the world of its concrete reality and not only converting objects into dollars but causing their "it-ness" or being to disappear. A particularly powerful statement of this idea occurs at the beginning of "The Ponds," in the passage (cited in Chapter 1) where Thoreau assails the marketing of huckleberries. He argues that nature's fruits "do not yield their true flavor" either to the man who raises them commercially or to their urban purchasers. The huckleberry cannot be tasted or even said to exist outside its native habitat: invariably it undergoes a fatal transformation en route from the countryside to the metropolis. What reaches Boston is not the fragrant berry itself but the "mere provender" that the fruit has become in being transported to the customer. Its bloom has been "rubbed off in the market cart" and its "ambrosial and essential part" extinguished by its conversion into an article of trade (p. 173).

Thoreau believes that along with the degradation of the physical object in exchange there occurs a shriveling of the individual. Men in the marketplace, according to *Walden*, do not relate as persons but as something less than human; they commit violence against their own natures in their incessant anxiety to induce others to buy their products or their labor. "The finest qualities of our nature," Thoreau says in a passage paralleling his discussion of the huckleberry, "like the bloom on fruits, can be preserved only by the most delicate handling. Yet we do not treat ourselves or one another thus tenderly" (p. 6). The laborer's self, his authentic being, has as little chance to survive the exchange process as a genuine huckleberry. To satisfy his employer, he has to suppress his individuality and become a mechanical thing: "Actually, the laboring man has not leisure for a true integrity day by day; he cannot afford to sustain the manliest relations to men; his labor would be depreciated in the market. He has no time to be anything but a machine" (p. 6). The final disappearance of the person, the most extreme form of absence, would be death, and Thoreau does in fact equate exchange with the deprivation of life. "The cost of a thing," he writes, "is the amount of what I will call life which is required to be exchanged for it, immediately or in the long run" (p. 31). Exchange brings about the ultimate alienation of man from himself; to engage in buying and selling is not merely to debase the self but to extinguish it, to hurry into death.

Thoreau's analysis of commodification has certain affinities with the Marxist critique of capitalism. His comments on the erosion of human presence in exchange evoke the notion of reification, a concept developed in the twentieth century by Georg Lukács. Reification refers to the phenomenon whereby a social relation between men assumes the character of a relation between things. Because they interact through the commodities they exchange, including the commodity of labor, individuals in the capitalist market confront each other not as human beings, but as objectified, nonhuman entities. They lose sight altogether of the subjective element in their activity. An important corollary to this loss of the person is a confusion of history with nature. By mystifying or obscuring man's involvement in the production of his social reality, reification leads him to apprehend that reality as a "second nature." He perceives the social realm as an immutable and universal order over which he exerts no control. The result is greatly to diminish the possibility of human freedom.[5]

Thoreau reaches a similar conclusion about the decline of liberty under capitalism: he portrays his townsmen as slave-drivers of themselves. The weakness of his position, a weakness to which we shall return, is that he launches his attack against history rather than in its name, with the result that he mystifies the temporality of his own experience, presenting it as natural or removed from social time. He is outspoken in debunking such "naturalization" when it functions as a way of legitimating social codes. In his disquisition on clothing, for example, he points out how the fetishism of fashion invests the merely whimsical with the prestige of inevitability. "When I ask for a garment of a particular form," he explains, "my tailoress tells me gravely, 'They do not make them so now,' not emphasizing the 'They' at all, as if she quoted an authority as impersonal as the Fates. . . . We worship not the Graces, nor the Parcae, but Fashion" (p. 25).

Thoreau constantly challenges the false identification of what "they" say or do with the course of nature. He maintains that social reality, to which men submit as though to "a seeming fate" (p. 5), is in fact made by men and subject to their revision. His neighbors, whose resignation only masks their desperation, do not adopt the customary modes of living out of preference but "honestly think there is no choice left" (p. 8). Although they deny the possibility of change and say, "This is the only way," Thoreau insists that they are mistaken, that "there are as many ways" to live as "can be drawn radii from one centre" (p. 11). His lack of deference toward his elders stems from the same impatience with a reified social reality. Old people, he finds, regard their own experience as exemplary and refuse even to contemplate alternatives to the existing order of things. But "what old people say you cannot do you try and find that you can" (p. 8). What they fail to realize, what Thoreau feels all his neighbors are unable to see, is that "their daily life of routine and habit . . . is built on purely illusory foundations." They "think that *is* which *appears* to be" (p. 96).

III

To negate the "curse of trade" during his stay in the woods, Thoreau supports himself by farming. This is the occupation followed by the majority of his neighbors, but his own experiment in husbandry differs significantly from the commercial agriculture prevalent in Concord. By building his own house and growing his own food, by concentrating on the necessaries of life and renouncing luxuries, he minimizes his dependency on others and removes himself as far as possible from the market economy. In keeping with his precept, "Enjoy the land, but own it not" (p. 207), he squats on soil belonging to someone else (Emerson, as it happens) and endeavors to "avoid all trade and barter" (p. 64). "More independent than any farmer in Concord," he claims to have learned from his experience that something approaching self-sufficiency is still practicable in mid-nineteenth-century America, if only "one would live simply and eat only the crop which he raised, and raise no more than he ate, and not exchange it for an insufficient quantity of more luxurious and expensive things" (pp. 55–56).

Something *approaching* self-sufficiency: Thoreau makes no attempt to disguise the fact that he is unable to emancipate himself completely from exchange relations. He freely "publishes his guilt," as he puts it (p. 59), that his venture at subsistence farming is not strictly speaking an economic success. He raises a cash crop of beans and uses the proceeds to give variety to his diet, and he is forced to supplement his income from farming by hiring himself out as a day laborer, the employment he finds "the most independent of any, especially as it required only thirty to forty days in a year to support one" (p. 70). He recognizes, in other words, the obsolescence of his program as a *literal* antidote to the ills of market civilization.

What Thoreau does affirm, and affirm consistently, is the possibility even in the nineteenth century of a way of life characterized by self-reliance and minimal involvement in exchange. Following the civic humanist tradition, he identifies this ideal with husbandry, and husbandry in turn supplies him with a metaphoric solution to the problems of the marketplace. Agriculture, he states, "was once a sacred art; but it is pursued with irreverent haste and heedlessness by us, our object being to have large farms and large crops merely" (p. 165). Thoreau makes a point of actually farming in the traditional way,[6] going down to the woods and living by himself, because he refuses to sacrifice the use value of husbandry to its symbolic value in the manner of Flint. He wants to earn his metaphor by dwelling "near enough to Nature and Truth to borrow a trope from them" (p. 245).

Thoreau has an acute sense of the relationship between commodity and symbolism — or rather of the commodified thinking concealed in symbolization. The commodity, like the symbol, is both what it is and the token of something else (i.e., money); on Flint's farm, the something else has totally displaced the concrete reality. To use farming as a trope for self-sufficiency without literally farming would be to perform in thought the same violation Flint commits on his land. Thoreau finds this commodified habit of mind to be the common practice of his contemporaries. "Our lives," he complains, "pass at such remoteness from its symbols, and its metaphors and tropes are so far fetched" (pp. 244–45). At Walden he redeems his own life from such distancing and loss of the real; he farms the land, as he says in "The Bean-Field," "for the sake of tropes and expression, to serve a parable-maker one day" (p. 162).[7]

Thoreau suggests that the values formerly associated with farming are available to all men, in all pursuits. "Labor of the hands," as he describes his hoeing, ". . . has a constant and imperishable moral, and to the scholar it yields a classic result" (p. 157). The moral yielded by *Walden* is that virtually any kind of workman can be a figurative farmer and any kind of work independent "labor of the hands." The centrality of this phrase to Thoreau's undertaking is suggested by its position at the very outset of the book; it appears in the opening sentence: "When I wrote the following pages, or rather the bulk of them, I lived alone, in the woods, a mile from any neighbor, in a house which I had built myself, on the shore of Walden Pond, in Concord, Massachusetts, and earned my living by the labor of my hands only" (p. 3). Labor of the hands is clearly meant to encompass intellectual as well as manual work. As Thoreau says in explaining what he lived for, "My head is hands and feet. I feel all my best faculties concentrated in it" (p. 98).

A difficulty that arises immediately with Thoreau's metaphoric solution to exchange is that it has the effect of privatizing a civic virtue. Farming as a way of life enjoyed the high standing it did in civic humanist thought because it was a training for participation in the public or political sphere. In *Walden*, as a figure for self-reliant labor, it has become a private virtue—a virtue without civic consequences. And there is no doubt that Thoreau hoped his text would result in some form of political awakening. Indeed, one of his principal objectives in writing *Walden* is to restore his countrymen to the freedom which they have lost under the market system. He moves to the woods on "Independence Day, or the fourth of July, 1845," because he considers this a civic enterprise, requiring a reformation or new foundation of American liberty (p. 84). A close connection can be seen here between the project of *Walden* and Thoreau's appeal at the end of "Civil Disobedience" for a founder or reformer whose eloquence will revive the polity. In the essay, which he wrote while working on the early drafts of the book, he criticizes the country's lawmakers for their failure to "speak with authority" about the government. Implicitly he projects a role for himself as a model legislator, one whose effectiveness will lie in his ability to inspire others through his words:

> No man with a genius for legislation has appeared in America. They are rare in the history of the world. There are orators, politicians, and eloquent men, by the thousand; but the speaker has not yet opened his mouth to speak, who is capable of settling the much-vexed questions of the day. We love eloquence for its own sake, and not for any truth which it may utter, or any heroism it may inspire.[8]

In *Walden* Thoreau assumes the duties of this reformer-legislator as a writer rather than a speaker because of the greater range and authority of literature. The orator, he says in the chapter "Reading," addresses the mob on the transitory issues of the moment, but the author "speaks to the heart and intellect of mankind, to all in any age who can *understand* him" (p. 102). Great writers, he adds, "are a natural and irresistible aristocracy in every society, and, more than kings or emperors, exert an influence on mankind" (p. 103). Twentieth-century readers, with their very different ideas about the functions of texts and the role of the writer, may find it difficult to take these statements seriously. But it is a mistake to treat *Walden* as though it were imbued with the modernist sentiment (to paraphrase W. H. Auden) that literature makes nothing happen. This kind of accommodation with "reality" — of reified consciousness — is precisely what Thoreau is arguing against in the book. Nor for the time and place is there anything especially unusual about his civic ambitions; on the contrary, they are perfectly consistent with the New England ideal of the literary vocation.

Lewis P. Simpson has shown that a conception of the writer as a spiritual and intellectual authority was particularly strong around Boston and Concord during the early decades of the nineteenth century. Simpson uses the term "clerisy," a borrowing from Coleridge, to designate the literary community that emerged at this time and sought to claim for men of letters the influence formerly exercised by the ministry. The wise and learned, it was felt, had a special obligation to educate the nation; through the practice of literature, they were to provide moral guidance and enlightenment.[9] While Thoreau was hardly a conventional member of the New England elite, he shared his culture's emphasis on the usefulness of the literary calling. He conceives *Walden* as a reforming text meant to produce results in the world, and hopes to be remembered, like the heroic writers whom he so admires, as a "messenger from heaven, [a] bearer of divine gifts to man" (p. 36).

But in this respect *Walden* is a notably different text from "Civil Disobedience": though both works begin, as it were, in the social world, *Walden* retreats into the self while "Civil Disobedience" calls for resistance to the government. This change can be seen in the book's very structure, its transition from "Economy" to "Conclusion," from Concord and Thoreau's neighbors to the inwardness of self-discovery. A mood of withdrawal totally dominates the final pages, as Thoreau urges his readers to turn their backs on society and look inside themselves. "Be a Columbus to whole new continents and worlds within you," he exhorts, "opening new channels, not of trade, but of thought. . . . [E]xplore the private sea, the Atlantic and Pacific Ocean of [your] being alone" (p. 321). The ending contains some of the book's best-known aphorisms, most of which revolve around the sentiment that "every one [should] mind his own business, and endeavor to be what he was made" (p. 326). The image left is of a solitary individual pursuing his own development, cultivating his own consciousness, in utter indifference to the common good. Such an image is not only radically at odds with the tone of *Walden*'s beginning; it also amounts to a distorted—and reified—reflection of the laissez-faire individualist pursuing his private economic interest at the expense of the public welfare.

Thoreau's unwitting kinship with social behavior he deplores can also be seen in his effort to create a myth of his experience. As the narrative progresses, he seems to grow intent upon suppressing all traces of autobiography and treating his two years at the pond as a timeless and universal experience. The patterning of the book after the cycle of the seasons contributes to this sense of the mythological, as does perhaps even more strongly the almost purely metaphorical character of the "Conclusion." In contrast to the specificity of the opening chapter, which takes place in Concord, Massachusetts, in the year 1845, the ending is situated in no time and no physical location. Thoreau declares open war on history: after ridiculing the "transient and fleeting" doings of his contemporaries, he vows "not to live in this restless, nervous, bustling, trivial Nineteenth Century, but stand or sit thoughtfully while it goes by" (pp. 329–30). The text's denial of history, its flight from Jacksonian America, paradoxically resembles the commodified mode of thought which Thoreau charges against his countrymen and which permits a Flint to perceive his fruits and vegetables as dollars. In an analogous way, Thoreau allows the mythic value of his Walden experiment to displace the actual circumstances of its occurrence. Moreover, his determination to empty his adventure of historical content replicates a basic feature of reified consciousness. As he himself has pointed out repeatedly, market society engenders a conflation of history with nature. By presenting its limited, time-bound conventions as eternal, the existing order in effect places itself outside time and beyond the possibility of change. Although Thoreau rigorously condemns his society's "naturalizing" of itself in this fashion, he can be charged with performing a version of the same process on his own life by erasing history from *Walden* and mythologizing his experiment at the pond.[10]

IV

The privatizing and antihistorical tendencies which blunt *Walden*'s critical edge reappear in Thoreau's attempt to devise a conception of reading and writing as unalienated labor. He is obliged to seek such a formulation because as a maker of texts, a would-be reformer in literature, he encounters the same problem that his neighbors experience in their daily transactions as farmers, merchants, and workmen: he has to confront the specter of the marketplace. In this area too Thoreau's rebuttal to exchange embroils him in difficulties he is unable to overcome. Indeed, the two goals he sets himself as an author, to initiate civic reformation while resisting the exchange process, turn out to be so incompatible by the mid-nineteenth century as to render their attainment mutually exclusive.

Trade, Thoreau keeps insisting, "curses everything it handles; and though you trade in messages from heaven, the whole curse of trade attaches to the business" (p. 70). Anything that is done for money, including the effort to instruct mankind, to be a "messenger from heaven" as Thoreau desires, is compromised by that very fact. Of his brief experience as a schoolteacher, he observes: "As I did not teach for the good of my fellowmen, but simply for a livelihood, this was a failure" (p. 69). In *Walden* he regularly refers to his readers as students — "Perhaps these pages are more particularly addressed to poor students," he says as early as the second paragraph (p. 4) — and he clearly sees the threat of failure hanging over his writing unless he can circumvent exchange in his dealings with his audience.

Thoreau regards life and presence, two qualities nullified by the capitalist market, as fundamental to his efficacy as an author-legislator. In censuring philanthropists, he says that their error is to distribute money rather than spending themselves. "Be sure to give the poor [i.e., poor students] the aid they most need, though it be your example which leaves them far behind" (p. 75). When he introduces himself on the first page as *Walden*'s narrator, he emphasizes his own determination to retain the "I" or the self in his writing, to speak in the first person, and he adds that he requires of every writer "a simple and sincere account of his own life, and not merely what he has heard of other men's lives" (p. 3). This conception of literature as synonymous with life and the person recurs throughout the book, for example, when Thoreau states of the written word that it "is the work of art nearest to life itself. It may be translated into every language, and not only be read but actually breathed from all human lips" (p. 102). But if words have to be alive to "inspire" the reader, there are two senses in which exchange turns them into dead letters and kills the text. Since the cost of a thing is the amount of life expended for it, the book as commodity becomes an instrument of death like any item sold on the market. It also suffers an internal demise, commodification destroying literature's "bloom" just as surely as it blights the fruits and flowers on Flint's farm.

The literary work as article of exchange and the author as tradesman was the accepted state of affairs when Thoreau wrote *Walden*. As Tocqueville noted after his visit to America, the aristocratic domain of letters had become in democratic-capitalist society "the trade of literature."[11] Thoreau, who claims to want "the flower and fruit of a man, that some fragrance be wafted from him to me, and some ripeness flavor our intercourse" (p. 77), views the situation of literary culture with dismay. The books read and written by his countrymen, he feels, are not literature at all but commodities with the impoverished nature of commodities. Singularly lacking in either fragrance or flavor, they are fit only to be consumed by "those who, like cormorants and ostriches, can digest" any sort of foodstuff (p. 104). To Thoreau, they are simply one more piece of merchandise in the unending stream of commerce which connects "the desperate city" to "the desperate country" (p. 8); and like the huckleberries transported to the Boston market from the country's hills, they lose their most essential qualities in transit. "Up comes the cotton, down goes the woven cloth; up comes the silk, down goes the woolen; up comes the books, but down goes the wit that writes them" (p. 116). Popular writers are "the machines to provide this provender," Thoreau contends, evoking his characterizations of both the huckleberry and the laboring man, and his neighbors are "the machines to read it" (p. 104–5). He proceeds to deliver a lengthy diatribe against fashionable literature and the public that devours it "with unwearied gizzard," concluding with the statement that "this sort of gingerbread is baked daily and more sedulously than pure wheat or rye-and-Indian in almost every oven, and finds a surer market" (p. 105).[12]

In addition to changing the text into a commodity and taking away its life and essence, the marketplace endangers Thoreau's literary-civic enterprise because it encourages the reader in his addiction to mediation. Mediation, the substitution or replacement of one thing or person by another, is the heart and soul of the exchange process. In "Civil Disobedience" Thoreau disapproves of money, the medium of exchange, on precisely the grounds that it "comes between a man and his objects, and obtains them for him," thereby reducing his capacity for self-reliance.[13] In *Walden* he states repeatedly that he wants the reader to obtain his objects by his own exertions (see his definition of a *"necessary of life,"* p. 12). To allow the reader to accept Thoreau's experience as a substitute for his own would be the literary equivalent of the use of money. "I would not have any one adopt *my* mode of living on any account," he declares; rather, "I would have each one be very careful to find out and pursue his *own way"* (p. 71). Reading or studying something should never become a substitute for doing it, according to Thoreau, who expresses disdain for the "common course" of instruction whereby the student (or reader) is required "to study chemistry, and not learn how his bread is made, or mechanics, and not learn how it is earned." " 'But,' " he continues, anticipating a probable critic,

> "you do not mean that the students should go to work with their hands instead of their heads?" I do not mean that exactly, but I mean

something which he might think a good deal like that; I mean that they should not *play* life, or *study* it merely, while the community supports them at this expensive game, but earnestly *live* it from beginning to end. How could youths better learn to live than by at once trying the experiment of living? [P. 51]

As Thoreau also points out, those who make a habit of depending on others through exchange and the division of labor court the risk of not being able to use their heads at all. "No doubt another *may* also think for me; but it is not therefore desirable that he should do so to the exclusion of my thinking for myself" (p. 46).

The reader who lets another do his thinking or his acting for him is a reader whose consciousness has been reified. He reacts to the words on the printed page with the same passivity and sense of noninvolvement as he feels in bowing to social reality. Most readers, in Thoreau's view, are in exactly this position; they limit themselves to books meant for deficient intellects and children and so "dissipate their faculties in what is called easy reading" (p. 104). To read in this feeble way, without exerting one's mind or relying on oneself, is merely to be confirmed in one's present condition. "Easy reading," like the writing which elicits it, obviously cannot promote the spirit of independence Thoreau seeks to nurture as the author of *Walden*.

Thoreau's task as a writer-reformer accordingly requires him to make a book which is not a commodity. To spare *Walden* the fate of the huckleberry, he has to ensure that like the pond it contains "no muck" and is "too pure to have a market value" (p. 199). He also has to find some way for the reader to eliminate mediation and achieve independence in his own right. And here again Thoreau has recourse to the civic humanist ideal of husbandry for his solution. He links authorship and agriculture and portrays both the artist and his audience as figurative husbandmen, extricating *Walden* from the marketplace by means of metaphor.

In "The Bean-Field" Thoreau draw a sustained comparison between composing a text and planting a crop. He likens himself at his hoe to "a plastic artist in the dewy and crumbling sand," and he speaks of "making the yellow soil express its summer thought in bean leaves and blossoms rather than in wormwood and piper and millet grass, making the earth say beans instead of grass" (p. 156–57). The writer as metaphorical farmer remains outside the exchange process and never deals in commodities because he never sells his crop for money. His text, which never reaches the Boston market, preserves its effectiveness as a living expression of his individuality.

Thoreau also depicts the reader as a laborer "of the hands" and contrasts the toil of reading *Walden* with the "easy reading" suitable to popular literature. He claims that the diligent student who sits alone with his books throughout the day and late into the night is "at work in *his* field, and chopping in *his* woods, as the farmer is in his" (p. 136). Such strenuous intellectual exertion is the price of comprehending *Walden*, which requires a "heroic reader" to emulate its heroic author (p. 106). "The heroic books, even if printed in the character of our mother tongue, will always be in a language dead to degenerate times; and we must *laboriously* seek the meaning of each word and line, conjecturing a larger sense than common use permits out of what wisdom and valor and generosity we have" (p. 100, italics added). The reader as symbolic farmer, tasked more by *Walden's* intricacies than by "any exercise which the customs of the day esteem" (p. 101), triumphs over mediation by having the same "laborious" experience at his desk that Thoreau has at the pond. Reading *Walden* becomes figuratively identical with being at Walden, a discipline in the mental self-reliance which enables one, or so Thoreau believes, to penetrate the "veil of reification."[14]

The qualification is in order because in metaphorizing reading and writing as activities outside history and the marketplace Thoreau disregards the realities of the text's evolution and his relation to the public. History forcibly enters *Walden* in the changes and additions made between the first draft and the published version, changes stretching over a period of nearly ten years. J. Lyndon Shanley, who has done the most thorough study of the original draft, finds that Thoreau enlarged the second half of the manuscript far more than the first, adding "more to the account of his life in the woods than to his criticism of contemporary ways," and that his major revisions were intended to emphasize the cycle of the seasons.[15] The development *within* the text, in other words, corresponds to a development *outside* the text, a shift in attitude suggesting a deepening estrangement from the social realm. Thoreau seems to have suffered a crisis of confidence in the likelihood of civic reform and the idea of his writing as a means of instigating it. Besides the addition of the "Conclusion," none of which appeared in the first draft, one change in particular is unequivocal in suggesting his disenchantment with the role of educator-legislator. In both versions he speaks of planting in his readers the seeds of sincerity, truth, and simplicity, to "see if they will not grow in this soil." But missing from the original manuscript is the sentence which comes next in the book: "Alas! I said this to myself; but now another summer is gone, and another, and another, and I am obliged to say to you, Reader, that the seeds which I planted, if indeed they *were* the seeds of those virtues, were wormeaten or had lost their vitality, and so did not come up" (p. 164).[16]

Between 1846, when he began *Walden*, and 1854, when he completed it, Thoreau had good reason to lose confidence in the viability of his civic aspirations. "Civil Disobedience" (1849) and *A Week on the Concord and Merrimack Rivers* (1849) had been published in that time; the first elicited no reaction whatsoever from the public, and the second has been described as "one of the most complete failures in literary history."[17] In the final version of *Walden* Thoreau himself alludes to the discouraging reception of his earlier work. He tells the story of an Indian who came to Concord to sell baskets but learned to his chagrin that the inhabitants did not want to buy any. The Indian wrongly supposed that he had done his part by making the baskets, "and then it would be the white man's to buy them. He had not discovered," comments Thoreau,

> that it was necessary for him to make it worth the other's while to buy them, or at least make him think that it was so, or to make something else which it would be worth his while to buy. I too had woven a kind of basket of delicate texture, but I had not made it worth any one's while to buy them. Yet not the less, in my case, did I think it worth my while to weave them, and instead of studying how to make it worth men's while to buy my baskets, I studied rather how to avoid the necessity of selling them. [P. 19]

The "kind of basket" woven by Thoreau prior to *Walden* was of course *A Week*, a book which sold so poorly, as he reveals in a journal entry for 1853, that he was obliged to take possession of "706 copies out of an edition of 1000." He confides to the journal, and the bravado does not hide his own feelings of hurt and vexation, "I believe that this result is more inspiring and better for me than if a thousand had bought my wares. It affects my privacy less and leaves me freer."[18]

Under the market system, there is no way for an author to exert influence to a significant degree without attracting a popular audience. If a book never reaches Boston, it is not likely to have much impact there. The influential writers praised by Thoreau enjoyed an "advantage" that was unavailable to him in the United States in the middle of the nineteenth century: the advantage of patronage by kings, noblemen, and warriors. Thoreau is caught in a contradiction of his own and history's devising: while he craves the authority of a founder, he refuses to view his text as a commodity and to accept "the necessity of selling" it. The failures of "Civil Disobedience" and *A Week* strengthen his antimarket resolution, but at the same time they force him to retreat from his ambition to reform the polity. Since he cannot shape popular opinion without large sales, he effectively abandons his civic project by striving to make *Walden* a difficult text at which the reader has to labor — hence a text which is inaccessible to the great majority of the public. "It is a ridiculous demand which England and America make," he writes in the "Conclusion," "that you shall speak so that they can understand you." And he goes on to voice defiant satisfaction that his own pages "admit of more than one interpretation," approximating the obscurity of the Walden ice (pp. 324–25). At this point Thoreau's celebration of figurative husbandry has become indistinguishable from the modernist credo of textual complexity, even incomprehensibility. The first draft of *Walden* was "Addressed to my Townsmen," but the last, colored by disappointment, seeks to exclude the many and narrow its appeal to a "fit audience, though few."[19]

Thoreau worked five years longer on *Walden* than he had originally intended. Expecting a success with his first book, he hoped to bring out the second as early as 1849; copies of *A Week* included the announcement that *Walden* would be published shortly.[20] But when it became evident that *A Week* was not selling, his publishers refused to issue *Walden*, and Thoreau spent five additional years revising and refining it. Since neither *A Week* nor the first draft of *Walden* is a masterpiece, this brief account of Thoreau's publishing difficulties suggests some final ironies of history. Insofar as *Walden* does "transcend" the age of Jackson, does rise above its historical moment as a consequence of its excellence as an artwork, it does so precisely because of the particular nineteenth-century circumstances under which it reached print. Its transcendence of history is rooted in the conditions of its production — its *belated* production — as a commodity to be marketed by publishers. And still more: there is the additional irony that *Walden* is its own most effective reply to Thoreau's denigrations of commercial enterprise. One need not even point out that the values of brotherhood and love, values conspicuously absent from *Walden*, are inextricably bound up with the principle of "exchange." On strictly aesthetic grounds, the text disputes the contention that "trade curses every thing it handles." Far from impairing the quality of *Walden*, commercial considerations conspired to make it a better work. *Walden* is the one undeniably great book Thoreau ever wrote, thanks in part to the operations of the marketplace.

Notes

1. Henry D. Thoreau, *Walden*, ed. J. Lyndon Shanley (Princeton: Princeton University Press, 1971). Page numbers included in the text refer to this edition.

2. Ralph Waldo Emerson, "Thoreau," in *The Selected Writings of Ralph Waldo Emerson*, ed. Brooks Atkinson (New York: Modern Library, 1950), p. 896. The standard view of *Walden*'s development is given by Walter Harding and Michael Meyer in their edition of *The New Thoreau Handbook* (New York: New York University Press, 1980), p. 51: "*Walden* may seem to begin in despair, but it ends in ecstasy."

3. Leo Marx has explored *Walden* from the perspective of pastoralism in *The Machine in the Garden: Technology and the Pastoral Ideal in America* (New York: Oxford University Press, 1964), pp. 242–65. Marx sees Thoreau's great foe as technology, the railroad in particular; I regard technology as simply one aspect of the market society that is his real adversary.

4. On the civic humanist tradition, see J. G. A. Pocock, *The Machiavellian Moment: Florentine Political Thought and the Atlantic Republican Tradition* (Princeton: Princeton University Press, 1975).

5. See Luckàc's *History and Class Consciousness: Studies in Marxist Dialectics* (Cambridge, Mass.: MIT Press, 1971), pp. 83–222. Also relevant is Roland Barthes, *Mythologies*, trans. Annette Lavers (New York: Hill & Wang, 1972), esp. pp. 109–59. A valuable discussion of reification and American literature appears in Carolyn Porter, *Seeing and Being: The Plight of the Participant Observer in Emerson, James, Adams, and Faulkner* (Middletown, Conn.: Wesleyan University Press, 1981), pp. 23–53, passim. On reification in Thoreau, the

best treatment is John P. Diggins, "Thoreau, Marx, and the 'Riddle' of Alienation," *Social Research* 39 (1972): 571–98.

6. The question of whether American farmers were ever really self-sufficient is much debated. Clarence H. Danhof, for one, has argued that the market orientation deplored by Thoreau did not come to dominate American agriculture until the nineteenth century. See Danhof's *Change in Agriculture: The Northern United States, 1820–1870* (Cambridge, Mass.: Harvard University Press, 1969.

7. Compare Thoreau's question in *A Week on the Concord and Merrimack Rivers*, ed. Carl F. Hovde, William L. Howarth, and Elizabeth Hall Witherell (Princeton: Princeton University Press, 1980), p. 382: "Is not Nature, rightly read, that of which she is commonly taken to be the symbol merely?"

8. Henry D. Thoreau, *Reform Papers*, ed. Wendell Glick (Princeton: Princeton University Press, 1973), p. 88. For a reading of *Walden* as a heroic text, see Stanley Cavell, *The Senses of Walden* (New York: Viking Press, 1972).

9. See Lewis P. Simpson, *The Man of Letters in New England and the South: Essays on the History of the Literary Vocation in America* (Baton Rouge: Louisiana State University Press, 1973), esp. pp. 3–31.

10. Compare Roland Barthes, p. 141: "The status of the bourgeoisie is particular, historical: man as represented by it is universal, eternal."

11. Alexis de Tocqueville, *Democracy in America*, ed. Phillips Bradley, 2 vols. (1835, 1840; rpt., New York: Vintage Books, 1945), 2:64.

12. Thoreau's outburst here brings to mind another prominent American author who was for a time his townsman: Nathaniel Hawthorne. In *The House of the Seven Gables* (1851), Hawthorne takes an equally dim — if rather more bemused — view of his potential audience. His image for the undiscriminating public, eager to devour whatever is available (including the latest literature) and always hungry for more, is little Ned Higgins, the Yankee schoolboy who patronizes Hepzibah's cent shop and feasts on gingerbread figures of everything from men to locomotives.

13. *Reform Papers*, p. 77.

14. Lukàcs, p. 86.

15. J. Lyndon Shanley, *The Making of "Walden": With the Text of the First Version* (Chicago: University of Chicago Press, 1957), pp. 57, 87; see also Lawrence Buell, *Literary Transcendentalism: Style and Vision in the American Renaissance* (Ithaca: Cornell University Press, 1973), pp. 309–10.

16. Compare Shanley, p. 11.

17. Harding and Meyer, p. 11.

18. Laurence Stapleton, ed., *H. D. Thoreau: A Writer's Journal* (New York: Dover Books, 1960), p. 107. Walter Harding discerns a strain of despair in Thoreau's journal for 1853–54 and speculates that he was discouraged because "his literary career seemed to have reached a stalemate." See Harding's *The Days of Henry Thoreau* (New York: Alfred A. Knopf, 1965), p. 329.

19. Shanley, p. 11.

20. See Shanley's "Historical Introduction" to the Princeton edition of *Walden*, p. 363.

The Great Bean Field Hoax:
Thoreau and the Agricultural
Reformers
Robert A. Gross*

I

Surely, no two figures of antebellum American culture make an odder couple than the fabulous, gaudy promoter of "The Greatest Show on Earth," Phineas Taylor Barnum, and the so-called Hermit of Walden, Henry David Thoreau. What starker contrast could there be, what more striking allegory of the fate of what Barnum once called "the Universal Yankee Nation" in the world of industrial capitalism and mass democracy? P. T. Barnum: the Connecticut farm boy who left the hard soil of his native Bethel to build an entertainment empire upon the sure foundations of well-advertised hoax and deceit. Henry David Thoreau: the much-traveled Concordian who seldom left home, yet established an enduring reputation for a "simple and sincere" way of life. How could one even imagine linking the name of the "prince of humbugs," the shah of Iranistan — the $150,000 Oriental palace Barnum built in Bridgeport, Connecticut — the popular lecturer on "The Art of Money-Getting," with that of Concord's artist of Kouroo, who proved in his $28.12½ hut by a pond that "a man is rich in proportion to the number of things which he can afford to let alone"?

Well, the *Knickerbocker* magazine of March 1855 did just that, joining Barnum and Thoreau together in an essay provocatively titled "Town and Rural Humbugs." "Beyond all question," the anonymous writer explained, "the two most remarkable books that have been published the last year are the 'Auto-biography of Barnum' and 'Life in the Woods' by Thoreau." The essay opened as a study in contrasts, with Barnum and Thoreau alike only in the fact that their opposing ways of life were equally unattractive:

> If anything is calculated to induce a man to see how few beans will support animal life [the reviewer said], we think it is a contemplation of the life and career of the great showman. If there is any thing calculated to reconcile us, not to the career of Barnum, but to whatever laborious drudgery may be necessary to procure good beefsteaks and oysters. . . . , it is the thought of those inevitable beans, that constituted so large a part of the *crop* of Mr. Thoreau, and that extraordinary compound of cornmeal and water, which he facetiously called bread.

*Reprinted from *Virginia Quarterly Review* 61 (Summer 1985):483–97, by permission of *Virginia Quarterly Review*.

But the difference involved more than a pot of beans. The reviewer had perceptively detected that Barnum and Thoreau stood apart, in distinctive ways, from the shams and illusions that entranced most of their country-men. The Connecticut showman, of course, profited richly by exploiting the illusions of the public; the "Concord philosopher, or modern Diogenes," as he was called, preferred simply to live by exposing them. In that difference from their contemporaries, the two were akin. Neither, it appeared, was easily fooled by what the mass of men took to be reality.

So far, so good. Then suddenly, the writer began probing further the resemblance between the two. And now it was more than similarity in difference. Both were artists, mixing nature and art in order to live "by their wits" and not by their hands. Barnum's physical concoctions—the Feejee Mermaid, the Woolly Horse—were matched by Thoreau's imagina-tive ones, like the battle between the ants. Both were "good-natured, genial, pleasant men," fleecing or scorning their fellows with equal cheerfulness. Both were "compassionate men," with an occasional moment of pity for the follies of humankind. And finally, "both were humbugs—one a town and the other a rural humbug."

A staggering conclusion to an essay which had opened with the claim that Barnum and Thoreau were "perfect antipodes to each other"! But nowhere did the writer explain precisely why he thought Thoreau a fraud. My guess is that it was those "horrid beans and that melancholy mixture of meal and water." Nobody, the author evidently believed, nobody could exist on that miserable fare. Obviously, then, Thoreau had invented the story of his stay at the Pond, beans and all, for the sake of assailing the shams and delusions of his neighbors. The ancient Diogenes would have been pleased.

Now, I want to argue that the *Knickerbocker* writer was onto something important about Thoreau, though he failed utterly to divine the hidden depths of *Walden*. Henry David Thoreau was no P. T. Barnum. But he did have a good many tricks up his sleeve. ". . . There are more secrets in my trade," he observed, "than in most men's, and yet not voluntarily kept, but inseparable from its very nature." Discovering those secrets provides for me much of the challenge and the delight in reading *Walden*. The one I propose to unravel now is what I have called "the Great Bean Field Hoax."

Thoreau's bean field, of course, occupies rich ground in *Walden* and in American literature. It forms the central part of his experiment in getting a living at the pond "by the labor of my hands only." The account of that venture, recording in fresh, imaginative detail Thoreau's progress in farming, from his wars with the woodchucks to his battle with the weeds, and conscientiously itemizing his "income" and his "outgoes" down to the last half-penny, purports to represent a true experience, practical proof of his belief that "to maintain one's self on this earth is not a hardship but a pastime, if we will live simply and wisely. . . ." But, as with everything in *Walden*, it is more than that. The epic of the bean field also shows off Thoreau in literary high spirits, playfully telling his husbandman's toils. Indeed, "The Bean-field" chapter, as one scholar has observed, represents "a microcosm of the entire *Walden*," an epitome of the techniques and the themes he uses throughout the book. The account of the beans thus could be said to realize perfectly Thoreau's Transcendental purposes, so integrating the details of experience with their higher meaning that the facts of the Understanding are subtly transformed into the facts of the Imagination.

But the essence of the hoax in 19th-century America was to accomplish a comparable conversion of fact into conviction through the painstaking marshalling of seemingly scientific evidence for outlandish claims. P. T. Barnum was the unchallenged master of the method; at his American Museum in New York City, natural curiosities were exhibited with such "an *appearance* of scientific validity" that the public could relish the challenge to determine what was authentic and what was not. Perhaps Thoreau discerned the technique during the three visits he made to the museum in the 1850's, but these came after *Walden* had been published; besides, Thoreau never evinced any suspicion of the displays, even of the horned "camelopards" he viewed that were only five feet long but stood 18 feet high. Then again Thoreau did not need any lessons from the master.

"The one great rule of composition. . . ," Thoreau proclaimed, "is to *speak the truth*. This 1st, this 2nd, this 3rd." But it was not a narrowly literal truth he had in mind. He could, to be sure, be impeccable about the facts when it suited his fancy, insisting, for example, on altering the proofs of *Walden* to reflect a 15-cent rise in the railroad fare from Concord to Fitchburg. "Here is warranty, if needed," remarks J. Lyndon Shanley, a distinguished scholar of the book, "for almost all the other facts in *Walden*, even down to the one cent listed as the cost of chalk." The trap for the unwary is easily set. Although the railroad fare is exact, although other details demonstrate a precise knowledge of the life of Concord, even stating the typical farm to be the 60 acres which every valuation list I have analyzed, from 1750 to 1850, also shows, it can be demonstrated that Thoreau wickedly assembled the "facts" of his bean field experiment, not to furnish a reliable agricultural report, but to carry out an elaborate spoof. His method was to mingle seeds of truth and fiction so artfully that the innocent reader would be led unhesitantly to swallow his beans. As Thoreau warned, "Books must be read as deliberately and reservedly as they were written." But Thoreau, as the *Knickerbocker* remarked, was also a compassionate soul. He carefully provides a creative reader with the clues to detect the witty incongruities of the facts and to laugh at the hoax. In the process, the larger mysteries of *Walden* are unveiled.

II

The targets of this well-constructed spoof were the agricultural reformers of the day, who carried on an incessant campaign throughout the antebellum era to alter the ways farmers used the land. New England agriculture, went the complaint, was slovenly, wasteful, inefficient, blindly ridden by ignorance and custom, heedless of the long-term damage being done to the land. The chief trouble was that farmers unthinkingly tried to do too much, cultivating far more land than they had the labor or capital to manage with any success. Everything was done "by halves" — "half-farming, half-tilling, and half-manuring" — without any foresight or plan. Farmers labor hard, it was conceded, far harder than they ought, but "to no kind of good purpose."

> Their work hurries them on [a New Hampshire writer lamented], and they have not time to make the necessary retrenchments and improvements; but continue (to use the common expression) 'slashing on, heels over head,' without consideration — zeal without improvement; thus they make perfect slaves of themselves, and never reform, pass through the world without enjoying the sweets of living — they follow their fathers' paths and swerve not.

This was a longstanding objection against American agriculture, dating back to the mid-18th century and deriving its inspiration and ideals from the English Agricultural Revolution. In this perspective, shaped by the Old World realities of abundant, impoverished labor and scarce, expensive land, intelligent farming was intensive farming, directed by educated, progressive gentlemen, whose wise example would be readily imitated by grateful and deferential small farmers. The reformers' vision, sadly, overlooked one fundamental economic reality: in the setting of the New World, it was rational for farmers to save on labor by exploiting land. Even after circumstances shifted, with crop yields falling and a rising population pressing on the soil, farmers stubbornly refused to change their ways. Instead, they increasingly headed west, where they could live less "thickly" and obtain an easier living from the land.

For the agricultural reformers, many of whom were New England clergymen with the conservative beliefs of the Federalist-Whig tradition, that was the real problem: the continuing exodus of farmers away from the East, away from the hallowed institutions of town and meeting house and into the potential disorder and irreligion of the frontier. It was to discourage this emigration that the Massachusetts Unitarian clergyman Henry Colman abandoned the ministry in the mid-1830's and sought out the official burden of conducting an agricultural survey of the state. "If the Survey results in no other good," Colman wrote Whig Governor Edward Everett in a covering letter to his first report, "it will present, I hope, in their true light the motives which the children of Massachusetts have to stay at home." To that end, Colman comprehensively summarized the expert wisdom of reform in a set of four reports between 1837 and 1841, including a survey of Thoreau's own Middlesex County. Farmers needed to rationalize and systematize their work; in the words of one of Colman's reforming predecessors, the Federalist Josiah Quincy, they had "YET TO LEARN THE IMMENSE PRODUCTIVE POWER OF A PERFECTLY CULTIVATED ACRE." Colman recommended a vast array of specific reforms—new crops, new fertilizers, new rotations—all gathered together under the belief that if farmers reduced their acreage, consolidated and perfected their methods according to the latest scientific advice of the agricultural improvers, carefully calculated their productions by the demands of the market, and withal, continued to practice Poor Richard's virtues of honesty, industry, and thrift; if they did all these things, then they would easily meet the test of agricultural competition from the West and prosper under God. Of course, they would never grow rich. But parson Colman knew that was not the goal of life. "Good husbandry," he thought, "promotes good morals." In Colman's Whiggish vision, the outcome would be a well-ordered commonwealth, knit together by public virtue and Christian love.

> Let the children of Massachusetts then love and honor their good old mother. Her soil may be hard; but labor compels it to be bountiful. Her climate may be harsh; but it gives strength and elasticity to the muscles, and the brightness of its own stars to the mind. Her voice in winter may sometimes be hoarse; and her face wrinkled and frowning; but her children will not love her the less for a sternness of discipline, by which she trains them up in habits of unremitting labor and self-dependence; and thus qualifies them to be the blessings and ornaments of their own community; the substantial pillars of the federal edifice; and the pioneers of learning, civilization, humanity, and religion in the boundless West.

Henry Thoreau had a long familiarity with the institutions and literature of agricultural reform, by the time he began hoeing beans at Walden. Although he had been raised largely in the commercial world of the central villages of New England and, briefly, in Boston, Thoreau could not escape the agricultural concerns of his neighbors. His own father, a storekeeper turned pencil-maker, belonged to the Middlesex Society of Husbandmen and Manufacturers, the local reform association that sought to forge a strong commercial alliance between the farmer and the tradesman, and the Thoreau family actively competed for prizes at the society's annual fairs. In the manufacturers' division, John Thoreau, Sr., won an award for his pencils in 1823. In the women's departments, Henry's Aunt Maria was once cited for a hearth rug, his sisters Helen and Sophia for their art work. Thoreau himself always took pride in his talent in the garden, especially the melon-patch, but "All that I ever got a premium for," he once recalled with amusement, "was a monstrous squash—so coarse that nobody could eat it." Thoreau was also a close reader of the agricultural press—close and selective. "In reading a work on agriculture," he advises in *A Week on the Concord and Merrimack Rivers*,

> we have to skip the author's moral reflections, and the words 'Providence' and 'He' scattered along the page, to come at the profitable level of what he has to say. . . . There is more religion in men's science than there is science in their religion. Let us make haste to the report of the committee on swine.

On the surface, there are noticeable affinities between Thoreau's ideas about agriculture and those of the reformers. Henry Colman decried luxury, encouraged self-sufficiency, and urged farmers to produce their own bread—all favorite themes of Thoreau. Thoreau was probably attracted as well by the improvers' ideal of "one perfectly cultivated acre," if only for its uncompromising spirit. It is striking that both in *A Week* and in *Walden* Thoreau accepted the reformers' critique as an accurate depiction of the contemporary state of farming. "Ancient poetry and mythology suggest, at least, that husbandry was once a sacred art," he lamented in *Walden*, "but it is pursued with irreverent haste and heedlessness by us, our object being to have large farms and crops merely." Having grown up in a Whig household, he took Whig ideas as a starting point in defining social reality—but not as his ultimate destination.

What radically divided Thoreau from the agricultural improvers was his refusal of intensive cultivation. Thoreau was appalled at the improvers' vision of a tame, polite landscape of apple orchards and market gardens. Excessive cultivation, he complained in *A Week*, ground down and pulverized the man along with the soil. It carefully cropped the independent, heroic spirit, fencing him in a solid wall of respectable institutions and "good manners." "There may be an excess of cultivation as well as of anything else until civilization becomes pathetic. A highly cultivated man—all whose bones can be bent! whose heaven-born virtues are but good manners." Worse, intensive farming was not only refined but also obscene. The gardener wooed nature too strenuously, laboring with a courtier's zeal for his reward. Far better for Thoreau was the independence of the Indian, who kept his dignity as he learned the ways of the woods. "If the [Indian] is somewhat of a stranger in [nature's] midst, the gardener is too much of a familiar. There is something vulgar and foul in the latter's closeness to his mistress, something noble and cleanly in the former's distance." In *Walden*, Thoreau redoubled the attack, pouring out his invective on the model farms, whose agricultural experiments filled the pages of the reformers' reports. The very thought of them raised a vile stench.

> A model farm! where the house stands like a fungus in a muck-heap, chambers for men, horses, oxen, and swine, cleansed and uncleansed,

all contiguous to one another! Stocked with men! A great grease-spot, redolent of manures and butter-milk! Under a high state of cultivation, being manured with the hearts and brains of men! As if you were to raise your potatoes in the church-yard! Such is a model farm.

No wonder, then, Thoreau boasted that his "was one field not in Mr. Coleman's [sic] report."

III

With Thoreau's disdain for model farms so explicit and so extreme, it becomes obvious that the bean field was no innocent agricultural experiment, whose success would be freely tested by the practical results. Thoreau sets up the account to suggest otherwise, slyly beginning "The Beanfield" chapter as an open inquiry into an as yet unsettled question. "What was the meaning of this so sturdy and self-respecting, this small Herculean labor [with the beans], I knew not. I came to love my rows, my beans, though so many more than I wanted. . . . But why should I raise them? . . . What shall I learn of beans or beans of me?" These are essential questions for Thoreau; exploring the meaning of labor, in its broadest sense, forms the central project of the chapter and of the book. But at the same time, what is about to unfold is a wonderfully malicious parody of agricultural reform literature, executed with a completely straight face. In the authentic spirit of P. T. Barnum and Davy Crockett, of the Yankee and the frontiersman, Thoreau concocts out of seemingly plausible, petty details a triumphant tall tale of man and beans.

Let me hasten to add I have no doubt Thoreau actually grew some beans. But why beans? "Wishing to earn ten or twelve dollars by some honest and agreeable method," Thoreau explains, he planted the seeds. Beans were a money crop from the start. It is a believable claim, unless one happens to know that beans were no commercial staple in Concord, in fact, had never been and would never be so in the agricultural history of the town. In the 1840's, when Thoreau's farming neighbors set about raising money, they planted grains — corn and oats; they made English hay, the epitome of the cash crop, intensively produced on upland meadows that at the reformers' urging, had been laboriously redeemed from bogs and swamps; they cut wood; and increasingly, after the coming of the railroad, they milked cows for the city. They did *not* grow beans. In 1850, half of the farmers in town listed no beans at all in their reports for the U.S. Agricultural Census. And of the 60 who did grow beans, only four raised as many as 12 bushels, Thoreau's total in 1846. Considering that he produced little else, Thoreau surely deserves to be regarded as the "bean king" of Concord. After all, the eccentric choice of crop led local farmers to christen Thoreau's field "the Paradise of Beans," and passersby could not resist the urge to offer the lessons of experience. "Corn, my boy, for fodder; corn for fodder."

It was not just idiosyncrasy that prompted Thoreau to grow beans. They were, in addition, a humble crop, familiar in every Concord home, so long associated with the New England farmer that they had come to stand as a national symbol of the Yankee. Thoreau's common white bush bean was the source of Boston's minor claim to distinction—the baked bean. The famous line about "good old Boston, The home of the bean and the cod," was invented only in 1910, but even in Thoreau's day, the Yankee was known by his beans. "This is the happy land of baked beans and pure religion," the humorist Artemus Ward observed in 1861. Another wit, Josh Billings, developed a considerable monologue on the subject:

> Next to rhy bread, beans hav been called by the poets, and philosphers the cumfort, and staff ov life. . . . Beans are az old az Esau, he sold out for bean porridge. . . . I luv beans, but dont hanker for them. But beans, and me wont quarrell. Baked beans are a grate necessity in Nu England, and not to hav a platter ov them for Sunday dinner, iz lookt upon thare az being stuck-up to the neighbors. One ov the old blue laws ov Massachusetts waz, 'thou shalt eat baked beans on Sunday.' I kan remember now ov eating baked beans, and rhy, and injun bread every Sunday, when i waz a boy, and luving it, bekauze i was obliged to.

In *Walden*, Thoreau delights in pretending to be the mythic Yankee, hardheaded, practical, industrious, regularly up for business by dawn. What could be more fitting, then, than to grow beans?

There is one more reason: beans were originally an Indian crop, the cultivation of which the English settlers had adopted from the natives along with Indian corn. Thoreau imaginatively identified with the independent Indian even more strongly than with the canny Yankee, and he was delighted to discover, by the arrowheads he turned up in the course of hoeing, "that an extinct nation had anciently dwelt here and planted corn and beans ere white men came to clear the land, and so, to some extent, had exhausted the soil for this very crop." Beans thus smacked of the wilderness; they were no kin to English hay.

> The crop of *English* hay is carefully weighed, the moisture calculated, the silicates, and the potash; but in all dells and pond holes in the woods and pastures and swamps grows a rich and various crop only unreaped by man. Mine was, as it were, the connecting link between wild and cultivated fields . . . so my field was, though not in a bad sense, a half-cultivated field. They were beans cheerfully returning to their wild and primitive state that I cultivated, and my hoe played the *Rans des Vaches* for them.

Thoreau not only defied the wisdom of his elders by specializing in beans. He happily ignored advice on many other matters as well. He planted late. He did nothing to improve the thin soil. No foul manures, no commercial, chemical fertilizers for this field! He left three feet between rows and 18 inches between plants; the *New England Farmer* that same year recommended around two feet and six inches, respectively. Thoreau's beans needed room to grow. He hoed them while they were still wet with morning dew: "I would advise you to do all your work if possible, while the dew is on." He claimed to have spent numerous hours cultivating them, from five a.m. to noon, day in, day out, yet somehow he never managed to cultivate them all, though they occupied fewer than two-and-a-half acres. Nor was he any more diligent about dealing with marauding woodchucks. He asked one old woodsman: "Mr. W., is there any way to get woodchucks without trapping them—" "Yes, shoot 'em, you damn fool." He declined the advice, until there was no choice: it was either him or the woodchucks. Supposedly, Thoreau laid a successful trap, but rather than end the creature's career of pillaging, he carried it two miles away, administered a schoolmasterly beating with a stick, then let the rogue go in peace. (Later on, he would devour its kinsman.) Who is he to decide, Thoreau asks, who should live and who should die? "These beans have results which are not harvested by me. Do they not grow for woodchucks also?"

Perhaps the most telling clue to Thoreau's satirical intent is the final accounting of his results. He presents us with a detailed balance sheet as his contribution to the literature of agricultural improvement, "for it is complained that Mr. Coleman [sic] has reported chiefly the expensive experiments of gentlemen farmers." The table of "outgoes" and "income" appears reassuring on the printed page, until one begins to inspect the figures closely, comparing them with the contemporary accounts of other bean farmers and with the scientific literature on bean culture. Thereupon emerges a sorry record of paltry results. Among Thoreau's co-workers in the bean fields of Massachusetts in the late 1840's and early 1950's, the "brag" crop was 35 bushels per acre, and the normal yield was around 20. Chanticleer could boast at best seven or eight. The futility of Thoreau's labors, in literal terms, is evident in still another way. Other bean cultivators required only one and a quarter to one and a half quarts of seed to produce a bushel of beans; Thoreau needed four quarts. But then, his rivals for the premiums were not supporting woodchucks with their crop. Thoreau did well in only one aspect of the bean business: he hired his labor cheap, giving only $3 per acre for ploughing, harrowing, and furrowing, when others paid twice that much. Even so, he grumbled that it was "Too much." Thoreau relished the pretence of being more tightfisted than old "Skin-Flint."

The point of all these Transcendental high jinks is, I think, to turn the sober literature of agricultural improvement, with its spiritually deadening obsession with crop rotations, manures, turnips, and tools, upside down. The conventional agricultural report of the day would proudly testify that the farmer had taken a rundown field or swamp, fit only for crickets and frogs, and by dint of heroic labor, rational planning, large doses of money, and, not uncommonly, exploitation of Irish laborers, had "raised [the land] from the dead and adorned [it] with life and beauty." By contrast, Thoreau claimed to have done just the opposite. He started with exhausted, barren land, did nothing to improve it, obtained little from it, and announced himself quite content. This was a novel achievement, not only in farming, but in American humor. Thoreau had transformed the frontiersman's tall story into a Transcendental small story, replacing the grandiose with the diminutive and, in the process, deflating the exaggerated material pretensions of his countrymen. At least one of his reviewers appreciated the jest. Writing in *Putnam's* in October 1854, Charles Frederick Briggs remarked that Thoreau's practical example in farming was unlikely to be imitated.

> As he was a squatter, he paid nothing for rent, and as he was making no calculation for future crops, he expended nothing for manure so that the results of his farming will not be highly instructive to young agriculturists, nor be likely to be held up as excitements to farming pursuits by agricultural periodicals.

Still, Briggs could take satisfaction in the fact that Thoreau had cultivated literature rather than beans.

> If Mr. Thoreau had been a practical farmer, we should not have been favored with his volume. . . . As it is, we see how much more valuable to mankind is our philosophical vagabond than a hundred sturdy agriculturists; any plodder may raise beans, but it is only one in a million who can write a readable volume.

Briggs' satisfaction in the exchange is today very much our own. Thoreau meant, of course, to "know beans," not to hoe them, in an imaginative demonstration of how a man's labor can be so invested with creative spiritual meaning that actor and object become one. "It was no longer beans that I hoed, nor I that hoed beans. . . ." As a symbolic project of self-culture, the bean field inverted agricultural reform for Thoreau's radical, individualistic purposes. Henry Colman urged farmers to reduce their acreage, improve their methods, particularly in markets, all for the sake of preserving a traditional, deferential way of life. Thoreau agreed on the need to cut back, but as a means of freeing farmers from the market and thereby enabling them to approach Nature as a source of spiritual growth. As a literary achievement, too, *Walden* derives its own lessons from agricultural reform. Thoreau labored in his fields so devotedly, he says, "if only for the sake of tropes and expression, to serve a parable-maker one day." The result was an intensive cultivation of prose, a literary equivalent of hothouse gardening, with Thoreau going over and over the same ground, grafting words with multiple meanings, until he achieved his own "perfectly cultivated acre." He had learned how to plant his message for the attentive reader and how also to cover it up. That was the secret of the "Great Bean Field Hoax."

Henry Thoreau and
the Wisdom of Words
Philip F. Gura*

In 1873 William Ellery Channing, nephew of the Unitarian divine, published a generous reminiscence of his longtime friend, Henry Thoreau; among the many salient hints about Thoreau's character strewn through *Thoreau: The Poet-Naturalist* is Channing's judgment that anyone reading Thoreau should be aware of his "philological side, — this needs to be carefully considered."[1] Given this early assessment by one of Thoreau's closest associates, it is surprising how long it has taken critics to appreciate how the complexity of Thoreau's writing derives in part from his interest in various eighteenth- and nineteenth-century philological theories. Even the most recent scholarship, while acknowledging the importance of the philosophy of language to the mythopoeic structure of *Walden*, does not stress a more important consideration, the relation of his language theory to the development of a teleology quite different from that of other transcendentalists.[2]

In a tangible way Thoreau's interest in and gradual assimilation of the theories of language current among his New England acquaintances convinced him that within the very structure of language was recorded an answer to what comprised the universe as far as man could know it. Thus, as Michael West has suggested, in Thoreau's writing philology often fuses with eschatology, but in such ways that Thoreau was better able not only to comprehend his relationship to the "currents of the Universal Being" but also to define further his philosophical differences from neo-Platonists like Emerson.[3] Certain parts of *Walden* reveal Thoreau's rejection of Emerson's notion of a tripartite correspondence among words / things / Spirit. Further, when the relationship between Thoreau's thoughts on language and his teleology is understood, there is more reason to consider the argument advanced by critics like Joel Porte, who believe that Emerson and Thoreau are best understood as "Transcendentalists in conflict." The ways in which Thoreau saw language stemming organically from empirical objects led to startlingly different conclusions from those proposed by his Concord neighbor.[4]

I

Thoreau agreed with Emerson's basic propositions on language outlined in such places as the fourth section of *Nature* and in "The Poet." For example, even in so late an essay as "Walking" (ca. 1850–52), Thoreau echoed Emerson's statement of how words were "signs of natural facts,"

*This essay was prepared especially for this volume and is published here with the permission of the author. An earlier version appeared in the *New England Quarterly* 52 (March 1979):38–54.

insisting that the true poet was a man who not only could "impress the winds and streams into his service, to speak for him," but "nailed words to their primitive senses" and made his speech so "fresh and natural" that it "would appear to expand like buds at the approach of Spring."[5] But, just as the most evocative vocabulary stemmed from an appreciation of how man's words originate in the observable phenomena of nature, so too did the poet have to realize how all nature was a metaphor for the spiritual life. "All perception of truth," Thoreau remarked in his journal, "is but the detection of analogy." Like Emerson, he believed that by assiduously studying nature one could arrive at the absolute ground of being. "How indispensable to a correct study of nature," he proclaimed, "is a perception of her true meaning." Becoming an interpreter of supranatural analogies as well as a natural historian, Thoreau believed that each fact would "one day flower into a truth."[6]

But if facts flowered into words as well as truths, what did this mean to the man who came so close to these natural facts and to their relationship to language that he detected truths decidedly untranscendental? Emerson had told Thoreau to go to nature to discern "higher laws," but what if these laws were not the ones Emerson expected to pervade the universe? Once nature was pointed to as the repository of a knowledge that could rehabilitate nineteenth-century man, Thoreau continued to sharpen his already keen mind on the analogies he discovered between the worlds of matter and spirit. But from his college days on, his mind had worked with language and nature in ways which evoked a world quite different from Emerson's.

This gradually increasing intellectual separation from Emerson was caused by extended study of seventeenth- and eighteenth-century philological theories, but in particular by those of Charles Kraitsir, the Hungarian immigrant who arrived in Boston in 1844 and who, with the support of Elizabeth Peabody, began proselytizing his novel manner of teaching languages.[7] In 1846, Peabody, the premier purveyor of language theory among the transcendentalists, issued his *The Significance of the Alphabet*, and shortly thereafter Thoreau owned a copy. In 1849 he found Kraitsir's ideas blazoned forth in Peabody's *Aesthetic Papers*, in which his own essay on resistance to civil government was printed. By the 1850s he had furthered his knowledge of Kraitsir's philology by reading his *Glossology: Being a Treatise on the Nature of Language and on the Language of Nature*, from which Thoreau copied pages into his commonplace book.[8]

Kraitsir's *Glossology* was an expanded version of the system on which he had lectured in Boston and which Peabody had assembled in a pamphlet from notes taken at those performances. In Kraitsir's preface to his longer work Thoreau read the assertion that any man who professed to believe in the spiritual life had to "consider it blasphemy to except the human mind and its manifestations in speech from the universal harmony of the world," a supposition that might have been found in the essays of

Emerson himself. Kraitsir's purpose in presenting his larger study thus was to further his assumption of how at the roots of all languages was a unity of meaning and symbol stemming from the fact that all men, "however diverse they might become by conflicting passions and interests, have yet the same reason, and the same organs of speech."[9] There was only a limited number of sounds man could make through his vocal organs, and thus the reason for the underlying unity of all tongues was a *physiological* one: the relationship between a man's consciousness and his organs of speech *was* language.

Kraitsir also stressed the higher purpose of language study. For example, he boldly declared that his book was not mere etymology but a tool designed for people who "wish to employ language for its divine ends, as a pole, so to say, whereon the tendrils of clear reason, benign humanity, and of chaste taste, climb up, in the direction of man's posture, towards the Source of Light."[10] Still caught in the webs of religious controversy that demanded anyone investigating language to square his discoveries with biblical revelation, Kraitsir assured the reader his study tended toward "an approximation of the various races and nations to that union into *one mankind*, which is admitted to have existed, by all earnest inquirers into language, and which is attested to by Gen., XI.1."[11] Kraitsir, then, was chasing nothing other than the phantom of uniformity for which many of his nineteenth-century contemporaries yearned, a unity demonstrating how, beneath their temperamental differences, men were one in the Oversoul.

II

In a passage that is critical to the distinction between Emerson's and Thoreau's philosophical positions, Kraitsir elaborated on his contention, seemingly conventional enough for the age, that words originated in the perception of the exterior world. Language, he explained, is

> a symbol, a paradigm, an index, a finger-board, pointing in one direction to what is brought in and how it is brought within us; in another direction, to what is uttered and how it is to strike the mind of our fellow men. Man is a mirror of, but also a mediator between, all objects felt without and within himself, as well as between these objects and his own spirit on the one side, and between his spirit and that of his neighbors on the other.[12]

Some impression, then, strikes a man; as important as what it does to him *internally* is what he does to make it *external* again, how through various sounds he *reflects* or *expresses* it to other beings. The complexity of this process of *reflection*, as well as the mediation that occurs when a piece of language is formed, fascinated Kraitsir and Thoreau, but remained a point about which Emerson did not offer any particular speculation.

To explicate further this idea of "reflection," Kraitsir distinguished between *speech* and *languages*. The former was a "necessary function of man's sensations" and arose "instinctively, involuntarily, yet in keeping with the divine harmony of the universe"; while the latter, in their multiplicity, were what eventually happened to speech when it was brought under the influence of local and personal circumstance. But the essentials of human speech, the way outer impressions were reflected to the world, were always and everywhere the same. "Each people's genetic powers of speech, peculiar in each, amalgamate the phonetic (sound) elements with the feelings and mental conceptions into an organic unity."[13] Speech became, in Kraitsir's felicitous phrase, "the explosion of reason," and the word itself—that is, the series of sounds of which it was composed—became a "new outward object, linking the world with man and man with man."[14] The sounds men uttered were conditioned as much by *how they were made*—by the vocal organs—as by *what caused them*; and the complex physiological and psychological relation that occurred when reason sought to explode into articulation provided the underlying unity to all human utterance. Kraitsir believed that there was a universal law as to why "spirit" broke into the atmosphere the way it did, that, while languages appear so different, in reality there was only *one* way words originally could be formed, "according to the triad" of the interaction of mind, thing, organ. The "germs" of all languages were the same, a fact arguing for the unity of man's spirit with the Oversoul.[15]

Continuing the discussion in his earlier pamphlet, he elaborated the relationship among the gutturals, labials, and dentals he had discovered in his research.[16] In his felicitous metaphor, these various types of sounds were the "strings" upon which the voice "performed" language:

> To excite in other men something to be guarded and cherished like our heart, we gutturalize; to indicate wind, wool, wood, water, or any other moving object, we lap with our lips; to denote fleeting, flea-like, free lively butter (flutter)-flies on a level prairie, we combine labials with linguals; when speaking about steady, staring, stiff, dead, still, stony stereotypes, or about dim, dull, dreary, dense, starving, indurated, enduring objects, we make a din at our teeth.[17]

One has to have a tin ear not to realize the seductive flavor of this kind of poetic argument; but Kraitsir knew that, while such concentrated examples were convincing, his contemporaries would have difficulty discriminating such concepts in groups of sentences. Like Emerson, who in *Nature* declared that "the corruption of man is followed by the corruption of language," Kraitsir noted that "the symbolism of sounds" had decreased by degrees "in consequence of the fading of the primordial poetry of the human mind." Sounds themselves were no longer symbols with readily apparent meanings, and the loss of "intuitiveness and liveliness" in language had been balanced only by a "greater compenetration of sound and thought."[18]

Communication had moved to a more abstract level; and if before the word had "painted vividly the idea man had of the nature of the object," now it was more likely to bring to mind "the total of its characters and relations, not unlike a spiritual tableau."[19] Kraitsir thought men had forgotten how a sound *itself* might symbolize something greater than the word in which it was contained. Thoreau became deeply interested in the science of glossology not only because of its "practical" application in making the assimilation of foreign languages easier, but also because its concepts suggested how the enterprise in which he was engaged, of returning "to the primitive analogical and derivative sources of words," was philosophically important.[20]

In his own etymological explorations Thoreau enjoyed discovering the oldest meanings of words, as if the archaeological treasure he sought would flower into a truth all the more striking because of its proximity to the time when it was first created. "I desire," he once bragged, "to speak somewhere without bounds, like a man in a waking moment, to men in their waking moments"; he was convinced that he could not "exaggerate enough to lay the foundation of a true expression."[21] To exaggerate one's language meant to go beyond the common bounds understood for each sound-symbol, a project involving the verbal excavation Thoreau had come to love as he struggled to get the better of words. Such exaggerated sounds were to be found, for example, in the classics; for him the "heroic" books always would be in a language "dead to degenerate times." In order to read, as well as to write, such great books, a man had to "laboriously seek the meaning in each word" and "conjecture a larger sense than common use permits of the wisdom and valor and generosity we have."[22] In such a frame of mind Thoreau approached the subtleties of Kraitsir's glossological theories.

III

This sketch of Kraitsir's ideas suggests how he raised the study of language and nature to a level that, to him, approximated a religious quest; and this, too, appealed to Thoreau. Indeed, as West recognizes in his essay on Kraitsir, for him the word was with God.[23] Even the glossology of the word for the deity suggested the insight: "The spirit is spread-ing, sprout-ing, go-ing; gas-like, a ghost (Germ. geist, self-acting), gush-ing, God's highest manifestation so far as it can be felt by us, in our spirit, especially in our mental faculties."[24] For Kraitsir the study of language became the best way to worship the universal spirit. In an image Thoreau himself frequently used, Kraitsir noted that the truly religious man had "to trace the papillon of language, from the egg, through all the metamorphoses" until he arrived at a knowledge of the spirit, insofar as he could know it. "Get, got = go + to = cause + end . . . symbol of first, of beginning, tending to an aim, and attaining it. Hence God and good. The latter is not an epithet of sickly sentimentality, but of reasonable conscious aim-viewing, of apt- or fitness."[25] The revelations at the end of these trails into the history of language amounted to teleological truth: Kraitsir believed language hinted at all we could know of God. It marked the highest point of mankind's attempt to comprehend the true Logos, a height which at all costs had to be scaled, just as the bottomless pond of Walden had to be probed as well as Thoreau could measure it.

Here then were more extraordinary propositions for Thoreau as he reworked the manuscript of *Walden*, ideas that brought him farther afield than Emerson had intended when he suggested that Thoreau begin looking to nature for an understanding of the spirit. Now the pursuit of the word, through its glossological symbols, became the highest consideration of man thinking. Instead of interpreting the works of Providence as had earlier New England saints, Thoreau puzzled over the verbal tracks societies left behind. What did the accumulated wisdom of the ages tell him? What was the secret of his fascination with, for example, Native American vocabulary or the etymological game playing of people like Richard Trench?[26] The answers lie in the manner in which language anticipated and confirmed the very philosophy Thoreau came to adopt.

Thoreau's most stunning use of the insights derived from Kraisir's theories (as well as from a lifelong reading in etymology) occurs in the "Spring" chapter of *Walden*. The pivotal passage comes at the moment when Thoreau has worked himself through the seasons of the year and again has arrived at spring, when from the promptings of the sun the land surrounding Walden Pond shows signs of metamorphosis.[27] After reporting on the condition of the ice as it begins to break in the pond, Thoreau shifts his attention to the thawing earth. "Few phenomena," he relates, gave him more delight "than to observe the forms thawing sand and clay assume in flowing down the sides of a steep cut in the railroad."

> When the first frost comes out in the spring . . . the sand begins to flow down the slopes like lava, sometimes bursting out through the snow and overflowing it where no sand was to be seen before. Innumerable little streams overlap and interlace one with another, exhibiting a sort of hybrid product, which obeys halfway the laws of currents and halfway that of vegetation. As it flows it takes the form of sappy leaves or vines, making heaps of pulpy sprays a foot or more in depth, and resembling, as you look down on them, the laciniated lobed and imbricated thalluses of some lichens; or you are reminded of coral, of leopards' paws or birds' feet, of brains or lungs or bowels, and excrements of all kinds. It is a truly *grotesque* vegetation . . . a sort of architectural foliage more ancient and typical than acanthus, chicory, ivy, vine, or any vegetable leaves. . . . The whole cut impressed me as if it were a cave with its stalactites open to the light. . . .
>
> The whole bank, which is from twenty to forty feet high, is sometimes overlaid with a mass of this kind of foliage, or sandy rupture, for a quarter of a mile on one or both sides, the produce of one spring

day. What makes this sand foliage remarkable is it springing into existence thus suddenly. When I see on the one side the inert bank, — for the sun acts on one side first, — and on the other this luxuriant foliage, the creation of an hour, I am affected as if in a peculiar sense I stood in the laboratory of the Artist who made the world and me, — had come to where he was still at work, sporting on this bank, and with excess of energy strewing his fresh designs about. I feel as if I were nearer to the vitals of the globe, for this sandy overflow is something such a foliaceous mass as the vitals of the animal body. You find thus in the very sands an anticipation of the vegetable leaf. No wonder that the earth expresses itself outwardly in leaves, it so labors with the idea inwardly. The atoms have already learned this law, and are pregnant by it. The overhanging leaf sees here its prototype. *Internally*, whether in the globe or animal body, it is moist thick *lobe*, a word especially applicable to the liver and lungs and *leaves* of fat, (λείβω, *labor*, *lapus*, to flow or slip downward, a lapsing, λοβος, *globus*, lobe, globe; also lap, flap, and many other words); *externally*, a dry thin *leaf*, even as the *f* and *v* are a pressed and dried *b*. The radicals of lobe are *lb*, the soft mass of the *b* (single lobed, or B, doubled lobed) with the liquid *l* behind it pressing it forward. In globe, *glb*, the gutteral *g* adds to the meaning the capacity of the throat. The feathers and wings of birds are still drier and thinner leaves. Thus, also, you pass from the lumpish grub in the earth to the airy and fluttering butterfly. The very globe continually transcends and translates itself, and becomes winged in its orbit. Even ice begins with delicate crystal leaves, as if it had flowed into moulds which the fronds of water plants have impressed on the watery mirror. The whole tree itself is but one leaf, and rivers are still vaster leaves whose pulp is intervening earth, and towns and cities are the ova of insects in their axils.

Seen in the light of Kraitsir's theories, this passage, so long inadequately understood, becomes clear proof that Thoreau's brand of transcendentalism differed considerably from that held by others within his New England circle. What Thoreau had done was to show how words, derived from the basic "germs" of sound as described most recently by Kraitsir but earlier by Antoine Court de Gebelin and others, are reflections of nothing less than the grand purpose of nature, that the "language of nature" could, indeed, be termed "the true Messiah," as the Swedenborgian Guillaume Oegger had once called it.[28] In man's earliest oral expression the "explosion of reason" since muffled by the baggage of civilized life, had reflected the great and eternal processes of birth, life, and death; that is, it displayed the inevitable *change* of which all life is made. Thoreau offered as his critical proposition that words were not merely steps to a higher reality but themselves *embodied* the reality, a thought most likely suggested to him by his reading in Kraitsir's philology. Working through this passage a bit more slowly, one discerns both Thoreau's philological strategy and the philosophical conclusion toward which his analysis of language brought him.

The most obvious metaphoric construct is the equation of the thawing sand, the raw earth itself, with an organic, vegetative force. The *sand* — the reader must be alert to the dental, fricative sounds of which the word is made, that is, that it represents "dormant" effect — begins to flow like *lava*. Streams *interlace* until the reader does not know if he is looking at a *living* stream or a *live* plant. Sappy *leaves* and *vines* appear as the thaw progresses; lichens are evoked, with their laciniated, lobed, imbricated thalluses. The dominant sounds become the liquid labials, and one sees a *living* organism that before was dead: leopards' paws, birds' feet, lungs and bowels emerge as the earth stirs into life.

But to Thoreau the sand foliage conjures yet another image, of the *innards* or bowels of the earth. He feels as though he stands in a cave flooded with light and later comments on the vast size of the "sandy rupture." He thinks himself in the workshop of God as He *overflowed* Himself, "strewing his fresh designs about" through an excess of divine energy. Here the reader witnesses nothing less than Thoreau's visionary metaphor for creation, life struggling to put itself forth, and, inevitably, how each individual existence again fades into the thin dentals and fricatives that denote death. The earth is filled with living, flowing, running, moving motions, and so labors with the idea of streaming life that it must project itself through the imagery of living things, in this case, leaves. The overhanging boughs become archetypal, and are "pregnant" with the laws that all atoms contain within themselves: here Thoreau reads his leaf with every philological tool Kraitsir, Court de Gebelen, and others bequeathed him. All begins internally, with the gutterals, as a lobe, thick and moist in its womblike position in the earth (and in a man's vocal organs) and then *slips* and *slides* outward, delivered finally to the *liquid labials* and ending as a leaflike sound, *dry* and *thin* when finally *externalized*.

The wordplay continues complex as Thoreau moves from a lumpish *grub* in the *earth* to the airy and fluttering *butterfly*. All metaphors in the passage follow this pattern; and, before the reader is aware of it, the philological sleight of hand has brought him from an insect to the entire globe: the world is but a "leaf" and subject to the same laws. Towns and cities are but the "ova of insects" in the axils of this organism (an image making one think of *Walden*'s last page, when the dormant grub emerges triumphant from the table after lying entombed for decades), and the railroad cut becomes nothing less than a parable for our entire natural existence!

Thoreau made the lesson explicit. It seemed that "this one hillside illustrated the principle of all the operations of nature." The creator of the world had "but patented a leaf."[29] But was this a type of *all* the operations of nature? Did "transcendence" mean that the globe, like the leaf, constantly translates itself, then to return to the frozen sand / death of winter?

"What Champollion will decipher this hieroglyphic for us, that we may turn over a new leaf at last?"[30] What Champollion, indeed, if not the curious Hungarian immigrant, and a handful of his New England disciples! In "The Poet" Emerson had maintained "nature has a higher end, in the production of individuals, than security, namely ascension, or the passage of the soul into higher forms." But could Thoreau hold this tenet, especially after being shown a parable of the laws of God's creation? The phenomenon of the flowing sand was so exhilarating that Thoreau finally had to turn to scatalogical puns to express his wonder at it:

> True, it [the sand] is somewhat excrementitious in character, and there is no end to the heaps of liver lights and bowels, as if the globe were turned wrongside outward; but this suggests at least that Nature has some bowels, and there again is mother of humanity. This is the frost coming out of the ground; this is Spring. . . . It convinces me that the earth is still in her swaddling clothes, and stretches forth baby fingers on every side. Fresh curls spring from the baldest brow. There is nothing inorganic.[31]

The hieroglyphic repeated throughout nature was nothing but the fact, so obvious to the trained observer of the natural world, that words are coextensive with natural facts, which are *themselves* nothing less than the reality men have been chasing. The world of birth and change and death is the ultimate secret to be read in nature, as well as in the highest mental activity of man, his language. Thoreau's insight was that life goes on and on in an unending cycle of constant change, and that, while individuals die, the totality of existence is ever in the finest health.

Viewed in light of language theory and natural history, the earth was not a "mere fragment of dead history, stratum upon stratum like the leaves of a book," but rather "living poetry, like the leaves of a tree which precede flower and fruit." This was not a "fossil earth," but a "living earth." Gallows humor presiding even at the sacred moment when Thoreau describes the end of all his wisdom, he reminds his readers to recall how the earth's ever-vital throes will heave "exuviae from their graves," that is, that the only thing sacred will be the motion, the great cyclical pattern of life which will outlive such man-insects as ourselves.[32]

In this "Spring" chapter, then, Thoreau offers a curious scene of resurrection. The only terms of spirituality lie, paradoxically, in metamorphosis. Immortality is man's transformation into the earth's elements so that the balance of energy might be maintained, other births brought forth. The deepest layers of language, of man's very articulation, reinforce this knowledge. As it had come to be understood by one who had not only the philological dexterity of Kraitsir but the practical naturalist's skills of an Agassiz, language was but the expression of the great cause-and-effect process that rules the world.

Concomitantly, in light of Thoreau's philological interests, a reading of *Walden* suggests that Thoreau's aesthetic gradually became one of "a purely sensuous life." The foundation of Thoreau's spiritual reality did not so much lie in a belief in transcendence of the physical world in which he, as well as his language, was rooted. One of *Walden's* main lessons is that man does not need to get anywhere: he is *there* already, surrounded by the literal ground of being from which he springs and to which he will return.[33]

This suggestion is voiced elsewhere in Thoreau's works. How else, for example, can one interpret such a passage from his journals:

> It is salutary to deal with the surface of things. . . . There is something invigorating in the air which I am peculiarly sensible is a real wind, blowing over the surface of a planet. I look out my eyes, I come to my window, and I feel and breathe the air. It is a fact equally glorious with the most inward experience.[34]

When the reader acknowledges that for the philologist *breath* and *wind* both derive from the root for *spirit*, the point is even more apparent. All around man flows that spiritual ether into which he has to plunge himself; furthermore, he has no sane reason to try to transcend it.

Recall as well this famous passage from *A Week on the Concord and Merrimack Rivers*:

> We need pray for no higher heaven than the pure senses can furnish, a purely sensuous life. Our present senses are but the rudiments of what they are to become. We are comparatively deaf, dumb and blind, and without smell or taste or feeling. Every generation makes the discovery that the divine vigor has been dissipated, and each sense and faculty misapplied and debauched. The ears were made, not for such trivial uses as men are wont to suppose, but to hear celestial sounds. The eyes were not made for such grovelling uses as they are now worn out by, but to behold beauty invisible. May we not see God?[35]

Here Thoreau displays an allegiance more to John Locke than to any Berkeleian idealist, for he believed that what is experienced sensually provides all the inspiration a man needs. In his passage the parody of religious language is explicit, and the prayer Thoreau raises is for man to approach the sacrament of life in the purest frame of mind possible, that of celebration. God is, indeed, visible everywhere, for any connotation to which the word "God" lends itself derives from the natural world. "Remember thy Creator in the days of thy youth," Thoreau confides to his journal. "Lay up a store of natural influences. Sing while you may, before the evil days come. See, hear, smell, taste, etc., while the senses are fresh and pure."[36] "I believe," he would later avow, "in the forest and in the meadow and in the night in which the corn grows."[37]

Lengthy philological research, as well as close study of natural history, taught Thoreau that man did not need to use the world for instruction toward a higher order of things. He was concerned with the ecstasy of feeling and the knowledge that he was alive and well because the same spirit that blew through him blew through all creation indiscriminately. It has taken critics until the 1970s to accept Channing's hint of Thoreau's deep involvement with philology and to see how closely his language provides the key to his meaning. Emerson strolling across a bare common at twilight had never peered into the very workshop of creation, and, in the two men's philosophies (of both language and life) that made all the difference.

Notes

1. William Ellery Channing, *Thoreau: The Poet-Naturalist* (Boston: Roberts Brothers, 1873; enl. ed., ed. F. B. Sanborn, Boston: Charles E. Goodspeed, 1902), 77.

2. Michael West has made the most extensive investigations into Thoreau's philological reading. See his "Charles Kraitsir's Influence on Thoreau's Theory of Language," *ESQ: A Journal of the American Renaissance* 19 (4th Quarter 1973):262–74; "Scatology and Eschatology: The Heroic Dimensions of Thoreau's Wordplay," *PMLA* 89 (October 1974):1043–64; "*Walden's* Dirty Language: Thoreau and Walter Whiter's Geocentric Etymological Theories," *Harvard Library Bulletin* 22 (April 1974):117–28; and "Thoreau and the Language Theories of the French Enlightenment," *ELH* 51 (Winter 1984):747–70.

3. See West, "Scatology and Eschatology," *passim.*

4. Joel Porte, *Emerson and Thoreau: Transcendentalists in Conflict* (Middletown, Conn.: Wesleyan University Press, 1966); Victor Carl Friesen, *The Spirit of the Huckleberry: Sensuousness in Henry Thoreau* (Edmonton: University of Alberta Press, 1984).

5. Bradford Torrey and Francis H. Allen, eds., *The Writings of Henry David Thoreau* (Boston: Houghton Mifflin Company, 1906), 5:232.

6. Torrey and Allen, *Writings*, 8:463; Thoreau, *Journal, Volume I: 1837–1844*, ed. John C. Broderick et al. (Princeton: Princeton University Press), 19. Also see Perry Miller, "Thoreau in the Context of International Romanticism," in *Nature's Nation* (Cambridge: Harvard University Press, 1967), 175–83.

7. The most accessible information on Kraitsir is in West, "Kraitsir's Influence"; my "Elizabeth Palmer Peabody and the Philosophy of Language," *ESQ: A Journal of the American Renaissance* 23 (3rd Quarter 1977):154–63, discusses the relationship of Peabody and Kraitsir and comments upon the latter's philological activity. Also see Thomas Wentworth Higginson, *Cheerful Yesterdays* (Boston: Houghton Mifflin, 1898), 86, 93, for a contemporary assessment of Kraitsir.

8. Charles Kraitsir, *The Significance of the Alphabet* (Boston: E. P. Peabody, 1846); and *Glossology: Being a Treatise on the Nature of Language and on the Language of Nature* (New York: C. B. Norton, 1854 [1852]). For documentation of Thoreau's reading in Kraitsir's work see West, "Kraitsir's Influence," 262, and Thoreau, "Extracts, Mostly Upon Natural History," Widener MS Collection, Harvard University, 130–31.

9. Kraitsir, *Glossology*, 10.

10. Ibid.

11. Ibid., 20. On the relationship of language theory to the problem of scriptural exegesis so prevalent in the early nineteenth century see my "The Transcendentalists and Language: The Unitarian Exegetical Background," in *Studies in the American Renaissance 1979*, ed. Joel Myerson (Boston: Twayne, 1979), 1–16; *The Wisdom of Words: Language, Theology, and Literature in the New England Renaissance* (Middletown, Conn.: Wesleyan University Press, 1981), 15–34; Jerry Wayne Brown, *The Rise of Biblical Criticism in America, 1800–1870: The New England Scholars* (Middletown, Conn.: Wesleyan University

Press, 1969); Hans W. Frei, *The Eclipse of Biblical Narrative: A Study in Eighteenth and Nineteenth Century Hermeneutics* (New Haven: Yale University Press, 1974), 165–202; and tangentially, Harold Durfee, "Language and Religion: Horace Bushnell and Rowland Hazard," *American Quarterly* 5 (Spring 1953):57–70.

12. Kraitsir, *Glossology*, 23.

13. Ibid., 25. Note particularly the word "organic." The common denominator among all the language theorists in whom the Transcendentalists were interested is the notion that in a previous age language stemmed organically from man's relation to the universe.

14. Ibid., 26.

15. Ibid., 144. In "Thoreau and the Language Theories of the French Enlightenment," West presents strong evidence that Thoreau knew and was influenced by Charles de Brosses, who postulated an organic, primitive language characterized by a close relation between an object and its vocalization, and whose work might have been known to Thoreau through Hugh Blair's summary of it in his *Lectures on Rhetorick and Belles Lettres* (1783), a common textbook of the day. In addition, West points to Antoine Court de Gebelin, whose works supported the ideas of de Brosses and whose ideas Thoreau definitely had encountered. West's discoveries are, of course, important, but it seems to me that with regard to the composition of *Walden*, Kraitsir's ideas, for all their similarity to those of de Brosses and Court de Gebelin, are the most important.

16. For a summary of Kraitsir's concept of the "germs" of language, see *Significance of the Alphabet*, *passim*; West's "Kraitsir's Influence," 267–71; and my "Elizabeth Peabody," 158–59.

17. Kraitsir, *Glossology*, 170.

18. *The Collected Works of Ralph Waldo Emerson*, ed. Alfred R. Ferguson et al., 4 vols. (Cambridge: Harvard University Press, 1971–   ), 1:20; Kraitsir, *Glossology*, 213. This theory is remarkably similar to that advanced by Rowland Gibson Hazard in his *Language: Its Connexion with the Present Condition and Future Prospects of Man[,] by a Heteroscian* (Providence, R.I.: Marshall and Brown, 1836), which the Reverend William Ellery Channing admired and Peabody knew well. See Durfee, "Language and Religion," *passim*, and my "Elizabeth Peabody," 156.

19. Kraitsir, *Glossology*, 213.

20. Thoreau, *Writings*, 8:462–63.

21. Thoreau, *Walden*, ed. J. Lyndon Shanley (Princeton: Princeton University Press, 1971), 324.

22. Thoreau, *Walden*, 100.

23. West, "Kraitsir's Influence," 270.

24. Kraitsir, *Glossology*, 159.

25. Ibid., 197.

26. For Thoreau's interest in native American vocabulary see my "Thoreau and John Josselyn," *New England Quarterly* 48 (December 1975):514–15, and "Thoreau's Maine Woods Indians: More Representative Men," *American Literature* (November 1977):377–82; for his reading in Trench, Gordon V. Boudreau, "Thoreau and Richard C. Trench: Conjectures on the Pickerel Passage in *Walden*," *ESQ* (2nd Quarter 1974):20: 117–24.

27. Thoreau, *Walden*, 304ff.

28. West, "Thoreau and the Language Theories of the French Enlightenment," 760–65. In 1842 Elizabeth Peabody published excerpts from Oegger's *The True Messiah; or The Old and New Testaments, According to the Principles of the Language of Nature*. Her translation of this French Swedenborgian's work had been an underground classic among the Transcendentalists and had circulated in manuscript as much as six years earlier. See my "Elizabeth Peabody," 162.

29. Thoreau, *Walden*, 308.
30. Ibid.
31. Ibid.
32. Ibid., 309.
33. Porte, *Emerson and Thoreau*: chapter six, convincingly argues this matter.
34. Thoreau, *Writings*, 10:312.
35. Ibid., 1:408.
36. Ibid., 8:330.
37. Ibid., 5:225.

Revolution and Renewal:
The Genres of *Walden*

Linck C. Johnson*

Few American books have received the attention that has been lavished upon *Walden*. Indeed, the relative neglect of Thoreau's masterpiece during the years following its publication in 1854 has been more than compensated by the scrutiny it has since received, especially by critics and scholars during the last few decades.[1] Thoreau's sources, his ideas, his rhetoric and style, and the structure of his narrative have all been studied in detail. But one of the most basic questions about *Walden* — what kind of book is it? — has not been fully explored, even by those who have offered the most probing and illuminating readings of the text.[2] The tendency to skirt the question is understandable, since few acknowledged classics seem so resistant to what is usually understood to be a generic approach. Among various analogies to the function of genre, students of the subject have suggested that it functions like a code of conduct established between the author, or host, and the reader, his guest. Its function has also been compared to that of a social institution, which, like a well-established genre, transmits certain cultural values.[3] Thoreau's hostility to all institutions is a central feature of *Walden*, in which he also mocks the sterile social codes of his day, so we might easily conclude that he was equally hostile to the conventions of any of the generic categories into which we might seek to place his book.

Although it contains a germ of truth, that conclusion distorts the relationship between genre and creativity, both as a general rule and in the specific case of *Walden*. As Alastair Fowler has observed, genre "is so far from being a mere curb on expression that it makes the expressiveness of literary works possible," since "their relation to the genres they embody is not one of passive membership but of active modulation."[4] *Walden* offers a

*This essay was written especially for this volume and is published here for the first time with the permission of the author.

fascinating example of the communicative power of such generic variation. In fact, a full appreciation of Thoreau's artistry requires an awareness of the subtle interplay among the genres embedded in various
chapters and embodied by the book as a whole. In "Reading," Thoreau
offers a paean to the "heroic books," especially the *Iliad*. But his celebration of that epic should not obscure the relationship between *Walden* and
other classical genres, especially the eclogue and georgic, or its connections to popular contemporary writings like Melville's *Typee*. Moreover,
Thoreau's ambitious narrative began as a comparatively simple and
straightforward lecture, a portion of what became "Economy," in which
he echoed utopian tracts and parodied contemporary manuals like Catharine Beecher's *Treatise on Domestic Economy*. In developing that
lecture into a book, Thoreau in later chapters adapted and combined
elements of numerous other minor or nonliterary genres, including agricultural reports, house pattern books, travel guides, natural history
writings, and the sketch, organizing his chapters in a way that also reveals
a debt to Emerson's *Essays* and *The Conduct of Life*.

In contrast to Emerson, however, Thoreau used genre to free himself
from generic restrictions. Although both writers struggled to attain a form
of literary self-reliance, they achieved such freedom of expression through
dramatically different means. Emerson, who was far more concerned
with style and subject matter than with literary form, sought in the
lecture-essay an escape from what he viewed as the confinement of the
major genres of English literature. Thoreau's cultural nationalism and
literary nonconformity was revealed in other ways, for he sought to exploit
the full generic repertoire without accommodating his narrative to the
demands of any single literary kind. Insofar as it belongs to any one genre,
Walden is probably most accurately defined as an autobiography. But just
as he integrated aspects of other American lives into his own autobiography, enacting in a single year a symbolic history of his country, Thoreau
incorporated into the genre of autobiography elements of many other
literary kinds, engaging in an oblique dialogue with the whole tradition of
European and American literature. *Walden* was thus an act of revolution
and renewal, as Thoreau at once subverted and restored the authority of
genre, the power of which helped him transform his experience into a
story both timely and timeless, individual and universal.

Since its third chapter, "Reading," offers the best guide to the severe
discipline required to read *Walden*, we might also expect the chapter to
contain some clues about the kind of book Thoreau wrote. Taking a hint
from his celebration of the *Iliad*, to which Thoreau makes numerous
allusions elsewhere in *Walden*, some critics have emphasized the Homeric
dimension of Thoreau's experiment at Walden Pond.[5] The commentary in
"Reading" may nonetheless reveal more about his attitude toward contemporary culture than about his own literary aspirations and intentions in
Walden. In the eighteenth century Fielding described his novel *Joseph*

Andrews as "a comic epic-poem in prose," partly to lend respectability to a new literary form by linking it to a more established and more respected form.[6] During the nineteenth century the reputation of the epic declined dramatically, especially in America, where it suffered from social and political as well as changing critical and aesthetic assumptions.[7] By elevating the *Iliad* and mocking the novel, which had begun to dominate the literary marketplace, Thoreau in "Reading" rejected the authority of American culture, as he elsewhere in *Walden* rejected the authority of American laws and institutions. By seeming to align himself with a genre that, like his way of living at Walden Pond, seemed outmoded and regressive, he also challenged America's cherished belief in universal human progress. "Reading" is therefore perhaps best understood as the aesthetic correlative of "Economy," for as Thoreau initially rejects a misguided faith in material progress, so he also questions the complacent faith in artistic and intellectual progress. "Men sometimes speak as if the study of the classics would at length make way for more modern and practical studies," he observes; "but the adventurous student will always study classics, in whatever language they may be written and however ancient they may be. For what are the classics but the noblest recorded thoughts of man?"[8]

Yet, as Thoreau emphasizes, the study of the classics is threatened by the materialism that infects all aspects of life in Concord. Early in "Economy," he describes the plight of "young men," his townsmen, whose struggle with "inherited encumbrances" is but one consequence of man's foolish effort to lie "up treasures which moth and rust will corrupt and thieves break through and steal" (*W*, 5). As his allusion to the sermon on the mount suggests, Thoreau in "Economy" is primarily concerned with the spiritual costs of such material gains. In "Reading," he implies that another consequence of the effort to accumulate property either for ourselves or for our posterity is the loss of a far more valuable and incorruptible birthright. Noting that classics like the *Iliad* "have carried their own serene and celestial atmosphere into all lands to protect them against the corrosion of time," he continues: "Books are the treasured wealth of the world and the fit inheritance of generations and nations" (*W*, 102). But most Americans, whose only measure of value is material success, ignore such "true books," turning instead to the popular products of the commercial press, books that are mass produced for a mass audience. "If others are the machines to provide this provender, they are the machines to read it," Thoreau contemptuously remarks: "The result is dulness of sight, a stagnation of the vital circulations, and a general deliquium and sloughing off of all intellectual faculties" (*W*, 104–5). "Reading," like "Economy," is thus in part a protest against the dehumanizing forces of a market economy, which debases both life and literature.

The *Iliad* serves Thoreau as a prime illustration of the values that had been lost during the rise of modern, commercial civilization: the simplicity, naturalness, and spirituality of the ancient Greeks. But his reaffirmation of those values in his own life and art does not necessarily imply that Thoreau sought to adapt the literary form in which he believed those values had been most triumphantly embodied. At no point in "Reading" or anywhere else in *Walden*, for example, does he actually use the term *epic*. Instead, he refers to the *Iliad* as one of the "heroic books," intentionally jumbling Homer together with others of "the heroic writers of antiquity" (*W*, 100). As Thoreau probably knew, from the Renaissance onward the epic was also called a *heroic poem*, that is, a poem relating the deeds of heroes. He used "heroic" in a different sense, not to describe the subject of the works but the spirit of the ancient writers, asserting that later writers had "rarely, if ever, equalled the elaborate beauty and finish and life-long and heroic literary labors of the ancients" (*W*, 103). Although he clearly sought to equal the ancient texts in his modern classic, simply to describe *Walden* as an epic would disguise the fact that Thoreau drew as much inspiration from the Hindu scriptures as from the *Iliad*, and that his book has more in common with Virgil's *Eclogues* and *Georgics* than with the *Aeneid*.

Indeed, the mode of the two books he worked on at Walden Pond is less heroic than pastoral, which in Thoreau's handling mingled elements of both the eclogue and the georgic.[9] In a journal entry jotted down in the summer of 1845 and later indexed as "houses on Merrimack," he observed: "I repeat it that if men will believe it — there are no more quiet Tempes or more poetic & Arcadian life than may be lived in these New E. dwellings — It seemed as if their employment by day would be to tend the flowers & herds — and at night like the shepherds of old to cluster & gives [*sic*] names to the stars."[10] As I have elsewhere suggested, that idealized vision probably owed less to Thoreau's recollections of his 1839 voyage on the Concord and Merrimack rivers, the subject of the book he began to draft immediately after moving to Walden Pond, than to both his idyllic life there and his reading of Virgil's *Georgics*.[11] In *A Week* Thoreau used allusions to pastoral and georgic verse to dignify the native inhabitants of New England, whom he associated with ancient simplicity and purity. "The husbandman is always a better Greek than the scholar is prepared to appreciate," he notes in the "Friday" chapter, where he depicts Concord's annual cattle show as a reenactment of ancient games and festivals.[12] In contrast, Thoreau in *Walden* introduces such classical elements only when depicting his own activities, attaining the ideal pastoral *otium* as he sits by his cabin, listening to the sounds of nature, reclines in his boat, fishing or playing his flute, and works in his bean field. At such moments the harmonies of pastoral and georgic verse resonate through the text, confirming Thoreau's successful escape from the debased husbandry and other exigencies of life in Concord.

But *Walden*, like some of the great pastoral poems Thoreau read, does not simply portray an escape from reality. On the contrary, he was probably drawn to the pastoral for much the same reason Virgil and Spenser chose it, because "pastoral provided a mode for the juxtaposition of contending values and perspectives."[13] In *Walden* the contest between the pastoral world (the pond and its environs) and the nonpastoral world (Concord and the America for which it stands) is far less even than it is in either the *Eclogues* or the *Shepheardes Calender*, in both of which social criticism is balanced by "a counterpoising awareness of the limitations of pastoral values and with that a greater sense of the multivalence of experience."[14] Nonetheless, just as Thoreau's withdrawal to the pond is in itself a criticism of society, so is his return to Concord at least an implicit acknowledgement of the claims of that society. The termination of his pastoral experiment, like the "Conclusion" of *Walden*, is not an end but a new beginning, a signal of his reengagement with a society from which Thoreau had never fully withdrawn, in either literal or literary terms. His explanation of his departure from Walden Pond is thus not nearly as puzzling as some of his readers believe, since from the very beginning of *Walden* it is clear that Thoreau has "several more lives to live" than either the pastoral world could accommodate or the pastoral mode could embody.

Although he drew upon a long and rich tradition of pastoral verse, Thoreau was also influenced by more recent and far more prosaic works. "I read one or two shallow books of travel in the intervals of my work," he confesses in "Reading," "till that employment made me ashamed of myself, and I asked where it was then that *I* lived" (*W*, 100). Despite his dismissive tone, Thoreau had a capacious and enduring appetite for travel books, to which *Walden* has some affinities.[15] At the opening of the book he emphasizes that he "would fain say something, not so much concerning the Chinese and Sandwich Islanders as you who read these pages, who are said to live in New England" (*W*, 4). The passage, of course, offers an early example of Thoreau's frequent wordplays, indicating that he was speaking, not to those who lived in what is called New England, but to those who are *said* to live, but who actually do not *live* in any meaningful sense of the word, in New England. In detailing those local conditions, however, Thoreau speaks as a traveler reporting on a distant and alien culture. As he portrays them, the activities, rites and rituals of his neighbors in Concord are every bit as exotic — and finally just as terrifying to the truly civilized man — as are those depicted in *Typee*, which Thoreau read soon after its publication in 1846.[16]

Thoreau borrowed a number of ingredients from the popular recipe developed by Melville and other writers of semifictional travel narratives. As Harold Beaver has remarked, "the formula for launching such adventures was simple enough: a young white (male of course, preferably alone) makes for some outpost — island, jungle, desert, prairie — as remote as possible from Victorian London or New York."[17] None of those outposts was more remote than Thoreau's cabin, though it was less than two miles from Concord. "If it were worth the while to settle in those parts near to the Pleiades or the Hyades, to Aldebaren or Altair, then I was really there, or at an equal remoteness from the life which I had left behind," he observes in "Where I Lived, and What I Lived For" (*W*, 88). He there emphasizes the timeless, celestial dimension of his pastoral world; but in later chapters he transforms the woods of Concord into a terrain as wild and unspoiled as those described in works like R. M. Ballantyne's *Hudson's Bay; or Every-Day Life in the Wilds of North America* (1848) and J. T. Headley's *The Adirondack; or Life in the Woods* (1849). In fact, Thoreau may have hoped to capitalize on the popularity of such accounts in some of his own works, including "Ktaadn, and the Maine Woods," published in 1848, and the book that first appeared in 1854 as *Walden; or, Life in the Woods*.

Among the transcendentalists Thoreau's original title no doubt recalled a text altogether different from those produced in such profusion by writers like Headley. The subtitle of *Walden* was probably borrowed from the English reformer Charles Lane, whose "Life in the Woods" appeared in the final issue of the *Dial* in April 1844.[18] Lane's article, a consideration of "the sylvan man in his native state," summarized the advantages of the forester's life, especially its closeness to nature (416). Lane also rejected the assumption that the elevation of thought and sentiment claimed by the civilized man was denied to "the unschooled savage," who had intuitive access to the highest truth (421). "No wonder need be then excited in our minds, when we occasionally hear of the young spirit, to whom the costliest education has been afforded, and before whom the whole world invitingly lies as a beautiful unexplored garden, every path free to his foot, turning, after a little experience, his course from the city towards the woods," Lane continued. But he added that the notion of trying an "experiment of a true wilderness life" was probably no more than "an interesting dream," since the white man was neither born nor nurtured for it. Noting that a few individuals had nonetheless undertaken such experiments, Lane asked:

> But will they succeed in wrestling against their increased natural needs, and their remaining civic wants, diminished as these may be? On trial, as on due consideration, it will be found that this is not a very promising course. By the time the hut is built, the rudest furniture constructed, the wood chopped, the fire burning, the bread grown and prepared, the whole time will be exhausted, and no interval remain for comfortably clothing the body, for an expansion in art, or for recreation by the book or pen. This but faintly promises to be the mode, by which the simple and pure of heart shall escape the pressures and burdens, which prevent the full and happy development of the soul. (422)

Thoreau rejected both the cautionary argument and the alternative mode of life offered by Lane. Indeed, *Walden* served as triumphant evidence that securing the necessities of life in the wilderness need not, as Lane insisted, leave no leisure "for recreation by the book or pen." Lane's alternative to a "recluse life" was a community or some form of "association" (423), a cause that had gained numerous recruits from the ranks of the transcendentalists. Like Emerson, Thoreau had turned down invitations to join Brook Farm, established by George Ripley and his followers in 1841, and Fruitlands, the short-lived community that Lane and Amos Bronson Alcott had formed in 1843 and abandoned in January 1844. Although it was addressed to his townspeople, the first lecture Thoreau delivered on his own utopian venture was also directed to the communitarians, whose belief in what Lane and others called "union" gave added edge to Thoreau's apologia for a solitary and withdrawn life. Following that lecture, delivered at the Concord Lyceum in February 1847, Emerson thus wrote Margaret Fuller, "Mrs Ripley & other members of the opposition came down the other night to hear Henry's Account of his housekeeping at Walden Pond . . . and were charmed with the witty wisdom which ran through it all."[19]

Despite its implicit challenge to association, many elements of Thoreau's account no doubt had the charm of the familiar to the communitarians. His goals at Walden Pond were not far different from Ripley's original objectives at Brook Farm, which he had outlined in a famous 1840 letter to Emerson, or from the ideals that had inspired the establishment of Fruitlands.[20] In "The Consociate Family Life," a letter published in numerous newspapers and periodicals in August 1844, Lane and Alcott had described their efforts "to attain simplicity in diet, plain garments, pure bathing, unsullied dwellings, open conduct, gentle behavior, kindly sympathies, serene minds."[21] In his equally high-minded though far more exuberant account of a similar effort, Thoreau adopted the language, rhetoric, and form of manifestoes like "The Consociate Family Life," an outline of a plan for "personal reform" designed to redeem fallen mankind from the abuses and corruptions of civilized society, including property, trade, and the hiring system. Like Alcott and Lane, whose letter was ostensibly prompted by "many inquiries by letter for a statement of our principles and modes of life," Thoreau also emphasized the interest others had expressed in his experiment, stating that he would not have delivered the lecture "if very particular and personal inquiries had not been made concerning my mode of life."[22]

Thoreau's glance at works like "The Consociate Family Life" may have been intended as a private joke, one that could be fully savored by only a small portion of his audience. From the beginning, however, Thoreau in *Walden* looked beyond such obscure works to far more familiar and imposing writings on social and domestic life, including Lydia Maria Child's *The Frugal American Housewife* (1832), a general guide to household management; *The Young Lady's Friend By a Lady* (1836), a popular book on etiquette written by Margaret Fuller's friend Eliza

Farrar, the wife of a distinguished Harvard professor; and, especially, Catharine Beecher's *Treatise on Domestic Economy*. In fact, the general subject and topical organization of Thoreau's first lecture, the germ of "Economy," suggests that it was at least in part a parodic response to Beecher's *Treatise*, one of the most influential of all manuals of domestic reform, which was first published by a small Boston firm in 1841 and reissued by Harper and Brothers in 1842, after which it was reprinted every year until 1856.[23] Compared with the national distribution and public acclaim Beecher's text gained, Thoreau's lectures and the published version of *Walden* constituted little more than a voice crying in the wilderness against the emerging ideology of domesticity. Emerson's characterization of the initial lecture as an account of Thoreau's "housekeeping" was therefore doubly ironic, since housekeeping, at least as Beecher and most other middle-class Americans used the term, was precisely what he sought to avoid at Walden Pond. "When we consider how our houses are built and paid for, and their internal economy managed and sustained, who does not wonder that the floor does not give way under the visitor while he is admiring the gewgaws upon the mantel and let him through into the cellar—to some solid and honest, though earthy, foundation!" Thoreau exclaimed. "Before we can adorn our houses with beautiful objects—the walls must be stript—and our lives must be stript, and beautiful housekeeping and beautiful living be laid for a foundation. Now what we call taste for the beautiful is most cultivated out of doors, where there is no house, and no housekeeper" (*FV*, 122).

Thoreau adopted some of Beecher's aims and method, but he worked toward a radically different end. Both the *Treatise* and *Walden* were efforts to combat the growth of acquisitive and commercial values; nonetheless, Thoreau clearly believed that Beecher and other proponents of domesticity were part of the problem, or at least that their proposed solutions were far more complicated than the problem itself. Consequently, although he and Beecher sought to simplify life, she did so by making the complexities of household maintenance understandable, while Thoreau sharply challenged the need for such elaborate maintenance. Beecher offered detailed advice to the housekeeper on every branch of domestic economy, which she believed should be "a regular part of the school education" of all young women, whose knowledge and experience did not prepare them to deal with the practical necessities of life.[24] Drawing on her own experience, Beecher divided the *Treatise* into chapters like "On the Preparation of Healthful Food"; "On Clothing"; "On the Construction of Houses", subdivided into sections on the economies of labor, money, health, and comfort; "On Economy of Time and Expenses"; and "On Giving in Charity." In his lecture and at greater length in "Economy"—in which the running chapter heads in the first edition of *Walden* also included "Clothing," "Shelter," "Building the House," "Architecture," "Bread," "Furniture," and "Philanthropy"—Thoreau offered his own detailed advice on such domestic matters, especially to "the class of poor students," young men whose education did not prepare *them* for life (*FV*, 106; cf. *W*, 4). In fact, what Kathryn Kish Sklar has suggested about the *Treatise*, that its success may have owed to Beecher's ability to combine ideology with advice, thus "demonstrating how these ideals could be realized," may also account for some of the later success of *Walden*.[25] The advice and ideologies of the two books were finally diametrically opposed, however, since Thoreau sought not to domesticate but to naturalize the life of mankind.

In mounting his attack on the overwhelming forces of domesticity, Thoreau operated like a literary guerrilla, lifting his weapons from his opponents' formidable array of writings. The embattled bachelor of *Walden* was at once the successor and a foil to a long line of bachelor narrators from Geoffrey Crayon of Irving's *Sketchbook* to Ik Marvel, the narrator of Donald Grant Mitchell's *Reveries of a Bachelor* (1850).[26] Sitting by the cozy fireplace of the small parlor in his humble farmhouse in the country, Ik Marvel constantly toys with the idea of matrimony, especially in "Home," the final reverie, where he imagines that he, his beautiful wife, and their three children are living in a substantial cottage. Thoreau's reveries are never invaded by thoughts of a wife, even when he sits by the fire on lonely winter nights. On the contrary, although in "House-Warming" he "sometimes dream[s] of a larger and more populous house," he hardly envisions a domestic home, since that rude and primitive hall would contain "all the essentials of a house, and nothing for house-keeping" (*W*, 243). Indeed, as recent critics have convincingly demonstrated, *Walden* is in part "a subversive parody of the house pattern book genre," a genre that was "steeped in the rhetoric of domestic tranquility."[27] By contrasting his single-room dwelling far from the village, Thoreau craftily offered an alternative, not simply to experiments like Brook Farm — his vision in "House-Warming" is profoundly communal — but also to the increasingly elaborate domestic designs found in books served up to an eager public by writers like Andrew Jackson Downing.

Like the design of his cabin, the structure of *Walden* was initially simple and utilitarian. The first version was an extension of Thoreau's 1847 lecture, a form that offered a good deal of freedom and flexibility. "Why should we write dramas, & epics, & sonnets, & novels in two volumes?" Emerson mused in his journal in 1839. "Why not write as variously as we dress & think? A lecture is a new literature, which leaves aside all tradition, time, place, circumstance, & addresses an assembly as mere human beings, — no more — It has never yet been done well."[28] Potentially, at least, the lecture offered Emerson a solution to a number of problems. Two years after he delivered "The American Scholar," with its ringing declaration of cultural independence, he hailed the lecture as "a new literature," a democratic alternative to the major genres that had dominated English and European literature. The lecture also promised to free the speaker from what Emerson viewed as the artificial constraints of more conventional genres. Implicitly, the lecture was a literary manifestation of self-reliance, the subject of the following entry in his journal: "The objection to conforming to usages that have become dead to you, is, that it scatters your force: loses your time, blears the impression of your character" (*JMN*, 7:225). Like conformity to domestic, social, and religious usages, for Emerson an adherence to the generic conventions of the drama, the epic, the sonnet, or the novel also resulted in a loss of the self. In contrast, the lecture allowed the speaker to be himself, merely a human being speaking to other human beings. Significantly, that was precisely the stance Thoreau assumed when he delivered "A History of Myself" at the Concord Lyceum in February 1847.

As Thoreau expanded his lectures on the Walden experiment into a book, he may also have taken some hints from the arrangement of Emerson's major works. Not surprisingly, given the close friendship between the two writers, Thoreau had jotted down a list of essay topics as early as 1840, when Emerson was revising the lectures included in *Essays*.[29] Following the publication of that volume in 1841, Thoreau began to plan a similar collection of essays, which he hoped to write while living at Flint's Pond. After he was denied permission to build a hut at the pond — a grudge Thoreau later repaid with interest in his scathing portrait of Flint in "The Ponds" — his interest had slowly begun to shift to narrative forms like the excursion, which he experimented with in "A Walk to Wachusett" and "A Winter Walk," both published in 1843. By the time *Essays: Second Series* was published in 1844, Thoreau had already begun to gather material for *A Week*, which he first called "An Excursion on Concord and Merrimack Rivers." *Walden*, too, described an excursion, but when Thoreau divided the original, unbroken narrative into chapters he arranged them topically rather than chronologically, as in the day-to-day divisions of *A Week*. A glance at the contents page of *Walden* reveals some of the same principles of organization that Emerson adopted in *Essays* and in *The Conduct of Life*, the lecture series he developed in the early 1850s, though the volume was not published until 1860. Emerson arranged the chapters in *Essays* in balanced pairs, for example "Prudence" and "Heroism," a dialectical arrangement Thoreau exploited from the very opening chapters of *Walden*, where "Economy," his dark depiction of the life of his townsmen, is played off against the luminous "Where I Lived, and What I Lived For."[30] Moreover, the overall movement of the book, which charts its narrator's evolution through various stages of self-culture, is similar to that of *The Conduct of Life*, which, as Lawrence Buell has observed, was organized "in accordance with Emerson's idea that 'there is a climbing scale of culture' from the material to the human to the intellectual levels."[31]

Paradoxically, however, what distinguishes *Walden* from Emerson's collections of essays is not only its greater unity but also its far greater variety. In contrast to the *Essays*, for example, in which the form and style of the twelve chapters is relatively invariable, the central sequence of eight of its twenty-four chapters illustrates the sometimes dizzying generic shifts and combinations in *Walden*. Describing his labors in "The Bean-Field," Thoreau creates a Transcendental version of the georgic while carrying out "an elaborate spoof" of the agricultural reformers of the day.[32] In the following chapter, "The Village," he turns his satirical eye back to Concord, offering a brief portrait that mocks the glowing reports of visitors to the town. In sharp and immediate contrast, Thoreau in "The Ponds" undertakes an extended tour of his "lake country," a loving topographical description that follows in the path of Wordsworth's *Guide Through the District of the Lakes*.[33] Thoreau's poetic tourist transforms himself into a rather intrusive reformer in "Baker Farm," a short story or sketch somewhat in the manner of popular magazine writers, which is followed by "Higher Laws," originally entitled "Animal Food," an austere tract that might have been written by any one of the anxious dietary, health, and sexual reformers of the day.[34] But such high seriousness is deflated by the self-mocking interchange between the hermit and the poet at the opening of "Brute Neighbors," a dialogue reminiscent of those in Izaak Walton's *The Compleat Angler*, which introduces a series of descriptions in which Thoreau combined the techniques of the fable and the mock-heroic with the detailed renderings characteristic of natural-history writings.[35]

The generic diversity of *Walden* is balanced and contained, not only by transitions between chapters and similar connective materials, but also by elements that Thoreau might have derived from a number of genres popular in the eighteenth and nineteenth centuries. The seasonal structure of the narrative recalls William Howitt's *A Book of the Seasons; or the Calendar of Nature* (1831), the subject of one of Thoreau's undergraduate essays, and James Thomson's *The Seasons* (1736), a long poem of natural description and philosophical meditation that Thoreau praised in the first draft of *A Week*.[36] His books probably also owe something to another form popular in the eighteenth century, the topographical poem, which Dr. Johnson defined as "*local poetry*, of which the fundamental subject is some particular landscape . . . with the addition of . . . historical retrospection or incidental meditation."[37] If Walden Pond is the central subject of the book it is also a mirror of the narrator of *Walden*, a fictionalized persona with a strong kinship to characters in contemporary novels. Thoreau's scorn for popular romances and other productions of "universal noveldom" was genuine (*W*, 105), but *Walden* is "the closest the Transcendentalists came to creating a major work of prose fiction."[38] It may, for example, be viewed as an ironic variant of sentimental novels of the period, since Thoreau offers an idyllic account of family life in the woods, where the narrator, Mother Nature, and God the Father share a home far removed from the crass commercial world *and* the oppressive domestic sphere. *Walden* may also be described as a bildungsroman, a novel of personal growth, though in the case of Thoreau's narrator, unlike his contemporary David Copperfield, we are from the beginning of the book left in little doubt about who will be the hero of the story.

Despite its fictional qualities, *Walden* is probably more accurately defined as an autobiography, a form every bit as variable and flexible as the novel. In fact, the term autobiography was not commonly used until the middle of the nineteenth century, when it began to be applied to a wide range of works.[39] Encouraged by Emerson, Thoreau dutifully read Carlyle, the subject of an extended lecture-essay he wrote during his first year at Walden Pond. "The before impossible percept, 'know thyself,' he translates into the partially possible one, 'know what thou canst work at,' " Thoreau commented in "Thomas Carlyle and His Works," published in 1847. "Sartor Resartus is, perhaps, the sunniest and most philosophical, as it is the most autobiographical of his works, in which he drew most largely on the experience of his youth. . . . We should say that he had not speculated far, but faithfully, living up to it. He lays all the stress still on the most elementary and initiatory maxims, introductory to philosophy."[40] Thoreau in his 1847 lecture on his mode of life at Walden Pond did much the same thing, defining the nature of man's proper work and offering a series of introductory maxims on true economy. But in *Walden* he clearly sought to go beyond *Sartor Resartus*, setting out on a path toward true self-knowledge, the final goal of the philosophy that Carlyle's vision failed to encompass.

Thoreau was nonetheless deeply ambivalent about the autobiographical impulse and its literary consequences. In December 1846, a few weeks before he delivered "A History of Myself," he jotted down a sharp critique of another of Emerson's heroes, Goethe, in his journal. Following that severe assessment of the German master's education and character, which was prompted by a reading of a translation of *Dictung und Wahrheit* published earlier that year as *The Autobiography of Goethe*, Thoreau in the following entry added: "When I am stimulated by reading the biographies of literary men to adopt some method of educating myself and directing my studies — I can only resolve to keep unimpaired the freedom & wakefulness of my genius. I will not seek to accomplish much in breadth and bulk and loose [*sic*] my self in industry but keep my celestial relations fresh" (*J*, 2:357). The spiritual cost of such industriousness was, of course, a central theme of his forthcoming lecture. On the other hand, Thoreau's determination to resist the gravitational pull of masters like Goethe raised a fundamental question about the purpose of both that lecture and the book that would grow out of it. Given his wariness toward literary autobiographies, how could Thoreau give an account of his activities at the pond without stimulating others simply to adopt his own methods of study and mode of life?

Thoreau's awareness of some of the problems inherent in autobiography helped shape *Walden*, which became a very different book from the one he first set out to write. In a review of *A Week*, published in 1849, James Russell Lowell remarked, "We must have our libraries enlarged, if Mr. Thoreau intend to complete his autobiography on this scale."[41] Lowell's strictures did not deter Thoreau from enlarging *Walden*, which he originally planned to publish shortly after *A Week*, but which he radically revised and expanded during 1851–54. Describing those late additions, Thoreau in a preface to the manuscript version explained that his object had been "chiefly to make it a completer & truer account of that portion of the author's life."[42] But he omitted the note, possibly because he recognized that, rather than a chapter of an autobiography, which the early versions resembled, *Walden* had become an autobiography in its own right. Whereas in the first version he noted that the account was a response to particular inquiries about his mode of life, he later added, "Moreover, I, on my side, require of every writer, first or last, a simple and sincere account of his own life" (*W*, 3). Although it is far from simple and something other than sincere, *Walden* finally offered such a full accounting, one in which Thoreau increasingly shifted the emphasis from his way of living, the focus of the early versions, to the larger cycles of life suggested by his year at Walden Pond. As a result, the book became less a literal guide to the conduct of life than a symbolic account of a life that at least potentially subsumed all other lives. Indeed, as William Howarth has observed, Thoreau's "story is an autobiography, but on a large scale: it uses one life as a metaphor for the entire course of human growth."[43]

Thoreau, whose millennial hopes for America made him all the more bitter about its social and cultural failures, was especially preoccupied with the history and experience of his countrymen. In *Walden* he consequently sought to work patterns from other American lives into the design of his own autobiography. For example, Thoreau consciously reversed the formula of captivity narratives like those of Mary Rowlandson, which he alluded to in "A Walk to Wachusett," and Hannah Duston, whose story he retold in the "Thursday" chapter of *A Week*.[44] Where Rowlandson described her captivity in terms of a series of "removes" from civilization to barbarism, Thoreau in the early chapters of *Walden* charts his own spatial, temporal, and finally spiritual removal from a barbaric civilization to a civilized wilderness. Similarly, where Duston was told that she would be forced to run the gauntlet, a threat that prompted her escape from the Indians, Thoreau encounters such a trial only when he returns to Concord, whose houses are arranged "so that every traveller had to run the gantlet, and every man, woman, and child might get a lick at him," as he wittily observes at the opening of "The Village" (*W*, 168). At the end of that chapter, Thoreau briefly describes his arrest for failing to pay the poll tax, thus lodging a formal protest against slavery. Among the most powerful literary weapons against slavery were slave narratives, to which Thoreau's story had some striking affinities. Noting that Thoreau moved to the pond shortly after the publication of *The Narrative of the Life of Frederick Douglass, an American Slave*, Michael Meyer has suggested that *Walden* may be read as "a white version of a slave narrative," since both books concern "human potential," while "each employs an emblematic life to dramatize the fulfillment of that potential."[45]

Walden bears an even stronger family resemblance to earlier American autobiographies, especially to some of the most widely known spiritual autobiographies.[46] Thoreau was possibly familiar with the *Journal of John Woolman*, which was praised by a host of nineteenth-century writers from Samuel Taylor Coleridge to the Quaker poet and abolitionist John Greenleaf Whittier, who noted on the final page of a copy of the *Journal* he sent to Emerson: "I find more wisdom in these pages than in any other book written since the days of the apostles. There is a true philosophy — a clear insight — a right estimate of things."[47] Thoreau, too, would have responded to Woolman's determined efforts to live a life according to principle, one that finally required him to lessen his "outward business," which had become a burden, in order to achieve a truer inward communion with God. Woolman's *Journal* anticipated many of the moral and social issues that loom so large in *Walden*, but Thoreau's language and imagery are less clearly related to Woolman's simple eloquence than to the complex rhetorical world of Puritan autobiographies. Just as Jonathan Edwards in his *Personal Narrative* charted the stages of his spiritual growth, or awakening, characterized by an influx of light that finally transforms the face of nature, so Thoreau charts the stages or seasons of his own spiritual growth, culminating in the great burst of refulgent light in "Spring." "The change from storm and winter to serene and mild weather, from dark and sluggish hours to bright and elastic ones, is a memorable crisis which all things proclaim," he announces. "It is seemingly instantaneous at last. Suddenly an influx of light filled my house, though the evening was at hand, and the clouds of winter still overhung it, and the eaves were dripping with sleety rain. I looked out the window, and lo! where yesterday was cold gray ice there lay the transparent pond already calm and full of hope as on a summer evening, reflecting a summer evening sky in its bosom, though none was visible overhead, as if it had intelligence with some remote horizon" (W, 312).

In that extraordinary moment of inspiration and revelation, Thoreau evokes the experience of the saints, the elect of the Puritan tradition in New England. Significantly, however, the autobiography to which he most directly alludes in *Walden* is that of a secular saint, Benjamin Franklin, whose dominant role in American history and culture Thoreau fully recognized. Reminding his pious and patriotic audience of the heroes of the past who had resisted the authority of the state, Thoreau in an 1848 lecture published in 1849 as "Resistance to Civil Government" asked: "Why does [the government] always crucify Christ, and excommunicate

Copernicus and Luther, and pronounce Washington and Franklin rebels?"[48] On a lighter note, Thoreau in *A Week* cited Franklin as one of two figures who would one day take their place in the mythology of America: "Who knows what shape the fable of Columbus will at length assume, to be confounded with that of Jason and the expedition of the Argonauts. And Franklin, — there may be a line for him in the future classical dictionary, recording what that demigod did, and referring him to some new genealogy. . . 'He aided the Americans to gain their independence, instructed mankind in economy, and drew down lightning from the clouds' " (*AW*, 60–61).

Walden is frequently viewed simply as a refutation of the instruction delivered by Franklin, whose precepts are mocked and parodied by Thoreau in "Economy."[49] Yet, although he identified Franklin as a crucial source of the materialism and commercial spirit of his countrymen, Thoreau perhaps gained from Franklin's *Autobiography* some important hints about how to shape a life story for the purpose of instruction. Like Franklin, Thoreau in *Walden* created an exemplary persona, one whose experience might serve as an example to the young, the rising generation to which both authors directed most of their attention. Carrying the additional burden of Emersonian self-reliance, Thoreau could not simply offer his life as one fit for imitation, but the major difference between *Walden* and the *Autobiography* is the result of divergent methods rather than of different intentions. The *Autobiography* is primarily didactic, a method of instruction Thoreau adopted in his early chapters, especially "Economy" and "Reading," but largely abandoned in the remainder of *Walden*. His book is consequently less didactic than heuristic, an account designed to inspire his audience to undertake the explorations and investigations adumbrated in "Conclusion," where Thoreau exhorts each individual to discover or invent a new, inward America, in effect becoming his own Columbus and Franklin.

Where Franklin offered fatherly advice, Thoreau spoke for the sons, offering a vigorous challenge to such paternal authority. Nonetheless, the example and influence of the founding fathers of New England and America are apparent in *Walden*. In depicting his growth from poverty and obscurity to wealth and fame, Franklin in the *Autobiography* charted his country's steady movement from dependence to independence, transforming his own life into national history. Thoreau used his experiences at Walden Pond in similar ways. He moved to the pond, of course, on Independence Day, and "Economy" may be read as his personal version of the "Declaration of Independence," which, like the original, contains a highly colored and exaggerated bill of particulars against the society from which he withdrew his allegiance. In his reenactment of American history, Thoreau fused the Revolution with the first break from England, the settlement of the Pilgrims and Puritans in *New* England.[50] *Walden* recalls both "A Modell of Christian Charity," John Winthrop's eloquent apologia for the Puritan mission to the New World, and William Bradford's *Of Plymouth Plantation*.[51] Like Bradford, Thoreau details the causes of his removal, describes his resettlement in detail, catalogs the resources of his new world, and finally confronts the greatest challenge to his mission, the "unspeakable cold" of a New England winter (W, 240), from which he triumphantly emerges the following spring. For all of his interest in local histories and topographical descriptions, which also left their mark on *Walden*, Thoreau's book is not local but national in its communal concerns. Writing at the very moment when America was fulfilling its Manifest Destiny to overrun the continent, Thoreau in *Walden* sought no less than to rewrite his country's history, depicting his life at the pond as an example of the new start that, even after two false starts, was still possible for man and his institutions in the New World.

Genre ultimately served Thoreau's literary and social purposes in *Walden*. Inspired by his reading of Homer and Virgil, as well of popular travel books, he envisioned his removal to Walden Pond as a withdrawal to a remote realm poised in his imagination between Arcadia and the wilds of North America. But his ongoing engagement with civilized society was revealed by his first lecture on the experiment, "A History of Myself." Despite its title, the focus of that lecture was the public world rather than his private experience. Assuming the posture of radical reformers like Alcott and Lane, Thoreau also consciously parodied and inverted the teachings of guides like Beecher's *Treatise on Domestic Economy*. In addition to his obvious challenge to the assumptions and values of his audience, Thoreau from the beginning challenged them to penetrate what he later called the "secrets" of his trade, which were "not involuntarily kept, but inseparable from its very nature" (W, 17). Those secrets included his manipulations of various genres, which like his complex and allusive style force the reader of *Walden* to be ever on the alert. His literary experiments corresponded to his experiment at Walden Pond, for as Thoreau moved there to test the limits of life so in *Walden* does he test the limits of language, rhetoric, and genre. An attempt to integrate elements of various ways of life into a new mode of living was thus paralleled by Thoreau's efforts to adapt and combine a wide range of rhetorical and generic modes in *Walden*. His pleasure in discovering that Wyman the potter once lived near Walden Pond—that "so fictile an art was ever practised in my neighborhood" (W, 261)—is understandable, since Thoreau himself sought to mold the seemingly fixed forms of literary art.

Thoreau consequently reshaped both history and autobiography. Alerted to some of the problems and limitations of autobiography by his reading of writers like Carlyle and Goethe, he endeavored to tell, not simply one man's story, but the story of mankind, whose tribulations he has shared and whose aspirations he carries with him to Walden Pond. By compressing the two years he spent at the pond into a narrative of a single year, Thoreau created a sweeping chronicle from ancient India to the settlement of America, the subsequent history of which is re-enacted in *Walden*. Like the Walt Whitman of "Song of Myself," the chameleonlike "I" of Thoreau's similar song assumes innumerable and overlapping guises, merging the Hindu sage with the Greek warrior, moving from simple shepherd through pious husbandman to rugged frontiersman, mingling with his own the experiences of European settlers and native Indians, of captive slaves and triumphant liberators. "Dante's praise is that he dared to write his autobiography in colossal cipher & make it universal," Emerson observed in 1844 (*JMN*, 9:85). By the time that comment appeared in "The Poet," published that fall in *Essays: Second Series*, Thoreau was already making plans to move to Walden Pond. But neither he nor Emerson could then have possibly anticipated that a decade later Thoreau's relatively brief and seemingly uneventful stay at the pond would be transmuted into another such universal autobiography, *Walden; or, Life in the Woods*. Indeed, he may later have requested that the subtitle be omitted because it limited the experience described in his book, which as *Walden* is simply identified with the "character" whose name and origins Thoreau considered in "The Ponds." "Perhaps on that spring morning when Adam and Eve were driven out of Eden Walden Pond was already in existence" (*W*, 179), he remarks in the chapter, offering a hint of what his year-long narrative powerfully suggests, that Walden Pond has witnessed the whole course of human history, from that first fall in the spring to the return to Eden in "Spring."

Notes

1. A useful guide to and through that commentary is provided by Walter Harding and Michael Meyer, *The New Thoreau Handbook* (New York: New York University Press, 1980).

2. See, for example, Charles R. Anderson, *The Magic Circle of Walden* (New York: Holt, Rinehart and Winston, 1968), an attempt to read the book "*as if* it were a poem" (vii). The starting place for a generic approach to *Walden* is Lawrence Buell, *Literary Transcendentalism: Style and Vision in the American Renaissance* (Ithaca: Cornell University Press, 1973), which contains an excellent discussion of the genres of Transcendentalist writing, including the conversation, the essay, the sermon, the excursion, and the autobiography.

3. Heather Dubrow, *Genre* (London: Methuen, 1982), 2–3.

4. Alastair Fowler, *Kinds of Literature: An Introduction to the Theory of Genres and Modes* (Cambridge: Harvard University Press, 1982), 20.

5. A notable example is Ethel Seybold, *Thoreau: The Quest and the Classics* (New Haven: Yale University Press, 1951), chapter 3, "The Homeric Experiment," 48–63. Thoreau drafted portions of what became "Reading" in the Journal of the early Walden period, when, as Seybold notes, "Greece and the classics were steadily in his thoughts" (51).

6. Dubrow, *Genre*, 11.

7. For a detailed discussion of changing attitudes toward the epic during the nineteenth century, see Donald M. Foerster, *The Fortunes of Epic Poetry* (Catholic University Press of America, 1962), chapters 2–4. As Foerster notes, in America the epic suffered from its

association with the derivative culture of the colonial period, as well as from the common view that heroic poetry embodied the values of aristocracy and social hierarchy.

8. *Walden*, ed. J. Lyndon Shanley (1971), 100, in *The Writings of Henry D. Thoreau*, ed. Walter Harding et al., 8 vols. (Princeton: Princeton University Press, 1971–19––). All subsequent references to this edition of *Walden* are cited as *W*, by page number.

9. The most convincing discussions of Thoreau's pastoralism are Leo Marx, *The Machine in the Garden: Technology and the Pastoral Ideal in America* (New York: Oxford University Press, 1967), 242–65; and John Seelye, "Some Green Thoughts on a Green Theme," in *Literature in Revolution*, ed. George Abbott White and Charles Newman (New York: Holt, Rinehart and Winston, 1972), 566–636. Marx treats *Walden* as "the report on an experiment in transcendental pastoralism" (242), a book with strong affinities to the Virgilian mode and to the tradition of American pastoralism, while Seelye emphasizes the political dimensions of that tradition, discussing the ways in which Thoreau mixed elements of the epic, the eclogue, and the georgic in *Walden*, the "original model" of which was *Robinson Crusoe* (617).

10. *The Writings of Henry D. Thoreau, Journal, Volume 2: 1842–1848*, ed. Robert Sattelmeyer (1984), 197. Hereafter cited as *J*, by volume and page number.

11. *Thoreau's Complex Weave: The Writing of "A Week on the Concord and Merrimack Rivers," with the Text of the First Draft* (Charlottesville: University Press of Virginia, 1986), 23. In that study I discuss the ways in which Thoreau in *A Week* combined various genres, especially the literary excursion and the pastoral elegy.

12. *The Writings of Henry D. Thoreau, A Week on the Concord and Merrimack Rivers*, ed. Carl Hovde et al. (1980), 338. Hereafter cited as *AW*, by page number.

13. Patrick Cullen, *Spenser, Marvell, and the Renaissance Pastoral* (Cambridge: Harvard University Press, 1970), 1.

14. Cullen, *Renaissance Pastoral*, 3.

15. The impact of such reading is discussed by John Aldrich Christie, *Thoreau as World Traveler* (New York: Columbia University Press, 1965).

16. Although Thoreau clearly read the book as a factual report, a true picture of life among the natives of the South Pacific (*J*, 2:315–18), *Typee* raises some interesting generic questions, especially concerning its status as autobiography or fiction. For a summary of various approaches and a discussion of the issue, see John Samson, "The Dynamics of History and Fiction in Melville's *Typee*," *American Quarterly* 36 (Summer 1984):276–90.

17. Introduction to *Moby-Dick; or, The Whale*, ed. Harold Beaver (New York: Penguin, 1972), 40.

18. Noting that Thoreau had chosen his original title before Headley's book was published, Walter Harding cites Lane's article as "a possible source" of the subtitle of *Walden*. Thoreau in a letter written in March 1862, two months before his death, asked his publishers to omit the subtitle in a new edition of the book. See *The Variorum "Walden" and the Variorum "Civil Disobedience,"* ed. Walter Harding (New York: Washington Square, 1968), 255. All quotations from Lane's "Life in the Woods" are from the *Dial* 4 (April 1844): 415–25, hereafter cited by page number.

19. *The Letters of Ralph Waldo Emerson*, ed. Ralph L. Rusk, 6 vols. (New York: Columbia University Press, 1939), 3:377–78. As Rusk notes, the records of the Concord Lyceum indicate that Thoreau's subject on 10 February was "History of Himself," and that on the 17th his subject was the "Same as last week." It is therefore not clear whether the second lecture was a repetition or a continuation of Thoreau's first lecture on the subject. For details concerning Thoreau's various lectures on the Walden experiment, see Walter Harding, "A Check List of Thoreau's Lectures," *Bulletin of the New York Public Library* 52 (February 1948): 78–87.

20. Ripley's letter, which Thoreau may have seen, is printed in Octavius Brooks

Frothingham, *George Ripley* (Boston: Houghton, Mifflin, 1882), 307–12. For an analysis of the ideas that brought Alcott and Lane together, see Richard Francis, "Circumstances and Salvation: The Ideology of the Fruitlands Utopia," *American Quarterly* 24 (May 1973):202–34.

21. All quotations from the letter are from the text printed in *Bronson Alcott's Fruitlands*, comp. Clara Endicott Sears (Boston: Houghton Mifflin, 1915), 41–52.

22. J. Lyndon Shanley, *The Making of "Walden," with the Text of the First Version* (Chicago: University of Chicago Press, 1957), 105. The first version, hereafter cited as *FV*, by page number, incorporated the lecture or lectures Thoreau delivered in February 1847. For an excellent discussion of the differences between the earliest Journal entries on his life at Walden Pond, where Thoreau focused on his private experience, and the public concerns and oratorical style of his first lecture, see Thomas Woodson, "The Two Beginnings of *Walden*: A Distinction of Styles," *ELH* 35 (September 1968):440–73.

23. The publication and impact of the *Treatise* are discussed by Kathryn Kish Sklar, *Catharine Beecher: A Study in American Domesticity* (New Haven: Yale University Press, 1973), 151–67, to which my comments on Beecher's aims and ideology are indebted. Emerson's wife Lidian owned a copy of the 1851 edition of the *Treatise*, as well as a copy of its supplement, the *Domestic Receipt Book* (1852); see Walter Harding, *Emerson's Library* (Charlottesville: University Press of Virginia, 1967), 24.

24. Miss Catharine E. Beecher, *A Treatise on Domestic Economy, For the Use of Young Ladies at Home, and at School* (Boston: Marsh, Capen, Lyon, and Webb, 1841), 41.

25. Sklar, *Catharine Beecher*, 161.

26. For a discussion of such "male sentimentalists," a rather condescending characterization of which Thoreau would no doubt have approved, see Ann Douglas, *The Feminization of American Culture* (New York: Alfred A. Knopf, 1977), 236ff.

27. Richard N. Masteller and Jean Carwile Masteller, "Rural Architecture in Andrew Jackson Downing and Henry David Thoreau: Pattern Book Parody in *Walden*," *New England Quarterly* 57 (December 1984):483–510.

28. *The Journals and Miscellaneous Notebooks of Ralph Waldo Emerson*, ed. William H. Gilman, Ralph H. Orth, et al., 16 vols. (Cambridge: Harvard University Press, 1961–82), 7:224. Hereafter cited as *JMN*, by volume and page number.

29. For a fuller discussion of Thoreau's early apprenticeship to Emerson, see *Thoreau's Complex Weave*, especially 202ff.

30. The arrangement of *Essays* is briefly discussed by Sherman Paul, *Emerson's Angle of Vision: Man and Nature in the American Experience* (Cambridge: Harvard University Press, 1952), 117–18.

31. Buell, *Literary Transcendentalism*, 162.

32. See James S. Tillman, "The Transcendental Georgic in *Walden*," *ESQ: A Journal of the American Renaissance* 21 (3rd Quarter 1975):137–41; and Robert A. Gross, "The Great Bean Field Hoax: Thoreau and the Agricultural Reformers," *Virginia Quarterly Review* 61 (Summer 1985):483–97.

33. Neill R. Joy, "Two Possible Analogues for 'The Ponds' in *Walden*: Jonathan Carver and Wordsworth," *ESQ: A Journal of the American Renaissance* 24 (4th Quarter 1978):197–205.

34. In "Thoreau's Buried Short Story," *Studies in Short Fiction* 1 (Fall 1963):16–20, E. Arthur Robinson compares "Baker Farm" to Gogol's "The Student." Thoreau's ambivalent relation to contemporary reform movements is admirably treated by Taylor Stoehr, *Nay-Saying in Concord: Emerson, Alcott, and Thoreau* (Hamden, Conn.: Archon Books, 1979).

35. The opening of the chapter is briefly discussed by Thomas Blanding, "Walton and *Walden*," *Thoreau Society Bulletin*, no. 107 (Spring 1969):3; and Robert Hodges, "The Fundamental Satire of Thoreau's Hermit and Poet," *Satire Newsletter* 8 (Spring 1971):105–8.

See also Raymond Adams, "Thoreau's Mock-Heroics and the American Natural History Writers," *Studies in Philology* 52 (1955):86–97.

36. *Thoreau's Complex Weave*, 384–85.

37. Quoted in the *Princeton Encyclopedia of Poetry and Poetics*, ed. Alex Preminger (Princeton: Princeton University Press, 1965), 858. Thoreau's experiments in topographical poetry, a form largely outmoded by the English romantic poets, included "When winter fringes every bough," at various times entitled "Fair Haven" and "Stanzas Written at Walden." For a comparison of "lococentrism" in the writings of Thoreau and Timothy Dwight, see Lawrence Buell, *New England Literary Culture: From Revolution Through Renaissance* (New York: Cambridge University Press, 1986), 319–34.

38. Buell, *Literary Transcendentalism*, 301.

39. James M. Cox, "Recovering Literature's Lost Ground Through Autobiography," in *Autobiography: Essays Theoretical and Critical*, ed. James Olney (Princeton: Princeton University Press, 1980), 123.

40. *The Writings of Henry D. Thoreau, Early Essays and Miscellanies*, ed. Joseph J. Moldenhauer et al. (1975), 254.

41. Lowell's review, which appeared in the December 1849 issue of the *Massachusetts Quarterly Review*, is reprinted in the *Thoreau Society Bulletin*, no. 35 (April 1951):1–3.

42. Quoted in Sherman Paul, *The Shores of America: Thoreau's Inward Exploration* (Urbana: University of Illinois Press, 1972), 295n.

43. William Howarth, *The Book of Concord: Thoreau's Life as a Writer* (New York: Penguin, 1983), 93.

44. Richard Slotkin has described *Walden* as "a unique synthesis of several genres of Colonial writing," including discovery and conversion narratives, observing that Thoreau's withdrawal to the wilderness also has similarities to captivity and hunter tales; see *Regeneration through Violence: The Mythology of the American Frontier, 1600–1860* (Middletown: Wesleyan University Press, 1973), 526.

45. Michael Meyer, Introduction to *Walden and Civil Disobedience* (New York: Penguin, 1983), 26. *Walden* is compared with Douglass's second autobiography, *My Bondage and My Freedom* (1855), by William W. Nichols, "Individualism and Autobiographical Art," *CLA Journal* 16 (December 1972):145–58.

46. G. Thomas Couser, *American Autobiography: The Prophetic Mode* (Amherst: University of Massachusetts Press, 1972), 67–69.

47. That copy of *A Journal of the Life, Gospel Labors, and Christian Experiences of that Faithful Minister of Jesus Christ, John Woolman* (1840), which Whittier sent as a gift to Emerson in 1853, is now in the Houghton Library, Harvard University. *Walden* and Whitman's "Song of Myself" are set against the background of Quaker autobiographical writing by Daniel B. Shea, Jr., *Spiritual Autobiography in Early America* (Princeton: Princeton University Press, 1968), 256–62.

48. *The Writings of Henry D. Thoreau, Reform Papers*, ed. Wendell Glick (1973), 73.

49. Couser, *American Autobiography*, 64–66. Thomas Cooley suggests that "Thoreau only half parodied Franklin's method," since both *Walden* and the *Autobiography* "may be regarded as character-building manuals written by men who already knew themselves surely enough to instruct others in the art of self-definition"; see *Educated Lives: The Rise of Modern Autobiography in America* (Columbus: Ohio State University Press, 1976), 15–16.

50. Thoreau's reenactment of the Great Migration and the settlement of the country is discussed by Stanley Cavell, *The Senses of "Walden"* (New York: Viking, 1972), 7–11.

51. Although the complete text of Bradford's account was not published until 1856, the manuscript had served as the primary source for other histories, including *Mourt's Relation* (1622), the earliest account of the planting of the colony, and Nathaniel Morton's history of

Plymouth, *New England's Memorial*, both of which Thoreau read by 1850; see my article, "Into History: Thoreau's Earliest 'Indian Book' and His First Trip to Cape Cod," *ESQ: A Journal of the American Renaissance* 28 (2d Quarter 1982):75–88.

The Social Ethics of *Walden*   Robert D. Richardson, Jr.*

I

The social and political case against Thoreau is that he is a self-sufficient anarchist, preferring nature to human society, putting the welfare of the individual above that of the community. The case has seldom been put better than it was by James Russell Lowell in an essay/review written several years after Thoreau's death. Lowell says Thoreau "was not merely solitary, he would be isolated, and succeeded at last in almost persuading himself he was autochthonous." Prescribing the cure, Lowell writes: "a greater familiarity with ordinary men would have done Thoreau good, by showing him how many fine qualities are common to the race. . . . He is not so truly withdrawn as exiled, if he refuse to share in their strength." It is, Lowell goes on, "a morbid self-consciousness that pronounces the world of men empty and worthless before trying it, the instinctive evasion of one who is sensible of some innate weakness." Lowell also disapproves of the emphasis on nature he found in Thoreau, which he associates with Rousseau and Chateaubriand. "The natural man," Lowell says, "like the singing birds, comes out of the forest as inevitably as the natural bear and the wildcat stick there. To seek to be natural implies a consciousness that forbids all naturalness forever. It is as easy — and no easier — to be natural in a *salon* as in a swamp." What Lowell understands by "Nature" is made clear in the next paragraph. "The divine life of Nature is more wonderful, more various, more sublime in man than in any other of her works. . . . In outward nature it is still man that interests us, and we care far less for the things seen than the way in which poetic eyes like Wordsworth's or Thoreau's see them." With a modern substitution of medicine for morality, Lowell concludes that Thoreau was not only wrongheaded but unhealthy: "To a healthy mind," Lowell insists, "The world is a constant challenge of opportunity. Mr. Thoreau had not a healthy mind, or he would not have been so fond of prescribing. His whole life was a search for the doctor."[1]

Lowell's assessment, or attack, as it is often seen, is hard and shrewd.

*This essay was written especially for this volume and is published here for the first time with the permission of the author.

Lowell can be dead wrong about some things. He thought Thoreau "had no humor," for example. But Lowell's view of Thoreau's selfishness and his retreat to nature have found many later independent reconfirmations. A hundred years later we are still hearing the same charges. Leon Edel thinks Thoreau went to Walden Pond because he felt so guilty about setting fire to the Concord woods that he literally shrank from his neighbors in town. Irving Howe, with his usual clarity and honesty, focuses on the political issue: "Except possibly by way of preliminary, Thoreau's vision of freedom did not depend upon or require communal experience." Howe also connects Thoreau's individualism with the anti-communal individualism of a later era: "Thoreau drives to an extreme a version of individualism that in later decades would lend itself to conservative bullying and radical posturing, both of which can undercut the fraternal basis of a democratic polity."[2]

Quentin Anderson associates Thoreau with Emerson and Whitman in what is perhaps the most sweeping modern attack on transcendental individualism. American individualism is, for Anderson, an unmixed curse:

> Individualism, insofar as it stands for the energy, inventiveness, and adaptability of Americans committed to commercial or industrial enter-prise, is a name for those personal qualities which foster impersonality in social and economic relations; the individualist is (again, in the very terms of the myth) the man who subjects others to himself through his shrewdness in gauging their appetites or anticipating their needs.

Anderson argues that it was Emerson, Thoreau, and Whitman that brought this about:

> In Emerson, society was not spurned; it was judged irrelevant to human purposes in the measure that it forced or encouraged each of us to assume a distinct role. Transcendentalism, which Emerson described as "the Saturnalia or excess of Faith" in individual powers and individual sufficiency, simply attempted to supplant society.

Throughout *The Imperial Self*, Thoreau is regularly associated with "the freezing absoluteness of the Emersonian disavowals. The satanic and the angelic are alike meaningless," says Anderson, "in the light of a consciousness which denies that our sense of ourselves is based on a reciprocal or dramatic or dialectic awareness of one another."[3]

Most recently, Jacques Barzun concedes, with deft elegance, that Thoreau has "helped create this country's view of itself." But in examining that view he can only praise Thoreau as a stylist, an impressionist, and an epigram maker after he humorlessly examines a list of "inconsistencies" in "Civil Disobedience." Barzun concludes: "as a guide to conduct, Thoreau's tract is worthless, and as a pattern for the conscientious feelings, it is deplorable."[4]

Allan Bloom, in *The Closing of the American Mind*, writes to defend the idea that "Nature should be the standard by which we judge our own lives and the lives of peoples," but he fails to find an ally in Thoreau, whom indeed he associates with anarchy and with wishing to leave civil society. Bloom's new analysis is remarkably close to Lowell's old one. Bloom notes how

> the first reaction to the self's maladaptation to society, its recalcitrance to the rationality of preservation and property, is the attempt to recover the self's pristine state, to live according to its first inclinations, to "get in touch with one's feelings," to live naturally, simply, without society's artificially generated desires, dependencies, hypocrisies. The side of Rousseau's thought that arouses nostalgia for nature came to the United States early on in the life and writings of Thoreau. . . . Anarchism in one form or another is an expression of this longing, which arises as soon as politics and laws are understood to be repressions, perhaps necessary, but nonetheless repressions of our inclinations rather than perfections of them or modes of satisfying them.[5]

If the usual attack on Thoreau is not fully satisfactory because it is too sweeping and general, so the usual defense of Thoreau fails to convince because it is too personal and particular. Thoreau's defenders would have us understand that Thoreau himself was active in Concord life, both as a teacher and as an organizer for the Lyceum, that he was a good friend and neighbor, not just to Ellery Channing and Emerson, but to farmers Minot and Rice, that he was a strong family person who helped his father in business and went on frequent outings with his sister Sophia, that he raised money for the Irish, helped blacks toward Canada and freedom, and hosted an Abolition Society annual meeting at his cabin by Walden Pond. All of this is true, but none of it addresses itself to what he wrote and said, except as a demonstration that his life was less antisocial than is sometimes supposed.

Nor can the debate be settled by selective quotation. *Walden* can be cited on both sides of many issues, and rather easily if one's irony detector is switched off. The misanthrope argument may quote, from "Visitors," Thoreau's stiff remark that "wherever a man goes, men will pursue and paw him with their dirty institutions," without noticing that he has just been talking about the institution of slavery. On the other hand, defenders of a supposed social Thoreau can quote him as saying "I think that I love society as much as most," without noting that Thoreau does not commit himself on how much "most" love it.[6] Thoreau's verbal texture is so complex (gloriously so), his irony and playfulness so pervasive that we do not feel that a few aphorisms or boldly declarative sentences can be conclusive either way. Individual lines and phrases do not outweigh the serious and long-held charges against him. Nor do defenses of *Walden* as a self-contained work of art. To be content with a strictly literary defense against social and political arguments is, for Thoreau, as for Ezra Pound, or anyone else, to avoid or trivialize the social and political issues.

II

It must be said at the outset that most of Thoreau's modern detractors at least do him the courtesy of taking him seriously, not only as an artist, but as a social critic. At the risk of occasionally stepping into the ironist's thickly laid traps, the writers who most seriously question Thoreau's teachings concede, by the quality of their attention, that he means what he says, that he has designs upon how we live our lives, and that his writings are more than aesthetic objects. Neither New Critical or deconstructive techniques will, *by themselves*, clarify the larger issues in Thoreau's work, for he himself habitually worked to break down the purely literary and verbal aspects of his work and call attention to the personal and social acts and choices underlying the words. He would have agreed with Walt Whitman that "no one will get at my verses who insists upon viewing them as a literary performance, or attempt at such performance, or as aiming mainly toward art or aestheticism."[7] Writing cannot be separated from life for Thoreau. It is linked to it, built upon it, dependent upon it. He once wrote: "nothing goes by luck in composition — it allows of no trick. The best you can write will be the best you are. . . . The author's character is read from title page to end." And a recent critic, Geoffrey O'Brien, has noted that "the sentences of other writers can be regarded as artifacts; Thoreau forces us to consider his as actions, so that any reading of him becomes a judgment of his life, and consequently of the reader's."[8] This is also true of most of the great writers of moral prose, from Plutarch and Montaigne to Wendell Berry and Jonathan Schell.

Thoreau did not underestimate the inadequacies of language. Indeed, for his time, he is remarkably aware of the arbitrary and limited nature of language. His critical position, like that of Emerson, resists the exclusions of some of the often-quoted critical aphorisms of modernism such as T. S. Eliot's saying "honest criticism and sensitive appreciation are directed not upon the poet but upon the poetry," or D. H. Lawrence saying "Never trust the artist. Trust the tale."[9] Thoreau, on the contrary, accepted the idea that there is *always* a poet behind the poem, a teller behind the tale. He does not reverse the dicta, nothing so predictable. He simply assumes that in the kind of writing he is doing (moral prose, wisdom literature, personal narrative, travel literature, literature of personal and social improvement and liberation) there is always an author and a reader as well as the text, and that, in all cases that matter, the author's life and the reader's life are more important than the text taken by itself. Since the text is written in order to change lives, to teach and instruct, the text cannot be *fully* understood apart from the trajectory to that intent.

Thoreau's intentions in *Walden* (which can be tracked and analyzed by his persistent rhetoric of intentionality) were social as well as individual, and his social concerns are put forward in five principal ways: the economic argument, the biological or ecological imperative, the psychological imperative, the awareness of limits, and the rhetoric or language of commonality.

III

The opening chapter of *Walden* does for the subject of economics what Emerson had done for history. Emerson had tried to shift attention from history as a vast objective record of the past, to history as read and interpreted by the individual. Not universal or even chronological history, but history as perceived by each person and validated in that person's life. "The student," said Emerson, "is to read history actively and not passively, to esteem his own life the text, and books the commentary." Thus, in the end, he thought, "all history becomes subjective; in other words, there is properly no History; only Biography."[10] So for Thoreau and economics. He tries to shift attention from the wealth of nations to the wealth or well-being of the individuals who make up the nation. Thoreau anchors public affairs in private ones, and he returns the word "economy" to its original Greek sense of "household management" or "domestic arrangements." As he tells the story of his own arrangements, his purpose is not so much to exalt self-sufficiency or isolation from others as it is to make a personal inquiry on behalf of all of us into the general human condition, into what we call the necessities of life. It is a freely chosen inquiry into fixed necessity, an experiment in essentialism. "It would be some advantage to live a primitive and frontier life," Thoreau says, early in *Walden*, and he immediately adds this significant qualifier: "though in the midst of an outward civilization, if only to learn what are the gross necessaries of life."[11]

Thoreau's calculations in this chapter read like a gloss or commentary on Adam Smith. Like Smith, Thoreau insists on calculating the cost as well as the price of things, and he gives a definition of cost that is similar to but somewhat broader than Smith's labor theory of value. "The cost of a thing," says Thoreau, "is the amount of what I will call life which is required to be exchanged for it, immediately or in the long run."[12] He calculates both the cost and the price of his Walden experiment not merely to crow about his personal achievement, but to make the argument that one, anyone, can spend a year as he did for about the cost of a year's tuition at a good private school, with money raised by day labor. It cost Thoreau, in round numbers, sixty dollars to set up house and live at Walden Pond for eight months. Tuition at Harvard was then fifty dollars an academic year, a Massachusetts day laborer made between 120 and 144 dollars a year, and Thoreau's income for his first eight months at the Pond was some forty dollars. Anyone able to settle for a used mobile home will find the same conditions still apply today.

Thoreau's personal economy and his domestic arrangements at Walden are rarely explained for their own sake. Indeed, his personal experience is often not very personal. When he is considering the necessity of clothing for example, he tells us little about what he wore. Instead he concentrates on what *one* needs, and from individual requirements, he moves on to consider the larger issues. "I cannot believe," he concludes,

> that our factory system is the best mode by which men may get clothing. The condition of the operatives is becoming every day more like that of the English; and it cannot be wondered at, since, as far as I have heard or observed, the principal object is, not that mankind may be well and honestly clad, but, unquestionably, that the corporations may be enriched.[13]

Just as Thoreau's personal economics are not a license to dominate others, so, here, as he generalizes about clothing, he is not simply antifactory or antimachine. From questioning his own motives he has moved to questioning corporate motives.

He has done the same thing with the railroads. Though he used them and, on occasion, enjoyed them as a new and energetic part of the nineteenth century, he has as sharp a sense of the economics underlying rail transportation as Ivan Illich. Speaking of building the railroad, Thoreau says,

> Men have an indistinct notion that if they keep up this activity of joint stocks and spades long enough all will at length ride somewhere, in next to no time, and for nothing; but though a crowd rushes to the depot, and the conductor shouts "All aboard!" when the smoke is blown away and the vapor condensed, it will be perceived that a few are riding, but the rest are run over.[14]

The point, here and in many other places in the chapter and the book, is that all sorts of projects involving the expenditure of money, even those presented as public benefits, must be evaluated finally by their effect on those individual people who collectively make up the public. When Thoreau presents himself as economic man, he does so not to isolate himself, but to speak as a typical, a representative individual.

IV

It had been a major point for Lowell that Thoreau devoted too much attention to nature and not enough to people. Men and women might be part of nature, for Lowell, but he insisted, as we have seen, that "the divine life of Nature is more wonderful, more various, more sublime in man than in any other of her works." Lowell's insistence here on human supremacy is a strongly felt protest against a side of Thoreau that thought differently. Thoreau could feel kinship with family, friends, neighbors, children, and disciples, but he could also feel kinship with a hawk ("it was not lonely but made all the earth lonely beneath it"), or with a white pine ("that tree is the symbol of my life"). He had made an even stronger claim for a pine in an article on the Maine Woods he had sent in 1857 to none other than James Russell Lowell, then editor of the *Atlantic Monthly*. "It [a pine tree] is as immortal as I am, and perchance will go to as high a heaven, there to tower above me still," Thoreau had written.[15] But when Thoreau received his copy of the magazine he was surprised to find that the sentence had been removed. The piece had been commissioned, Lowell had worked on Emerson to get it, then had changed it, ignoring Thoreau's attempt to restore it in proof stage. Thoreau was furious. He sent off a blistering letter self-righteously accusing Lowell, at length, of meanness, cowardice, expurgation, bigotry, and timidity. Lowell's later review of Thoreau, which I have been citing, was a getting even, but the issue is not one of name-calling, or even of character. It is a genuine difference in principles.

The nineteenth-century name for the issue was pantheism versus Christian theism. Thoreau was accused of being a pantheist, by Horace Greeley among others. The twentieth-century version of the issue is usually framed as some sort of ecological imperative versus the necessary subjugation of nature by the (divinely ordained) dominant species. Many would argue that it is still a religious issue. For Henry Thoreau, the human is different from other animals, but not necessarily better. He sees, in "Brute Neighbors" and "Winter Animals" and in parts of "Sounds" and "Spring," no reason why humans should privilege themselves about other forms of life. Pushed to its extreme, this view leads to the conclusion that not only animals, but plants and even minerals are, in some sense, alive. An ocean is neither animal nor vegetable, but it can surely die. The planet is itself alive. This is the significance of the great clay-bank scene in *Walden*'s next to last chapter, "Spring." Thoreau follows, and improves on, Linnaeus's magisterial dicta that "Stones grow (or increase), plants grow and live, and animals grow live and feel" ("*lapidae crescunt, vegetabile crescunt et vivunt, animali crescunt vivunt et sentiunt*"). After watching the earth-expressing art work of the thawing sand and clay flowing down the side of a newly dug railroad cut, Thoreau concludes "there is nothing inorganic. . . . The earth is not a mere fragment of dead history, stratum upon stratum like the leaves of a book, to be studied by geologists and antiquarians chiefly, but living poetry like the leaves of a tree, which precede flowers and fruit, — not a fossil earth, but a living earth."[16]

In a recent issue of *Raritan*, George Kateb claims that the democratic individualism of Emerson, Thoreau, and Whitman is the foundation for our "best defensive idealism in the age of the nuclear solution." Individualism, he notes, challenges both nuclear statism and "the auxiliary of nuclear statism, state activism." Kateb puts the general argument thus:

> I believe that individualism in some of its developments after the seventeenth century contains the substance of the saving thoughts and

feelings. The great work of Emerson, Thoreau, and Whitman comprises the main development, and the phrase "democratic individuality" perhaps best names their idealism. It grows out of the individualism of personal and political rights, and out of the related idea of individual sovereignty or free being, but represents their completion and ultimate greatness. This crowning work turns out to be central to the task of conceiving an attachment to existence that withstands all temptations to go along with policies that may lead to human and natural extinction. It offers itself for an enlistment never imagined by its devisers and propounders.[17]

The whole of *Walden* but especially "Spring" is a case in point. Much of the lasting power of *Walden* is its persuasive argument for our adopting a new attachment to the earth. Perry Miller once noted that shortly after the collapse of his romance with Ellen Sewall, Thoreau turned his affections toward nature. This has been seen mainly in personal, psychological terms as an act of displacement or substitution, an invalid emotional retreat. We need to see this in a fuller context, however, and to remember that for Thoreau himself, affection for nature was not a substitute for human affection. The two were linked. "A lover of Nature is preëminently a lover of man. If I have no friend, what is Nature to me?"[18] What we now can see is that it is not Lowell's narrow Christian exaltation of the human, but Thoreau's insistent linking of humans with the rest of life on the planet and with the planet itself that will lead to our salvation if anything can. It is Thoreau not Lowell who exhibits the fuller social responsibility in articulating the biological and ecological imperative, an imperative that has become much more urgent since Thoreau's time.

V

In psychological terms, the social ethic is expressed in *Walden* as what Erik Erikson calls "generativity," that is "the concern for establishing and guiding the next generation." Neither Thoreau nor any of his siblings had children, but Thoreau's generative attitude expressed itself in many ways as has been perceptively discussed by Richard Lebeaux. Thoreau was an effective and admired teacher, a substitute father for Emerson's children, and leader of huckleberry parties for Concord children. He nursed his brother and his father, he acquired and encouraged disciples and followers such as Blake, Brown, Ricketson, Cholmondely and others, he spent more years being head of the Thoreau household than he did at Walden Pond. It is also true that the overall direction of Thoreau's thought and writing from *Walden* to the late unpublished manuscripts on "The Dispersion of Seeds," and "Notes on Fruits" is a movement from economy to ecology, from autonomy to interrelatedness. The center of *Walden* is Thoreau's insistence on the necessity of individual freedom or autonomy; the center of the late writings is generativity itself, the relation of parent to offspring, the natural mechanics of reproduction and regeneration. The opening chapter of *Walden*, "Economy," ends with Thoreau telling the parable of the cypress, which the Persians called azad or free because it bears no fruit. "The Dispersion of Seeds" manuscript opens with a similar comment, this time from the Roman Pliny, about trees that bear no fruit. But Pliny, with Thoreau's approval, now adds, significantly, "these trees are regarded as sinister (or unhappy, infelices) and are considered inauspicious."[19]

But we need not look only at the end of Thoreau's career. *Walden* itself shows a marked passage from the spirit of freedom in "Economy" to the regenerative spirit in "Spring" and "Conclusion." These impassioned chapters close the book with a complex, many-sided account of the coming of spring. The point is not to strengthen one's faith in resurrection or immortality so much as to strengthen our faith in the natural phenomena that underlie and give point to those ideas. Thoreau describes not Christian regeneration (and certainly not regeneration through violence) but the natural rebirth of the year. Alfred North Whitehead began his 1929 book on *The Function of Reason* by pointing out

> history discloses two main tendencies in the course of events. One tendency is exemplified in the slow decay of physical nature. With stealthy inevitableness, there is degradation of energy. The sources of activity sink downward and downward. Their very matter wastes. The other tendency is exemplified by the yearly renewal of nature in the spring.[20]

Walden, especially in its late chapters, is our major celebration of the force of natural renewal which underlies and which alone makes possible any individual or social renewal.

In his funeral eulogy of Thoreau, Emerson chided his young friend for having had no ambition: "Instead of engineering for all America, he was the captain of a huckleberry party."[21] Perhaps it is clearer to the late twentieth century than it could have been to Emerson—or even to Thoreau—that no concern for the next generation can ignore the now diminished regenerative power of nature. In any case, Emerson was wrong this time. The captain of the huckleberry party had a truer concern than the engineer for the generations to come.

VI

The fourth way in which *Walden* urges us toward socially responsible actions and lives is Thoreau's acceptance of life within limits. One of his modern successors, Wendell Berry, has persuasively shown how the concern about living within limits is very much the same problem as the problem of maintaining a human scale in a world of ever larger buildings, cities, roads, and machines: "The reason is simply that we cannot live except within limits, and these limits are of many kinds: spatial, material, moral, spiritual. The world has room for many people who are content to live as humans, but only for a relative few intent upon living as giants or as gods."[22] *Walden* is a decisive rejection of the Faustian spirit of insatiable striving. Where Faust was willing to bet that he could never be satisfied with the passing day, no matter how lovely or pleasing, Thoreau took the exact opposite position, vowing to live *his* life fully, however mean it might be, and so not come to the end of it only to find that he had not lived. Where Faust required supernatural and superhuman aids and the whole world at his feet, Thoreau was content with the merely human and with Concord. Although Genesis 1:26 stands to the contrary, Thoreau did not believe that human beings should press for dominion everywhere. He respected the American Indians for thinking the tops of mountains to be places where humans never went.

Limits protect diversity and pluralism. Thoreau thought civilized life rested on, and required wildness as a base. For wildness to survive either for itself or as the raw material of civilized life, limits between the tame and the wild must be observed. "Our village life would stagnate," Thoreau says, "if it were not for the unexplored forests and meadows which surround it." His explanation not only recognizes limits, it insists on our *need* for limits. "We need to witness our own limits transgressed, and some life pasturing freely where we never wander." From its careful inventory of basic necessities to his ecstatic revelling in a "land and sea . . . infinitely wild, unsurveyed and unfathomed by us because unfathomable," *Walden* is an exercise in living within limits.[23] Nature may be limitless, but human beings, as part of nature, have definite limits.

VII

All of these arguments, the economic, the ecological, the generative, and the need for limits are advanced in *Walden* in a language strongly marked by the rhetoric, not of community but of commonality. *Walden* is, of course, a first-person narrative, famously so. "In most books, the 'I' or first person, is omitted," Thoreau says in the second paragraph of the book; "in this it will be retained; that in respect to egotism, is the main difference." Now he shifts pronouns: "we commonly do not remember that it is, after all, always the first person that is speaking."[24] Thoreau's hint that there may be more than simple self-absorption in his account is corroborated when we notice that, in addition to "I," "we" is a word that comes rather easily to him. He uses "we" 447 times in the book. ("I" is used 1817 times, "me" 310, "my" 727, "us" 106, "our" 294).[25] In general, it is not an editorial, royal, or imperial "we." It is in most cases a true plural or collective. And it is not just the frequency of the word, it is where it is used that is interesting.

In the opening paragraphs of *Walden* we find far more instances of

"I" than "we" until we come to the culminating fifteenth paragraph, which begins "I think we may safely trust a good deal more than we do." This paragraph uses "we" sixteen times. Not just here, but elsewhere in the book, Thoreau tends to work along with his narrative and descriptive mode, generally using "I" until he comes to a summing up. Then he switches from the declarative and description to the imperative mode, to using "we" to express ethical conclusions, moral imperatives, judgments, suggestions, manifestoes, and calls to action. The climactic paragraph, third from the end, of "Spring," beginning "Our village life would stagnate . . . ," uses "we" ten times. The fourth from the last paragraph in "Conclusion," beginning "How long shall we sit in our porticos practising idle and musty virtues," uses "we" thirteen times, and the last paragraph of the book says "Only that day dawns to which we are awake," when he might so easily have written "to which I am awake." Over and over we notice the collective first-person plural in moments of moral seriousness; "when we consider," "we might try," "we should live," "we may waive," "let us spend," and so on. The very language of *Walden* creates the impression that while the experience at the pond is Thoreau's own, the conclusions and lessons to be drawn from it are common property, not just his but ours. The social ethic functions in *Walden* even — perhaps especially — at the all-important but nearly invisible level of grammar.

VIII

But even granting that there is some cogency in each of these cases, and that there is, to some degree, a measure of long-range social concern in *Walden*, it remains true that the central and insistent focus of the book is inescapably on the question of individual well-being, and the chief reform called for is of the self. No one has more forcefully described the limits of transcendental individualism than Orestes Brownson who wrote, in 1840, in "The Laboring Classes.":

> The truth is, the evil we have pointed out [the "actual condition of the working man today"] is not merely individual in its character. It is not, in the case of any single individual, of any man's procuring, nor can the efforts of any one man, directed solely to his own moral and religious perfection, do aught to remove it. What is purely individual in its nature, efforts of individuals to perfect themselves, may remove. But the evil we speak of is inherent in all our social arrangements, and cannot be cured without a radical change of those arrangements.[26]

The "answer" given by both Thoreau and Emerson to Brownson's challenge is that indeed our efforts should not be "solely" directed to our own individual moral and religious perfection. We must live social lives and perform social actions, and those social values and actions are rooted in and grow from our fundamental existence as individual, autonomous beings. Yet our autonomy only has significance, can only be conceived of, by considering our connections with others. Emerson's best definition of self-reliance or self-trust is that it is "not a faith in a man's own whim or conceit as if he were quite severed from all other beings and acted on his own private account, but a perception that the mind common to the Universe is disclosed to the individual through his own nature."[27] Thoreau saw a similar connection between the personal and the social. He observed in his woodchopper friend Alek Therien "a certain positive originality," which he said "amounted to a re-origination of many of the institutions of society."[28] Thoreau's own individualism was also of the kind that serves as the basis for society rather than a rejection of it or a refuge from it. Indeed it has been observed that American transcendentalism has a "submerged vein of collectivism" running through it, and that for most of its practitioners it had a strong social and ethical imperative, leading them from the schoolroom and the study into active advocacy for social and political causes.

Yet there are very real dangers in advocating any program of self-cultivation or self-development, what the Germans call *bildung* and what Robert Bellah calls "expressive individualism." Thomas Mann was much interested in the effect of the cult of personal cultivation, — "inwardness," he called it — in Germany:

> The idea of a republic meets with resistance in Germany chiefly because the ordinary middle-class man here, if he ever thought about culture, never considered politics to be a part of it, and still does not do so today. To ask him to transfer his allegiance from inwardness to the objective, to politics, to what the peoples of Europe call *freedom*, would seem to him to amount to a demand that he should do violence to his own nature, and in fact give up his sense of national identity.[29]

The challenge to modern American individualism, which is based in part on transcendental individualism, is to connect the goal of self cultivation not only with the goal of social cultivation, but also with the goal of personal, social, and political freedom. And this is precisely where transcendentalism has something to offer. Much of it is a working out of Kant's categorical imperative, which itself makes general social applicability the test of individual actions. "Act only on that maxim [principle] through which you can at the same time will that it should become a universal law."[30] Gandhi's ethic, derived in part from transcendentalism, makes a similar connection in different terms. "Home Rule equals Self Rule and Self Rule equals Self Control. Only he who is master of himself can be master of his 'house,' and only a people in command of itself can command respect and freedom."[31]

The special power and cogency of *Walden* lies in its awareness that political freedom and a social life compatible with that freedom rest on respect for individual autonomy. *Walden* does not talk as much as it might about the social world to be built on this autonomy, but that is because it is intent on getting the foundations right. To build a free and a just society on that foundation is our task still, and if there are inevitably dangers in overvaluing the autonomous human being, it is also true that no better foundation has been proposed. "If you have built castles in the air," Thoreau says toward the end of *Walden*, "your work need not be lost: that is where they should be. Now put the foundations under them." *Walden* is not the castle in the air, it is the foundation.

Notes

1. James Russell Lowell, "Thoreau," *North American Review* 101 (1865):597–608; rpt. in *Approaches to Walden*, ed. Louriat Lane, Jr. (Belmont, Calif.: Wadsworth, 1961), 31–38.

2. Leon Edel, letter to the editor, *New York Times Book Review*, 14 December 1986, 37; Irving Howe, *The American Newness* (Cambridge: Harvard University Press, 1986), 34–35.

3. Quentin Anderson, *The Imperial Self* (New York: Alfred A. Knopf, 1971), 4, 5.

4. Jacques Barzun, "Thoreau the Thorough Impressionist," *American Scholar* 56, no. 2 (Spring 1987):258.

5. Allan Bloom, *The Closing of the American Mind* (New York: Simon and Schuster, 1987), 38, 171.

6. *Walden*, ed. J. Lyndon Shanley (Princeton: Princeton University Press, 1971), 140, 171.

7. Walt Whitman, "A Backward Glance o'er Travel'd Roads," in *Prose Works 1892*, ed. Floyd Stovall, 2 vols. (New York: New York University Press, 1964), 2:731.

8. Thoreau, *Journal, Vol. 1: 1837–1844*, ed. John C. Broderick et al. (Princeton: Princeton University Press, 1981), 276; Geoffrey O'Brien, "Thoreau's Book of Life," *New York Review of Books*, 15 January 1987, 46.

9. T. S. Eliot, "Tradition and the Individual Talent," in *Selected Essays: 1917–1932* (New York: Harcourt, Brace, 1932), 7; D. H. Lawrence, *Studies in Classic American Literature* (New York: Viking, 1964 [1923]), 2.

10. Emerson, "History," in *Essays: First Series*, ed. Alfred R. Ferguson and Jean Ferguson Carr (Cambridge: Harvard University Press, 1979), 6.

11. *Walden*, 11.

12. Ibid., 31.

13. Ibid., 26–27.

14. Ibid., 53.

15. *The Correspondence of Henry David Thoreau*, ed. Walter Harding and Carl Bode (New York: New York University Press, 1958), 515–16.

16. Carl Linnaeus, *Philosophia Botanica* (Vienna: Trattner, 1763), 1.

17. George Kateb, "Thinking about Human Extinction," *Raritan* 6, (Fall 1986–Winter 1987): no. 2, 2–3.

18. Thoreau, *Journal*, ed. Bradford Torrey and Francis H. Allen, 14 vols. (Boston: Houghton Mifflin, 1906), 4:163.

19. See Richard Lebeaux, *Young Man Thoreau* (Amherst: University of Massachusetts Press, 1977), 244, esp. notes 15 and 17; *Walden*, 79; "The Dispersion of Seeds," MS Howarth F 30, p. 1.

20. Alfred North Whitehead, *The Function of Reason* (Princeton: Princeton University Press, 1929; rpt. Boston: Beacon Press, 1958), Introductory Summary, n.p.

21. Emerson, "Thoreau," *Atlantic Monthly* 10 (August 1862); rpt. in *Thoreau: Man of Concord*, ed. Walter Harding (New York: Holt, Rinehart, and Winston, 1960), 29.

22. Wendell Berry, *The Unsettling of America: Culture and Agriculture* (1977; 2d ed., San Francisco: Sierra Club Books, 1986), 222.

23. *Walden*, 317, 318.

24. Ibid., 3.

25. Marlene A. Ogden and Clifton Keller, *Walden: A Concordance* (New York: Garland, 1985).

26. Orestes Brownson, "The Laboring Classes," *Boston Quarterly Review* 3 (July 1840):358–95, excerpted in *The Transcendentalists*, ed. Perry Miller (Cambridge: Harvard University Press, 1950), 439.

27. "Ethics," in *The Early Lectures of Ralph Waldo Emerson*, ed. Stephen E. Whicher, Robert E. Spiller, and Wallace E. Williams, 3 vols. (Cambridge: Harvard University Press, 1959–1972), 2:151.

28. *Walden*, 150.

29. W. H. Bruford, *The German Tradition of Self-Cultivation* (Cambridge: Cambridge University Press, 1975), vii.

30. Immanuel Kant, *Groundwork of the Metaphysic of Morals*, ed. H. J. Paton (New York: Harper and Row, 1964), 88.

31. This formulation is from Erik H. Erikson, *Gandhi's Truth* (New York: W. W. Norton, 1969), 217.

INDEX